RAF Bomber Command Profiles

115 Squadron

RAF Bomber Command Profiles

DESPITE THE ELEMENTS

115 Squadron

Chris Ward

An imprint of
MENTION THE WAR PUBLICATIONS

This edition first published 2019 by Mention the War Ltd., 32 Croft Street, Farsley, Pudsey, LS28 5HA.

This squadron profile has been researched, compiled and written by its author, who has made every effort to ensure the accuracy of the information contained in it. The author will not be liable for any damages caused, or alleged to be caused, by any information contained in this book. E. & O.E.

Cover design: Topics - The Creative Partnership www.topicsdesign.co.uk

A CIP catalogue reference for this book is available from the British Library.

ISBN 9781911255420

Also by Chris Ward:

Dambusters- The Definitive History of 617 Squadron at War 1943-1945
by Chris Ward, Andy Lee and Andreas Wachtel, published 2003 by Red Kite.

Dambuster Crash Sites
by Chris Ward and Andreas Wachtel, published 2007 by Pen and Sword Aviation.

Dambusters. Forging of a Legend
by Chris Ward, Andy Lee and Andreas Wachtel, published 2009 by Pen and Sword
Aviation.

Images of War: 617 Dambuster Squadron at War
by Chris Ward and Andy Lee, published 2009 by Pen and Sword Aviation.

1 Group Bomber Command. An Operational History
by Chris Ward with Greg Harrison and Grzegorz Korcz, published 2014 by Pen and
Sword Aviation.

3 Group Bomber Command. An Operational History
by Chris Ward and Steve Smith, published 2008 by Pen and Sword Aviation.

4 Group Bomber Command. An Operational History
by Chris Ward, published 2012 by Pen and Sword Aviation.

5 Group Bomber Command. An Operational History
by Chris Ward, published 2007 by Pen and Sword Aviation.

6 Group Bomber Command. An Operational History
by Chris Ward, published 2009 by Pen and Sword Aviation.

Other RAF Bomber Command Profiles published by Mention the War Ltd.
75(NZ) Squadron
83 Squadron
101 Squadron
103 Squadron
106 Squadron
138 Squadron
300 Squadron
617 Squadron

Contents

Introduction

RAF Bomber Command Squadron Profiles first appeared in the late nineties, and proved to be very popular with enthusiasts of RAF Bomber Command during the Second World War. They became a useful research tool, particularly for those whose family members had served and were no longer around. The original purpose was to provide a point of reference for all of the gallant men and women who had fought the war, either in the air, or on the ground in a support capacity, and for whom no written history of their unit or station existed. I wanted to provide them with something they could hold up, point to and say, "this was my unit, this is what I did in the war". Many veterans were reticent to talk about their time on bombers, partly because of modesty, but perhaps mostly because the majority of those with whom they came into contact had no notion of what it was to be a "Bomber Boy", to face the prospect of death every time they took to the air, whether during training or on operations. Only those who shared the experience really understood what it was to go to war in bombers, which is why reunions were so important. As they approached the end of their lives, many veterans began to speak openly for the first time about their life in wartime Bomber Command, and most were hurt by the callous treatment they received at the hands of successive governments with regard to the lack of recognition of their contribution to victory. It is sad that this recognition in the form of a national memorial and the granting of a campaign medal came too late for the majority. Now this inspirational, noble generation, the like of which will probably never grace this earth again, has all but departed from us, and the world will be a poorer place as a result.

RAF Bomber Command Squadron Profiles are back. The basic format remains, but, where needed, additional information has been provided. Squadron Profiles do not claim to be comprehensive histories, but rather detailed overviews of the activities of the squadron. There is insufficient space to mention as many names as one would like, but all aircraft losses are accompanied by the name of the pilot. Fundamentally, the narrative section is an account of Bomber Command's war from the perspective of the bomber group under which the individual squadron served, and the deeds of the squadron are interwoven into this story. Information has been drawn from official records, such as group, squadron and station ORBs, and from the many, like myself, amateur enthusiasts, who dedicate much of their time to researching individual units, and become unrivalled authorities on them. I am grateful for their generous contributions, and their names will appear in the appropriate Profiles. The statistics quoted in this series are taken from The Bomber Command War Diaries, that indispensable tome written by Martin Middlebrook and Chris Everitt, and I am indebted to Martin for his kind permission to use them.

Finally, let me apologise in advance for the inevitable errors, for no matter how hard I and other authors try to write "nothing but the truth", there is no such thing as a definitive account of history, and there will always be room for disagreement and debate. Official records are notoriously unreliable tools, and yet we have little choice but to put our faith in them. It is not my intention to misrepresent any person or Bomber Command unit, and I ask my readers to understand the enormity of the task I have undertaken. It is relatively easy to become an authority on single units or even a bomber group, but I chose to write about them all, idiot that I am, which means 128 squadrons serving operationally in Bomber Command at some time between the 3rd of September 1939 and the 8th of May 1945. I am dealing with eight bomber groups, in which some 120,000 airmen served, and I am juggling around 28,000 aircraft serial numbers, code letters and details of provenance and fate. I ask not for your sympathy, it was, after all, my choice, but rather your understanding if you should find something with which you disagree. My thanks to you, my readers, for making the original series of RAF Bomber Command Squadron Profiles so popular, and I hope you receive this new incarnation equally enthusiastically.

My thanks also, as always, to my gang members, Andreas Wachtel, Steve Smith, Greg Korcz and Clare Bennett for their unstinting support, without which my Profiles would be the poorer. I appreciate the generosity of Steve Roberts, Mark Every and Ken Delve at the Marham Aviation Heritage Centre, not only for spending some hours with me and allowing me access to the extensive photo archive, but also for scanning the many photos and sending them to me for inclusion in this book. Finally, my appreciation to my publisher, Simon Hepworth of Mention the War Ltd., for his belief in my work, untiring efforts to promote it, and for the stress I put him through to bring my books to publication.

Chris Ward. Skegness, Lincolnshire. March 2019.

Canadian Gavin Hall was a rear gunner. This photo is dated July 1943, at which time 115 Sqn was stationed at RAF East Wretham.

Narrative History

115 Sqn group photograph at RAF Marham, 1937. The aircraft is a Handley Page Harrow, subsequently to be replaced by the Vickers Wellington.

Formed on the 1st of December 1917, 115 Squadron did not see action until it arrived in France in September 1918, from where it conducted bombing operations against German industrial targets for what remained of the Great War. Following its return to England, it was disbanded in October 1919, and spent most of the inter-war years on the shelf. Reformation took place on the 15th of June 1937 at Marham, and, on the 3rd of April 1939, it became the fifth unit in the Command to equip with Wellingtons. With this type on charge, and, as one of 3 Group's front line squadrons, 115 Squadron spent the last few months of peace preparing for the inevitable impending conflict.

September to December 1939

The squadron Operations Record Book contains the build-up to war, the entry for the 1st of September 1939 referring to German forces occupying the city of Danzig and launching a ground and air offensive across the frontier. This prompted an order to disperse the squadron's aircraft in anticipation of air attacks. The entries for the 2nd and 3rd spoke of the ultimatum by the British and French governments and the failure by the Germans to respond positively by 11am on the 3rd, concluding with the line "so Britain and France are at war with Germany". There had already been drama at Marham on the 28th of August, when the 3 Group A-O-C, Air Commodore Thomson, had been killed in a tragic incident. He had been watching the loading of a Wellington, when a bomb slipped, sending onlookers retreating, and he had the misfortune to be struck by a rotating propeller, which killed him instantly. He would be succeeded by AVM "Jack" Baldwin, who would remain in post for the ensuing three years. When war was declared, 3 Group was poised for action, and was confident in the validity of the theory, that the self-defending bomber formation would always get through to its target in daylight in sufficient numbers to find and destroy its objectives. As the theory had never been tested in battle, its flaws had not yet become apparent, but 3 Group was to be one of those, whose crews would be sacrificed in learning valuable lessons.

115 Squadron was under the command of W/C Rowe, who had been in post since March, with the recently-arrived S/L Glencross, late of 214 Squadron, in command of A Flight and S/L Bowles of B Flight. The squadron was put on two-hours readiness at 07.30 on the 6th on reports that the German fleet had put to sea, but the order was cancelled at noon. The next week saw the squadron withdraw its aircraft to a rearward location at Elmdon near Birmingham, while others spent time exercising at Carew Sheriton

in South Wales, although there were frequent visits to Marham to pick up personnel and equipment. The squadron would not be involved in the early skirmishes arising out of armed

reconnaissance operations to the north-west German coastal regions in search of enemy naval forces. In fact, it did not operate for the first time until the 8th of October, when orders were received for six aircraft to join others from 99 Squadron to attack elements of the German fleet off the Norwegian coast. The 99 Squadron Wellingtons arrived over Marham at 15.40 to prompt the departure at 15.55 of the 115 Squadron aircraft containing the crews of S/L Bowles, F/L Guthrie, F/Os Newman and Pringle and F/Sgts Boore and Groves. Each was carrying a load of 500 pounders, which they still had on board when they returned between 19.15 and 19.55 to report having failed to locate the enemy warships.

Anson N5239 at Grangemouth, October1939 (Ollar Collection)

It was a relatively gentle final quarter of the year for the squadron, when compared with the experiences of other 3 and 5 Group front line units, which attempted daylight forays over the North Sea in search of enemy shipping. There were no further operations for the squadron during October and November, but plenty of exercises and stand-by operations orders kept the crews on their toes. Marham welcomed G/C Keith as successor to G/C Lloyd as station commander on the 27th of November, and S/L Bowles was posted to command fellow Marham residents, 38 Squadron on the 30th as successor to W/C Adams, just as the squadron was being prepared for a posting overseas to Egypt. This left a vacancy for a B Flight commander at 115 Squadron, which was filled by the arrival of S/L du Boulay.

December began with a North Sea sweep on the 1st by three aircraft containing the crews of F/Os Pringle, Gibbs and Donaldson. They took off at 12.20, and encountered a small flotilla of destroyers and minesweepers, towards which they dived with their bomb doors open. Deck markings suggested that the vessels belonged to the Royal Navy, and no bombs were released. Defensive fire from the intended targets failed to score any hits, and there is still a question as to whether or not they were enemy ships after all. The squadron dispatched three sections of three aircraft each at 09.05 on the 3rd, to join up with elements from 38 and 149 Squadrons, with S/L Glencross, F/O Gibbes and P/O Barber acting as section leaders. The aircraft taking part were N2875, N2876, N2877, N2899, N2900, N2947, N2949, N2950 and N2989, and their destination was Heligoland, which they reached at 11.45, before bombing shipping at anchor from 10,000 feet. Hits were claimed on a cruiser and a trawler, while the late release of a hung-up bomb caused it to land on a flak battery on the shore, the first RAF bomb to fall on German territory.

Squadron photo with a Wellington, in 1939

It should be understood, that rules of engagement at this time precluded attacks on land, in case of reprisals by the enemy, and this left ships at sea as the only permissible targets. However, accidents happen, and such incidents would, ultimately, lead to the abandonment of such restrictions. The Wellingtons were forced to run the gauntlet of anti-aircraft fire, which was accurate for height, but little damage was sustained. Enemy fighters appeared once out of range of ground fire, and one was reported to have been shot down. One Wellington lost contact with the formation, but arrived home with the others shortly after 14.00, riddled with holes, but, otherwise, not majorly damaged. It was confirmed later that a minesweeper had been sunk.

Flying into the jaws of the waiting BF109s and BF110s on the 14th of December, five out of twelve 99 Squadron Wellingtons were shot down, and four days later, twelve of twenty-four from 9, 37 and 149 Squadrons suffered a similar fate. Following these disasters, when an overall 50% loss rate was incurred, the policy of unescorted daylight operations was re-appraised. A sweep off the Norwegian coast on the 24th involved fifteen Wellingtons from Marham, nine of them provided by 115 Squadron. The first section of six took off at 10.45 with F/Os Pringle, Gibbes and Donaldson the senior pilots on duty. They were followed away shortly after 11.00 by S/L Glencross, F/L Newman and F/O Wells, who were bound for the same general area off Norway. The first section observed no enemy warships, and managed to return to Marham to land before darkness fell. The second section, which was expected back at around 17.00, encountered flak ships, the fire from which, during the course of bombing them, damaged F/L Newman's N2948. By the time they reached England, at around 18.00, fog had compounded the difficulties of landing in darkness, and news eventually came through that F/L Newman had baled-out his crew, and had landed at Martlesham Heath. The lack of hydraulics had led to a crash, from which he walked away, but his second pilot, P/O Gayford, had broken an ankle on landing by parachute. Unaccountably, S/L Glencross was placed under arrest for disobeying orders, although the precise nature of the charge against him was not made apparent in the ORB. Happily, he was released from custody on

Christmas Day pending an enquiry. On the 27th, by which time the "Phoney War" and the harsh winter were restricting operational activity to a minimum, W/C Mills was appointed as the new commanding officer in succession to W/C Rowe, who was posted to Maintenance Command at Andover.

January 1940

The New Year brought with it an increase in the severity of the winter conditions, and it would be towards the end of February before the season's grip had loosened sufficiently to allow unrestricted flying. What little operational flying was possible during January involved North Sea sweeps under Operations Instructions 20 and 21, undertaken by S/L du Boulay and F/Sgt Boore on the 2nd, in the only two Wellingtons that could be fired up in the extreme cold. Three managed to get away on the 3rd captained by the newly-promoted F/L Pringle and F/Os Donaldson and Wood, and nine on the 5th, in sections of six and three led by S/Ls Glencross and du Boulay respectively, all of which were completed without incident. There were discussions concerning "nickel" (leaflet) operations, for which advice was sought from 4 Group, which had been conducting such flights from the outset, and was the only group fully trained in the art of flying by night. F/Sgt Powell took off shortly after midnight on the 13th with P/O Wickenkamp as second pilot, and headed for Hamburg on a nickelling sortie under Operations Instruction 22, to deliver what ACM Harris would later refer to as toilet paper. They returned at 07.00 after an uneventful sortie and having fulfilled their brief. At 11.00 on the 20th W/C Mills led P/O Barber's section of three Wellingtons on a sweep under O.I 20 and 21, and returned after three-and a half hours with nothing to report. F/L Pringle and F/Os Donaldson and Wood conducted another sweep in the early afternoon of the 23rd, and this concluded the squadron's operational activity for the month after twenty-one sorties.

115 Sqn senior officers with a Wellington, early 1940 at RAF Marham

February 1940

Wellington N2948 lies wrecked at Marham on 24th February 1940. The aircraft crashed on take off whilst being piloted by F/O E. G. Scott

Operations began for the squadron with an intended North Sea sweep on the 1st for which six Wellingtons were made ready. F/L Pringle and F/Os Donaldson and Gibbes departed Marham at 10.50, to be followed ten minutes later by S/L du Boulay and F/Os Statham and Wood. The plan called for them to proceed from base to a position a hundred miles east of Skegness, before turning north and patrolling for a further hundred miles. However, by the time they had reached the coast, the weather had deteriorated to such an extent that the operation was abandoned, and the two sections descended through the cloud at thirty-second intervals before returning safely to land at 13.00 and 13.15. The weather remained unfavourable for the next week-and-a-half, and it was the morning of the 11th before another sweep could be conducted over the same beat. W/C Mills joined S/L Glencross and crew in N2876 at the head of a section of six aircraft taking off at 11.45 and flying into heavy cloud. Aircraft lost contact with each other from time to time, and F/O Wells became detached altogether from the others after passing through two layers of cloud. He emerged from the murk at around 300 feet above sea level, and spotted a lifeboat which was checked out and found to be empty. With no prospect of regaining the formation, he turned for home and landed at 14.00. F/L Newman's section caught site of a large tramp and two destroyers ploughing a course of 230 degrees, but lost contact with the two remaining aircraft of S/L Glencross's section, and it was decided to return home, where they landed safely at 15.00.

Orders were received on the morning of the 20th for A Flight to be at readiness for night operations against elements of the German navy off Heligoland. It was 23.50 before W/C Mills and crew took off in challenging weather conditions, and they were followed into the air at 00.15 and 00.20 by F/Os Wells and Scott respectively. An inaccurate weather forecast adversely affected navigation, and the freezing-up of the Heligoland Bight made the coastline difficult to identify, as a result of which, the intended targets were not located. W/C Mills landed at Ratcliffe at 07.30 to report encountering enemy fighters, but being uncertain as to whether or not they had attacked. He also reported attempting to bomb a destroyer, but a technical issue had caused the bombs to hang-up. F/Os Wells and Scott landed at North

Coates, and all three Wellingtons returned to Marham in the late afternoon. The 24th was devoted to training, and it ended with the squadron suffering its first aircraft casualty of the war. F/O Scott and crew were in the process of taking off in N2948 when the Wellington struck a tree and returned immediately to earth. The fuselage broke in two and the front turret was ripped off before the wreckage was consumed by fire, but, remarkably, only superficial injuries were sustained by the occupants. The leap year threw up a 29th of February, and fifteen minutes before its end, F/Sgt Boore took off in N2987 to deliver leaflets to the Baltic port and ancient Hanseatic (free trade) city of Lübeck.

March 1940

The 1st of March was just fifty-five minutes old when S/L du Boulay and crew departed Marham in N2989 for similar duties over Wilhelmshaven, Cuxhaven and Brunsbüttel. Both crews were safely back on the ground by 06.30 have completed uneventful sorties. During the course of the month the squadron operated on just four occasions, launching seventeen sorties for the loss of one Wellington during training.

The residents of Marham awoke on the 1st to a glorious morning with a cloudless sky but a chill east wind. There were no operations, but a fairly intensive training program occupied the first week of the new month, with pinpoints for the cross-country-exercises as far apart as Tiree, Guernsey and Aldergrove. P/O Barber took off at 10.15 on the 4th for a cross-country flight taking in Land's End, but returned at 14.30 with a faulty throttle control. During the course of the landing a Verey pistol was accidentally fired and the Wellington was set on fire. There were no crew casualties, but the Wellington sustained considerable damage, although it was not declared to be a write-off. W/C Andrew "Square" McKee arrived on the 7th to conduct an investigation into the forced landing by S/L Glencross, which may be a reference to the latter's arrest on Christmas Eve. Six Wellingtons were made ready on the morning of the 9th for a special sweep to be conducted by two sections of three, the first taking off at 11.15 led by F/L Pringle. They set course from base to a position twenty-five miles east of Sheringham at 53°N and 2°E with orders to proceed to 55.20N and 1.00E, which put them around ninety miles off Blyth on the Northumberland coast. The weather conditions of heavy cloud were unhelpful, and P/O Donaldson became detached from the others, ultimately returning over Wells, while F/L Pringle and F/O Gibbes made landfall further north. They all reached Marham at the same time, however, at 14.45, fifty minutes after F/L Newman, F/O Wells and P/O Gayford had departed to reconnoiter the same beat. F/O Wells returned early with W/T failure, and, after the others landed at 16.30, they reported observing the superstructure of a large steamer that had sunk in the shallow waters of the Wash.

On the 15th 3 Group sent aircraft in search of enemy shipping at sea, for which sweep F/L Pringle and F/Os Donaldson and Gibbes took off at 10.20. They picked up a sighting report from another section, which led them to the location of the target vessels, a minesweeper and a patrol boat. P/Os Barber, Gayford and F/Sgt Powell took off at 15.00 to join a 9 Squadron element to carry out an attack, but they were unable to find them at the reported location and returned empty-handed. These three crews were in action again on the following day, taking off in the late morning for a special sweep that found nothing of interest. That evening F/L Pringle and crew took to the air at 20.00 for a nickeling and reconnaissance sortie over north-western Germany's coastal region, and they were followed fifteen minutes later by F/O Wood and crew. Cloud rendered both sorties unsuccessful, but F/L Pringle dropped leaflets over Wilhelmshaven and encountered blue searchlights. A convoy was sighted at 54°N and 05°E and reported, before a hydraulics failure forced them to fly home with bomb doors open. F/O Wood's brief was to reconnoiter the River Elbe, and pinpointed on Hitzacker to the south-east of Hamburg. They reported a few enemy aircraft and an aerodrome with boundary and beacon lights clearly visible, and anti-aircraft

115 Sqn Wellington Formation

fire and searchlights at Hamburg and Brunsbüttel. They also noted a German village close to the Dutch frontier which was not blacked out.

The policy of bombing restraint still held firm, but this was a situation about to be brought to an end. At dusk on the 16th fourteen JU88s had attacked elements of the Royal Navy at Scapa Flow in the Orkneys. Five of the attackers made a low pass and hit HMS Norfolk, killing four officers, while the remaining aircraft delivered high explosives onto Hatston aerodrome and Bridge of Wraith on the road between Kirkwall in the east and Stromness in the west. Two cottages were damaged, and a twenty-seven-year-old civilian was inadvertently killed by a stray bomb. As an act of retaliation, Bomber Command was ordered to attack the German seaplane base at Hörnum on the Island of Sylt, an operation carried out over a six-hour period on the night of the 19/20th, first by Whitleys of 4 Group and, later, by Hampdens of 5 Group. Enthusiastic claims by returning crews told of major damage to the target, but sadly, by the time that photographic reconnaissance took place on the 6th of April, there was no evidence to support the claim. Such over-optimistic claims of success would become a recurring theme and would eventually return to haunt the Command. Earlier in the day of this momentous first strike against Reich territory, 115 Squadron suffered its first crew fatalities of the war. While being ferried to Vickers at Weybridge, N2987 suffered an engine failure, and crashed near Huntingdon while F/O Statham was attempting a forced-landing. Second pilot, F/O Fanshawe and two others on board lost their lives, while F/O Statham, and the two remaining occupants sustained serious injury.

Two sections took off for a routine sea sweep over the usual beat at 13.50 on the 20th led by F/L Newman and P/O Barber, but nothing of interest was spotted and all returned without incident at 16.00 and 16.30. The squadron made ready four Wellingtons for nickeling and reconnaissance duties on the 21st, and they took off between 19.15 and 19.30 in the hands of F/L Newman, F/O Wells and P/Os Barber and Gayford and their crews. Poor weather conditions prevented reconnaissance of the area between Hamburg and

Boizenberg to its south-east along the Elbe, but their seemed to be flooding at Hamburg, and searchlights were active over Cuxhaven, while flak-ships were operating south-west of the Frisian Island of Terschelling. Leaflets were dropped over Hamburg and Bremerhaven, the latter revealing itself to be the location of oil storage tanks, and searchlight batteries along the Frisian chain assisted greatly with navigation.

S/L Marwood-Elton was posted to the squadron on the 23rd to succeed S/L Glencross as A Flight commander, on the latter's posting to Stradishall for operations room duties. One is left wondering if the recent enquiry chaired by W/C McKee was behind the transfer. The funeral of F/O Fanshawe took place at 15.00 with full military honours, and, at 20.00 that evening, N2950 took off with F/Sgt Powell at the controls, only to blow a cylinder just after a course had been set for north-western Germany for a reconnaissance sortie. The Wellington just failed to make the runway on return for a forced-landing and crashed at 20.10, before being consumed by fire. The occupants all managed to make their escape and sustained only slight injuries. The incident did not prevent F/O Donaldson and crew from getting away at 20.15 or F/O Gibbes five minutes later, but both would encounter low cloud in their respective briefed operating areas. The former was tasked with reconnoitering the Elbe-Weser Canal near Hannover, which they picked up first at Wunstorf, north-west of the city, and found strings of barges, floods, and two trains moving at high speed. With cloud down to 300 feet, however, further reconnaissance was pointless, and they returned home to land at 02.10. Half an hour later F/O Gibbes landed to report ten-tenths cloud at 500 feet over Bremen and Bremerhaven, which had severely compromised his efforts to fulfil his orders.

S/L Solbe and crew arrived from 214 Squadron at Stradishall on the 27th, and one must assume that he had been posted in with a view, ultimately, to being appointed to the role of flight commander, although this did not happen. At 19.40, F/O Scott and crew took off for nickeling and reconnaissance duties over northern Germany, but were back in the circuit two hours later after their W/T failed. The two new flight commanders led a section each for the first time operationally on the 28th, S/L Marwood-Elton taking off at 10.00 for a North Sea sweep with F/L Newman and F/O Wells in tow, while S/L Solbe, F/O Boore and F/Sgt Boore departed at 15.00 for the same general area. Nothing of interest was spotted, and each section landed safely after no more than two-and-a-half hours aloft. The father of the RAF, Lord Trenchard, visited the station during the afternoon. As unfolding events in Scandinavia began to attract attention, the squadron received orders on the 30th to prepare to move to Kinloss in Scotland, while 9 Squadron took up residence at Lossiemouth for a temporary attachment to Coastal Command. The advance party left Marham by rail on the 31st led by the squadron adjutant, P/O Smith. During the course of the month the squadron operated on twelve occasions, dispatching thirty-seven sorties for the loss of two Wellingtons on home soil and three crew members.

April 1940

Those remaining at Marham awoke on the 1st to heavy rain and a southerly gale, which would not have helped preparations for the departure for Kinloss of the main body of ground personnel and equipment. The advance party arrived at noon and set about the task of preparing the way for the remainder of the squadron. The main party, under the command of P/O Rankin, left Marham at 17.00 and boarded trains for the long journey north, leaving the aircraft and crews to follow on next day. The 2nd dawned fine and dry with a less strident southerly wind to help push them to their new home. B Flight took off at 10.40 and A Flight thirty minutes later led by W/C Mills, and, once the main party had arrived at 17.00, the reunited squadron got on with the business of settling in. Their new role required them to fly reconnaissance patrols off Denmark, and the crews attended a lecture on ship recognition on the following afternoon. The squadron spent the ensuing few days on stand-by for an operation, but it was the 7th before they were called into action, twelve Wellingtons taking off between 11.05 and 11.15 to join up with elements of 9 Squadron. W/C Mills was the senior pilot on duty, although he was flying as second pilot to S/L du Boulay, while S/L Marwood-Elton led A Flight. Their orders were to square-search an area of the North Sea off Denmark's western coast from south to north, beginning around seventy miles out and ending in sight of land. Their quarry was an enemy flotilla comprising a cruiser and six destroyers, which, in the event, was not located, despite a search lasting from 13.45 to 15.25. Through avoiding 9 Squadron during the turn for home, A Flight became somewhat adrift, and was set upon by BF110s, which concentrated their attacks from the beam. The Wellingtons maintained a tight formation and took no evasive action in an attempt to prevent any from becoming stragglers, but N2949 and P2524 were shot down in flames into the sea. and there were no survivors from the crews of P/Os Gayford and Wickenkamp respectively. Three other aircraft were hit by cannon and machine gun shells, and petrol tanks were holed in each case, damage which would require them to be returned to Vickers for repair. The survivors landed after more than seven hours aloft, and one report suggested that an enemy fighter had been destroyed. S/L Marwood-Elton sustained a slight wound, as did AC2 Bax of F/O Scott's crew, but they would soon return to duty. These were the first 115 Squadron failures to return from operations, and, by war's end, the squadron would hold the record for the most aircraft lost.

On the 9th, German forces marched unopposed into Denmark, and began sea and airborne landings in southern Norway. The British and French governments responded by dispatching forces by sea to attempt their own landings at Narvik in the north. Prevented by the extreme range from directly supporting this operation, Bomber Command was ordered to focus its efforts against the southern airfields, from which the enemy was launching its airborne troops into battle, and shipping on the main route from Germany. On this opening day of the campaign, B Flight was on stand-by to attack the German cruisers Köln and Königsberg at Bergen, and the six Wellingtons took off shortly before 16.00 with S/L du Boulay the senior pilot on duty. F/Sgt Boore had to switch to the reserve aircraft, which delayed his departure by ten minutes, but he had caught up by the time the target area was reached. Attacks were carried out from between 6,000 and 2,500 feet, and S/L du Boulay claimed a hit with a 500 pounder on the stern of one of the vessels. P/O Donaldson's P9235 sustained a little damage from light flak, but all returned safely either side of 21.00. F/L Pringle and F/O Wells were the section leaders when six of the squadron's Wellingtons took off either side of 15.30 on the 10th with orders to attack a cruiser at berth in Christiansand harbour. They had covered around seventy miles when a recall order was received from 18 Group, and they landed back at Kinloss shortly before 17.00.

Sola airfield at Stavanger was the target for two sections of three aircraft each on the evening of the 11th, that comprising F/O Scott, P/O Barber and F/Sgt Powell and their crews departing first at 18.00 to be followed ten minutes later by S/L du Boulay, F/O Wood and F/Sgt Boore. W/C Mills was flying as second pilot to S/L du Boulay, whose section carried out an attack with 500 pounders from 1,000 feet, claiming hits near the runway and a possible petrol fire. The second section ran in at between 200 and 300 feet, but missed the aerodrome and found itself the target for fierce and accurate anti-aircraft fire, which brought down P9284 to crash in flames. There were no survivors from the crew of P/O Barber, and F/Sgt Powell and crew almost suffered a similar fate after P9271 was hit three times, damaging the hydraulics and wounding F/Sgt Powell and gunner, LAC Hodgson. However, the wounded pilot brought the damaged Wellington home to a wheels-up landing, for which he was awarded the DFM, thus becoming the first in 115 Squadron to be decorated for gallantry. P9235 was hit by a single shell, which seriously wounded F/O Scott's navigator, Sgt Smith, and his role was taken over by the second pilot, Sgt Newberry. Later in the day, a force of eighty-three Wellingtons, Hampdens and Blenheims took part in the largest Bomber Command operation of the war to date, against shipping off Stavanger.

115 Sqn F/Sgt Boore DFM, 7th April 1940

F/L Pringle, F/O Gibbes and F/O Donaldson took off at 02.00 on the 14th for a return to Sola aerodrome, and flew out in formation to reach the target area while it was still dark. They stooged around for thirty minutes until there was sufficient light to carry out their attacks, and, between them, in the face of spirited opposition, delivered fourteen 250 pounders among aircraft lined up on each side of the runway. F/O Gibbes then carried out a strafing run on the seaplanes in the fjord, before all returned safely to land by 07.30. This proved to be the final offensive action for the squadron under the banner of Coastal Command, as orders were received later in the day to return to Marham. W/C Mills talked about the squadron's Kinloss operations in a BBC broadcast at 21.00 on the 18th, and he and S/L du Boulay later recalled their experiences for an American radio audience. F/O Laslett and F/Sgt Moores continued their training with a special sweep each over the North Sea on the 22nd, but observed nothing of interest during their two-hour and twenty-minute sorties. On the 23rd the squadron contributed three Wellingtons to a 3 Group effort of twelve tasked to attack the aerodrome at Westerland on the island of Sylt. Fellow Marham residents 38 Squadron provided three aircraft and the remainder came from 9 Squadron at Honington. The 115 Squadron element, consisting of S/L du Boulay and F/Os Laslett and Wood, took off either side of 21.00, and, as far as could be ascertained, delivered an effective attack in the face of intense anti-aircraft fire. F/O Wood, in particular, found it difficult to escape the attention of the defences, having arrived in the later stages of the raid. S/L Marwood-Elton took off 19.05 on the 26th to carry out a reconnaissance of Stavanger, ahead of a force of eighteen Wellingtons and Whitleys, whose crews had been briefed to attack the aerodrome, shipping and oil-storage facilities. He reached the target area at 20.15 to find heavy cloud obscuring the ground, and reported back to group, which sent out a recall signal.

Operations continued in support of this ill-fated campaign, and the squadron was next called into action on the night of the 30th, when dispatching F/L Pringle and F/Os Donaldson and Gibbes at 18.25. They were to join forces with six Wellingtons each from Mildenhall and Feltwell and three from Honington to attack Stavanger (Sola) aerodrome with 250lb GP bombs, some of them with up to twelve-hour delay fuses. F/O Donaldson was baulked by another aircraft during his first run, but carried out a second one, before returning home independently of the others. F/L Pringle and F/O Gibbes came home together as far as the English coast, and the former made it back to Marham without difficulty, while F/O Gibbes struggled to establish his whereabouts in conditions of poor visibility and low cloud and having lost his W/T. While cruising at 1,000 feet R3154 hit high ground at Spaunton Moor, north-west of Pickering in Yorkshire, and crashed, killing the second pilot and navigator and slightly injuring the pilot and two others. During the course of the month the squadron operated on nine occasions, dispatching forty-two sorties for the loss of four Wellingtons and three complete crews.

May 1940

The Scandinavian misadventure was in its final stages by the time the squadron carried out its first offensive activity of the new month, after spending most of the first seven days and nights training and ferrying. Three aircraft each from 115, 37 and 75(NZ) Squadrons were made ready for a further attack on Sola aerodrome at Stavanger on the evening of the 7th. F/L Newman led the 115 Squadron element with F/Os Scott and Laslett, and they took off at 19.30 with a load of six 250 pounders each. Poor weather was encountered in the target area, and only F/L Newman, approaching from the east, managed to locate the aerodrome and deliver his bombs. The remaining eight crews apparently searched long and hard, but failed to find it through the cloud. On the 9th, the A-O-C and Vickers chief test pilot, Mutt Summers, came for lunch, and, that evening, F/Sgt Moores took off at 19.30 to for an anti-mining patrol in the Husum-Flensburg area. He was followed into the air at 20.45 by F/O Wells and crew bound for the Kolding region of Denmark, a little further north, and, finally, by S/L Marwood-Elton and crew at 22.00 with Esbjerg as their destination. They observed no activity, but attracted a little attention from searchlight and flak batteries before returning safely after a round trip each of between six and six-and-three-quarter hours. As they lay in their beds in the early hours of that morning, they were unaware that the first phase of the war had just ended, and, that what was about to unfold would end for good the pretence and shadow boxing that had characterized the previous eight months.

At dawn on the 10th of May, German forces began their advance through Luxembourg and into Holland and Belgium, prompting all RAF leave to be cancelled along with the Whitsun holiday. On that day also began the massacre of the French-based Battle and Blenheim squadrons of the AASF. Thrust into an unequal fight, the cumbersome Fairey Battles would be no match for the marauding BF109s and BF110s, to say nothing of the murderous ground fire from the defensive positions alongside the canals and bridges that the Germans had been allowed to establish unopposed. Over the ensuing days the Battles would be mercilessly hacked down, and the supporting Blenheim squadrons, along with those of the home-based 2 Group, would fare little better. At 00.45 on the 11th S/L du Boulay led a section of three Wellingtons into the air having been briefed to attack Waalhaven aerodrome at Rotterdam, which had been captured by airborne forces earlier in the day. F/L Newman's section took off thirty minutes later, and, together, they formed a thirty-six-strong 3 Group force in concert with six aircraft from 38 Squadron, a dozen from Mildenhall and six each from Honington and Feltwell. A reduction in the standard quantity of petrol allowed each Wellington to carry twelve 250 pounders, and returning crews reported they had been put to effective use against all parts of the aerodrome and parked aircraft. F/Sgt Boore alone failed to find the target, and brought his bombs home, while S/L du Boulay had two hang up.

Dutch forces laid down their arms on the 14th, before the squadron had a further opportunity to support them. The Germans began their drive through the Ardennes on the 15th, prompting the first strategic bombing of mainland Germany by Bomber Command. Sixteen communications and industrial targets in the Ruhr were selected for attack by a force of ninety-nine Wellingtons, Whitleys and Hampdens, the first occasion on which bombs were to be dropped east of the Rhine. The 3 Group crews had been briefed to attack oil production sites near Duisburg at the western end of the Ruhr, and this almost certainly included Homberg on the north-western outskirts of the city, but they were also given marshalling yards and road and rail movements as alternative objectives. The squadron put up eight Wellingtons in four sections of two, and F/L Pringle was the first to take off at 20.55 in P9299, which developed engine problems and forced him to return. One of his crew, AC Butler, reported sick and would not be on board the replacement Wellington, P9229, in which F/L Pringle eventually departed Marham as the last away at 23.35. S/L Marwood-Elton was the senior pilot on duty, and took off at 21.20, with the others following behind at regular intervals. The crews arrived in the target area to find thick cloud, which made it very difficult to establish their precise location. The winds encountered turned out to be the opposite of those forecast, and crews were blown south of their intended track on the way home. F/O Scott ordered his crew to bale out when R3152 ran low on fuel, and he and second pilot, P/O Moore, landed the Wellington near Barbey in France. F/O Laslett also landed in France, near Poix, while F/O Wells ran into a fierce electrical storm over southern England, but managed to find Marham where he touched down at 04.00. F/L Pringle fell foul of the inaccurate wind forecast, and was then given a reciprocal course, which took him further south to ultimately fly into high ground between Bernay and Rouen, some twenty miles from the French coast. F/L Pringle and three others were killed on impact, and a gunner, Cpl Fallows, died soon afterwards. This represented Bomber Command's first casualty of strategic bombing.

The speed of the enemy advance forced the Air Ministry to divert elements of the heavy squadrons away from their strategic role during the last two weeks of the month, and deploy them against troop concentrations and communications in Belgium and France. 115 Squadron briefed nine crews on the 17th for attacks on road targets in concert with nine from 38 Squadron, eighteen from Mildenhall and twelve from Feltwell. S/L Marwood-Elton was the senior pilot on duty as they departed Marham at intervals between 22.15 and 00.30, each carrying a dozen 250lb bombs with a mixture of instant and delay fuses for use against bridges over the Meuse near Namur and at Givet and Dinant, road junctions at Gembloux and marshalling yards in the Ruhr. They would not have been told that a dawn attack by twelve Blenheims of 82 Squadron at Gembloux had resulted in eleven of them failing to return. News came through at the last minute that the French had re-occupied Namur, and crews assigned to it who had not yet taken off were diverted to other targets. The weather conditions of nine-tenths cloud with some rain and haze added to the difficulties caused by considerable anti-aircraft activity and night-fighters, but returning crews claimed to have inflicted heavy damage on the bridges at Namur and Dinant and on the road junction at Gembloux. They arrived back over East Anglia to find fog, and F/O Gibbes took advantage of a break in the cloud to find a field in which to land at Markstey near Colchester. There R9300 remained until a track had been prepared and all removeable equipment taken out to reduce the take-off weight. On the following day the squadron contributed F/Os Laslett, Scott and Sheeran and P/O Morris to a 3 Group return to Gembloux and Namur, for which they took off between 22.45 and 23.53 with similar bomb loads to those employed twenty-four hours earlier. Three of them successfully carried out their assigned tasks, two hitting the bridges and one a railway junction, but the fourth one failed to locate the target.

A and B Flights prepared five Wellingtons each on the 20th for operations that night against road targets in the areas of Cambrai, Guise, Hirshon and St-Quentin. Take-off was staggered between 21.15 and 00.35, with S/Ls Marwood-Elton and du Boulay the senior pilots on duty. Returning crews claimed hits on troops and convoys and road junctions, but any success was marred by the failure to return of two crews. R3152 received a first class bearing somewhere near Le Havre, but nothing further was heard, and it was later found to have crashed in that general area, taking with it P/O Morris and his crew. There were no survivors either from the crew of F/Sgt Moores in P9298, and their current burial location suggests that they came down in Belgium. During the course of the 21st news filtered through that German forces had entered Arras and were pushing a wedge between Sedan and Liege on their way to Boulogne. That night F/Os Laslett and Wood took off after 22.00 to join four others from 38 Squadron and forty-two from 37 and 75(NZ) Squadrons at Feltwell to attack road crossings at Namur and Dinant and marshalling yards at Aachen. Haze made target identification a problem, but F/O Wood returned with claims of hits near the entrance to a bridge at Dinant. F/O Laslett and crew failed to return in P9297, and news was received eventually that all had survived their forced-landing near Poix, before falling into enemy hands.

F/Os Gibbes and Wells were the 115 Squadron participants in a 3 Group effort against Belgian road targets at Hal and Gembloux and bridges at Namur and Dinant on the night of the 22/23rd. The squadron had detailed eight Wellingtons, but the risk of fog led to six being scrubbed, and F/O Wells, after taking off at 21.25, responded to an erroneous recall signal, and came home. F/O Gibbes had taken off ten minutes earlier, and pressed on to deliver an attack on a road convoy. Later on the 23rd, German forces were reported to be in Boulogne, but operations for that night involving 3 Group remained focussed on the Belgian/Franco frontier region, with road and railway targets selected in the Chimay region in the south-west of Belgium and Liart, situated just across the frontier in France. Crews had to be recalled from leisure activities in local towns after having been stood-down, and S/L Marwood-Elton, F/Os Donaldson and Wood and F/Sgt Boore took off either side of 22.30 to join forces with forty-seven other 3 Group Wellingtons. Road, railway and anti-aircraft defences were hit at Chimay and Hirson, but only one aircraft located the railway at Liart. Marham waved off twenty Wellingtons on the evening of the 26th, eight of them containing 115 Squadron Crews. They became airborne during a ninety-minute slot either side of midnight briefed to attack road and railway movements of troops in an area covering Brussels, Wavre, Lier and Herentals and also Antwerp aerodrome. S/Ls du Boulay and Marwood-Elton were the senior pilots on duty as the squadron element headed for the target area, five carrying an increased load of fourteen 250 pounders, two with fifteen and F/O Donaldson with sixteen. F/Sgt Boore was forced to turn back with a.s.i problems, but the others pressed on to deliver their loads onto road convoys, railways and anti-aircraft defences along with Antwerp aerodrome. F/O Donaldson lobbed in at Manston to refuel before heading home to land at 05.10.

The 27th was the day on which the net began to close on the BEF, which was becoming squeezed into an ever-decreasing pocket at Dunkerque. That night brought operations against similar targets in the Menin-Brussels-Hal area, for which 115 Squadron contributed three Wellingtons to an overall 3 Group force of thirty-six aircraft. The departures of F/L Newman and F/Os Gibbes and Scott were again spread over a ninety-minute period from 21.30, and each Wellington carried a load of fifteen 250 pounders. On return, between 00.55 and 03.14, crews reported attacking road convoys, railways and searchlight concentrations, and one claimed to have hit the entrance to a bridge. On the 28th King Leopold of the Belgians ordered his forces to capitulate, doing so against the wishes of his cabinet, and causing the left flank of the Allied Army in the north to become exposed. That night 115 and 38 Squadrons each dispatched ten Wellingtons to support a 3 Group assault on tactical targets in the Dixmude-Poperinge-Cassel-Gravelines-Roulers region of north-eastern Belgium. They took off between 22.35 and 00.55 with S/Ls du Boulay and Marwood-Elton the senior pilots on duty, and all but two located their assigned targets at Roulers and Aire, where bombs were dropped into the towns themselves. On the 30th the squadron identification code letters were changed from BK to KO, and news came through that the wreckage of F/O Morris's Wellington had been found near Le Havre with six bodies on board.

The final operation of the month was mounted on the night of the 30/31st, when ten Wellingtons each from 115 and 38 Squadrons took to the air with eight from Mildenhall to attack targets in the Ypres, Torhout and Dixmude area. Take-off for the 115 Squadron brigade was spread over ninety minutes, and both flight commanders were in action leading from the front. Eight of the Wellingtons were loaded with fifteen 250 pounders, while two carried seven 500 pounders, and all made it to the target area, where poor visibility hampered their efforts. Two returning crews reported hitting Torhout and four Roulers, while the others were defeated by the conditions. During the course of the month the squadron operated on fourteen nights, dispatching eighty-two sorties for the loss of four Wellingtons and the better part of four crews.

June 1940

It had also been decided at high level, that attacks on Germany's oil industry would have a serious effect on the enemy's war effort, and Bomber Command was accordingly ordered to direct a large proportion of its resources to the "Oil Plan". However, priorities would change almost as often as the weather, and, by the third week of the month, oil would find itself relegated to third place. On the 1st of June the DFC was awarded to W/C Mills, S/L du Boulay and F/O Donaldson, and, posthumously, to F/L Pringle, and there was a DFM for F/Sgt Boore and a posthumous MBE (Military Division) for F/O Wickenkamp. That night 115 and 38 Squadrons contributed eight Wellingtons each to disrupt enemy movements around Socx, Rexpoede and Furnes in France. They took off between 21.30 and 22.25 with F/L Wells the senior pilot on duty. Four crews assigned to Rexpoede returned to report bombing the target, two others bombed Furnes as an alternative, and the two remaining crews failed to locate a suitable target and returned with their fourteen 250 pounders still on board. At debriefing it became clear that the early arrivals had benefitted from fires burning on the ground, while the smoke from these and cloud had hampered those following later. On the 2nd all air gunners were promoted to sergeant rank, thus creating upset among the long-serving regulars, who had mostly spent many years to progress beyond AC2 rank, with the prospect of achieving three-stripe status still in the distant future.

S/L du Boulay joined the station HQ staff on the 3rd for operations room duties pending his posting to 6 Group (Training) at the conclusion of his tour. He would return to the operational scene in March 1942 as the commanding officer of 103 Squadron. S/L Dabinett was posted in from 149 Squadron on the 3rd as the new B Flight commander. He had been in action on the very first day of the war, when leading a section in search of enemy shipping in the Schillig Roads. On the evening of his arrival at Marham the station dispatched eighteen Wellingtons to join a similar number from Feltwell to attack oil refineries and coking ovens at Monheim, situated between Cologne and Düsseldorf in the Ruhr. The nine 115 Squadron crews had been briefed for the refineries with marshalling yards at Cologne as an alternative target, and took off between 21.33 and 22.54 with S/L Marwood-Elton the senior pilot on duty. He was forced to turn back early on with an engine problem, by which time F/O Wood had also aborted his sortie because of a faulty a.s.i. The others pressed on to the target area, where six scored hits on the refinery, setting off fires, and one went for the marshalling yards at Reisholz in Düsseldorf.

The 5th brought the conclusion of the Dunkerque evacuation, which had seen 338,000 men miraculously plucked off the beaches and returned to England's shores. That night the squadron contributed S/L Marwood-Elton and F/O Donaldson to operations intended to hinder the movement of German columns from Cambrai in France in the west to Aachen and Düren across the German frontier in the east. The 115 Squadron pair took off shortly before 22.00, and, having experienced difficulty in identifying the briefed target, carried out attacks on a railway junction at Eschweiler, situated a few miles to the north-east of Aachen. Both Marham squadrons provided five Wellingtons on the night of the 6/7th to join a dozen others from 149 Squadron for an operation to disrupt military communications at Hirson and between Amiens and the Channel. S/L Dabinett was the senior pilot on duty for his first sortie with the squadron, and he was last away at 23.47, some hour and twenty minutes after P/O Powell had set the ball rolling. Two crews were assigned to Hirson, where hits were claimed on the railway, while three others with a roving commission bombed enemy convoy movements on a road and lights in a wood. The squadron prepared ten Wellingtons on the 8th for operations that night against bridges over the Somme at St-Valerie and Picquiny, and motor convoys on roads between Etaples and St-Valerie and out of Montreuie. They were part of a 3 Group effort of thirty-six aircraft, and took off between 21.56 and 23.50, with S/L Dabinett again the last to depart and he and S/L Marwood-Elton the senior pilots on duty. Four crews had been briefed to attack Picquiny Bridge, and one located it to strike home with three 500 pounders. The other three found alternative targets, while two of the remaining crews started fires in the Foret-de-St-Michel, three with a roving commission attacked road convoys and another targeted Abbeville aerodrome.

Italy declared war on the 10th, the day on which British and French forces finally withdrew from Norway to bring down the final curtain on the ill-fated Scandinavian adventure. An intended operation that night against concentrations of troops and vehicles in the Black Forest was cancelled, and replaced by an attack on roads at Laon and La Fere a dozen miles to the north-west. 115 Squadron dispatched four Wellingtons shortly after 22.00 with F/Os Donaldson and Scott the senior pilots on duty. Two unspecified aircraft bombed road access points out of La Fere, and another delivered a single bomb on Laon, the remainder of the load having hung up. The fourth crew failed to locate its target and brought its bombs home. R3150 developed engine trouble, which persuaded P/O Moore to bale out three of his crew, before landing safely at Watton. W/C Mills and S/L du Boulay attended an investiture at Buckingham Palace on the 11th each to receive their DFC from the hand of HM King George VI. Back at Marham the squadrons were warned that operations over Italy would soon begin from bases in the Marseilles area of southern France. News came through on the 13th that German forces were in Reims and just a dozen miles from Paris, and raids on Italy were cancelled. That night a 3 Group force of sixty-five Wellingtons was sent to attack communications centres and harass the movement of troops on the approaches to the French Capital. The effort was directed largely at forest locations at Pont-de-L'Arche, Les Anderleys, Vernon, Fleury Forges, Gournay, Gisors, Beauvais, Creil, Werberie and Soissons. The ten 115 Squadron participants took off between 22.00 and 23.32 with S/L Dabinett the senior pilot on duty. A Flight crews had been briefed to attack targets at Vernon, and reports at debriefing described fires and explosions, a gap in a bridge, a ship on fire at Dieppe and an aircraft crashing in flames near Rouen. This was almost certainly the only casualty of the operation, a 9 Squadron Wellington, that crashed at Doudeville, between Rouen and the coast, killing all on board. The B Flight section attacked targets in the Foret-de-Creil to the north-east of Paris, and returning crews reported fires and explosions.

German forces entered Paris on the 14th by which time a front had been established from the Maginot Line in the east to Le Havre in the north-west. By the middle of June, the battered remnants of the AASF had all evacuated the continent, and most of the former Battle squadrons would become part of a reconstituted 1 Group equipped with Wellingtons. The doomed fight to save France continued on the night of the 14/15th with attacks on troop concentrations and fuel and ammunition dumps in the Black Forest. 115 Squadron briefed S/L Dabinett and P/O Moore, who took off at 22.10 with orders to attack a section of forest between Baden-Baden and Bühl to the south-west. Weather conditions in the target area consisted of torrential rain and thunderstorms, despite which, fires were started. S/L Dabinett landed at Boscombe Down and P/O Moore at Harwell, and both returned to Marham later in the day. It was announced on the 16th that the French Prime Minister Reynaud had resigned and that the aged Marshal Petain had succeeded him. Also on this day, orders came through that operations over Italy were back on, and six crews were briefed for a take-off at 06.00 on the 17th. In the event, the 115 Squadron contribution would be cancelled, but ten Wellingtons from 99 and 149 Squadrons did carry out attacks on industrial targets at Genoa, launched from a base in southern France. 3 Group put up sixty Wellingtons for bombing operations over the Ruhr on the night of the 17/18th, of which five represented 115 Squadron, while F/O Sheeran flew as a reserve for an unserviceable 38 Squadron aircraft. They took off between 21.33 and 21.55, with S/L Marwood-Elton the senior pilot on duty, but F/O Sheeran was forced to return early with a faulty a.s.i. The target for the 115 Squadron element was a synthetic oil refinery at Wanne-Eickel, located a couple of miles north of Gelsenkirchen and Bochum. One crew reported dropping a stick of bombs across the northern end of the target, another claimed direct hits, and a third described causing fires and explosions. P/O Poultney reported attacking an aerodrome north of the Barmen half of Wuppertal, and observed strikes on buildings.

3 Group detailed twenty-six Wellingtons from six squadrons on the 18th to be employed against oil targets at Hamburg and Bremen, a power station, an explosives factory at Leverkusen in the Ruhr and a mine dump at Barge, twenty-five miles south-west of Wilhelmshaven. Three of the 115 Squadron crews were assigned to Hamburg and four for Barge, and they took off between 21.30 and 22.05 with W/C Mills undertaking his first operation for some time, flying with F/L Newman and crew. There was no evidence of fires as the Barge element arrived at the target, but what they left behind could be seen for some fifty miles into the return trip. There was no mention by the squadron scribe of the outcome at Hamburg, but local reports described six large fires. The squadron made ready a dozen Wellingtons on the 21st for operation against aircraft storage facilities on aerodromes at Oldenburg to the west of Bremen and Rotenburg to the east, with marshalling yards at Bremen as alternatives. They took off between 21.30 and 21.59 with S/Ls Dabinett and Marwood-Elton the senior pilots on duty, but P/O Gibbes was back on the ground after twenty minutes for an undisclosed reason, and F/O Poultney also returned early with overheating engines. The remainder pressed on, and returned up to six-and-a-half hours later to report hitting hangars and causing explosions and fires, while mixed results were claimed at marshalling yards. F/L Wells reported attacking Hörnum seaplane base on Sylt, and observed flames on the water become extinguished. F/O Fraser inadvertently landed L7845 with wheels up, and, no doubt, had an uncomfortable interview with his commanding officer on the following day.

France had been seeking peace terms since the 17th, and accepted the German and Italian offers, which would come into effect on the 25th, leaving Britain to fight on alone. From that moment the country would be gripped by invasion fever, and the rest of the world would await its collapse under the Nazi assault, America predicting just three weeks before that occurred. In the meantime, eleven 115 Squadron crews were briefed on the 24th and told they would join forces with fifty-nine others from the group in what would be its largest deployment yet in one night. The targets were dockyards, oil plants, aircraft factories and marshalling yards in northern Germany and the Ruhr, with six of the 115 Squadron element assigned to an aircraft factory at Deichhausen, north-west of Bremen, three to marshalling yards at Düsseldorf and two to a synthetic oil plant at Dortmund. They took off either side of 22.00 with S/Ls Dabinett and Marwood-Elton the senior pilots on duty, but encountered thick cloud and thunderstorms, which hampered their efforts to locate the briefed targets. F/L Wells carried out a dive-bombing attack from 3,000 to 1,000 feet on shipping at Ijmuiden, and then hit the dock at Den Helder as a last resort target. Lemwerder aerodrome was attacked to the north-west of Bremen, probably as an alternative to the Deichhausen factory. P/O Gerry jettisoned his bomb load ten miles west of Oldenburg after an engine caught fire and remained in flames all the way home to a safe landing at 02.46.

News was received on the 25th that W/C Mills was to be posted to Bassingbourne, and that S/L Dabinett was to succeed him as commanding officer. The hand-over would take place officially on the 30th when W/C Mills actually departed Marham. Before then there were operations to prepare for, the first on the night of the 26/27th, when the squadron made ready eleven Wellingtons, ten to attack the aerodrome at

Handorf near Münster and a singleton for a similar target at Dortmund. They departed Marham either side of 22.00 with S/L Marwood-Elton the senior pilot on duty, and encountered some thunderstorms in the target area. F/L Newman narrowly missed a collision with balloons by taking violent evasive action just as his bomb-aimer was pressing the tit, but his bombs may have added to the hits and fires reported by returning crews. P/O Fraser experienced engine trouble, and nearly turned L7845 on its back by diving too steeply, but managed to bomb a truck carrying a searchlight. The squadron detailed a dozen Wellingtons for operations on the night of the 28/29th, but F/O Gibbes would fail to take off because of engine trouble. The first section of five aircraft departed between 20.30 and 20.50 bound for Evreux aerodrome near Paris and led by S/L Marwood-Elton. F/L Wells failed to locate the target and bombed ships at Le Havre as a last resort target. The second element of six aircraft took off either side of 22.00 with F/L Newman the senior pilot on duty, and Hamm marshalling yards as their destination. F/O Donaldson returned early with engine trouble, and F/O Poultney went for an alternative objective, Handorf aerodrome, which he hit with five bombs and set off fires while night-flying was in progress. The remainder of this section reported causing fires within the marshalling yards.

At noon on the 30th the whole station paraded as the A-O-C presented a DFM each to Sgts Smith and Moir. The squadron was photographed afterwards, and W/C Mills bade farewell to the station. Anti-invasion measures were put in place from this day, which required three crews to stand at readiness from sunset until the following morning to take off at short notice. That night six crews departed Marham between 21.34 and 21.47 as part of a 3 Group effort against troop concentrations and dumps located in forests in the Frankfurt area. The squadron's target area was between Frankfurt and Babenhausen some fifteen miles to the south-east. All returned safely to report fires and orange explosions from sheds. This was the final operation of the month, during the course of which the squadron had undertaken twenty operations, dispatching 114 sorties without loss.

July 1940

W/C Mills departed Marham for his new post on the 1st, allowing the newly-promoted W/C Dabinett to settle into his office. He presided over his first operation on the 2nd, another hot, sunny day, which caused the Marham ground crews and armourers to perspire profusely as they prepared six Wellingtons from each squadron for the night's activity. They were to join forces with twelve others provided by 37 and 75(NZ) Squadrons at Feltwell to attack industrial targets in and around the Ruhr. The 115 Squadron crews had been briefed for marshalling yards at Soest, situated on the north-eastern rim of the Ruhr Valley, and Schwerte, a south-eastern suburb of Dortmund, and they took off between 21.40 and 21.57 with F/O Poultney the senior pilot on duty. Unfavourable weather conditions over Germany hampered target location and identification, but one returning crew claimed fire-bursts and explosions at Soest, which was confirmed by a second crew, another delivered seven 250 pounders in a stick on the Schwerte yards, also observing explosions and fires, and a third hit a blast furnace in Dortmund with similar results.

F/O Gibbes and crew were posted to Lossiemouth on the 3rd in accordance with the policy to rest crews who had been operating constantly. This was before the standard tour of thirty sorties was instituted. F/L Wells was posted to Stradishall on the 4th, the home of 214 Squadron, and two long-standing members of his crew were also rested. This was also the day on which the Royal Navy took over the home-based remnant of the French fleet, and destroyed the remainder at berth in Oran in North Africa in one of the war's most controversial actions. That night Marham and Feltwell dispatched twenty-six Wellingtons between them to continue the assault on marshalling yards and industrial targets. S/L Marwood-Elton was the senior pilot on duty as the five 115 Squadron participants got away in a thirty-three-minute slot either side of 22.00, three of them assigned to the Focke-Wulf aircraft factory in Bremen, and two to the

RAF Marham

Schwerte marshalling yards. In the event, hazy conditions over north-western Germany made target location difficult, and the Bremen trio went instead for alternative targets, including the docks at Emden and Stade aerodrome on the west bank of the Elbe near Hamburg. Meanwhile, further to the south, hits were claimed on the track and buildings within the marshalling yards at Schwerte, and yellow explosions were observed

The 5th was a glorious summer's day, but the 6th brought overcast, which possibly provided more comfortable conditions for the ground crews who had to prepare seven Wellingtons from each squadron for operations that night over north-western Germany. The target for the entire 115 Squadron effort and four from 38 Squadron was the Blohm & Voss shipyards at Hamburg, for which they took off between 21.13 and 22.11 with F/L Newman the senior pilot on duty. Adverse weather conditions, which included ten-tenths cloud and electrical storms, combined with intense flak and searchlight activity to play havoc with attempts to locate the target, and two crews brought their bombs home, while a third jettisoned its load after the pilot was thrown from his seat by flak explosions. Two crews reported bombing the docks area at Emden, but were unable to assess the results because of complete cloud cover. One crew bombed the entrance to Kiel harbour at Brunsbüttel, before delivering a stick across the south-western corner of Emden docks, and all aircraft returned safely to land between 02.00 and 04.02. The squadron made ready eight Wellingtons on the 8th to send back to north-western Germany for another crack at the Blohm & Voss yards at Hamburg and the naval dockyard at Wilhelmshaven. They took off either side of 22.00

28

with F/Os Donaldson, Scott and Wood the senior pilots on duty. They again encountered cloud and were subjected at both locations to a heavy bombardment from the ground in the form of flak set to detonate at 14,000 feet. Three returning crews reported attacking the Blohm & Voss yards and one the dockyard at Wilhelmshaven, but cloud obscured the results.

What would become known as the Battle of Britain got under way on the 10th, and began at Marham at 06.00 with a dive-bombing attack by a lone enemy aircraft, which dropped a stick of bombs across a road just beyond the married quarters occupied by the WAAFs. On the following evening, while P9236 was being prepared for a long-range night photography sortie to Stettin, a firing pin from a flash bomb was accidentally removed, causing it to explode. This burst the overload petrol tank and the Wellington was consumed by the resultant fire, thankfully, without serious injury to any ground personnel. The twenty-six-year-old S/L Patrick Foss arrived on the 12th from 15 O.T.U. at Harwell, where he had been since the 2nd of June following a spell at 3SFTS. He had joined the RAF in 1932 to learn to fly with a view to a career in civil aviation, but the war had taken priority and his role at Marham was to immediately assume command of B Flight following the elevation of the newly-promoted W/C Dabinett. The C-in-C Bomber Command, Air Marshal Portal, visited the station on the 14th, while the ground crews were busy preparing eleven 115 Squadron Wellingtons for operations over the Ruhr that night. They took off between 21.43 and 23.10 bound for the Nordstern synthetic oil plant at Gelsenkirchen and the Eiffeltor marshalling yards at Cologne, with S/L Foss the senior pilot on duty. Last away, P/O Gerry and crew, experienced engine problems shortly after take-off, and returned thirty-five minutes later after jettisoning the bomb load. The remainder would experience mixed fortunes, particularly so the three assigned to the oil plant at Gelsenkirchen. One crew reported hitting the target and causing fires, a second had their bombs hang up and the third brought their load home after cloud obscured the ground. Three aircraft attacked nearby Buer aerodrome, hitting hangars and extinguishing lights, another caused fires and explosions at the Eiffeltor marshalling yards, while yet another attacked the aerodrome at Vught in Holland and also set off fires. One crew at an undisclosed location succeeded in halting flak by firing off two red cartridges, but also had the navigator and wireless operator pass out at 16,000 feet through lack of oxygen.

Hitler gave orders on the 15th to prepare Operation Sealion, the invasion of the British Isles, and this was the same day upon which the squadron was ordered to have twelve aircraft and crews on stand-by in case of invasion. This would be a requirement every fourth day thereafter, until the threat no longer existed. Eight Wellingtons were made ready for operations on the 18th, to join forces with others from the group to attack Diepholz aerodrome, situated some fifty miles south-west of Bremen, and also the Focke-Wulf aircraft plant in Bremen itself. They departed Marham between 21.20 and 22.03 with S/L Marwood-Elton the senior pilot on duty, and it again turned into a night of mixed fortunes. One aircraft over Bremen had its bombs hang up, while two others failed to locate the target, one bringing its load home and the other flying on to Emden, where hits were claimed and fires started. Another unnamed crew attacked a bridge over a canal and caused a large fire. P/O Fraser attacked a railway near Rheine within a dozen miles of the Dutch frontier, and, for his troubles, was engaged three times by BF110s from astern and then by one on the beam while on a parallel course. The Wellington's gunners fired six hundred rounds at the assailant from two hundred yards, observing the tracer to strike home, after which the enemy disappeared from view. Sgt Gregory reported severe icing conditions, and dived down to eventually dislodge the accretion at 9,000 feet before pulling out at 7,000 feet. P9227 failed to return with the relatively inexperienced crew of P/O Hunkin, and news ultimately filtered through to confirm their survival in enemy hands. This was the first 115 Squadron crew to go missing since F/O Laslett on the night of the 21/22nd of May.

115 Sqn Wellington P9227 18/19th July 1940. Piloted by P/O W H C Hunkin. Shot down by Flak on operation to Bremen. All crew survived and became POW's. (Aircrew Remembered- Michael Beckers collection.)

During the course of the 20th another batch of battle-hardened airmen was posted out for non-operation duties. That night eleven aircraft were made ready for operations, and, not for the first time, the squadron and 3 Group ORBs are at variance. According to 3 Group records three crews were briefed for the marshalling yards at Soest and six for an oil target in Bremen, while the squadron scribe confirms the Soest element, but lists the Lindenthal aircraft park to the north of Leipzig in eastern Germany and an aircraft stores in Göttingen, a university town some twenty-five miles north-east of Kassel in northern Germany, as the other objectives. There were also two crews, those of P/O Powell and F/O Wood, taking part in ongoing experiments to generate artificial smoke to obscure potential targets from enemy bombers. Their task on this night was purely reconnaissance to assess the performance of the system over Slough, Tolworth and South Wales. Their conclusion was that it identified the location of a target, but did not hide it from prying eyes. S/Ls Marwood-Elton and Foss were the senior pilots on duty as the others departed Marham between 21.45 and 22.25 and encountered cloud over enemy territory. This prevented any assessment of results by those crews actually locating their targets, and this was typical of operations for the period, during which small numbers of aircraft were sent ineffectively against multiple, wide-ranging targets. This was a policy which would continue until early 1942, and which diluted the effectiveness of operations at a time when few bombs were finding the mark anyway. Although not fully appreciated at the time, it was a token gesture, which was frittering away the finest pre-war crews for little or no return. As the Battle of Britain gained momentum overhead, enemy airfields joined the list of targets, stretching the Command's slender resources still further, and to this would soon be added a campaign against the Channel ports from which the expected invasion was to be launched.

Training occupied the ensuing week, and the experienced F/O Donaldson DFC was posted to Bassingbourne on the 26th for a period away from operations. Finally, after the long lay-off a dozen crews were briefed to attack oil storage facilities in Hamburg and drop nickels, while P/O Barr and crew carried out an exercise with a barrage balloon W/T warning device over Harwich. S/L Marwood-Elton was the senior pilot on duty as the main element departed Marham between 21.20 and 22.07, and P/O Barr was last away at 22.40. Cloud over north-western Germany intervened to make target identification a challenge, and those releasing bombs were unable to make an assessment of results. F/O Poultney returned early with an unserviceable artificial horizon, and the others drifted back between 02.15 and 04.05 to report attacking alternative targets including Borkum and Stade aerodromes, a seaplane base at Zwischenau, Bremen docks and Lauenburg? F/O Donaldson related his operational experiences in a BBC broadcast on the 29th, and Marham was treated to a visit by an envoy of the President of the United States, accompanied by a U.S. naval attache and A/C Slessor, who all arrived by air with a fighter escort on the afternoon of the 30th.

That evening the weather caused a reduction in the number of 3 Group aircraft being detailed for operations against oil plants and marshalling yards combined with nickelling. 115 Squadron briefed six crews for the oil plant at Monheim, situated on the East Bank of the Rhine just north of Leverkusen in the Ruhr, and two for Soest marshalling yards, and they took off between 21.03 and 21.22 with F/O Poultney the senior pilot on duty. Heavy cloud obscured the ground, and only one aircraft each attacked the two assigned targets, the crews reporting explosions, presumably seen as flashes through the cloud. One aircraft returned with its bomb load intact, and the remaining five crews reported bombing last-resort targets including an aluminium works at Cologne, aerodromes at Courtrai in Belgium and Duisburg and an anti-aircraft battery at Rheine. On the 31st the recently promoted F/L Scott was posted to Bassingbourne to rest as an instructor, and F/Ls Wells and Newman were awarded the DFC. During the course of the month the squadron carried out fifteen operations (assigned targets) and dispatched seventy-three sorties for the loss of two Wellingtons and one crew.

August 1940

The Marham squadrons were not involved in the new month's opening salvoes on the night of the 1/2nd, but detailed a dozen Wellingtons each on the 2nd for operations that night against oil targets in Hamburg and marshalling yards at Hamm. S/L Foss was the senior pilot on duty as eleven 115 Squadron Wellingtons took off between 21.07 and 22.05, nine heading for Hamburg and two to Hamm, situated just to the north-east of the Ruhr. P/O Alexander and crew returned early with engine trouble, leaving the others to press on to their respective targets. Flak and searchlight activity at Hamburg was intense, and the glare prevented some crews from making an identification of the aiming-point. Four crews ultimately bombed the refinery, two straddling the target, another observing the bombs to fall into an adjacent wood and the other hitting nearby dock installations causing clouds of white smoke. Hamburg's Altona docks on the North Bank of the Elbe were attacked as an alternative target, as were the docks at Emden and a railway junction south of Hamburg. One aircraft returned with its bombs still on board after they hung up. S.O.S signals were received for around thirty minutes from the squadron's R3202, which seemed to indicate it gaining and losing altitude as its engines began to fail on the way home from Hamburg. The last signal at 01.45 fixed it at about one hundred miles north-east of Marham. W/C

P/O G R Torrance (Pilot)   *P/O R W Pryor (Pilot)*   *Sgt J Dempsey (W/Op/AG.*   *Sgt J M Croft (Air Gnr).*

Target, oil refinery Hamburg, Germany. 2/3 August 1940
Ditched 0200 off the island of Rottum, Netherlands. The aircraft was found in 1980.

Dabinett and crew were among those conducting a search at first light, but, despite extensive efforts by air and sea, nothing was found. The bodies of F/O Gerry and three of his crew eventually came ashore at various points on the Dutch coast, and it was established later that the Wellington had ditched off the little island of Rottumerplaat, some eight miles west of Borkum in the Waddenzee at 02.00.

The objectives for operations on the night of the 5/6th were the heavy cruiser Gneisenau, which was in the floating dock of the Germania shipyards at Kiel, oil refineries in Hamburg and the marshalling yards at Hamm. 115 Squadron made ready six Wellingtons for Kiel and three for Hamm, and they departed Marham either side of 21.30 with S/L Foss the senior pilot on duty, supported by the newly-promoted F/L Lynch-Blosse. The weather conditions of cloud and haze over north-western Germany were not conducive to a precision attack, and two crews brought their bombs home, while P/O Moore reported diving down to 4,000 feet to bomb the U-Boot construction yards at Kiel. One crew claimed hits on Schiphol aerodrome and another on the Hamm marshalling yards, but, all-in-all, it was another frustrating night of ineffective effort. It was a similar story on the night of the 8/9th, when the squadron contributed ten Wellingtons to an attack on the Bismarck at berth in Hamburg. W/C Dabinett was the senior pilot on duty, supported by S/L Marwood-Elton, and all got away safely either side of 21.00 only to encounter ten-tenths cloud in the target area along with intense flak and searchlight activity. Many crews either jettisoned their bombs or brought them home, and just one crew reported bombing a power generator building in Bremen without observing results. Sir Archibald Sinclair, the Secretary of State for Air, visited Marham on the 10th, and, no doubt, watched the preparation of twenty 115 and 38 Squadron Wellingtons for operations that night against the Bismarck at Hamburg and marshalling yards at Soest and Hamm. Both squadrons put up eight for Hamburg and two each for the marshalling yards, the 115 Squadron pair briefed for those at Soest. They took off between 21.44 and 22.49 with no pilots on duty above pilot officer rank, and once more encountered unfavourable weather conditions in the form of cloud. Four returning crews claimed to have carried out attacks on the primary target, but, aside from some bomb bursts in the docks to the west, no assessment could be made. Other crews attacked alternative targets in the form of aerodromes at Bomlitz in Germany and Twente in Holland and Wilhelmshaven docks.

Ollar, Woor, Peters, Gregory, Wessels and Palmer after their crash at Hillsden, August 1940
(Ollar Collection)

On the way to Berlin 28ᵗʰ August 1940 (Ollar Collection)

S/L Mulholland was posted in from 20 O.T.U on the 12th to assume command of A Flight after the posting of S/L Marwood-Elton to Lossiemouth for instructional duties on the following day. Born in Sydney Australia in 1908, Norman Mulholland had joined the RAF in 1933 on a Short Service Commission, and was serving with 148 Squadron within a month of the outbreak of war. He would be a spectator of the preparations for the night's operation to bomb the Messerschmidt aircraft factory at Gotha in central Germany, for which the Marham squadrons briefed nine crews each to join forces with ten from Honington. The 115 Squadron element took off between 20.46 and 21.45 with, again, no senior pilots on duty, and, on reaching the target area, they encountered ten-tenths cloud and generally poor weather conditions, which persuaded one crew to bring its bombs home and another to jettison them. Others carried out attacks on the primary target without observing results, and alternative objectives of Borkum aerodrome and Amsterdam docks also received attention. The 3 Group A-O-C, AVM Baldwin, visited Marham on the 14th, while the ground crews were preparing aircraft for industrial targets at Frankfurt in the south and Lünen in the Ruhr, but Bomber Command HQ changed the target to the Blaye oil depot situated on the banks of the Gironde near Bordeaux in south-western France. The number of 115 Squadron aircraft required was reduced to six, of which only five are listed as departing Marham either side of 20.30 with F/L Lynch-Blosse the senior pilot on duty. Returning crews reported many hits in a successful attack, which set off fires that were observed to be intensifying as the aircraft withdrew. P/O Fraser and F/O Robertson landed at Boscombe Down, the former with a dead engine, while F/O Poultney and Sgt Gregory force-landed at Brancaster and Bicester respectively with empty petrol tanks.

Seven 115 Squadron crews were assigned to three targets on the night of the 16/17th, for which S/L Foss and F/L Lynch-Blosse were the senior pilots on duty. Four crews were briefed for the Junkers aircraft factory at Bernberg, situated to the south of the Ruhr, two for an aluminium aircraft components factory in Frankfurt, and one for the marshalling yards at Hamm. The briefing was attended by ACM Sir W. Brook-Popham and his guest, F/L Rod Learoyd of 49 Squadron, who had just been awarded a Victoria Cross for his part in an attack on the Dortmund-Ems Canal four nights earlier. The ORB does not specify targets/crews as six of them took off between 20.40 and 21.02, but the departure much later at 21.43 of P/O Alexander and crew suggests that they were the lone 115 Squadron representatives at Hamm. At Bernberg, F/L Lynch-Blosse dived down to 2,000 feet on his second run over the target, and delivered all of his bombs onto the factory. His aircraft was hit by flak, which led to a tyre bursting on landing. Returning crews claimed this as a successful operation, as was that at Frankfurt, where crews had to run the gauntlet of accurate flak fired through the cloud.

S/L Mulholland was the senior pilot on duty for the first time on the night of the 22/23rd, when the squadron contributed seven Wellingtons to attacks on industrial and railway targets. Take-off was spread over more than ninety minutes either side of midnight, with three crews heading for the oil plant at Bottrop in the Ruhr and one each to the marshalling yards at Mannheim in southern Germany, Soest and Hamm north-east of the Ruhr, and Koblenz, some forty miles south-east of Cologne. Ten-tenths cloud covered much of the target areas, despite which some successful individual attacks were claimed, one by an unidentified 115 Squadron crew at Bottrop, which resulted in explosions. In addition to the bombing of the marshalling yards at Hamm, Koblenz and Mannheim, an electrical power station was targeted at Duisburg, as was the De Mok seaplane base. Returning from Mannheim short of fuel, R3276 struck a line of trees near Corpusty, some fifteen miles north-north-west of Norwich, and crashed at 05.15 alongside the Saxthorpe-Heydon road, severely injuring Sgt Cook and three of his crew including the front gunner, Sgt Watts, who succumbed soon afterwards in hospital.

Following a Luftwaffe raid on the 24th, in which some bombs were inadvertently dropped on central London, a retaliatory raid on Berlin was mounted by around fifty mostly Wellingtons and Hampdens on the night of the 25/26th. It was, at best, a token gesture, which succeeded only in destroying a wooden summer house in a resident's garden, but it did at least give lie to Goering's boast, that no enemy aircraft would penetrate deep into Reich territory. From this point on, Germany's Capital would become a regular destination for small numbers of aircraft, although few were to actually find the mark with their bombs. Included among the targets for 3 Group on the night of the 26/27th were a fuel store at Frankfurt and a chemicals factory in Cologne, and 115 Squadron was ordered to prepare six Wellingtons for the former and one for the latter. They took off either side of 21.00 with S/Ls Foss and Mulholland the senior pilots on duty, and appear to have experienced favourable weather conditions. Returning crews reported a successful attack at Frankfurt, where heavy flak and searchlight activity was encountered, and P/O Alexander and crew were set upon by an enemy fighter. Some sixty rounds were fired back from the Wellington, and the assailant was seen to dive down and disappear. The marshalling yards at Koblenz lay on the route between Cologne and Frankfurt, and one unspecified crew reported dropping its bombs there.

The squadron's first visit to Berlin was scheduled for the night of the 28/29th, when eight crews were briefed to bomb power stations in the Klingenberg district and on Tempelhof aerodrome, while one other was assigned to a Messerschmidt/Focke-Wulf aircraft factory at Mockau, a northern suburb of Leipzig. W/C Dabinett was the senior pilot on duty as they departed Marham either side of 21.00 to make their way eastwards, but P/O White was forced to turn back with engine trouble, and jettisoned his bombs into the sea before landing. Once over Germany the force had to run the gauntlet of flak and searchlights, and haze in the target areas made observation difficult. Despite that, returning crews claimed to have caused explosions and set off fires that could be seen more than fifty miles into the return journey. Such was the morale-boosting effect of attacking Germany's capital city, that the crews were photographed on the 30th by Movietone News and Fox Photos for screening in cinemas. The final operations of the month for 115 squadron involved a return to Berlin to attack the Henschel aircraft factory and aerodrome at Schönefeld on the south-eastern edge of the city, and also marshalling yards at Hamm, Soest and Osnabrück. A dozen aircraft were made ready, nine for Berlin and one each for the marshalling yards, and they took off during a one-hour slot either side of 21.00. The warm air and following wind made it difficult for the less experienced pilots to climb away, and, once over enemy territory, they found haze and searchlight glare prevented them from identifying ground detail. As a result, no 115 Squadron crews found the briefed target in Berlin, but one unnamed crew bombed a gas works at Tegel on the city's north-western edge. Others selected alternative and last resort targets in the form of a railway junction at Hildesheim, a factory in the Bentheim region close to the Dutch frontier and aerodromes at Braunschweig (Brunswick), Burg, Stendal and Texel. Two brought their bombs home, while those briefed for the marshalling yards appear to have attacked as briefed. During the course of the month the squadron operated on eleven nights and dispatched ninety-seven sorties for the loss of two Wellingtons, one complete crew and the incapacity of another.

September 1940

Since the middle of August the Battle of Britain had been intensifying, and would reach its climax in two weeks. In the meantime, the likelihood of invasion continued to dominate the minds of the authorities and the populace, and Bomber Command would turn its attention now upon the build-up of barges and landing craft in Channel ports. There would also be an attempt to set fire to forests using "Razzle", a new incendiary device conceived by the boffins. The purpose of the deforestation policy was to prevent their use for concealment, and 115 Squadron's introduction to what, ultimately, would prove to be a damp squib, came during its first night of operations of the new month. A dozen crews were briefed, and informed that they would be operating in concert with others from the group to attack forests, carry out reconnaissance at other locations and continue the assault on marshalling yards. F/L Lynch-Blosse was the senior pilot on duty as nine crews departed Marham either side of 21.00, six of them to fly due east to the Harz mountains south of Hannover, while three others continued on the same heading to the Grünewald Forest north of Berlin. Of the three remaining crews, one each was assigned to the marshalling yards at Schwerte and Hamm and the third to reconnoitre an area of the Black Forest near Strasbourg to check on the results of the previous night's attack. F/O Robertson and crew returned early with port-engine trouble, leaving the others to press on to their respective targets, and, those reaching the Harz were successful in causing explosions and fires which remained visible for some fifty miles into the return trip. The attacks on the marshalling yards also appeared to be effective, but cloud in the Berlin area prevented crews from carrying out their briefs there.

Orders came through on the 6th for similar operations to be mounted that night, for which 115 Squadron again detailed twelve Wellingtons. Six crews were briefed to attack the Black Forest with Razzle, while four others targeted a power station in Berlin and two attended to railway sidings in a northern suburb of Brussels. They took off between 21.07 and 22.25 with S/L Mulholland the senior pilot on duty, and those heading south to the Germany's frontier region with France and Luxembourg would return at first light with enthusiastic claims of setting off large fires, although a stuck shutter prevented photographic evidence in support. Low cloud over Berlin persuaded one crew to bring their bombs home, and the remaining three were unable to comment on the outcome of their efforts. One of them also unleashed a few bombs on an aerodrome near Hannover. P/Os McAfee and Pate reported attacking the Brussels marshalling yards and stirring up a hornet's nest of flak immediately afterwards, but made it home in one piece to tell their story. The 7th was the day on which the Luftwaffe carried out its first major raid on London, an event which, ultimately, would change the course of the Battle of Britain. All leave was cancelled, and those currently enjoying life away from their stations were recalled.

There would be no response from Marham until the 9th, when the squadron was ordered to make ready nine Wellingtons for operations that night against railway targets at Berlin, Krefeld, Hamm, Brussels and Ehrang, the last-mentioned situated in the Saarland near the Luxembourg frontier. Four crews were briefed to attack Charlottenburg station in Berlin, two the marshalling yards at Brussels and one each the marshalling yards at Krefeld, Hamm and Ehrang. S/L Foss was the senior pilot on duty among the Berlin-bound element as they took off between 21.35 and 22.22, leaving S/L Mulholland and the remainder to depart Marham after midnight. The Berlin contingent was again thwarted by cloud, and none, it seems, reached it. The attack on Brussels went well, and much damage was claimed by returning crews, but most others sought out alternative and last resort targets, including railway installations and a blast furnace at Essen, railway installations at Liege, and aerodromes at Diepholz, Celle, Schiphol and Brüggen.

F/L Lynch-Blosse and crew were posted to Mildenhall on the 10th, where he would be appointed flight commander with 149 Squadron on promotion to squadron leader rank. In early May 1942 he would be posted to command 44 (Rhodesia) Squadron, one of 5 Group's finest and the first in the Command to be equipped with the Lancaster. On his first operation, on the night of the 8/9th, he would lose his life with the rest of his crew. F/O Robertson was promoted to flight lieutenant rank to compensate for the departure of F/L Lynch-Blosse to 149 Squadron. The Marham squadrons were back in the briefing room on the 11th, where eleven crews from each unit were told of that night's operations against invasion barges at Ostend and marshalling yards at Cologne, Mannheim and Ehrang. Take-offs were spread over a two-hour period between 19.49 and 21.48, with S/L Mulholland among the first to depart and the senior pilot on duty. He was bound for southern Germany, and he is recorded as hitting a railway and small bridge at Namur in Belgium, which, presumably, occurred on the way home. The Ostend element of five carried out their attacks from around 3,000 feet, facing little opposition in the process, and returned safely to report seeing many barges and fires. The 3 Group ORB recorded this as a successful night's work.

Sgt Norman Stent

RAF Marham 1940. Ollar, Palmer, Woor and pilots Stent and Wessels (in front)   (Ollar Collection)

Post-flight refreshments while waiting to de-brief. F/O Gale is third from left.

Intelligence de-briefing after first Bomber Command raid on Berlin 1940

F/O. W. E. Gale and crew giving a 'thumbs-up' to Wellington 'Pinocchio' on 5th September 1940

More than fifty aircraft from 3 Group were made ready for operations on the 14th, of which six each from the Marham squadrons were detailed to attack the Luftwaffe HQ in the Chateau d'Argenteuil near Nivelles in the Forest of Seignes in Belgium, a building situated just half a mile east of the Waterloo memorial commemorating Wellington's victory over Napoleon in 1815. They took off first, between 21.00 and 21.25 led by S/L Foss, to be followed either side of 22.00 by six other crews led by S/L Mulholland, who had been briefed to attack marshalling yards at Brussels, Hamm and Krefeld. Weather conditions were not ideal, and ten-tenths low cloud over the Luftwaffe HQ prevented three crews from locating it. Two returning crews claimed near misses, while a third was hit by light flak. Other primary and alternative/last resort targets attacked were a power station at Brussels, railway yards at Hamm and Rheine, a road, railway and river at Arnsberg and an aerodrome near The Hague. The Battle of Britain reached its climax on the following day, the 15th, when around 1,500 aircraft were involved in pitch battles and skirmishes between dawn and dusk, and the Luftwaffe lost more than sixty, twice as many as RAF Fighter Command.

On the 17th leave for Bomber Command crews was reinstated, although, in the absence of firm intelligence that the invasion was off, attacks on invasion ports would continue throughout October, as would the Battle of Britain at a much-reduced intensity. During the course of the 17th a dozen 115 Squadron Wellingtons were prepared for operations that night. Eleven crews were briefed for an attack on ships and invasion barges at Calais, while the all-NCO crew of Sgt Stent would target the marshalling yards at Ehrang. They took off first at 20.05 to be followed between 20.55 and 22.14 by the main section, which included both flight commanders. Ten aircraft reached Calais, and attacked from between 4,000 and 10,000 feet, causing explosions and fires in locks, docks and basins. Some were exposed to intense light flak and searchlights, a proportion of which came from flak ships moored five miles off the coast, while others experienced little opposition. Sgt Stent dropped two sticks of bombs across Ehrang marshalling yards from 1,500 feet, and also caused explosions and a violent fire.

On the 20th, thirteen Wellingtons from each squadron were loaded with bombs and fuel for the continuing campaign against invasion barges. Calais and Ostend were the targets for seven and six aircraft respectively, and they took to the air between 22.48 and 00.15 with both flight commanders once more on the Order of Battle. They encountered very intense light and heavy flak, some again from flak ships,

Wellington RAF Marham September 1940
(Ollar Collection)

which followed them out to sea, and searchlight glare was partly responsible for the failure to observe results. One crew dived from 6,000 to 2,000 feet to deliver their second attack, and made their third from 10,000 feet in view of the intensity of the opposition. All returned safely to Marham, two with flak damage, and reported many explosions and fires across the docks at both locations. Le Havre and Ostend were the destinations for six and four 115 Squadron Wellingtons respectively on the 22nd, although it would be 00.57 on the 23rd before the first one got away. S/L Mulholland was the senior pilot on duty as they headed south in good weather conditions, which would hold for the entire operation. The crews at Ostend faced intense heavy and light flak, while there was little effective opposition at Le Havre, but both targets received an estimated seventeen-and-a-half tons of bombs, according to the 3 Group ORB, much of it to good effect. P/O Cookson and crew had to make an emergency landing at Ford on the south coast because of flak damage, and P/O Pate and crew reported spotting a rectangular dinghy containing four men midway between Ostend and the Suffolk coast.

G/C Groom succeeded G/C Keith as station commander at Marham on the 24th, and presided over the preparation of a dozen Wellingtons from each squadron for further operations that night against barge concentrations in invasion ports, this time Le Havre and Boulogne. The first section of five aircraft took off between 20.28 and 20.50, and they were followed between 21.12 and 21.45 by a second section of four in which S/L Foss was the senior pilot on duty. Finally, S/L Mulholland led away the last three participants between 00.13 and 00.16, it is believed, to back up the first five at Le Havre, leaving the second section to take care of business at Boulogne. At Le Havre crews mostly made two runs across the aiming-point delivering a stick of bombs on each occasion, and setting off explosions and fires. A few enemy fighters were seen, including a BF109 which climbed up a searchlight beam in pursuit of P/O Noble's aircraft. The rear gunner fired 150 rounds at it, and that put an end to the engagement. Intense heavy flak was encountered at Boulogne, particularly from flak ships moored in the harbour entrance, and shells followed the retreating bombers until they were five miles out to sea. With the arrival of the moon period on the 26th, operations over the next two weeks would be reduced to every third night.

The night of the 27/28th brought a return to attacks on marshalling yards while the anti-invasion campaign continued at Le Havre. The group and squadron ORBs differ slightly, but both Marham squadrons contributed six Wellingtons for the French port, while 115 Squadron also sent a single aircraft each to two marshalling yards at Cologne, including Gremberg, and one in Mannheim. S/L Mulholland was the senior pilot on duty as take-off began at 20.15 and went on until Sgt Miles's departure at 22.08 for a flight that lasted just twelve minutes. His was one of four sorties to end prematurely, three because of engine trouble and one with an unserviceable rear turret. Only two returning crews claimed success at Le Havre, one producing a massive explosion that could be seen from seventy miles away. One aircraft is recorded as attacking Boulogne, but cloud prevented an assessment of results. The duo assigned to the Cologne marshalling yards was thwarted by ten-tenths low cloud, and this completed a generally unsatisfactory night's work for the group.

The Command detailed more than a hundred aircraft on the last night of the month to attack a variety of targets across Germany. 115 Squadron made ready a dozen Wellingtons, five of them assigned to the Air Ministry building in Berlin's Leipzig Strasse, four to the oil refinery at Leuna near Merseburg, situated west of Leipzig, and the remaining three to the marshalling yards at Osnabrück. They took off between 18.44 and 19.53 with the Osnabrück-bound trio the last to depart and F/L Robertson heading for the Capital as the senior pilot on duty. P/Os Alexander and Roy returned early with technical issues, leaving the others to press on to their respective targets. The 3 Group ORB suggests that Berlin was

RAF Marham, September 1940. Sgt Stent (Pilot), Sgt Forrester (Pilot) Woor Peters Palmer Ollar (Ollar Collection)

located without difficulty, despite the presence of cloud, and seventeen returning crews would claim to have identified and aimed their bombs at the Air Ministry building. Local reports, however, record just six bombs falling in Berlin, and none hitting the intended aiming-point. One of the 115 Squadron element failed to locate the city, and bombed the aerodrome at Rottenburg as an alternative. At Osnabrück around forty searchlights sprang suddenly into life and co-operated with night-fighters. Sgt Dyer and crew reported being set upon by three ME110s and having to dive down to 2,000 feet to evade them. They also observed three aircraft going down in flames, and two of these are believed to have been R3292 and T2549, which failed to return with the crews of Sgt Wessels and P/O Steel respectively. P/O Steel and his navigator were the only survivors, and they soon found themselves in enemy hands. During the course of the month the squadron operated on eleven nights and dispatched 118 sorties for the loss of two Wellingtons and crews.

October 1940

F/L Claydon was posted in from 3 Group HQ on the 1st, the day on which it was decided that F/L Robertson should be paid for his elevation in rank. On the 5th, Sir Charles Portal's brief spell as C-in-C ended with his appointment as Chief-of-the-Air-Staff, and he was succeeded by Sir Richard Peirse. Peirse's masters would present him with a long list of targets, which included a continuation of the oil plan, and attacks on industry and railways in Germany and Italy. It would be a relatively quiet month for 115 Squadron, and, indeed, for the whole Command, as the pace of operations slackened with the diminishing threat of invasion, and the deterioration of weather conditions. There were no operations for the Marham squadrons until the 7th, when eight crews from each were briefed to attack the Viktoria Chemicals factory and a gas works in Berlin, while four others from 115 Squadron and five from 38

Squadron took part in Operation Lucid at Calais in support of the Royal Navy. The Berlin force took off first, between 18.53 and 19.23, with no pilots on duty above pilot officer rank, and they found the weather conditions in the target area to be generally good. Six of the squadron's participants reported bombing as briefed, and observing large explosions and fires visible from some sixty-five miles into the return journey. One returning crew reported bombing an aerodrome at Bahrenfeld, presumably the one north-west of Hamburg, and another the marshalling yards at Schoneberg, north-east of the Ruhr. The "Lucid" element, which departed Marham between 01.05 and 02.45 led by S/L Mulholland, had the task of dropping incendiaries south of the town of Calais to silhouette it for a naval bombardment from the sea. Three of them fulfilled their brief in the face of an intense searchlight and flak response, only for the Royal Navy to cancel its participation at the last minute.

The primary target for the Marham squadrons on the night of the 9/10th was the oil refinery at Wesseling, south of Cologne, for which 115 Squadron made ready eight Wellingtons plus three more for the marshalling yards at Koblenz, Ehrang and Cologne. They were airborne between 22.00 and 23.06 with S/Ls Foss and Mulholland the senior pilots on duty, and, mostly encountered cloud and haze. Crews returning from Wesseling reported fires and explosions, but none was able to provide a detailed assessment. One crew returned with its bombs, while another attacked Koblenz marshalling yards and one bombed a last resort target, Haamstede aerodrome on the island of Schouwen at the mouth of the Scheldt. A Wellington from 9 Squadron went down in the Wash on the way home, and F/L Claydon and crew were among those searching in vain for the crew later on the 10th. Wide-ranging oil-related sites at Hannover and Magdeburg and an aluminium works at Grevenbroich were intended to occupy eighteen Wellingtons from Marham on the night of the 11/12th, along with others from Mildenhall to add weight at the last-mentioned, situated north-west of Cologne. Take-offs for the nine 115 Squadron participants took place between 19.32 and 20.24 with S/L Foss the senior pilot on duty and F/L Claydon flying as second pilot to P/O Hamman. Once over enemy territory the crews encountered thick cloud, which stretched almost to ground level, and some were forced to jettison their bombs because of severe icing. None from 115 Squadron reached the primary targets, and alternatives were sought out, although two crews were unable to find anything worthy of their attention, while a third suffered bomb-release failure. Aerodromes at Moerkerke (Rotterdam) Schiphol and De-Kooy were attacked along with Ostend harbour, but it represented scant return for the effort expended.

Similar weather conditions over north-western Germany on the night of the 13/14th were responsible for another wasted effort. 115 Squadron had prepared eleven Wellingtons to attack Bismarck, Scharnhorst and Gneisenau at berth in Kiel, while a single aircraft participated in a raid on an oil plant at Gelsenkirchen in the Ruhr. The first section of five departed Marham between 18.40 and 18.53, to be followed between 19.04 and 19.25 by the second section of five led by S/L Mulholland. This left the final pair to take-off at 20.10 and 20.18, but all encountered ten-tenths low cloud and severe icing conditions that forced them to either jettison their bombs or bring them home. It was starboard-engine failure that persuaded P/O Pate to let his go, although it was successfully restarted after thirty minutes and a safe return accomplished. Orders came though on the 15th for a return that night to Kiel to attack Scharnhorst and Gneisenau and for others to try again at the Gelsenkirchen oil plant. Eleven 115 Squadron Wellingtons were air-tested, bombed and fuelled-up for the night's work, nine for Kiel and two for Gelsenkirchen, and took off between 18.54 and 20.01 with S/L Mulholland the senior pilot on duty. Weather conditions were much improved, but cloud over north-western Germany again made precision bombing impossible, and loads were dropped in the general area of the docks and shipbuilding yards, where some explosions were observed. The Gelsenkirchen duo reached and bombed the target, which was already burning well as they arrived on the scene, and 3 Group was able to confirm that 75% of crews had bombed the primary targets before returning safely home.

Another busy day awaited the Marham ground crews and armourers on the 20th as orders were received to prepare a dozen Wellingtons from each squadron for operations against the Blohm & Voss shipyards in Hamburg and the Grevenbroich aluminium works. Nine 115 Squadron crews were briefed for the former, with instructions to look out for the Bismarck as well, and three for the latter. The main element took to the air between 18.00 and 18.45 with F/L Claydon the senior pilot on duty, leaving Sgts Middleton and Miles and P/O Roy to set off for the Ruhr up to an hour later. The weather over Hamburg was fine but hazy with a little ground mist, and five returning crews reported dropping their bombs across the docks where Bismarck was believed to be. They reported bombs bursting and causing fires, and one large explosion was observed. The visibility in the Ruhr area was typically reduced by the ever-present blanket of industrial haze, and bombs were released on dead-reckoning (DR), although one crew decided to find an alternative objective, and dropped two 500 pounders on the oil refinery at Wesseling. Marham was to provide two-thirds of the aircraft for operations on the night of the 24/25th, which were to be directed at an oil refinery, an electricity power station and the Bismarck in Hamburg and a target at Rotterdam, probably the oil-storage facilities. 115 Squadron detailed nine Wellingtons for Hamburg, four of them for the Bismarck, and two for Rotterdam, and the main element took off between 17.50 and 18.35 with S/L Foss the senior pilot on duty. Eight-tenths cloud again intervened to provide challenging conditions for the attackers, but returning crews claimed that fires had been started at the oil plant and also at the Blohm & Voss shipyards. The freshman crews of Sgts Miles and Forrester departed Marham at 04.30 for Rotterdam, and were back within three hours having bombed through cloud without observing results.

Marham was ordered to prepare twenty-four Wellingtons for operations on the 27th, but this number was reduced to twenty-one by cancelling three 38 Squadron sorties. The target for eight of the 115 Squadron crews was a benzin plant at Magdeburg, while the remaining four went for an oil refinery in Gelsenkirchen, and take-off took place between 17.55 and 19.53 with both flight commanders on duty. Weather conditions over enemy territory were not helpful, and only the first four crews to arrive reported bombing at Magdeburg through developing cloud and haze, and a number of fires were observed. By the time the others arrived, ten-tenths cloud had completely obscured the ground, and most found a last-resort target to attack in the form of an aerodrome. P9283 lost its starboard engine thirty miles out from the Dutch coast on the way home, and crashed near Oulton in Norfolk, severely injuring P/O Rodger and three of his crew.

The 28th brought the posting to 214 Squadron of P/Os Alexander, Hamman, McAfee and Noble, while F/O Proctor moved in the opposite direction. Orders were issued on the 29th for Marham to supply three Wellingtons and crews from each squadron for the reinforcement of Malta. At midnight P/O Pate and Sgts Dyer and Forrester took off under the leadership of S/L Foss for what would be a transit flight of around eight hours. At 01.00, T2613 collided with a balloon cable at Langley in Buckinghamshire and crashed onto the railway station at Iver, where it was consumed by fire. P/O Pate and his four crew members lost their lives. Sgt Forrester and crew were forced to turn back with wireless failure, and the inability to draw fuel from the overload tank, and this left Sgt Dyer and crew, presumably with S/L Foss, to complete the journey with the 38 Squadron trio. S/L Foss would survive the war and pass away in 1996. The final operation of the month involved attacks on ports for which 115 Squadron contributed six Wellingtons. Three crews were briefed for Flushing (Vlissingen) on the island of Walcheren at the mouth of the Scheldt, two for Antwerp and one for Emden, and F/L Claydon was the senior pilot on duty as they departed Marham between 17.15 and 18.09. The squadron ORB made no mention of Flushing, and records two aircraft attacking Emden and causing explosions and fires which spread rapidly. At Antwerp two aircraft dropped eighteen 500 pounders, some with long-delay fuses, and also caused three fires, one of which was still visible from thirty miles away. During the course of the month the squadron operated on nine nights, and dispatched ninety-six sorties for the loss of two Wellingtons and one crew in crashes at home.

November 1940

The winter weather would begin to take a firmer hand during November, but the first week produced isolated days of unseasonably fine, even hot conditions. While the squadron remained at home on the night of the 1/2nd, other elements of the Command visited Berlin and Magdeburg, before a few days' lull preceded wide-ranging operations over Germany, Italy and the Occupied Countries on the night of the 5/6th. 115 Squadron made ready nine Wellingtons, seven to attack the docks at Bremerhaven and two for a similar target at Flushing. They took off between 17.15 and 17.55 with no senior pilots on duty, but a S/L Lasbrey flying as second pilot to P/O Todd. All reached their assigned targets in moderately good weather conditions, and the Bremerhaven element dropped a total of twenty-eight 500 pounders and nine hundred 4lb incendiaries, causing many fires. The Flushing duo of Sgt Morson and P/O Bois delivered a dozen 500 pounders and 240 incendiaries, and returned to report large fires in the docks area. Of ninety-one aircraft committed to operations on the night of the 7/8th, sixty-three were detailed to attack the Krupp armaments-producing complex in the Ruhr city of Essen. 115 Squadron contributed eight Wellingtons, which took off between 18.00 and 18.40 with S/L Mulholland the senior pilot on duty and S/L Lasbrey again accompanying P/O Todd. Six of the Marham crews claimed to have reached the target to find low cloud developing, and delivered their bombs before returning to report many fires burning. Two crews arriving a little later were thwarted by the cloud, and found alternative targets in Düsseldorf, which were also left burning. The 3 Group ORB claimed a successful operation, but the reality was that the fires were probably at decoy sites, and few, if any bombs actually landed in Essen. Hitting Ruhr targets would prove to be an insurmountable problem until technology could provide the answer, which would not be until early 1943.

It was the early hours of the 11th before the squadron was next called to arms, this time to attack the Scholven-Buer synthetic oil refinery at Gelsenkirchen, for which seven crews were briefed. S/L Mulholland was the senior pilot on duty as they departed Marham either side of 02.30, and he was supported by the newly-promoted F/L Van. Six claimed to have reached and bombed the target, causing large explosions and fires, while one attacked the inland docks at Duisburg and also reported setting off fires. The following night brought a return to the Ruhr for another attempt to hit the Scholven-Buer oil plant, and the eight participants took off either side of midnight led again by S/L Mulholland and F/L Van. The weather forecast proved to be inaccurate, and twenty miles after crossing the enemy coast they ran into thick, heavy, ice-bearing cloud, which persisted all the way to the target and back to the English coast. Bombing could only be carried out by DR, the cloud making it impossible to assess results, and the only consolation for a wasted effort was the safe return of all aircraft. 38 Squadron had, by now, begun the process of moving out of Marham before transferring lock, stock and barrel to the Middle-East to join 37 Squadron from Feltwell. Both units would spend the remainder of the war overseas, and 115 Squadron would have Marham all to itself for a short period.

Eleven crews attended briefing on the 14th to learn that six of them were to attack the Schlesiger railway station in Berlin that night, while five others would have an oil plant in Gelsenkirchen as their objective. During the course of the afternoon, however, intelligence suggested that the Luftwaffe was preparing to launch a major operation from Schiphol aerodrome near Amsterdam, and it was decided to send the Gelsenkirchen element there instead. They departed Marham for their respective destinations between 18.40 and 20.10 with S/L Mulholland heading for Berlin as the senior pilot on duty. Sgts Maloney, Marriot and Miles returned early with technical problems, the first-mentioned suffering an undercarriage collapse as L7810 touched down at Marham. The others pressed on, and those assigned to Berlin returned to claim having scored hits on the railway track and station buildings. The 3 Group ORB records that

Sgt H J Morson DFM (Pilot)

In November, 1940, Sgt Morson was the captain and Sgt Gleverley the wireless operator of a 115 Sqn Wellington which successfully attacked a target in the vicinity of Berlin.

On the return journey, intense anti-aircraft fire was encountered over Hamburg which severely damaged the aircraft.

Despite this, Sgt Morson set a direct course for base, which necessitated flying across the Heligoland Bight and, although many difficulties were overcome, he was unable to maintain height and was finally forced down into the sea from where he was rescued. For his actions, he received the DFM.

Sgt Morson resumed duties as a test pilot but in 1943 suffered a disastrous crash in the typhoon he was piloting. His burns were treated by Sir Archibald McIndoe, becoming one of the surgeon's first "Guinea pigs". He was honourably discharged from the RAF in 1944.

T2509 was on the way home from Berlin when it was hit by flak at a position 09.00E, which would put it over north-western Germany, perhaps in the Hamburg defence zone. Bill Chorley, however, suggests that the Wellington was still outbound when hit, and was forced to turn back. Whatever the truth, an engine caught fire, and, although the flames were extinguished, the engine was dead, and Sgt Morson and crew began the sea-crossing on the remaining good engine. Had the fuel reserves lasted they might have made landfall, but a ditching became necessary some forty miles off the Norfolk coast at 04.10, and they would endure a chilly fifteen hours in a dinghy before rescue boats arrive to pick them up. Sadly, second pilot, Sgt Dean, had drowned, but the others were in good shape, and the pilot and wireless operator would ultimately be awarded the DFM. Those attacking Schiphol aerodrome claimed successful results, but no details were provided.

Although S/L Lasbrey had been flying as second pilot to P/O Todd for a number of operations, he was not officially posted to the squadron from Bassingbourn until the 16th. That night he would perform that role again in the Todd crew for an operation by a force of 130 aircraft on Hamburg. 115 Squadron prepared ten Wellingtons for the main event, while the freshman crew of P/O Rash and crew were assigned to the night-fighter aerodrome at Soesterberg in Holland. The senior pilot on duty was F/L Van as they took off between 19.07 and 20.15, although F/O Proctor is recorded as departing at 21.00, only to be back on the ground seventy-five minutes later. Those pressing on encountered unhelpful weather conditions, and less than half of the crews reported bombing in the target area. Among them were four from Marham, who reported ten-tenths cloud over the city, which prevented any assessment of results. Intense flak added to the challenges, and enemy fighters were very much in evidence. F/L Van's R1034 was badly shot up, and P/O Tindall's T2606 was attacked by four ME110s, which resulted in the front gunner sustaining severe wounds. The Wellington was force-landed at Bircham Newton in Norfolk, where the gunner lost his fight for life. P/O Roy crash-landed P9299 at Wittering, the crew walking away with minor scrapes and bruises. These were the fortunate ones, as two other 115 Squadron Wellingtons failed to return altogether. P9286 fell victim to the night-fighter of Oblt Egmont Prinz zur Lippe-Weissenfeld, and crashed at 02.05 at Winkel, in the middle of the Den Helder peninsular north-east of

RAF Marham November 1940. Ollar Davidson P/O Petley P/O Currie Munby May

Alkmaar, Holland, with no survivors from the crew of Sgt Larkman. R3213 came down at Am Falkenberg, on the south-western approaches to Germany's Second City, and Sgt English died with his crew.

38 Squadron completed its move out of Marham on the 22nd as the aircrew flew out to Malta. It was business as usual for seven 115 Squadron crews who attended briefings to learn of that night's operations for five of them to an aerodrome at Bordeaux in south-western France, while S/L Lasbrey and F/L Claydon attacked the inland docks at Duisburg-Ruhrort. This would be the former's first sortie as S/L Foss's successor as B Flight commander, and he took off at 19.18, twelve minutes behind F/L Claydon. One of them bombed at Essen as an alternative target, and they landed an hour apart either side of midnight. S/L Lasbrey actually waited for the Wellingtons bound for France to take off before he touched down at 00.28, and, no doubt, watched P/O Tindall return a little over an hour after departing as the result of an unserviceable intercom system. The four crews assigned to Bordeaux arrived home between 08.00 and 09.00, three of them to report bombing the hangars and causing large explosions and fires, while the fourth had attacked the docks at Lorient on the way home. After two nights on the ground eight crews were briefed for operations on the 24/25th when Hamburg's Blohm & Voss shipyards was the primary target, while two other crews went to bomb the docks at Boulogne. S/Ls Mulholland and Lasbrey were the senior pilots on duty as they took to the air between 17.12 and 17.38 and headed for their respective targets in relatively good weather conditions. By the time they were ready to run in on the intended aiming-points cloud had all-but obscured the ground, hiding the targets and the results of the bombing. When they came home either side of midnight, all claimed to have delivered their bombs across the targets and witnessed large fires and explosions, but it was based on impression rather than sight.

218 Squadron was posted in to Marham on the 25th to occupy the accommodation left vacant by the departure for the Middle-East of 38 Squadron. The squadron had served with the AASF in France as a Fairey Battle unit, and had been decimated, before being withdrawn and transferred to 2 Group, with which it had flown Blenheims. It would now spend the next few weeks working up to operational status on Wellingtons. F/O Roy was posted to Lossiemouth on the 27th for a rest, before a collection of important visitors descended upon the station at teatime. His Majesty King George VI, C-in-C Sir Richard Peirse and the A-O-C, AVM Baldwin, inspected the operations room and intelligence section and observed the briefing for the night's main operation against railways communications and a goods station in Cologne. Afterwards they called in at the watch office and flare-path, and watched the early departures before dining in the officers' mess. Take-offs were spread throughout the evening between 18.30 and 00.05, with S/L Mulholland the senior pilot on duty and first away followed by Sgt Marriott. P/O Loder and Sgt Ralls departed shortly before 19.30 on freshman sorties to Boulogne, and F/L Van and Sgt Miles two hours later bound for Cologne. P/O Todd and crew took off alone at 22.00, to be followed by S/L Lasbrey and F/O Proctor fifty minutes later, leaving P/O Bois and Petley to set off after midnight. They found weather conditions to be better than of late, despite which, fewer than half of the sixty-two crews reported bombing the primary target. The 3 Group ORB was more upbeat, however, and suggested it had been a successful night. The V.I.Ps remained at Marham to meet returning crews, or, at least, those arriving back before midnight. Five officer pilots were posted in from Bassingbourn at this time, P/Os Salmon, Bailey, Kirk, Robertson and Dickie, and probably brought their crews with them, although this is not recorded. During the course of the month the squadron operated on nine nights and launched eighty-four sorties for the loss of three Wellingtons and two crews.

December 1940

As a safeguard against any German decision to reconsider an invasion, pressure would be maintained on occupied ports for the time being. F/L Claydon was posted to Harwell on the 4th for instructional duties, but he would return to the operational scene as the commanding officer of 3 Group's 90 Squadron in November 1942. Persistent fog kept 3 Group on the ground until the night of the 4/5th, when twenty-nine Wellingtons were made ready, fifteen for a trip across the Alps to Turin, while the remainder were to attack unspecified industrial targets in Düsseldorf. F/Ls Proctor and Van were the senior pilots on duty as the Turin-bound element of five took off between 17.38 and 17.53 and headed for the Channel. P/Os Bois, Rash and Tindall departed Marham for the Ruhr between 21.00 and 21.20, but ran into adverse weather conditions in the form of ice-bearing ten-tenths cloud, and P/O Bois bombed at Gremberg in Cologne in error for the primary target. P/O Tindall found Düsseldorf, while P/O Rash dropped his bombs over Dortmund, but it was another example of a wasted effort. Matters proceeded much more smoothly east of the Alps, where crews were able to identify the unnamed primary target, and, if not, the Fiat works as an alternative. The 115 Squadron participants returned safely either side of 03.00 to report causing fires and explosions, and the 3 Group ORB declared the operation to be a great success.

Diverse operations on the night of the 8/9th included attacks on U-Boot bases in France for 3 Group. Twenty-seven Wellingtons were detailed for Bordeaux, of which seven were to be provided by 115 Squadron, while three others from Marham attended to Lorient, where a huge concrete structure was being built by the Germans on the Keroman peninsular to house up to thirty vessels and their crews. They took off between 17.15 and 18.20 with S/L Lasbrey the senior pilot on duty, but engine problems curtailed his sortie, leaving the remainder to press on to their respective targets with F/L Proctor now the most senior pilot. The bombing at Bordeaux was described by returning crews as successful, with a number claiming direct hits on U-Boots, and a photograph revealed a fire in a warehouse and on a motor vessel. Any celebration on the part of the 115 Squadron crews on a good night's work was marred by the loss of P/O Tindall and crew, who all lost their lives when T2520 flew into a hill near Tradegar in south Wales at 03.12 after straying off track on the way home from Bordeaux. The southern German city of Mannheim began to attract attention, beginning on the night of the 10/11th, when Marham remained inactive and other elements of 3, 4 and 5 Groups joined forces to attack industrial targets. 3 Group was to take the lead, but extensive cloud on the outward route led to just two Wellingtons from the group reaching the target area, and the operation was ineffective.

Twenty-eight Wellingtons were detailed to return to Mannheim twenty-four hours later, the 11/12th, with 115 Squadron providing eight of them, but three were cancelled and F/L Proctor returned early with engine trouble. The practice of allowing squadrons or even individual crews to determine the details of their sorties led to a lack of concentration of bombs at targets, and this night's take-off times demonstrate the problem. P/O Todd departed at 17.16, almost two hours ahead of P/O Bois, who was soon back on the ground with engine problems. It was 23.25 before Sgts Bright and Hartland took to the air, and only the former returned to land at 06.10. What happened to T2466 and the crew of Sgt Hartland has never been established, but the last fix placed it some twenty miles west of Flushing. No trace of the aircraft and its occupants has ever been found, and the assumption must be that it disappeared into the Channel or North Sea. At debriefing the complete failure of the Marham effort was revealed, when poor weather conditions were blamed for just one aircraft reaching the target area to bomb, while the other two had jettisoned their loads. Briefings took place on the 15th for industrial targets in Berlin, Frankfurt and Kiel, for which a force of seventy-one Hampdens, Wellingtons and Whitleys was made ready. 115 Squadron detailed five aircraft for Berlin and two for Frankfurt, the former taking off either side of 00.30 led by S/L Lasbrey, and they were followed shortly after 02.00 by the latter pair consisting of Sgts Maloney and Marriott and their crews. S/L Mulholland was also in action on this night, and took off at 00.40 to attack the docks at Kiel. This turned into a successful operation by the standards of the period, and bombs were seen to fall into the naval dockyard and also into the town. S/L Mulholland brought back a photograph, which earned praise from the C-in-C. The Frankfurt raid was also described as successful, while weather conditions over the Capital prevented an assessment of the results there.

Mannheim again came under the spotlight on the night of the 16/17th, in what was intended as a retaliatory raid following recent heavy Luftwaffe attacks on English cities, most notably Coventry in November, but also the sustained assault on London that had been in progress since September. The original plan called for two hundred bombers to "destroy" Mannheim under Operation "Abigail Rachel", but this was thwarted by predictions of poor weather over many of the stations, and a force of 134 aircraft would eventually take to the air. Almost half of these were Wellingtons, and those in the van, principally from 3 Group, contained the most experienced crews, whose brief was to start fires in the city centre with incendiaries. This would be an early example of area bombing, although no such admission would be forthcoming to the general public. 3 Group put up sixty-one Wellingtons, of which six represented 115 Squadron, and they departed Marham either side of 23.00 with W/C Dabinett the senior pilot on duty, flying with F/L Proctor and crew, and S/L Mulholland in support. The weather conditions proved to be generally good with little cloud and a full moon, despite which, the "Pathfinder" crews failed to locate the intended city-centre aiming-point. This led to a scattered attack, which fell mainly into residential districts, where almost five hundred buildings were destroyed or damaged by incendiary and high explosive bombs. A small-scale return to Mannheim by 3 and 4 Groups on the night of the 18/19th involved just twenty-six aircraft, of which eight were provided by 115 Squadron. They took off either side of 21.00 with S/Ls Lasbrey and Mulholland the senior pilots on duty, and headed south in conditions of cloud and poor visibility, which persisted throughout the operation. All returned safely some seven hours later, six to report bombing in the target area and two having attacked last-resort objectives.

The Command detailed 125 aircraft for operations on the night of the 20/21st, when the main target was to be Berlin. French and Belgian ports were also on the menu, and the freshman crews of P/Os Salmon and Sands were briefed for Ostend, while six of their 115 Squadron fellow crews found themselves assigned to the German Capital. The leading five of the main element took off between 23.30 and 23.55, with S/L Lasbrey the senior pilot on duty, and P/O Loder and crew were last away thirty-five minutes behind. The freshmen had to wait until 04.00 before their turn came, and they departed Marham thirty minutes apart and in the company of the first two operational Wellington sorties by 218 Squadron. The weather conditions were generally favourable, and all returned safely, most to report attacking their primary target. S/L Mulholland was awarded a DFC on the 22nd, and celebrated by taking part in that night's operations for which he and S/L Lasbrey were the senior pilots on duty. Ten crews were originally briefed for a return to Mannheim, and one to the docks at Antwerp, and take-off was accomplished safely between 17.15 and 18.03. Although the squadron ORB was not specific, return times suggest that P/O Salmon turned back with technical difficulties, and was back on the ground in a little over thirty minutes, S/L Mulholland attacked Flushing as an alternative target, while P/O Saunders made it all the way to Antwerp to attack his primary. Most of the Mannheim element reached and bombed the target, where poor visibility hampered a clear view of results. One 3 Group crew described Mannheim as being ablaze on both sides of the River Rhine, but there was no local confirmation.

The second wartime Christmas came and went, and the festive period was extended to some extent at Marham by the absence of operations until the night of the 29/30th, when the two squadrons were handed Hamm marshalling yards as their target. 115 Squadron contributed just four Wellingtons, which took off between 16.58 and 17.30 with F/L Proctor the senior pilot on duty. They encountered adverse weather conditions of heavy ice-bearing cloud, and only one crew reported locating and bombing the primary target, while the others either jettisoned their load or brought it home. Sadly, a sight of the New Year was denied to P/O Salmon and his crew, who perished in T2465 after it came down somewhere between the German frontier and the target. During the curse of the month the squadron operated on nine nights and dispatched sixty-eight sorties for the loss of three Wellingtons and crews. The year had begun with the unreality of the Phoney War, before it exploded into life with the German advance through the Ardennes in May. It had been a backs-to-the-wall effort by the Command, and, in terms of effectiveness, it was little more than punching the air, representing more of an irritation to the German war effort than a threat. The New Year would bring nothing to increase optimism, and the hard-pressed crews of Bomber Command would continue to tread water for at least the next twelve months.

January 1941

A second successive harsh winter played its part in restricting operations as the New Year dawned. Most of the effort in January would be directed at ports in Germany and France, and Bremen was to find itself featuring on the first three nights. 3 Group contributed forty-seven Wellingtons to the three-wave attack on the night of the 1/2nd, of which eight represented 115 Squadron. S/L Lasbrey was the senior pilot on duty as they took off during a period of two-and-a-quarter hours between 16.50 and 19.05, but Sgt Milton was back after just forty-three minutes with engine problems, and was followed in by F/L Proctor for the same reason. P/O Petley took off at 17.50 as part of the second wave, but also returned early with a faulty engine. The first wave of aircraft produced some effective bombing, which hit the Focke-Wulf aircraft factory in the southern suburb of Hemelingen, and others caused fires which spread to the city centre and left a glow in the sky visible from a hundred miles away. 115 Squadron remained at home for the next two nights, before being ordered to prepare six Wellingtons for operations on the 4th. At briefing the crews learned that five of them were to attack an enemy cruiser at berth at Brest, while the sixth was assigned to an unspecified objective at Duisburg. Take-off was spread between 17.35 and 20.08, with F/Ls Proctor and Van the senior pilots on duty, and no indication in the ORB as to which target individual crews were assigned. Duisburg was found to be cloud-covered and the bombs were brought home, and cloud interfered also with visibility at Brest, persuading one crew to return with their bombs, while four

W/C A C Evans Evans
115 Sqn Commanding Officer
20th January 1941 – 19th May 1941

others delivered theirs but were unable to make an assessment of results. This proved to be the final operation for F/L Proctor, who was posted to 20 O.T.U at Lossiemouth on the 7th.

The naval ports of Wilhelmshaven and Emden were posted as the targets for operations on the night of the 8/9th, the former in an attempt to hit the battleship Tirpitz. Six 115 Squadron crews were briefed, and they took off between 21.04 and 21.35 with F/L Van the senior pilot on duty and the last to depart. Conditions in the target area were good, and most of the thirty-two participating crews reported straddling the vessel or scoring near misses. 115 Squadron delivered some seven tons of bombs, and there were no losses from any of the Command's activities. Although the warship was not hit, heavy damage was inflicted on a number of areas within the town, and local authorities described it as the first large-scale raid to be dealt with by the emergency services. The only non-coastal target selected for a heavy raid during the month was the important oil town of Gelsenkirchen, situated towards the north-eastern end of the Ruhr. 135 aircraft were made ready on the 9th, but 115 Squadron was not invited to take part, and briefed the freshman crews of P/O Saunderson and Sgts Marriott and Palmer to attack the oil storage tanks at Rotterdam. They took off between 17.15 and 17.31, and all reached and bombed the target, delivering their loads of mostly 500 pounders and observing explosions and fires. The raid on Gelsenkirchen was not a success after cloud intervened to hide the ground from the second wave crews, and most bombed alternative targets.

Orders were received on the 12th to prepare five 115 Squadron Wellingtons for very long-range operations that night. Two crews were briefed for Regensburg in south-eastern Germany, where a Messerschmidt aircraft factory was known to exist, two for Turin and one for Venice, and they took off between 21.30 and 23.43. The squadron ORB is not helpful, but, according to take-off times and flight durations, it can be deduced that Sgt Bright and crew were assigned to Venice, in company with others from 149 Squadron, and this was perhaps the only time that Bomber Command sorties was sent to this city on Italy's north-eastern coast. S/L Lasbrey and P/O Bois were likely those heading for Turin, while Sgt Milton and P/O Rash had Regensburg as their destination. Remarkably, all crews returned safely having carried out their briefs and having spent between nine and eleven hours aloft. R1179 overshot its landing and crashed into the boundary fence, causing considerable damage to the Wellington, but not to S/L Lasbrey and his crew, who were able to walk away without injury. The 3 Group ORB described the raids on Italy as particularly successful, with a number of low-level strafing attacks on an aerodrome and a large liner, but reported that cloud had compromised the Regensburg sorties.

The previously-mentioned operation against an oil-related objective at Gelsenkirchen pre-empted a new Air Ministry directive issued on the 15th, which prophesied a critical period for Germany's oil situation over the succeeding six months. A list of seventeen oil targets was drawn up, the top nine of which represented 80% of Germany's domestic production. It would be February before Peirse began to implement his orders, and, in the meantime, Wilhelmshaven continued to feature prominently, with the first of three further raids for the month taking place on the night of the 15/16th. 115 Squadron briefed eight crews for the naval stronghold, and two freshmen, believed to be P/Os Kirk and Saunderson, for Rotterdam, departing Marham between 17.48 and 19.40 with S/Ls Lasbrey and Mulholland the senior pilots on duty. The 3 Group ORB makes reference to a highly successful raid on the main target, which caused fires visible up to 130 miles into the return flight. Local reports confirmed the effectiveness of the attack, and listed dockyard offices and administrative buildings in the town as among those destroyed or damaged. The squadron was rested when Wilhelmshaven was targeted again on the following night, an operation that, this time, inflicted only slight damage. The squadron had not been in action again by the time that W/C Evans-Evans arrived from 11 O.T.U at Bassingbourn on the 20th to succeed W/C Dabinett as commanding officer. The larger-than-life W/C "Tiny" Evans-Evans was one of the Command's characters, who would enjoy a colourful career until his untimely death on operations early in 1945. W/C Dabinett would be posted to Harwell in February pending a permanent reassignment, and would have to relinquish his acting wing commander rank. He would return to the operational scene at the end of July 1942 as the commanding officer of 12 Squadron, a post in which he would remain until February 1943. S/L Mulholland was posted to the 3 Group Training Flight at Stradishall on the 23rd, and F/L Van was promoted to acting squadron leader rank to succeed him as A Flight commander. As events turned out, 115 Squadron would not operate again before the end of the month, and did not, therefore, take part in the sixth attack of the month on Wilhelmshaven on the night of the 29/30th. During the course of the month the squadron operated on just six nights, and dispatched thirty-eight sorties without loss.

On the 25th of August the newly-promoted W/C Mulholland would be appointed as the first commanding officer of 458 Squadron RAAF, which had been formed in New South Wales in the previous month, and arrived in England as the second RAAF unit to join RAF Bomber Command. In January 1942 the squadron was told to prepare for an overseas posting, and, on the 22nd of February, the day on which AM Sir Arthur Harris ascended the throne of Bomber Command, W/C Mulholland set off with two other crews on the 1,400 mile trip to Malta. Two Wellingtons arrived, but W/C Mulholland's did not, and it was learned later that it had been shot down into the Mediterranean Sea with just one survivor.

February 1941

The first nine nights of February would be devoted largely to small-scale raids on French ports, and 115 Squadron operated for the first time during the month on the night of the 4/5th, when sending four freshman crews to bomb the docks at Le Havre. They took off either side of 17.30, and flew into ten-tenths cloud thirty miles out from the Norfolk coast and encountered icing conditions. Poor visibility at the French coast prevented any from locating the target, and three returned with their bombs while the fourth jettisoned them over the sea. P/O Petley was posted to 15 O.T.U at Harwell on the 7th at the end of his tour of operations, while ten Wellingtons were made ready for an operation that evening against the docks at Boulogne. Eight were loaded with five 500 pounders and two cans of incendiaries, and two with a 1,000 pounder, three 500 pounders and a single 250 pounder. They departed Marham either side of 20.30 with S/Ls Lasbrey and Van the senior pilots on duty and W/C Evans-Evans flying as second pilot to the latter, while another new arrival, F/L Clyde-Smith, formerly of 218 Squadron, flew with P/O Bois. They all arrived in the target area to find a layer of cloud at 14,000 feet, but good visibility below that level, which enabled photographs to be brought back. Bombing took place from between 7,000 and 12,000 feet, and most of the loads were seen to fall across the docks and quays, returning crews reporting large explosions and fires, the glow from which was observed by some as they approached North Foreland on the Kent coast.

The month's "big" night saw a force of 222 aircraft made ready for an operation to Hannover on the 10th, of which 102 Wellingtons were provided by 3 Group, one of them assigned to photographic reconnaissance duties. A further seventeen Wellingtons with freshman crews and three Stirlings were dispatched by the group to attack oil storage tanks at Rotterdam, the latter type making its operational debut, and this represented the war's first one-hundred effort by any Group. 115 Squadron briefed five crews from A Flight and six from B Flight for the main raid, including both flight commanders, and W/C Evans-Evans again joined S/L Van as second pilot. They took off between 18.25 and 19.32, and all arrived in the target area where nine to ten-tenths cloud obscured the ground and made an accurate assessment of the outcome impossible. Ten crews reported bombing in the target area from around 12,000 feet, and many fires were observed. P/O Rodgers was the only one from the squadron unable to identify the primary target, and he dropped his bombs on Minden as he flew back towards the west, claiming that his bombs fell across canals, roads and railway installations on the north-eastern edge of the town. He encountered a strong head-wind on the way home, but descended to 6,000 feet to make machine-gun attacks on two Dutch aerodromes, before finding a pinpoint on the enemy coast, which took him across the North Sea to a red flashing beacon at Swaffham. He switched on his navigation lights after narrowly missing two other Wellingtons returning without lights, but this attracted the attention of Hptm Rolf Jung of 4/NJG2, whose fire hit R1084's port engine, causing it to explode. The Wellington lost height at such a rate that the crew was unable to bale out, and a crash-landing was carried out at 01.45 on a single railway track in a cutting at Narborough, five miles north-west of Swaffham. The crew members scrambled clear before their aircraft was consumed by fire, and only the rear gunner sustained an injury, which involved his left arm. 173 other crews claimed to have attacked their industrial targets within the city on this momentous night for 3 Group, and the 3 Group ORB surmised that considerable damage had resulted. No report is available from Hannover to confirm the effectiveness or otherwise of the operation.

On the following night 3 Group detailed fifty-three Wellingtons for operations against Bremen and Hannover again, of which ten were to be provided by 115 Squadron. Six crews were briefed for Bremen and four for the return to Hannover, and they departed Marham between 18.06 and 19.00 with W/C Evans-Evans the senior pilot on duty supported by S/L Lasbrey. The night turned into something of a disaster, as poor weather conditions prevented most crews from reaching their respective targets. Sgt Whittaker and crew were, perhaps, the only ones from the squadron to report bombing in the area of their primary target, and they dropped their bombs on a searchlight and flak concentration. A widespread and unexpected fog developed over parts of England as the aircraft headed home, and congested airwaves made it difficult for crews to establish their position and communicate with their bases. As a result, a total of twenty-two aircraft crashed or were abandoned by their crews. Eleven were from 3 Group, and three of them belonged to 115 Squadron, including R3238, which contained the squadron commander and his crew. They baled out near Saffron Waldon in Essex and came safely to earth, although W/C Evans-Evans sustained an ankle injury. P/O Clarke and crew vacated R1004 over Cambridgeshire, and the Wellington crashed in Histon Rd, Cambridge, killing three elderly ladies and burning out two houses. Finally, R1238 crashed after hitting an obstacle on approach to Finningley, and came down short of the runway. Sgt Whittaker and his crew emerged unscathed, but the Wellington was wrecked.

The oil offensive opened at Gelsenkirchen on the night of the 14/15th, when just nine of forty-four Wellington crews claimed to have bombed the Nordstern refinery as briefed, while others took part in a raid on a plant at Homberg to the north-west of Duisburg. 115 Squadron remained at home on this night, but responded to orders on the 15th to make ready nine aircraft for operations that night. The main target was the Holten synthetic oil refinery at Sterkrade in Oberhausen, for which the squadron briefed eight crews, while a single freshman crew would join others from the group in attacking the docks at Boulogne. They took off between 18.11 and 18.57 with F/Ls Clyde-Smith and Giles the senior pilots on duty, and P/O Ralph, it is believed by his description of the weather conditions in the target area, bound for Boulogne. The Ruhr was hidden beneath its blanket of haze, and, on this occasion, extreme darkness, while an unusually high number of searchlights were operating to create a glare that prevented

A 115 Sqn armourer supervises the manouvering of a 1000lb bomb, with Wellingtons in the background sitting at their dispersals.

identification of ground detail. P/O Saunderson dropped his bombs over the Ruhr from 11,000 feet and observed flashes, and fires also from loads delivered by others. Sgt Milton bombed the docks at Duisburg and witnessed a large explosion, and P/O Curry dropped his incendiaries in the vicinity of the primary target, but saw nothing as a result. Sgt Bright delivered all of his bombs across the target, causing fires, among which was a small green one lasting about ten minutes. P/Os Bois and Loder could only report bombing over the Ruhr from around 11,000 feet, while F/L Clyde-Smith specified Duisburg and an aerodrome at Eindhoven as the recipients of his hardware. P/O Ralph described ten-tenths cloud with a base at 5,000 feet and bad weather, through which he bombed from 12,000 feet and observed flashes and explosions.

The weather caused operations to be cancelled over the ensuing nights, and it was the early hours of the 23rd before 115 Squadron was next called to arms. Nine crews were briefed to join twenty others from the group to attack a Hipper Class cruiser at Brest, and they took off between 02.38 and 03.08 with S/L Van the senior pilot on duty. P/O Clarke and crew returned early with faulty trimming gear and artificial horizon, but landed too far down the runway, and, despite applying the brakes and turning to starboard, T2511 could not be brought to a halt in time. The Wellington sustained serious damage after crashing into trees on the western side of the airfield, but the crew was able to walk away. The others pressed on to encounter poor weather conditions over the target, and few were able to find the vessel. S/L Van attacked the target from 6,500 feet in the face of intense flak, which damaged the hydraulics system and necessitated an emergency landing, which was accomplished with little further damage to the aircraft. While returning in R1221, Sgt Milton and crew sent a Q.D.M. request at 08.25, and were instructed to proceed to Feltwell, which was acknowledged. Five minutes later the Wellington hit a tree at East Winch, five miles south-east of King's Lynn, and crashed in flames killing all on board. At debriefing, Sgt Bright's rear gunner, P/O Mills, reported an engagement with a ME110 eight miles north of Morlaix on the French coast. He opened fire and poured six hundred rounds into the cockpit of the enemy aircraft, which was some 500 feet below on the port quarter. The night-fighter dipped its port wing and banked away, upon which, on instructions from the rear turret, Sgt Bright stall-turned to starboard to bring the rear turret once more to bear. A further four hundred rounds shot off the port tail-fin and rudder, before the enemy dived through cloud at 4,000 feet and was lost from sight. That evening, L7810 took off at 19.43 for a freshman sortie to Boulogne carrying six 500 pounders and 120 x 4lb incendiaries. The squadron ORB has Sgt Lloyd as the pilot, but it is believed that he was flying as second pilot to P/O Arthurs. At 20.47 a request was received at Hull for a fix, which was acknowledged, but no further communication took place and the Wellington failed to return. It was established later that it had crashed in the vicinity of Pihen-les-Guines, six miles south of Calais, and that all on board had perished.

F/L Fletcher and Sgt Pike became the latest pilots to be posted in when they arrived from Bramcote and Bassingbourn respectively on the 24th. The squadron and group ORBs are at variance concerning the targets for the night of the 25/26th. The 115 Squadron record shows five aircraft being prepared for operations against Wilhelmshaven and Boulogne, while its 3 Group counterpart details five aircraft for Düsseldorf among twenty-five others from Marham, Wyton and Stradishall, plus a photo-reconnaissance aircraft from Oakington. In all, eighty aircraft were dispatched, the 115 Squadron element taking off between 18.50 and 19.27 with F/L Clyde-Smith the senior pilot on duty. They all claimed to have reached the target area, where nine to ten-tenths cloud obscured the ground, and they bombed from between 9,000 and 13,000 feet onto the glow of existing fires and the flashes from searchlights and flak. Some observed the reflections of bomb bursts, but it was impossible to assess the outcome. In fact, according to local reports, fewer than ten bomb loads had fallen in the city, and damage was negligible. It was a similar story at Cologne on the following night, although 115 Squadron remained on the ground on this night. The month ended with an attempt by a mixed force of 116 aircraft to bomb the Tirpitz in Wilhelmshaven harbour on the night of the 28th. 115 Squadron briefed eight crews, and they took off between 22.37 and 23.54 with S/L Lasbrey the senior pilot on duty. P/O Kirk and crew were back in a little over an hour after engine trouble curtailed their sortie, but the others reached the target area to deliver their bombs from around 9,000 feet, mostly from east to west. Some fires were seen and a deep red glow, but cloud again prevented crews from observing the fall of their bombs, and no report was forthcoming from Wilhelmshaven. During the course of the month the squadron operated on nine nights and dispatched sixty-seven sorties for the loss of six Wellingtons and two crews.

March 1941

March's operations began with a return to Cologne by a mixed force of 131 aircraft, whose crews had been briefed to attack two aiming-points. 3 Group contributed fifty-seven Wellingtons, although none from 115 Squadron, and fifty crews returned to claim having bombed in the target area. A local report confirmed a useful raid, which inflicted damage to buildings and docks on both banks of the Rhine close to the city centre. Orders were received on the 2nd to prepare for an attack that night on a Hipper class warship at berth at Brest, for which 115 Squadron detailed six Wellingtons from A Flight and three from B Flight. They departed Marham between 18.17 and 19.15 with F/L Clyde-Smith the senior pilot on duty. They were each carrying six semi-armour-piercing (SAP) 500 pounders, and two also had a single 250lb armour-piercing (AP) in their bomb bay. They arrived over the French coast to find generally good weather conditions and good visibility, although it seems that cloud slid in during the course of the raid, and P/O Curry and Sgt Palmer would cite ten-tenths cloud as the cause of their failure to locate the aiming-point. The former decided to attack the docks at Lorient as an alternative, but was thwarted by oil leaking onto the bomb-aimer's clear-vision panel from the front turret, preventing him from aiming accurately. After a rapid loss of altitude from 8,000 down to 1,500 feet on the way home, P/O Curry was forced to jettison his bombs over the sea, before making it home to a safe landing. Sgt Palmer ran short of fuel and landed at Chalmy Down in Somerset. The remainder carried out their attacks from between 8,500 and 12,000 feet, and a number of bomb bursts were observed along with a series of white explosions. The operation ended badly for 115 Squadron with the failure to return of R3279, which was the sole casualty. A weak transmission was received from Sgt Elliott and crew at 01.00, and then nothing further until a message from came through from Dartmouth that an aircraft had been seen to dive into the sea off Torbay. A Lysander rescue aircraft was sent out, and two parachutes were observed floating on the surface, one of them attached to the body of the wireless operator, Sgt Fenwick. The second pilot was Sgt Pike, who was on his first operation since joining the squadron a week earlier. It was a sobering start to the month, but thankfully, the squadron would negotiate the rest of it without loss.

Yet another raid was mounted against Cologne on the night of the 3/4th, but the only bombs recorded by the city authorities fell into the western outskirts. Thereafter, minor operations held sway for a week, largely because of unfavourable weather conditions, and it was during this lull, on the 9th, that C-in-C Peirse received a new Air Ministry directive, which changed the emphasis of operations. The continuing heavy losses of shipping in the Atlantic at the hands of U-Boots forced the War Cabinet to target this menace, and its partner in crime, the Focke-Wulf Kondor long-range maritime reconnaissance bomber. Until further notice, these were to be hunted down where-ever they could be found, at sea, in their bases, at their point of assembly and in the component factories. A new target list was drawn up, headed by Kiel, Hamburg and Bremen, each of which contained one or more U-Boot construction yards. The last-mentioned was not only home to U-Boot manufacture on the north bank of the Weser in the Vegesack district in the north-west, but also boasted a Focke-Wulf factory in the Hemelingen district south-east of the city centre. Also identified as targets in the directive were the French ports of Lorient, St-Nazaire and Bordeaux, where U-Boot bases and support facilities existed.

It was the 12th before Marham was next able to return to the offensive on a night of maximum effort in line with the new directive. Three major operations were posted involving eighty-eight aircraft for Hamburg, eighty-six for Bremen and seventy-two for Berlin. 115 Squadron prepared eight Wellingtons, four for the Focke-Wulf aircraft factory at Bremen with the crews of F/O Kirk, P/Os Saunderson and Loder and Sgt King, while the others, containing the crews of F/Ls Clyde-Smith and Giles, P/O Bois and Sgt King would head for Berlin. They took off between 18.55 and 19.31 before setting course for their respective targets, where, it seems, fine weather conditions were encountered. More than fifty Wellington crews were briefed to attack the Focke-Wulf factory, while Blenheims targeted the city centre. The 115 Squadron participants bombed from between 9,000 and 13,000 feet and observed explosions and fires, but only P/O Saunderson claimed to have seen his bombs straddle factory buildings. It was a similar story over the Capital, where bombing was carried out also from between 9,500 and 13,000 feet, and F/L Clyde-Smith watched his load fall into railway yards. All returned safely after modestly effective raids, F/L Giles bringing back a slightly damaged R1063 courtesy of the Berlin flak defences. The Hamburg operation was the most successful, however, as a result of twenty high explosive bombs and a few hundred incendiaries falling into the Blohm & Voss U-Boot yards.

Twenty-four hours later, 139 aircraft took off to return to Hamburg in an attempt to repeat the success. It would have been 140 aircraft had F/L Giles not been forced to abandon his sortie before take-off because of the failure of his oxygen system. This left seven 115 Squadron aircraft to participate in the main event and F/O Knight and crew to undertake a freshman sortie to Rotterdam. They took off between 19.55 and 20.56 with F/L Clyde-Smith the senior pilot on duty, and the recently-arrived F/L Fletcher accompanying him as second pilot. F/O Kirk and crew were back on the ground within two-and-a-quarter hours after the heating to the rear turret failed, but the remainder reached the target area, where they

A group of 115 Sqn personnel watch on as an effigy of Hitler is symbolically hanged in March 1941.

found hazy conditions and met fierce opposition from the ground and in the air. R1034 had both turrets rendered inoperable by a ME110, but Sgt King's front gunner managed to get one barrel working and fired fifty rounds into the enemy fighter, which turned away. The bombs were dropped onto a bend in a railway track a mile north of the aiming-point from 3,000 feet, and, on return, the crew reported a large red fire, which remained visible for some thirty-five minutes. P/O Bois dropped his bombs from 9,600 feet on a south-west to north-east heading to the south-west of the aiming-point, and reported that they caused a large, red fire. P/O Saunderson and crew reported two large fires already burning as they arrived, and they delivered their bombs to the east of the Aussen-Alster lake in what must have been the Eilbek district of the city. P/O Loder's bombs were released a quarter of a mile south-west of the aiming-point, but evasive action prevented sight of their impact. Two major flak hits inflicted damage to the bomb doors and tail-plane of R1471, but they made it safely home along with the others. The operation was highly effective for the period, starting more than a hundred fires in the city, thirty of which were classed by local authorities as large.

Despite the fact that the new directive had taken the emphasis away from oil-related targets, Gelsenkirchen was attacked on the night of the 14/15th, and the Hydriewerk-Scholven refinery was left badly damaged and temporarily out of action. 115 Squadron sat this one out, but briefed four crews for an attack on the U-Boot pens at Lorient on the 15th, which one must assume referred to the giant construction on the Keroman peninsular to the south of the main docks area of the town. They took off in a five-minute slot to 18.40 with F/L Clyde-Smith the senior pilot on duty, and encountered poor visibility in the target area. Returning crews reported delivering their loads of predominantly 250lb SAP bombs from around 10,000 feet on the north side of the docks behind the power station and on the docks below the lower bridge. Large explosions were observed, but it was impossible to interpret accurately the events on the ground. Thick fog at home forced all crews to land at airfields in the west country. F/L Fletcher's short spell with the squadron ended on the 16th with his posting to 75(NZ) Squadron at Feltwell, while Sgt Taylor moved in the opposite direction. The squadron was not involved in the operations against Bremen and Wilhelmshaven on the night of the 17/18th, but briefed six crews on the 18th to join ninety-three others to attack Kiel that night. S/Ls Lasbrey and Van were the senior pilots on duty as they departed Marham between 19.17 and 19.28, and all reached the target area to find the naval port obscured by ten-tenths cloud. Despite the conditions, returning crews were confident that their bombs, delivered from between 10,000 and 12,000 feet, had fallen into the town area, and reported the flash of explosions reflected in the clouds. Local reports confirmed an effective raid, which inflicted damage on the Deutsche Werke U-Boot yard and the town centre.

Poor visibility hampered attempts to bomb the U-Boot base at Lorient on the night of the 21/22nd, for which Sgt King and crew were the sole 115 Squadron participants in a force of sixty-six aircraft. They took off at 04.01 carrying six 500 pounders and a load of incendiaries, and brought them all home at 06.39 after failing to locate even the enemy coast, let alone the target. Operations were posted and cancelled thereafter, and, by the time the next offensive activity took place on the 27th, F/L Curry had been posted in from Wyton on the 22nd to assume acting squadron leader rank and succeed S/L Van as A Flight commander on the latter's admission to Ely hospital. The freshman crews of P/O Knight and Sgts King and Thompson were briefed for a raid on the docks at Dunkerque, and took off between 19.46 and 20.00 only to encounter ten-tenths cloud obscuring the enemy coast. Sgt Thompson flew along the coast from Dunkerque to Calais and from Calais to the Scheldt Estuary area without being able to identify ground detail, and brought his six 500 pounders and two small-bomb-cannisters (SBCs) home. P/O Knight was also unable to locate the target and returned his bombs to store. Sgt King and crew found the target by the light of flares from other aircraft, and delivered a stick across docks 4 to 8 from 12,000 feet on a west to east heading.

A flurry of postings brought new crews to the squadron during the final week of the month. On the 29th, the German cruisers Scharnhorst and Gneisenau were reported to be off Brest, and by the following morning they had taken up residence. This was to be the start of an eleven-month-long saga, which would divert valuable resources away from strategic bombing, and cost the Command dearly in effort, aircraft and crews. During the course of the day a force of 109 aircraft was made ready to attack the port and its lodgers, and among these were ten 115 Squadron Wellingtons, five from each flight. They took off between 19.40 and 20.18 with S/L Lasbrey the senior pilot on duty, most carrying six 500 pounders and a number of 4lb incendiaries. Sgt Thompson and crew returned early because of excessive vibration, leaving the others to press on to the target area in conditions of good visibility but extreme darkness. The operation was conducted in two waves, the first of which was able to identify the ships, before cloud slid across the coastal region to hamper the later arrivals. The 115 Squadron crews carried out their attacks over the dry docks from between 7,500 and 12,000 feet, but failed to observe bomb bursts, which suggests that they were part of the second wave. As events turned out, no hits were scored, and this would be typical of the dozens of attacks launched against the enemy vessels for the remainder of the year and beyond. The month had brought operations for the squadron on eight nights, and forty-nine sorties had been launched for the loss of a single Wellington and crew.

April 1941

Brest was again the main focus of attention at the beginning of April, but small forces of Hampdens operating by daylight on the 1st and 3rd were recalled because of a lack of cloud cover. A mixed force of ninety aircraft was made ready to attack the port on the night of the 3/4th, for which 3 Group contributed fifty-two aircraft, including a single Stirling. The 115 squadron element of ten Wellingtons took off between 18.26 and 19.08 with S/L Lasbrey the senior pilot on duty. Shortly before 20.00 Sgt Martin and crew set off on their freshman sortie to Rotterdam, where they found seven-tenths cloud and haze. They were unable to locate and identify the oil storage tanks, and landed at 00.06 with their bomb load intact. It was a similar story for the others, who also encountered cloud and haze at the French coast, that allowed them only brief glimpses of the docks area. On his return S/L Lasbrey reported that he had located the target through five-tenths cloud and only slight haze, and delivered his bombs on a south-west to north-east heading across dock No 1, without observing the results. F/L Clyde-Smith bombed from 12,000 feet, and, forty seconds after release, observed a very large, brilliant-white explosion. F/O Kirk and Sgt Palmer went in at 7,500 feet, the former identifying the target only by the intensity of the flak, while the latter watched the burst from five of his bombs straddle the target from south-west to north-east. Sgt King flew across the aiming-point from east to west at 11,500 feet, and watched his bombs explode slightly too far to the west. F/L Giles and P/Os Bois, Loder and Saunderson all returned with their bombs, and managed to avoid the attention of enemy intruders in the skies near Marham. T2560 was attacked over the airfield itself, but the assailant disappeared into the poor visibility after Sgt Palmer's rear gunner fired twenty rounds at it, after which a safe landing was carried out at 01.26. Just six minutes earlier, and five miles west of King's Lynn, Sgt Thompson's R1470 had crashed after being shot down by the JU88C of Lt Heinz Völker of 1/NJG.2, and there were no survivors.

On the following night, while 115 Squadron rested, a predominantly Wellington force returned to Brest, and, although the ships again escaped damage, one bomb fell into the dry dock occupied by the Gneisenau, and failed to explode. Her captain decided to move the ship out into the harbour while the bomb was dealt with, and, while there, she was struck by a torpedo delivered by a Coastal Command Beaufort, in what was virtually a suicide attack. The Beaufort was immediately shot down, and the crew killed, but the pilot, F/O Campbell, was posthumously awarded the Victoria Cross. Damage to the Gneisenau was severe, and the repairs were to take six months to complete. Never the less, operations against the warships would continue, and Wellingtons were the predominant type in an attack on the night of the 6/7th, which failed in the face of bad weather. 115 Squadron launched two freshman sorties on this night captained by S/L Curry and Sgt Martin, the former undertaking his first since joining the squadron. They took off either side of 20.15 and set course for Calais, but returned with their bombs still on board around three hours later after encountering the same unfavourable weather conditions as the Brest force.

In contrast, there were perfect conditions for a raid on Kiel on the night of the 7/8th, for which a force of 229 aircraft was made ready, including a dozen Wellingtons belonging to 115 Squadron. They departed Marham over a two-hour period from 19.17 with S/Ls Curry and Lasbrey the senior pilots on duty, and only P/O Knight returned early after the hydraulics system failed. Arriving in the target area the others found clear skies and bright moonlight, which diffused the glare of the searchlights and allowed ground detail to be identified. The squadron participants attacked from between 10,000 and 13,000 feet, and reported their bombs falling all around the aiming-point, some observing results and others not. Many fires and explosions were reported, and the success of the five-hour-long operation was confirmed by local accounts of widespread damage to buildings in the naval dockyard, civilian housing, industrial units, and to the Germania Werft and Deutsche Werke U-Boot yards, which had to be shut down for a number of days. The operation was repeated on the following night, for which a reduced force of 160 aircraft was made ready. 115 Squadron briefed nine crews, who took off between 21.34 and 22.12 with S/L Lasbrey the senior pilot on duty. F/O Kirk turned back with engine problems and jettisoned his bombs into the sea, but the remainder pressed on to the target, where they were greeted by virtually clear skies and excellent visibility. Bombing took place from between 8,500 and 13,000 feet and many explosions and fires were reported, the latter visible for some fifty miles into the return journey. The main weight of the attack fell this time into the town itself, and produced a death toll of 125 people, with

Armourers prepare to bomb up an unidentified 115 Sqn Wellington at Marham

a further three hundred injured, and this was almost certainly the highest number of casualties at a German urban target to date.

An inconclusive raid on Berlin on the night 9/10th did not involve 115 Squadron, but orders came though on the 10th to prepare ten Wellingtons as part of a force of fifty-three Wellingtons, Blenheims and Manchesters for yet another crack at Brest. S/L Curry was the senior pilot on duty as the 115 Squadron element took off between 19.15 and 19.33, and all arrived in the target area to carry out their bombing runs from between 9,000 and 13,000 feet. Visibility was good enough to determine that the attack was centred on the docks area where the German cruisers were at berth, but few crews saw anything other than the flash of their hardware exploding. The consensus of returning crews was that it had been an effective raid, which was confirmed some time later when reports were received that four bombs had struck the Gneisenau, killing or wounding over a hundred crew members and German workers. The same target was posted at Marham on the 12th, and 115 squadron was ordered to make ready four Wellingtons from each flight to join fifty-eight other aircraft for that night's attack. S/L Curry was first off the ground at 19.32, followed shortly afterwards by S/L Lasbrey as the other senior pilot on duty. Weather conditions were less favourable than of late, and heavy cloud sat over the target area, obscuring it from view. All but one of the squadron's participants dropped their bombs, mostly from between 9,000 and 13,000 feet, basing their aim on the amount of flak coming up at them through the cloud. F/O Knight caught a glimpse of the docks through a small hole in the cloud when flying at 15,000 feet, and let his entire load go, but could not observe the outcome. S/L Lasbrey also made a positive identification of the port, and delivered a number of 250 pounders over the southern dock before pushing on to the alternative target of Lorient to drop his 500 pounders. In fact, quite a proportion of the force also attacked Lorient, where visibility was described as good. Sgt Bright turned back when a short distance south of Brest after assessing the conditions to be too difficult, and he brought his bombs home.

The same furrow was to be ploughed again on the night of the 14/15th, for which 115 Squadron bombed-up and fuelled eight Wellingtons as part of an overall force of ninety-four aircraft. They took to the air between 23.11 and 23.41 with S/L Curry the senior pilot on duty, and all reached the target area to bomb from between 9,000 and 14,000 feet through sufficient amounts of cloud to be unable, in most cases, to observe the results. Crews chose a variety of headings, Sgt Bright flying west to east when caught by a searchlight beam, which caused his bombs to overshoot and hit barracks east of the river. P/O Loder observed green flashes as his bombs burst near the dry dock, but he knew he had not hit the target ships. Attention returned to Kiel on the night of the 15/16th, for which a force of ninety-six aircraft was prepared. 115 Squadron was not invited to take part, but dispatched the freshman crews of P/Os Bailey and Robertson at 20.44 and 20.59 respectively to bomb the docks at Calais. As they climbed through 4,000 feet they began to pick up ice, and decided to jettison all or part of their bomb loads before returning to base. The Kiel operation did not achieve the success of the recent raids after cloud intervened, and damage was light in comparison.

The focus remained on north-western Germany on the night of the 16/17th when Bremen was selected as the target for a force of 107 aircraft. 3 Group put up fifty-three Wellingtons, of which eleven represented 115 Squadron, and they took off between 21.10 and 22.35 with S/L Curry the senior pilot on duty. Adverse weather conditions greeted them in the target area, and only a quarter of returning crews claimed to have bombed there. The main problem was eight to ten-tenths cloud with a base at around 4,000 feet, which allowed glimpses of the ground but no opportunity to take aim. Bombs were dropped indiscriminately from between 8,500 and 14,000 feet into the general docks area or the town, guided by the flash of explosions, the glow of fires and the evidence of searchlight and flak activity. Having seen the cloud facing him, Sgt Rogers even flew away for fifteen minutes, before returning to find no improvement and emptying his bomb bay from 12,000 feet. On the way home P/O Loder machine-gunned Leeuwarden aerodrome in northern Holland from 4,000 feet.

Briefings took place across the Command on the 17th for two aiming-points in the city of Berlin, but adverse weather conditions rendered the raid ineffective. Marham was excluded from operational duties on this night, and, apart from a single freshman sortie by a 218 Squadron crew, the station dispatched only training flights until the evening of the 22nd. The target then was Brest and its lodgers, and the operation was a 3 Group show involving twenty-four Wellingtons and two Stirlings. 115 Squadron contributed ten Wellingtons, which took off between 19.58 and 20.14 with S/L Lasbrey the senior pilot on duty. They encountered no cloud in the target area, but the haze and extreme darkness combined with the formidable Brest flak and searchlight defences to largely prevent accurate bombing, and returning crews were able only to report the flash of bomb bursts. Fog at Marham forced crews to fly further west to find somewhere to land, and most lobbed in at Abingdon. Sgt Palmer decided to land at Wroughton in Wiltshire, but T2560 crashed four miles south-south-east of Swindon during the final approach, and the second pilot, Sgt Shaw, failed to survive.

After a couple of nights at home, 115 squadron was back on the Order of Battle on the night of the 25/26th, having been ordered to prepare eight Wellingtons in a force of sixty-two aircraft to attack Kiel, which had been visited also on the previous night. While this operation was in progress, four freshman crews from Marham, three of them belonging to 115 Squadron, were to bomb the naval docks at Emden. They took off between 20.56 and 21.21 with S/L Lasbrey the senior pilot on duty, and all reached their respective target areas to find favourable weather conditions. R1509 lost its heating system fifteen minutes into the outward flight, but Sgt King and crew pressed on, only to fail to locate the target, and bombed a searchlight concentration as an alternative. On his arrival over Kiel, S/L Lasbrey observed a large fire already burning, and he watched his hardware fall between the armoury plant and the docks. Bombing took place from between 10,000 and 16,000 feet, and returning crews reported many explosions, and fires so bright that they illuminated the cockpit some 15,000 feet above. Sgts Anderson and Smith and P/O Bailey attacked Emden also from between 10,000 and 16,000 feet, but only the last-mentioned observed bomb bursts.

The long-serving F/L Giles was posted to HQ 6 Group (Training) on the 28th at the end of his tour, and acting S/L Curry was finally granted an increase in salary for his additional responsibilities. Marham was excluded from an ineffective raid on Mannheim on the night of the 29/30th, but orders were received on the 30th to prepare for operations that night against Kiel. 115 Squadron made ready eleven Wellingtons to contribute to the overall force of eighty-one aircraft, but Sgt Rogers reported sick and his sortie was cancelled. The remainder took off between 20.00 and 21.18 with both flight commanders on duty, and all but one reached the target area to find it obscured by cloud. A proportion of the force bombed on estimated position, including six from 115 Squadron, who let their loads go from between 14,000 and 16,000 feet, some claiming to observe results, others not. S/L Curry brought his bombs home after failing to locate the primary or a worthwhile last resort target. Local reports suggested that no bombs fell within the town or port, and the fires may have been at a decoy site. During the course of the month the squadron operated on twelve nights and dispatched 104 sorties for the loss of two Wellingtons and one crew.

May 1941

Hamburg was selected to host the first major raid of the new month, for which ninety-five aircraft departed their stations in the late evening of the 2nd. 115 Squadron did not take part in what was claimed as an effective attack, which caused twenty-six fires but no major damage. Attention began to shift from Brest as a primary target, relegating it temporarily to secondary importance as German cities came more into the spotlight. The main effort on the night of the 3/4th was directed at Cologne, for which a force of 101 aircraft was made ready, while 115 Squadron prepared ten aircraft as part of a 3 Group force of thirty-three Wellingtons and Stirlings to maintain some pressure on Brest. They took off between 21.15 and 21.38 with S/L Curry the senior pilot on duty, and nine of them carrying a single 2,000 pounder along with 500 and 250 pounders. P/O Robertson jettisoned his load as R1500 struggled to gain sufficient height by the time the enemy coast hove into view, although a second entry in the ORB claims the bombs were dumped in error. Sgt Sayers and crew failed to locate the target, and, on the way home, R1280 shed a propeller, forcing Sgt Sayers to execute a crash-landing as his good engine began to fail. He just failed to make Oakington airfield and came to earth at 04.00 just north of the railway station, five miles north-west of Cambridge, and all walked away from the scene unharmed. Meanwhile, the remainder had carried out their attacks from between 11,000 and 14,000 feet in excellent weather conditions, and returned to report many fires, some of them large, and bomb bursts across the docks area.

There would be just two major raids on Brest during the month, and these would also take place during the first week. The first was scheduled for the night of the 4/5th, and involved ninety-seven aircraft, of which forty-four were provided by 3 Group. There were claims of direct hits on Scharnhorst and Gneisenau, but these were not confirmed. 115 Squadron sat out this operation, and spent the 5th preparing nine Wellingtons for an attack that night on Mannheim. This was to be a major undertaking involving 141 aircraft, half of them Wellingtons, of which the Marham squadrons were to provide nine each. The 115 Squadron element took off between 22.56 and 23.29 with S/L Curry the senior pilot on duty and P/O Saunderson and crew flying in W5459, a Mk II Merlin-powered variant with the squadron's first 4,000lb "cookie" on board. The more powerful Mk II was being fed in small numbers into all Wellington units specifically as "cookie" carriers. They flew all the way to southern Germany over a blanket of ten-tenths cloud, which hampered navigation, but 120 returning crews claimed to have bombed in the target area. P/O Saunderson reported bombing on a north-westerly heading, slightly south-east of the aiming-point, and observing a huge, red, circular explosion emanating from his cookie, with a mushroom cloud

Above and overleaf: 115 Sqn Wellington R1379 was shot down by a night fighter on the Hamburg raid of 10ᵗʰ May 1941. The pilot, Sgt. J Anderson, lost his life but the rest of crew survived and became POWs.

of smoke rising out of the centre. His squadron colleagues also delivered their loads into the target area, but cloud prevented them from observing results. A local report claimed that around twenty-five bomb loads hit the city, causing only modest damage, mostly to residential property.

A force of 115 aircraft set off for Hamburg on the evening of the 6th, with Feltwell, Stradishall and Wyton providing the 3 Group element of forty-three aircraft. The attack was dogged by poor visibility, and, despite the claims of eighty crews to have bombed in the target area, local reports suggested otherwise. Orders came through on the 7th to prepare for the second Brest operation, which was to be conducted by eighty-nine aircraft, including nine belonging to 115 Squadron. S/L Curry was the senior pilot on duty as they took off between 22.30 and 22.57, each Wellington carrying a 2,000 pounder, six 500 pounders and three 250 pounders. The conditions over the French coast were excellent, and crews were able to identify ground detail, including the enemy warships. All crews delivered their loads across the target area, some observing bursts, while others were prevented from doing so by searchlight glare and flak avoidance. Returning crews claimed hits on the vessels, but, again, there was no confirmation.

Instructions were received on the 8th to prepare for a busy night of operations with the main emphasis on north-western Germany. 188 aircraft were detailed to return to Hamburg, while 133 others were assigned to Bremen, and, with the minor operations also taking place, the 364 sorties dispatched by the Command would be the highest to date by a clear ninety-nine. 115 Squadron briefed ten crews, including that of S/L Curry, and P/O Saunderson and F/O Kirk would each take a cookie-carrying Mk II to Germany's Second City, where the effort was to be divided between the shipyards and the main town area. They departed Marham between 22.02 and 22.18, and only Sgt King and crew had to return early with intercom issues, leaving the others to press on. Excellent visibility greeted their arrival over Hamburg, where fires were already burning and the flak defence was intense. S/L Curry added to the fires with his incendiaries, and other crews reported observing explosions, particularly from the 4,000 pounders. Returning crews were confident that they had delivered a telling blow, and this was borne out by local reports which described eighty-three fires, thirty-eight of them classed as large, and the destruction of ten apartment blocks by a single cookie. A death toll of 185 people was also the highest to date at a German target. The simultaneous raid on Bremen was also moderately effective, local reports confirming widespread bombing but no significant industrial damage.

The twin cities of Mannheim and Ludwigshafen, which faced each other from the East and West Banks respectively of the Rhine in southern Germany, would feature prominently on the Command's target list throughout the war. In time, as the bomber fleet expanded, their relative positions would be incorporated into the plan of attack, to exploit the "creep-back" phenomenon common to most heavy raids. That was for the future, however, and the plan for the night of the 9/10th was to send a force of 146 aircraft, of which fifty Wellingtons were provided by the 3 Group stations of Feltwell, Honington, Stradishall and Wyton, while Marham remained inactive. The operation was modestly successful, destroying fifty-three buildings of a military, war-industry, commercial and residential nature, and damaging many more, whilst rendering a total of 3,533 people temporarily or permanently homeless.

On the 10th, the first anniversary of the German advance into Holland and Belgium, and of Churchill's appointment as Prime Minister, orders were received across the Command to prepare 119 aircraft for an operation that night against the shipyards, the city and the Altona power station in Hamburg. 115 Squadron loaded nine standard Wellingtons with a mixture of 500 and 250 pounders and incendiaries, and a single Mk II with a cookie for the main event, and one further aircraft for a small-scale raid on Berlin, and they took off between 22.17 and 22.35 with S/L Lasbrey the senior pilot on duty. It is believed that Sgt Smith and crew were Berlin-bound, but failed to reach it because of extreme cold and an inability to maintain height. According to the ORB, P/O Saunderson delivered his cookie from 19,000 feet, but, as this was substantially higher than normal, it was probably a misreading of 10,000 feet. It detonated violently about five hundred yards north-west of aiming-point B, and produced a red glow, "like the centre of an inferno" that lasted for several minutes, in the light from which could be seen houses. The crew also reported that about twenty-five flak guns ceased firing for a few seconds. The only other report came from Sgt Martin and crew, who dropped a stick across a railway junction from 13,000 feet and set off fires in the town. R1379 failed to return to Marham, and the crew of Sgt Anderson was duly posted missing. It would be some time before news came through that the Wellington had been shot down by Lt Eckart-Wilhelm von Bonin of II/NJG1 after being coned in searchlights over Tönning on the western coast of the Schleswig-Holstein peninsular. Five members of the crew survived to fall into enemy hands, but, sadly, the pilot died in the crash.

3 Group contributed sixty five Wellingtons and a Stirling for a return to Hamburg twenty-four hours later, the 3 Group contingent representing the main component of a force of ninety-two aircraft, whose crews had been briefed to attack the Blohm & Voss shipyards. The 115 Squadron element of ten departed Marham between 22.26 and 22.42 with S/L Curry the senior pilot on duty, and only P/O Bailey and crew were unable to carry on because of a failure to maintain height and a problem with the intercom system. As they flew back towards England they were attacked by a ME110, but neither aircraft sustained damage. The others found Hamburg without difficulty in excellent weather conditions, and delivered their bombs from between 12,000 and 16,000 feet, S/L Curry, P/O Loder and Sgt King doing so on a north to south heading, while F/O Kirk was flying east to west. Many large fires were observed, and Sgt Martin and crew reported a blaze in a main oil-storage tank and others in the Holzhafen district on the East Bank of the Elbe, south-east of the city centre. A simultaneous attack on Bremen attracted the bombs of Sgt Rogers and crew onto the Atlas Werke shipyard, after they mistook the River Weser for the Elbe. The Hamburg operation was declared a success, and local reports confirmed that the city had taken some punishment during this series of three raids in four nights, although there was no mention of significant industrial damage.

Three sergeant pilots and their crews were posted across the tarmac from 218 Squadron on the 15th, and would soon be in action on behalf of their new masters. An inconclusive raid on Hannover that night did not involve the Marham squadrons, but orders were received on the 16th to prepare for the first of a series of operations against the Rhineland Capital city of Cologne. 115 Squadron loaded eleven Wellingtons with a mix of 500 and 250 pounders along with SBCs of incendiaries, and they took off between 22.24 and 23.14 with S/Ls Curry and Lasbrey the senior pilots on duty and the newly-arrived Sgt Madgewick and crew undertaking their first operation with the squadron. Weather condition between base and the target were good, but a slight haze over Cologne became more dense as the raid progressed. All of the 115 Squadron participants reached the target and carried out bombing runs on a variety of headings from around 14,000 feet. S/L Curry suffered a hang-up on his first attempt to bomb, and eventually released his load with the jettison switch, which caused an overshoot to the north-west of the city. Sgt Smith was unable to identify the precise aiming point, and dropped his bombs in the vicinity of the Hohenzollern Bridge, the rail and road crossing between the main railway station on the West Bank and the Kalk marshalling yards. Returning crews described explosions and fires, but the reducing visibility precluded any meaningful assessment. Local reports claimed just seven high explosive bombs fell in the city to cause minor damage, and, certainly, none commensurate with the effort of sending a force of ninety-three aircraft. This proved to be the final operation of the month for 115 Squadron, while the Command returned to Cologne on the night of the 17/18th to deliver another largely ineffective attack, which was followed up by a failure at Kiel twenty-four hours later.

A flurry of postings signalled a change at the top for the squadron with the arrival of S/L Sharp from 214 Squadron at Stradishall on the 19th. He was immediately promoted to acting wing commander rank (unpaid), on the imminent departure of W/C Evans-Evans for Polebrook, a move which would take place

The 4000 lb 'Cookie' was intended to break open buildings, thereby enabling incendiaries to ignite the interior. It was a devastating weapon in Bomber Command's arsenal.

during the following week. As the new commanding officer arrived, P/O Saunderson was posted to 15 O.T.U at the end of his tour, and F/L Clyde-Smith went to 218 Squadron. Sgt King was the next pilot to be posted out, also at the end of his tour, and his destination on the 23rd was 23 O.T.U at Pershore. On the 27th, the Bismarck met her end in the North Atlantic, and a force of Wellingtons and Stirlings was sent in search of her escort, the Prinz Eugen. 115 Squadron had been put on stand-by from 04.00, but was not called into action, and no contact was made with the enemy warship. During the course of the month the squadron operated on seven nights and dispatched seventy sorties for the loss of two Wellingtons and one crew.

June 1941

June and July were to be significant months for the Command, as its performance began to be monitored in order to provide an assessment of its effectiveness for the War Cabinet. The project was initiated by Churchill's chief scientific advisor, Lord Cherwell, who handed the responsibility to David M Bensusan-Butt, a civil-servant assistant to Cherwell working in the War Cabinet Secretariat. June began with preparations on the 2nd for a raid that night on Düsseldorf, for which a force of 150 aircraft was assembled. Just one Wellington was detailed by 115 Squadron, which was also to provide a single aircraft for a small-scale 3 Group operation to Berlin involving eight Stirlings and three Wellingtons. F/L Bailey and crew took off for the Capital in Mk II W5459 at 22.45 carrying a 4,000 pounder, but lost the use of their rear turret to mechanical failure, and decided to join in at Düsseldorf instead. The cookie was released from 14,000 feet and caused a large, green flash followed by what was described at debriefing as an evil red glow. P/O Evans and crew departed Marham an hour after their colleagues, but encountered icing conditions which prevented them from climbing beyond 12,000 feet, upon which they returned home with their seven 500 pounders. Two thirds of the crews reported bombing as briefed over the Ruhr in conditions of partial cloud and industrial haze, but local reports described only scattered bombing and minor damage. S/L Lasbrey had now concluded his tour and was posted to Marham station HQ to be succeeded as a flight commander on the same day by S/L Sindall, who arrived from somewhere within 3 Group.

Having evaded all attempts by sea and air to find her following the loss of Bismarck, Prinz Eugen finally joined Scharnhorst and Gneisenau at Brest early in the month. 3 Group sent a force of thirty-three aircraft to target them on the evening of the 7th, but the enemy activated a smoke-screen, and no hits were scored or aircraft lost. S/L Curry was the second flight commander to finish a tour during the early part of the month, and he was posted to 21 O.T.U at Moreton-in-Marsh to be succeeded by the newly-promoted S/L Knight. Feltwell and Marham were notified of another raid on the enemy warships planned for the night of the 10/11th, for which an overall force of 104 aircraft was made ready. 115 Squadron briefed six crews, who took off between 01.22 and 01.40 with S/L Knight the senior pilot on duty. The enemy was waiting, and the smoke-screen effective as S/L Knight carried out a gliding attack from 15,000 down to 12,000 feet, releasing his bombs on a south-easterly heading and failing to observe their detonation beneath the smoke. Others from the squadron bombed from between 10,400 and 14,000 feet, and, despite claims of straddling the location of the ships, it seems that they emerged unscathed again, as did the attackers. Sgt Smith and crew failed to locate the target, and jettisoned their bombs some twenty miles north of the French coast to save fuel for the return journey.

On the following night Düsseldorf and Duisburg were the main targets for ninety-two and eighty aircraft respectively, but it seems that most of the bombs fell on Cologne, where damage was inflicted on the main railway station and the Rhine docks. 115 Squadron sat this one out, but dispatched the freshman crew of P/O Evans just before midnight to attack the docks at Boulogne. They located the target without difficulty and delivered their seven 500 pounders and incendiaries from west to east across the entrance to docks 4 and 5 from 10,000 feet.

The night of the 12/13th was to be a busy one devoted to attacks on railway installations at four locations in Germany. 3 Group was handed the important hub of Hamm, situated north-east of the Ruhr, and a force of eighty-two aircraft was made ready of which a dozen represented 115 Squadron. They took off between 23.34 and 00.05 with S/L Knight the senior pilot on duty, and the recently-arrived S/L Sindall flying as second pilot with F/L Bailey. They were each carrying a single 1,000 pounder and a varying number of 500 and 250 pounders. R1721 lost an engine while outbound, and the bombs were jettisoned in order to maintain height. During final approach to Marham, the second engine cut, and the Wellington struck trees before crashing on the edge of the airfield at 03.05. The rear gunner, Sgt Aikenhead, sustained serious injury, to which he would succumb on the 15th, while his crew colleagues were able to walk away apparently unscathed. P/O Duff and crew brought their bombs home, but the other squadron participants located the target area in conditions of ground haze, and found it a challenge to identify the precise location of the marshalling yards. Bombing took place from between 9,000 and 14,500 feet, but no assessment was possible. A local report stated that seven bombs fell in the town, six of which exploded with minimal effect, while the seventh, containing a delayed action fuse, killed two bomb-disposal men.

A force of 110 aircraft was assembled on the 13th for an attack that night on Brest and its resident enemy warships. Ten 115 Squadron Wellingtons took off between 00.20 and 00.57 with the new flight commander, S/L Sindall, the senior pilot on duty. All reached the target area to be greeted by the usual effective smoke-screen, which combined with searchlight dazzle to prevent identification of the aiming-point. Only Sgt Reid and crew decided to hang on to their bombs rather than dump them indiscriminately into the smoke, while the others delivered their loads from between 9,500 and 12,000 feet, S/L Sindall doing so onto a nearby flare-path. All then returned safely with nothing of use to report to the intelligence section at debriefing.

The second half of the month would see Cologne and Düsseldorf become the main focus of attention, and, from the night of the 15/16th, the two cities would be attacked simultaneously on no fewer than eight nights by forces of varying sizes. 115 Squadron made ready eleven Wellingtons on the 15th for an attack that night on the Gereon marshalling yards and goods station on the West Bank of the Rhine in the centre of Cologne, and two others for a freshman operation to Dunkerque. The main element took off between 23.15 and 23.35, each carrying a 1,000 pounder along with mostly 500 pounders, and with S/Ls Knight and Sindall the senior pilots on duty. Sgts Matthews and Payne departed at 00.13 and 00.25 respectively to join eight other Wellingtons and two Whitleys at the French coast. Sgt Payne and crew experienced engine problems with R1805 and brought all but one of their bombs home, leaving Sgt Matthews to deliver his load between docks 3 and 4 and start three small fires. Sgt Berney also reported overheating engines while outbound for Cologne, which prevented him from climbing, and he brought his bombs back. The others pushed on to find ten-tenths cloud over the target area, and carried out their attacks on estimated positions, before returning to report a few fires. Local reports suggested that four or five bomb loads had hit the city, and they had caused only minor damage.

On the afternoon of the 17th, P/O Evans took R1517 for an air-test in preparation for the night's operations, which, for 115 Squadron, meant Düsseldorf and Hannover. Having reached 500 feet the Wellington turned through 180° before diving towards the ground to level out only at the last second, and crash two miles north-east of Swaffham in Norfolk, where it burst into flames. There were seven men on board, including a member of ground crew, and five of them were killed outright, while the Canadian second pilot died in hospital, and only the rear gunner emerged more-or-less unscathed. While twelve crews attended briefing, their Wellingtons were being fuelled and bombed up, ten for Düsseldorf and two for Hannover. By the time of take-off, between 23.31 and 23.59, one sortie had been scrubbed, and it is believed that this was one of those intended for Hannover. S/L Knight set course alone for northern Germany in Wellington Mk II W5449, and carrying a cookie and 500 pounders, which were dropped from 14,000 feet in conditions of poor vertical visibility. A large red flash was observed through the haze and smoke, and his camera captured a photograph, which, in the event, was not helpful in plotting the fall of the bombs. S/L Sindall was the senior pilot on duty among the Ruhr-bound contingent, which lost Sgt Belsey and crew when overheating engines and an inability to climb forced them to turn back when close the Belgian coast. F/L Bailey and crew were in the other Mk II in use on this night, but diverted from the primary target after the rear turret became unserviceable. They delivered their cookie from 11,000 feet over an unspecified location south of the target area, and witnessed a large flash, followed by a red mushroom of smoke and dust rising upwards, which then lay over the area for some thirty seconds. Sgt Smith was unable to identify the aiming-point, and dropped his load onto what appeared to be a large factory building, which resulted in a fire and a number of electrical flashes. The others bombed from between 10,000 and 14,000 feet, mostly after picking up the Rhine as a reference point, and returned safely having been prevented by the poor visibility from assessing the outcome.

While 115 Squadron remained at home, other elements of the Command attacked Bremen and Brest on the night of the 18/19th, and Cologne and Düsseldorf twenty-four hours later. The squadron detailed eleven crews for an operation against Kiel on the night of the 20/21st, for which the battleship Tirpitz was the principal target. The two Mk IIs were loaded with a cookie each and the others with 500 and 250 pounders, and ten of them departed Marham between 22.28 and 22.59 with S/Ls Knight and Sindall the senior pilots on duty. It was 00.15 before Sgt Belsey took to the air in W5459, and he soon realised that he would not reach the briefed target before the raid was over. He decided to find an alternative objective, and dropped his cookie from 17,000 feet onto a flak and searchlight concentration in the Westerhaven district of Rotterdam, but was prevented by cloud from seeing the result. The others pressed on, unusually for a night raid, with a fighter escort, and reached the Schleswig-Holstein region of north-western Germany, where they encountered low cloud and haze. Despite the poor visibility, they picked out sufficient coastline to fix their general position, and delivered their bombs from between 12,000 and 16,000 feet, mostly using searchlight and flak concentrations as an aiming-point. It was not possible to observe the results, but S/L Knight reported a red glow through the clouds some five minutes after bombing, while local reports suggested that few bombs had found the mark.

Cologne, Düsseldorf and Bremen were targeted by elements of the Command before 115 Squadron was next called to arms on the 23rd, when ten crews attended briefing. Eight learned that they were to join fifty-four other Wellingtons and Whitleys to attack Cologne, while two would be flying Mk IIs in a return to Kiel in company with a predominantly Stirling and Halifax force. They took off between 22.55 and 23.48 with S/L Knight the senior pilot on duty, and P/O Foster and Sgt Belsey bound for Kiel, where they found excellent conditions. The former dropped his cookie from 14,000 feet onto the aiming-point, and witnessed a multi-coloured explosion followed by a large mushroom of fire. The latter let his 4,000 pounder go from 15,000 feet and saw it explode two hundred yards east of the aiming-point, flinging much debris into the air and silencing the flak and searchlight batteries for thirty seconds. This was almost certainly the bomb which, according to local sources, appeared to detonate in the air above an open space, where a crowd was watching an aircraft successfully evade a large searchlight cone. As it turned out, W5449 sustained damage to the starboard wing and fuselage and the bomb-aimer's clear vision panel, but made it safely home to report what appeared to be a successful raid, but was, in fact, not. The Cologne force found the Rhineland Capital to be hidden beneath a cloak of industrial haze, and bombs were delivered from between 12,500 and 15,000 feet, although only a few were reported by local authorities to have landed within the city. On return and short of fuel P/O Sharpe decided to put T2963 down at the emergency landing strip at Woodbridge on the Suffolk coast using the Lorenz Beam to guide him in. However, the Wellington clipped trees, possibly because of faulty equipment, and ended up on the ground at Debach some three miles north-west of the runway, eventually coming to rest embedded in a row of council houses at Moat House Farm, injuring one member of the crew, who subsequently died on the 25th.

Cologne, Düsseldorf and Kiel were the main targets posted on the 26th, all to be attacked by modest forces of fifty-one, forty-four and fifty-nine aircraft respectively. 3 Group supported the raids on Cologne and Kiel, and provided all thirty-two Wellingtons for the former, of which ten belonged to 115 Squadron. They took off between 23.35 and 23.51 with S/L Sindall the senior pilot on duty and each carrying a 1,000 pounder and five 500 pounders. R1501 failed to become airborne after Sgt Skillen retracted the undercarriage prematurely, and the Wellington skidded to a halt against the boundary fence, where it caught fire and was destroyed when the bombs went off. There were no injuries, but a number of houses on the married quarters site sustained damage. They others flew through violent electrical storms over the Channel as they made their way to the target area, and, so bad were the conditions, that S/L Sindall, P/O Foster, P/O McSweyn and Sgt Smith all turned back after failing to negotiate a passage around or over them. Sgt Matthews and crew were ensnared in a searchlight cone over Antwerp, and jettisoned their bombs safe as they spiralled down to make their escape. F/L Bailey and crew reached as far as Eindhoven in southern Holland before dropping their load on a flak and searchlight concentration from 9,000 feet. The others, Sgts Belsey, Reid and Wallace and P/O Duff, found ten-tenths cloud over the Rhineland, and all bombed from between 8,000 and 12,000 feet on estimated position guided by the flash of flak and searchlights. They returned home safely with little to report beyond the atrocious weather conditions, except, that is, for Sgt Wallace, who revealed that his rear gunner, Sgt Mercer, had abandoned the aircraft over Maastricht on the way home.

Bremen was selected to host the main effort on the night of the 29/30th, for which a force of 106 aircraft was made ready, while twenty-eight other aircraft were prepared for Hamburg, where the railway station was the briefed aiming-point. 3 Group supported both operations, providing twenty-seven Wellingtons for Bremen, of which nine represented 115 Squadron, while two of the three Mk IIs in use on this night were destined for Hamburg in the hands of S/L Sindall and F/L Bailey and their crews. They took off between 22.59 and 23.15 with W/C Sharp first away on his maiden sortie since taking command of the squadron. Sgt Matthews was forced to turn back after his intercom system failed, and he jettisoned part of his bomb load. The others pressed on to encounter good weather conditions over north-western Germany, and S/L Sindall watched his bombs fall from 13,500 feet onto the western side of Hamburg on a run from south to north. P/O Foster dropped his cookie from 16,500 feet onto the approximate location of the railway station, and witnessed a large, yellow explosion followed by a fire, which gave off volumes of white smoke. Meanwhile, seventy miles to the south-west, bombing was being carried out at Bremen from between 11,000 and 15,000 feet, and returning crews reported fires and bursts, but could not assess the accuracy of their work. Sgt Smith and crew drifted off track outbound and found themselves off the island of Heligoland. With time running short they turned towards Bremerhaven, and dropped a stick of bombs across the town from west to east.

On return from Bremen, R1508 crash-landed on the airfield at Manby in Lincolnshire, but Sgt Payne and his crew emerged unscathed. F/L Bailey and crew failed to return in W5459, and it was established later that the Wellington had been shot down by a night-fighter flown by Hptm Walter Ehle of II/NJG1, and had crashed at 01.52 a little more than two miles south-west of Bremen with no survivors. The loss of the experienced F/L Bailey DFC and his crew would be felt keenly at Marham. Also missing was the crew of P/O McSweyn RAAF in R1509, which was hit by flak over the target, before being raked by cannon fire from a ME110. It became necessary to abandon the Wellington to its fate, and all but the rear gunner reached the ground safely. Sgt Gill, who had been badly wounded during the fighter attack, and had landed in the branches of a tree, released his parachute harness and fell forty feet to the ground, where he was captured along with four others of the crew. He was taken to hospital, only to lose his fight for life on the following day. P/O McSweyn managed to evade capture for three days, until being apprehended while attempting to steal a ME110 on a Luftwaffe airfield. He eventually escaped from prison camp, and made his way back to England to be awarded a Military Cross. (Bomber Command Losses. Vol 2. W R Chorley.) F/L Litchfield was posted in from 11 O.T.U at Bassingbourn on the 29th. During the course of the month the squadron operated on eleven nights and dispatched ninety-seven sorties for the loss of seven Wellingtons and three crews.

July 1941

There was little change for the crews as July's operations progressed, with the familiar names of Brest, Bremen and Cologne all featuring in the first week's target list. An attack on the first-mentioned on the night of the 1/2nd resulted in a bomb exploding inside the Prinz Eugen, killing sixty of her crew. Bremen, Cologne and Duisburg were the targets for the night of the 2/3rd, and it was in support of the first-mentioned, the largest raid of the three, that 115 Squadron made ready seven Wellingtons among a 3 Group contribution of forty-four aircraft. P/Os Duff and Foster were the senior pilots on duty as they departed Marham between 23.15 and 23.23, and all arrived in the target area to find a layer of thin cloud and ground haze. They delivered their loads of 500 and 250 pounders and 4lb incendiaries from between 12,500 and 16,000 feet, and watched them fall in or close to the aiming-point, setting off many fires. P/O Duff reported a large fire burning twenty miles west of the target, and P/O Foster and crew described their X9663 coming under attack four times by a ME110, during which encounter it sustained damage to the tail-plane, rear turret, fixed aerial and port propeller.

The large and industrially important Ruhr city of Essen, home of the giant Krupp armaments producing complex, would become the principal target of the next commander-in-chief, but at this stage of the war it merited only modest attention. On the night of the 3/4th, ninety Wellingtons and Whitleys were sent against it, while Wellingtons and Hampdens returned to Bremen, but cloud cover at both locations prevented accurate attacks. 115 Squadron stayed at home for these, but prepared ten Wellington on the 4th for operations that night against Brest. Sixty-five Wellingtons and twenty-three Whitleys took off in the late evening, the 115 Squadron element taking to the air between 22.35 and 22.44 with S/L Sindall the senior pilot on duty. They encountered the expected and effective smoke-screen, which persuaded S/L Sindall to drop his bombs from 15,000 feet in a single stick along the coastline south of Brest's Port de Commerce. The others bombed from between 11,000 and 15,000 feet, and observed flashes beneath the smoke, but could not ascertain any detail. R1772 picked up some flak damage in its port wing and the compass failed, but P/O Duff brought it safely home to a landing at Chivenor. X9671 was engaged by a ME110, which Sgt Wallace's rear gunner, Sgt Parsons, shot down

Münster was another occasional objective, and had not been attacked for five months when it was selected as the target for attention on three consecutive nights, beginning on the 5th. 3 and 4 Groups combined to send ninety-four Wellingtons and Whitleys winging their way to north-western Germany, and those reaching the target claimed a successful raid in good weather conditions. 115 Squadron did not take part, but was called to arms to provide ten Wellingtons twenty-four hours later as part of an all-3 Group force of forty-seven Wellingtons for the same target, while 109 other aircraft returned to Brest. The Münster-bound element departed Marham between 23.20 and midnight with S/Ls Knight and Sindall the senior pilots on duty and carrying bomb loads made up principally of 500 pounders and SBCs of 4lb incendiaries. X9672 returned early after it was attacked outbound by an enemy night-fighter, the fire from which killed Sgt Berney's rear gunner, Sgt Kerruish. The others all made it to the target, where bombing was carried out from between 12,500 and 14,000 feet, and returning crews reported numerous fires, as many as forty, one of which was estimated by Sgt Wallace and crew to have been three miles long and a mile wide. This crew also reported being engaged by an unidentified enemy night-fighter, which was driven off by return fire, before a JU88 subjected X9671 to a prolonged, eight-minute attack, which also ended inconclusively. Sgt Matthews and crew were less fortunate, and all perished when R1063 was attacked by Oblt Helmut Woltersdorf of 4/NJG.1 and crashed into the sea at 02.17 off the Frisian island of Schiermonnikoog. A message from the stricken Wellington suggested that the pilot had been attempting a controlled ditching. Despite the claims of an effective raid, local authorities reported only thirty incendiaries hitting the town and no casualties.

Just three 115 Squadron crews were briefed for a return to Münster on the night of the 7/8th, and these were captained by S/L Sindall, F/L Litchfield and Sgt Rawlings. They were part of an all-3 Group force of forty-nine Wellingtons on a night when Cologne was the principal target, while 4 Group attended to railway yards at Osnabrück. The Marham element took off between 23.31 and 23.43 and headed across the North Sea to make landfall via the Dutch Frisians. F/L Litchfield and crew suffered an engine problem, and sought out an alternative target for their nine 500 and three 250 pounders along with incendiaries. They found a built-up area to the north-west of Münster, which they attacked from 10,000 feet, believing it to be Burgsteinfurt. As they retreated towards the North Sea they observed two large fires, which remained visible for sixty miles into the return journey. S/L Sindall delivered his load from 11,500 feet on a northerly heading, and watched it fall to port of the marshalling yards. Sgt Rawlings let his go from 14,000 feet onto a railway south of the target, and observed a fire start, which began to spread rapidly. Meanwhile, Cologne was suffering its most destructive raid of the year, which resulted in housing damage and over sixty large fires.

A new Air Ministry directive issued on the 9th signalled an end to the maritime diversion, which had been in force since March. It was now assessed, that the enemy's transportation system and the morale of its civilian population represented the weakest points, and that Peirse should direct his main effort in these directions. A new list of targets was drawn up, which included the main railway centres ringing

Sgt N L Johnson RCAF (Courtesy of Michel Beckers, Aircrew Remembered)

Wellington Z8788 was the only aircraft that failed to return having been shot down by Flak Battery 252 which was positioned at the Alfa Hotel at Mariakerke (Above right)

the industrial Ruhr in order to inhibit the import of raw materials, and the export of finished products. Railways were relatively precise targets, and were to be attacked during the moon period. On moonless nights, the Rhine cities of Cologne, Düsseldorf and Duisburg would be easier to locate for "area" attacks, and, when less favourable weather conditions obtained, Peirse was to send his force to more distant objectives in northern, eastern and southern Germany.

Aachen, a city on Germany's western frontiers with Holland and Belgium, was selected on the 9th to host its first major raid of the war, and sustained, what for the period, was heavy damage to commercial and residential property at the hands of a 4 and 5 Group force. While this was in progress, a predominantly 3 Group force of Wellingtons was attacking Osnabruck, 120 miles to the north-east. The same three 115 Squadron crews employed for the Münster operation were joined by P/O Pooley, and they took off between 23.12 and 23.18 loaded with three 500 pounders each, along with a single 250 pounder and SBCs of incendiaries. P/O Pooley and crew were unable to locate the primary target, and, as an alternative, bombed a railway in an unidentified built-up area from 14,000 feet, setting off a fire which burned very brightly. On return X9671 was force-landed at Northolt without injury to the crew, and the Wellington was soon returned to active duty. S/L Sindall attacked the primary target from 14,000 feet, and it was during the homeward leg that the engines began to falter. It was decided that the crew should bale out, which they did near Oxford, while the pilot remained with W5710 to attempt a landing. Shortly afterwards the engine issue seemed to cure itself, and he put the Wellington down at Brackley, where he learned that four of his crew had landed safely, but the rear gunner had sustained a broken leg. Sgt Rawlings bombed from 12,000 feet and F/L Litchfield from 14,000, and both landed away from Marham because of the poor visibility over East Anglia. At debriefing there were reports of bomb bursts and fires, but local authorities claimed that no bombs had fallen in the town.

The night of the 10/11th was devoted to an attack on Cologne, which involved 130 Wellingtons and Hampdens, but no participation by 115 Squadron. Adverse weather conditions in the target area rendered the raid totally ineffective, and damage was light in the extreme. Sixty-nine Wellingtons were made ready on the 13th for operations against the ports of Bremen and Emden and the U-Boot-manufacturing yards at Vegesack on the North Bank of the Weser north-west of Bremen. The Bremen raid was to be a 3 Group show involving forty-seven Wellingtons, of which six belonged to 115 Squadron, while a seventh, captained by Sgt Cook, targeted Emden. They began taking off at 23.00 with S/L Sindall the senior pilot on duty, but soon encountered heavy cloud and icing conditions between 12,000 and 14,000 feet, which would prevent most from reaching their objectives. Sgt Prior turned back with port engine problems and jettisoned his bombs into the sea, and Sgt Cook, unable to locate his primary target because of cloud, attacked a convoy of six vessels from 100 feet in the face of a spirited light flak response. The ships were of an estimated 5,000 tons each, separated by roughly one hundred yards, and the bombs were observed to fall within twenty yards of the centre one. S/L Sindall and P/O Pooley bombed on e.t.a from 11,000 feet and Sgt Berney from 15,000 feet, while F/L Litchfield let his go from 10,000 feet onto the island of Borkum, but no assessment of the results could be made by any of them. R1502 failed to return with the others, and it was eventually established that it had fallen victim to the night-fighter of Oblt Egmont Prinz zur Lippe of 4/NJG.1 while outbound over Holland, and had crashed at 00.28 south-south-east of Medemblik on the eastern side of the Den Helder peninsular. Happily, Sgt Reid and all but one of his crew survived to become PoWs.

The squadron remained at home on the following night while Bremen and Hannover were targeted by other elements of the Command, both of which claimed successful raids. 3 Group was ordered to attack Duisburg on the night of the 15/16th, and 115 Squadron prepared five of the thirty-eight Wellingtons detailed. They departed Marham either side of 23.00 with S/L Sindall the senior pilot on duty, but he and his crew were back within the hour because of an engine problem. F/L Litchfield, P/O Pooley and

Sgt Prior reached the approximate position of the target, which was shrouded in cloud, and bombed from between 11,000 and 13,000 feet in the face of intense anti-aircraft fire. R1222 was shot down by Hptm Walter Streib of 1/NJG.1, and crashed near Weert in southern Holland at 01.45, probably on the way home, and there were no survivors from the crew of F/Sgt Cook. Hamburg was the primary target on the night of the 16/17th, while 115 Squadron dispatched the freshman crews of Sgts Payne and Trench to bomb the docks at Boulogne. They took off at 00.31 and 00.35 respectively, and bombed on e.t.a from 11,000 and 13,500 feet through dense cloud, which prevented them from observing the results.

The squadron sat out operations against Cologne on the nights of the 17/18th and 20/21st, before attention shifted to southern Germany on the 21st, when Frankfurt was selected to host the first of many operations against it during the remainder of the war. 115 Squadron was not to be involved, but five of its crews would be heading for the same region of Germany to attack Mannheim, and they took off between 22.39 and 22.45 with P/O Pooley the senior pilot on duty. (He is shown in the ORB as a flight lieutenant, but a two-step promotion is unlikely, and the entry is probably an error. However, F/L and P/O ranks in respect of this officer seem to be interchangeable in the ORB.) Four crews returned safely to report finding the target under a blanket of ground haze, and bombing it from 14,000 to 15,000 feet. Three believed their bombs to have fallen within the city, while Sgt Trench's probably hit Ludwigshafen on the opposite bank of the Rhine. Local reports would claim only three high explosive bombs detonating along with a few incendiaries, from which only slight damage resulted. Z8788 crashed in Belgium, and there were no survivors from the crew of Sgt Payne, who was named as the captain in the squadron ORB, while Bill Chorley names Sgt Johnston RCAF as first pilot. Frankfurt and Mannheim were attacked again twenty-four hours later while 115 Squadron remained at home.

A major daylight assault had been planned on the warships at Brest, weather permitting, to be carried out on the 24th. On the previous day, a reconnaissance aircraft spotted the Scharnhorst at La Pallice, some two hundred miles further south, and this forced a last-minute alteration to the schedule. It was decided to send a force of Halifaxes to attack the Scharnhorst, while Wellingtons carried out the original plan, Operation Sunrise, at Brest. Three Fortresses of 2 Group's 90 Squadron were to begin proceedings by bombing from very high level to draw up the fighters, while a force of Hampdens performed a similar diversionary role at a less rarefied altitude under an escort of Spitfires. It was hoped that this would distract the enemy defences sufficiently to provide the unescorted seventy-nine Wellingtons of 1 and 3 Groups with a clear run on the target. 115 Squadron briefed the A Flight crews of S/L Sindall, P/O Pooley and Sgt Prior, who departed Marham between 11.40 and 11.50 and headed for Land's End for the sea crossing. As the force approached the target in clear conditions, the crews had no difficulties in identifying ground detail, and ran in in vics of three. Unfortunately, the diversionary measures failed to provide the hoped-for protection, and the Wellingtons were set upon by BF109s and BF110s and were forced to run the gauntlet of intense flak. S/L Sindall bombed from 15,200 feet on a north-east to south-west heading, and saw his first bomb fall into the water some ten yards from one of the warships lying alongside the mole. He observed other bomb bursts among a number of vessels, before being engaged by a BF109, which was claimed as destroyed. The Wellington was hit by flak, which damaged the hydraulics to the rear turret, but a safe return was accomplished. P/O Pooley and crew came under attack from a BF109 after the rear turret had been rendered inoperable by flak. Despite this, the front gunner poured fire into the assailant, which was seen to spin down vertically with thick smoke emanating from the engine. They continued on their bombing run, but were unable to plot the fall of their bombs. Sgt Prior and crew bombed the Gneisenau from 14,500 feet, and claimed two direct hits, while the other five 500 pounders fell short, and the bombs from two other neighbouring aircraft were observed to explode alongside the jetty. On return the Prior crew claimed to have shot down one BF109E and one F variant, while their X9671 displayed flak damage to a wing and petrol tanks. Ten Wellingtons and two Hampdens were lost to flak and fighters, but returning crews claimed six hits on Gneisenau, and those claimed by the Prior crew were confirmed by others from the squadron.

That night, 3 Group sent thirty-one Wellingtons to join forces with a similar number of 5 Group Hampdens to attack the shipyards in Kiel. 115 Squadron briefed the freshman crews of Sgts Rawlings, Trench and Wallace, who took off at 22.20, each carrying two 500 pounders, a single 250 pounder and six SBCs of incendiaries. They bombed from 14,000 to 14,500 feet in hazy conditions which prevented an accurate assessment of results, and local reports suggested minimal damage. The squadron had now concluded its account for the month, and was not, therefore, involved in raids on Hannover and Hamburg on the night of the 25/26th, and Cologne on the night of the 30/31st, when bad weather conditions contributed to a disappointing attack. During the course of the month the squadron operated on ten nights and one day, and dispatched fifty-nine sorties for the loss of four Wellingtons and crews.

August 1941

Hamburg, Berlin and Kiel opened the new month's operational account on the night of the 2/3rd, for which 3 Group detailed aircraft from eleven of its squadrons, but left 115 Squadron on the ground. There was no significant success to report, other than five large fires at Hamburg. Frankfurt was posted as the main target for the night of the 3/4th, for which 3 Group prepared aircraft, only for its participation to be scrubbed and Hannover substituted. The 3 Group ORB showed forty-one aircraft taking part, including five representing 115 Squadron, but only four of them took off, and the actual figure involved is probably the thirty-four mentioned in Martin Middlebrook's Bomber Command War Diaries. The 115 Squadron quartet departed Marham in a six-minute slot from 22.36, with F/L Litchfield the senior pilot on duty, and P/O Pooley again shown as a flight lieutenant. Each was carrying a 1,000 pounder and four 500 pounders, and, it seems, all made it deep into northern Germany. The squadron ORB tells us that engine trouble forced F/L Pooley and crew to return early when five miles south-west of an untraced location, which was probably Hildesheim, situated within twenty miles of the target. His flight time of seven-and-a-half hours was the longest of the night, which could be explained by a return flight on reduced power. F/L Litchfield bombed from 12,000 on e.t.a and evidence of a flak location, while Sgts Trench and Rawlings bombed from 14,000 and 16,000 feet respectively without observing any results.

Southern Germany was the destination for 260 aircraft on the night of the 5/6th, for which 3 Group detailed eighty-one aircraft, divided predominantly between Mannheim and Karlsruhe, with a few others assigned to Frankfurt and six freshmen for Boulogne. The five 115 Squadron Wellingtons took off between 22.45 and 22.51 with F/L Litchfield the senior pilot on duty and F/L Pooley shown again in his elevated rank, which is now probably correct. They were each carrying a 1,000 pounder with 500 pounders and incendiaries to complete the loads, which were intended for railway yards at Mannheim. The weather conditions were good enough to allow ground detail to be identified, despite which, F/Sgt Edwards and crew were unable to locate it and brought their bombs home. F/L Pooley, P/O Duff and Sgt Prior delivered their loads from between 13,000 and 15,500 feet, and watched them fall within a relatively short distance of the aiming-point. R1471 failed to return to Marham, and it was established later that F/L Litchfield and his entire crew were in enemy hands, although the circumstances of their loss have not been determined. On the following night the main targets for forces of modest size were Frankfurt, Mannheim and Karlsruhe in southern Germany, while 3 Group sent nine freshman crews to Calais to join forces with elements of 4 and 5 Groups. Sgt Scholes and his crew were the only 115 Squadron participants, and took off at 22.30 carrying five 500 pounder and two SBCs. They ran into icing conditions on the way to the French coast, and returned within ninety minutes with the bombs still on board.

Essen escaped with only superficial damage on the night of the 7/8th, while crews returning from the important railway yards at Hamm on the same night reported smoke rising to around 11,000 feet. The freshman 115 Squadron crew of Sgt Hill was briefed to represent the squadron at Boulogne, for which they took off at 22.20, but returned their bombs to store after failing to locate the target. The night of the 8/9th saw forces of fifty-four and forty-four aircraft take off for Kiel and Hamburg respectively to attack the shipyards at both locations and a railway target at the latter. The 3 Group contribution of twenty-six Wellingtons included five from 115 Squadron led by S/L Sindall, and they departed Marham between 22.11 and 22.19 bound for the Blohm & Voss shipyards. They reached north-western Germany to find ten-tenths cloud, and three delivered their bombs on e.t.a from between 12,000 and 18,000 feet, observing fires but no detail. Sgt Wallace joined in at Kiel, and let his load go from 15,500 feet onto the town area on the west side of the Sound and between two large fires. P/O Duff carried out a gliding attack from 13,000 on an alternative target after failing to locate the primary.

Among small-scale operations on the night of the 11/12th was one of significance directed at Mönchengladbach, situated on the south-western edge of the Ruhr. 3 Group provided twenty-one Wellingtons from Marham, ten of them belonging to 115 Squadron, and two of these would be conducting the first trial of the new Gee navigation device. They took off between 00.25 and 00.43 with S/L Sindall the senior pilot on duty, and it was while outbound that Sgt Prior's intercom failed. It is believed that he reached the target area and delivered some of his bombs from 14,000 feet, before jettisoning two 500 pounders in the Wash and landing some two hours ahead of the next to return. The others encountered heavy cloud over the target and bombed from between 12,000 and 15,000 feet in the face of a spirited flak defence, which caused some damage to S/L Sindall's W5710. A number of small fires were reported, some of which were white, but no further assessment was possible in the conditions.

The night of the 12/13th was to be a busy one for 3 Group, which made ready 125 aircraft for operations to Hannover, Berlin and Essen, along with freshman sorties predominantly to French ports. 115 Squadron briefed two crews for Hannover, that of Sgt Wallace RNZAF flying in the Gee-equipped Z8853 Wellington as the trial of the device continued, and seven for Essen. They took off between 21.26 and 21.42 with P/Os Scholes and Wood the senior pilots on duty, and those assigned to Essen all reached the target area, where they encountered eight to ten-tenths cloud and bombed from between 12,000 and 17,500 feet without observing any results. T2563 had reached East Anglia on return when it was set upon by a JU88C intruder flown by Ofw Peter Laufs of 1/NJG.2, which attacked four times and eventually shot the Wellington down at 02.20 to crash at Scottow, four miles south-south-west of North Walsham in Norfolk. The rear gunner lost his life in the incident, but P/O Wood came through entirely unscathed, while the four remaining members of his crew sustained various injuries. Sgt Wallace and crew failed to return in Z8835, and the cause of the loss, and whether it occurred before or after bombing, is not known. The second pilot has no known grave, but the rest of the crew was buried at Soltau, some forty miles north of Hannover. What is known is that the Gee box was not fitted with a self-destruct system, and probably fell into enemy hands.

On the 14th, W/C Trevor Freeman was appointed as the new commanding officer in place of W/C Evans-Evans. The latter would eventually gain the rank of group captain, and, in 1944, become the station commander at Coningsby, the home of 83 and 97 Squadrons, which had been posted back to 5 Group from the Pathfinders in April 1944, to act as the heavy element in 5 Group's own marker force. "Tiny" Evans-Evans would never lose his desire to be "one of the boys", and he occasionally took a Lancaster on operations with a scratch crew, despite his immense bulk fitting somewhat uncomfortably into the confined space of the cockpit. He was a popular figure, and was a buffer between the crews, who were disgruntled at being posted from 8 Group, and the abrasive and unpopular 54 Base commander, A/C "Bobby" Sharp. On the night of the 21/22nd of February 1945, G/C Evans-Evans climbed into an 83 Squadron Lancaster with a 97 Squadron crew, and set off to attack the Mittelland Canal at Gravenhorst.

The crew that took Queen Wilhelmina's Birthday Gift to the Dutch 31ˢᵗ August 1941. (Including 3ʳᵈ from left, S/L Percy Pickard DSO) (Ollar Collection)

115 Sqn Commanding Officer W/C Freeman Killed on air operations, 17 December 1943. L-R: F/L F H Denton DFC, W/C E G Olson, S/L J Gamble, W/C T O Freeman DSO, DFC.

He did not return, and died with all but one of those on board. W/C Freeman was a New Zealander, who had been an original member of the New Zealand Flight, which became the nucleus of 75(NZ) Squadron in April 1940. He completed a tour with that squadron, and was awarded a DFC.

The new commanding officer presided over his first operation and casualty on the night of his appointment, another busy one for 3 Group, which detailed aircraft for operations against Hannover and Magdeburg. The 115 Squadron element of eleven Wellingtons was assigned to railway station aiming-points in Hannover and took off between 21.00 and 21.42 with S/L Sindall the senior pilot on duty. This was to be the final trial of Gee before the device was withdrawn to be put into full production for distribution in early 1942. Nine crews reached the target area, where the weather conditions were reasonably good, although cloud drifted across in patches to obscure the aiming-points at times. Bombing took place from between 12,000 and 16,000 feet, and returning crews reported many fires, although no confirmation was forthcoming from local sources. Sgt Thompson experienced port-engine failure before reaching the target, and dropped his bombs on an unidentified urban area before returning early. R1500 came down in the North Sea in a controlled ditching, and a fix of its position allowed a search for Sgt Alway and his crew to begin. A dinghy was spotted, but it was lost in bad weather before a launch could reach it, and, although further efforts were made, no contact was made. The remains of the pilot and rear gunner eventually came ashore on the German coast and now lie in the Sage War Cemetery at Oldenburg.

It was on the 18th, that the previously-mentioned Butt Report was released, and its disclosures made available to send shock waves reverberating around the Cabinet Room and the Air Ministry. Having studied hundreds of photographs taken during night operations in June and July, Mr Butt concluded that only a fraction of the bombs had fallen within miles of their intended targets. This swept away at a stroke any notion that the Command was having an effect on Germany's war effort, and demonstrated the claims of the crews to be over-optimistic. This was probably not a revelation to senior figures in the Command and the RAF generally, who had known all along that bombing operations were largely ineffective. Of more concern was the fact that this would provide further ammunition for those calling for the dissolution of an independent bomber force, and the redistribution of its aircraft to other causes, such as the U-Boot campaign in the Atlantic and to counter reversals in the Middle East. The report was a bitter blow to the reputation of C-in-C Sir Richard Peirse, whose period of tenure would be forever unjustly blighted by its criticisms.

As the contents of the Butt Report were being digested, a hundred aircraft were made ready for operations that night against railway targets in Cologne and Duisburg. 115 Squadron detailed nine Wellingtons for the latter, including a Mk II, which was loaded with a cookie and 500 pounders, while the others had 500 and 250 pounders winched into their bomb bays along with incendiaries. They took off between 23.10 and 23.53 with S/L Sindall the senior pilot on duty, and arrived in the target area to find good conditions but the usual industrial haze, which made it difficult to identify ground detail. Bombing was carried out between 10,000 and 16,000 feet, and returning crews were satisfied that they had landed their bombs in the target area, reporting bursts but nothing specific in terms of damage. P/O Duff and crew were in the Mk II, W5449, and were unable to locate the primary target, deciding instead to drop their cookie from 12,000 feet onto the south-western edge of the city of Bonn. On their way home over the Zuider Zee (Ijsselmeer), Sgt Berney and crew observed an aircraft fall in flames and break up into three pieces, and this was almost certainly a Wellington belonging to fellow Marham residents, 218 Squadron.

The squadron was not required to operate thereafter for a week, during which period other elements of the Command were sent to Kiel on the 19/20th, Mannheim on the 22/23rd, Düsseldorf on the 24/25th, Karlsruhe on the 25/26th and Cologne on the 26/27th, none with any degree of effectiveness. It was while the Cologne raid was in progress that 115 Squadron dispatched the freshman crew of Sgt Murdoch at 20.55 with orders to attack the docks at Boulogne. They dropped their load of six 500 and two 250 pounders from 14,500 feet onto dock No 4, and started several large fires, which combined to form one huge conflagration that remained visible for forty miles into the return journey. Mannheim was selected to host its second major raid in the space of five nights on the night of the 27/28th, for which 115 Squadron prepared ten Wellingtons in a 3 Group effort of thirty aircraft, with 1, 4 and 5 Groups putting up the remaining sixty-one. They departed Marham between 20.05 and 20.45 with S/Ls Knight and Sindall the senior pilots on duty. P/O Scholes was forced to turn back with a rear turret malfunction, and F/Sgt Edwards got as far as the Ardennes before excessive vibration persuaded him to jettison his bombs. F/L Pooley was unable to locate the primary target, and dropped his bombs from 12,000 feet onto the town of Oppenheim, situated about ten miles to the west of Darmstadt. On return he headed for Swanton Morley, but the communication between the station and Wellington failed, and empty petrol tanks persuaded the crew to bale out, leaving X9672 to crash at 03.10 near North Walsham in Norfolk. The others found the target area and delivered their bombs from between 12,000 and 16,000 feet, observing bomb bursts and fires but no detail. Sgt Keating had both engines cut out when at 3,000 feet, presumably on the way home, but they restarted after three minutes and a safe landing followed. S/L Sindall and crew were making for Honington, but were notified of an air-raid in progress, and, with fuel reserves dwindling to critical levels as they crossed the coast near Cromer, they left W5710 to its fate, and it came down near Alburgh in Norfolk. P/O Foster was attempting to land R1468 at West Raynham in conditions of heavy rain and poor visibility, but the Wellington came to grief at 03.30 on the airfield and was consumed by fire after the crew had scrambled clear.

Honington and Marham were not called upon to provide aircraft for 3 Group's contribution to a raid on Duisburg on the night of the 28/29th, when claims of success were not confirmed by local reports. Both of the above stations along with Feltwell and Stradishall were busy on the 29th, however, preparing sixty-nine Wellingtons for that night's operation to Mannheim, whose residents were, no doubt, beginning to feel persecuted after facing four attacks in a week. A total of ninety-four aircraft set off, while 143 others also made their way towards southern Germany to target Frankfurt. 115 Squadron dispatched nine aircraft between 20.13 and 20.31 with S/L Knight the senior pilot on duty, and each carrying two 500 pounders, a single 250 pounder and six SBCs of incendiaries. They soon encountered electrical storms and icing conditions, which caused Sgt Keating and crew to turn back at 21.09 and land at 22.46, and they were followed forty-five minutes later by S/L Knight and crew, who had been beaten by the same adverse weather, and had bombed a wharf in the Hook of Holland from 4,000 feet on the way home. Cloud in the general target area added to the difficulties for the others, and, having failed to locate either the primary or suitable secondary objective, P/O Duff and crew experienced complete W/T failure, and also turned back with their load intact. Sgt Edwards and crew were, likewise, unable to locate the target, and bombed an unidentified built-up area from 9,000 feet after catching a glimpse of it through a gap in the cloud. The remaining aircraft delivered their loads on e.t.a or flak and searchlight concentrations from between 12,000 and 17,000 feet, and could offer no assessment of the outcome at debriefing. X9826 was seen over Martlesham Heath being pursued by an enemy aircraft, and crashed near the airfield at 02.12 killing Sgt Murdoch and four of his crew outright, and mortally wounding the other crew member, who succumbed two days later. This concluded the month's operations for 115 Squadron, but other elements of the Command attacked Cologne and Essen on the night of the 31st, producing poor results in the face of unhelpful weather conditions. During the course of the month the squadron operated on twelve nights, dispatching seventy-five sorties for the loss of eight Wellingtons, four complete crews and one additional airman.

September 1941

The 1st of the new month brought better weather conditions over western Germany, and Cologne would host its second raid on consecutive nights before it was over. Thirty-four Wellingtons were made ready at Marham and Honington, and they were to share airspace over the Rhineland with twenty Hampdens from 5 Group. Nine 115 Squadron aircraft took off between 20.05 and 20.32 with W/C Freeman the senior pilot on duty for the first time, supported by S/L Knight. Five were carrying a 1,000 pounder each, and all had an assortment of 500 and 250 pounders on board along with SBCs of incendiaries. Sgt Prior and crew found that X9877 was unwilling to climb fast enough to attain a respectable height in time for action over enemy territory, and dropped their 1,000 pounder and the rest of their load on the docks at Ostend from 11,000 feet as an alternative. They watched the big bomb fall into the water off the harbour entrance, closely followed by the others at the entrance to the docks, after which the gunners shot out eight searchlights. The others all managed to locate the target in good visibility, and deliver their loads from between 11,000 and 17,000 feet, before returning to report many fires. Some crews, however, were aware that decoy fires had been lit away from the target, and local reports suggested that they had attracted many bomb loads.

Following a disappointing attempt to hit Frankfurt on the night of the 2/3rd of September, which did not involve 115 Squadron, a mixed force of 140 aircraft was made ready on the 3rd to continue the assault on Brest, which had taken something of a back seat since Operation Sunrise in July. Detailed to renew acquaintances with the enemy warships that night were eleven crews representing 115 Squadron led by S/L Knight, and they departed Marham between 19.26 and 20.03, carrying between them two 2,000 pounders, one 1,000 pounder, fifty-eight 500 pounders and a single 250 pounder. Sgt Hill was back on the ground at 19.58 after R1772 suffered wireless failure, and his unscheduled landing slightly delayed the departure of P/O Scholes and crew. As the force made its way towards Land's End the weather over eastern England began to raise questions, and the 1, 4 and 5 Group aircraft were recalled, leaving 3 Group to go on alone along with four aircraft that had failed to pick up the recall signal. P/O Scholes was just five miles from the target when the starboard engine failed, and he jettisoned his bombs as he turned back. W5684 was sinking fast as it arrived over the Devon coast, and the decision was taken to abandon it to its fate, which was a crash at Horrabridge, three miles south-east of Tavistock. The crew landed safely by parachute, although P/O Scholes was reported to have sustained some kind of injury. The remaining squadron participants bombed from between 9,000 and 14,000 feet, and were among fifty-three crews who reported bombing in the target area, but an effective smoke screen forced them to do so on estimated positions. Fog over East Anglia forced all aircraft to land away from Marham.

A major raid on Berlin was planned for the night of the 7/8th, for which six aircraft types made up the force of 197, and, as was generally the case in a mixed force, more than half of them were Wellingtons. By far the largest contribution was from 3 Group, 115 Squadron making ready seven aircraft for this operation, three for Kiel and two freshmen for the docks at Boulogne. As usual, the ORB is not clear as to which crews were assigned to the main operation, but Sgt Dutton and W/O Snowden and their crews were the freshmen bound for the French port, and took off at 20.03 and 20.06 respectively. They found fires already burning around dock No 4 as they arrived on the scene, and added to the damage from 14,500 feet while on a north-westerly heading. Sgts Hill and Thompson and P/O Trench were the next to depart Marham, between 20.07 and 20.23 bound for Kiel, but Sgt Thompson crashed almost immediately onto the flare-path after the flap to the port fuel tank was left open. The crew was able to walk away from X9755, which would eventually be put back into service. P/O Trench dropped his bombs on the important naval base in a single stick from 16,000 feet on a north-westerly heading, and observed fairly large orange flames result.

The Berlin contingent finally got away between 20.43 and 21.05 with S/L Knight the senior pilot on duty. A night-fighter latched onto R1332, and its fire caused damage to the starboard wing, pitot head, IFF aerial and the leading edge of the starboard tail-plane. The rear gunner managed to get off fifteen rounds before one of the barrels jammed, and Sgt Berney brought the Wellington home with its bombs still on board to claim the ME110 as shot down. Sgt Rawlings and crew experienced navigation problems as they approached Berlin, and turned back towards the west, dropping their bombs from 15,000 feet onto a searchlight-protected built-up area, which they later identified as Magdeburg. F/Sgt Edwards found a camouflaged factory twenty miles south-east of Berlin, and bombed it from 16,000 feet, causing an enormous fire which was still visible from a hundred miles into the return journey. S/L Knight, P/O Foster and Sgt Prior attacked Berlin from between 12,000 and 15,000 feet, and observed bursts but nothing definitive. Among fifteen aircraft failing to return from the Capital was 115 Squadron's R1798, which was shot down by ace night-fighter pilot, Oblt Helmut Lent of 4/NJG.1, over northern Holland, and crashed at 04.58 near Drachten, some twenty miles from the coast, with no survivors from the crew of F/Sgt Keating RCAF. R1772 also failed to return after being brought down in the target area of Kiel, and this resulted in the death of the pilot, Sgt Hill, and the capture of his crew. Berlin had sustained some useful if not excessive damage in mostly northern and north-eastern districts, and Kiel reported a few bombs and some damage but no casualties. The three failures to return from Kiel brought the total of missing aircraft to a new record high in a single night of eighteen.

The first sizeable raid of the war on Kassel, situated to the east of the Ruhr Valley, took place on the night of the 8/9th in the absence of a 115 Squadron contribution, and modest success was gained without loss. Orders were received on the 10th to prepare six Wellingtons for a trip across the Alps that night to attack the arsenal at Turin, while others went for the main railway station. 3 Group provided fifty-one of the seventy-six-strong force, including fourteen from the Marham units, and the 115 Squadron element took to the air either side of 20.00 with W/C Freeman the senior pilot on duty. Because of the distance and need to maintain altitude to cross the mountain range, each Wellington was carrying only 1,750lbs of bombs. There were no early returns on a night of favourable weather conditions, and the only impediments to accurate bombing were haze and drifting smoke as the attack developed. Five of the 115 Squadron crews delivered their bombs from between 13,000 and 15,000 feet, while, according to the ORB, W/C Freeman dropped his from 2,000 feet. All returned safely to report many fires, some large and remaining visible for sixty miles into the return flight.

Frankfurt was posted as the target on the 12th, for which a force of 130 aircraft was assembled. 115 Squadron made ready eight Wellingtons for the primary target, and two for the freshman crews of Sgts Ellis and Soames to take to Cherbourg. The latter pair took off first at 19.40, and bombed from 12,500 and 10,000 feet respectively on estimated positions through cloud, before returning safely. The remainder departed Marham between 21.00 and 21.22 with S/L Knight the senior pilot on duty and P/O Duff the only other officer pilot. They all reached the target area to find it concealed beneath thick cloud, which forced them to bomb from between 13,000 and 16,000 feet on estimated positions based on the layout of flak and searchlight concentrations. Some bomb bursts were observed, and one crew saw fires through a gap in the cloud. Another reported an RAF aircraft being shot down and exploding on impact, and, as only one was lost in the target area, this was almost certainly X9670, which belonged to fellow Marham residents, 218 Squadron. Happily, the crew all survived to fall into enemy hands. The Frankfurt authorities reported seventy-five high explosive bombs hitting the city and its surrounds, along with more than six hundred incendiaries, and, although a number of fires resulted, damage was not serious. Some bombs fell on Mainz, situated twenty miles away to the south-west. It appears that S/L Knight was posted to 11 O.T.U on the following day at the conclusion of his tour, and his reward would be to drop to his substantive rank of flying officer.

The squadron sat out an operation to Brest on the night of the 13/14th, when the smoke screen again thwarted all attempts to pinpoint the German warships. 115 Squadron was also not required for a raid on Hamburg's shipyards two nights later, which resulted in extensive damage in various parts of the city. The first of two all-Wellington raids on Karlsruhe was carried out on the night of the 16/17th, for which the squadron briefed a dozen crews, one of which was later withdrawn. There would also be a freshman sortie by Sgt Bruce and crew to Le Havre, and they took off first at 19.09. They reached the French coast to find good bombing conditions, and delivered their bombs on a north-westerly heading from 12,000 feet, observing them to straddle No 7 dock, and the incendiaries to start fires visible for twenty miles into the return journey. Those bound for southern Germany were all airborne by 19.27 with S/L Sindall the senior pilot on duty, but Sgt Thompson and crew were forced to return early with an engine issue. The remaining ten aircraft reached the target to deliver their bombs from between 7,000 and 13,500 feet in good weather conditions but intense darkness. Sgt Ellis believed he was aiming at buildings, but discovered it was a wooded area. Sgt Dutton found what he believed to be a blast furnace, and saw his bombs start a fire, followed three minutes later by a large explosion, which blew up building stretching for two hundred yards and left others on fire. The others reported bomb bursts and fires, but no local report was available to confirm the outcome of what the crews felt was a successful night's work.

The Baltic port of Stettin on Germany's eastern frontier with Poland, and now situated in Poland as Szczecin, would provide a new destination for seven 115 Squadron crews on the night of the 19/20th. The round-trip of almost twelve hundred miles was only a little shorter than the one to Turin, and would require them to be airborne for up to nine hours. This would be the first operation for S/L Coleman, who had arrived from 15 O.T.U on the 11th, probably in the acting rank of flight lieutenant, to succeed S/L Knight as a flight commander. They took off between 21.27 and 21.56 with a small bomb load, which reflected the need for maximum fuel. They arrived in the target area to find favourable weather conditions and with briefed aiming-points, but these were difficult to identify. A standard area raid ensued, the 115 Squadron crews bombing from between 10,000 and 14,000 feet, some observing bursts and fires and dummy fires four miles to the south. It is not known how successful this raid was, but Stettin would experience a torrid time from 1943 onwards at the hands of four-engine heavy bombers.

The weather started to hamper operations at this time, and a recall signal was sent to aircraft outbound over the North Sea for Berlin on the night of the 20/21st. 115 Squadron was not involved, and, during a period of relative activity, S/L Sindall was posted to 27 O.T.U on the 23rd after serving the squadron with distinction, and it would be a number of weeks before his successor was appointed. 104 aircraft were outbound for far-flung targets on the night of the 26/27th, when another recall signal brought most of them home. 115 Squadron had dispatched three freshman crews to Emden between 18.42 and 18.50, and Sgt Hulls and crew responded to the recall and jettisoned their bombs at 20.48 before returning safely. Sgt Leslie and crew failed to pick up the signal and bombed the target from 14,000 feet on estimated position based on searchlight and flak activity, and also returned safely. R1332 failed to return with the crew of Sgt Horabin, from whom an S.O.S message had been received, stating that an engine was on fire. The Wellington is known to have come down off the Frisians, and only one body eventually came ashore on the north German coast. *(The squadron and group ORBs both name Sgt Horabin as the captain, not Sgt Farnan as stated by Bill Chorley in Bomber Command Losses for 1941.)*

The month ended with simultaneous operations on consecutive nights against Stettin and Hamburg. The first of these was posted on the 29th, when thirteen 115 Squadron crews attended briefing to learn that ten of them would be undertaking the long slog to north-eastern Germany, while three would be flying a standard-range trip to north-western Germany. Sgts Hulls, Bruce and Ellis took off for Hamburg between 19.37 and 19.46 as part of an overall force of ninety-one aircraft, but Sgt Bruce was unable to gain sufficient altitude to risk an incursion into enemy airspace, and headed south to drop his bombs from 12,500 feet onto docks 2 and 6 at Calais, setting off fires that were visible from the other side of the Channel and from some distance inland. S/L Coleman was the senior pilot on duty among the Stettin-bound element, which departed Marham between 20.52 and 21.21 for what, for most, would be a flight of up to nine hours, and, in the case of Sgt Leslie and crew, not far short of ten. They were still outbound when the Hamburg element reached its target area to encounter fairly heavy opposition from the ground and searchlight glare that prevented accurate bombing. Even so, nine fires erupted and more than eleven hundred people were bombed out of their homes in exchange for the loss of two Wellingtons, both from 115 Squadron. X9910 was shot down by the night-fighter of Oblt Ludwig Becker of 4/NJG.1, and crashed at 22.52 near Winschoten in north-eastern Holland, killing Sgt Hulls and all but the rear gunner, who was taken into captivity. X9673 fell victim to the night-fighter of Feldwebel Kalinowski of 6/NJG.1, and crashed at 00.26 about a dozen miles south of the target with no survivors from the crew of Sgt Ellis. Bombing conditions at Stettin were good, with only slight haze to blur ground detail, and attacks were carried out from between 7,500 and 14,000 feet. Returning crews were unable to offer an assessment of the outcome, but explosions and fires were reported, a number of crews referring to one large, red blaze to the north of the town. Opposition was fairly light, but Sgt Runagall's X9877 picked up a little flak damage. This was the final operation in a month which had seen the squadron operate on nine nights and dispatch eighty-three sorties for the loss of six Wellingtons and five crews.

October 1941

The weather at the start of October was entirely unsuitable for operations, and only 115 Squadron from the 3 Group fold was ordered to prepare aircraft for an operation to Stuttgart on the night of the 1/2nd. Two had actually taken off when a recall signal was sent, and when the next set of orders came through it was for targets much closer to home on the occupied coast. 3 Group put up eighty-nine aircraft to target Rotterdam, Dunkerque and Antwerp, and called upon 115 Squadron to provide nine Wellingtons for the first-mentioned and three freshman crews for Dunkerque. The freshman crews of Sgts Brown, George and P/O Wiley got away first shortly before 19.00, with the remainder hot on their heels between 18.59 and 19.08 with S/L Coleman the senior pilot on duty. Those bound for the French coast encountered hazy conditions, and delivered their bombs from between 11,000 and 15,000 feet, observing them to fall into the docks area and the adjacent canal, but were unable at debriefing to provide an accurate assessment. Sgt Morton and crew were some ten miles from the Dutch coast when an overheating engine made it clear that they would not reach bombing height. The bombs were jettisoned live into the sea and they turned for home. The others all reached Rotterdam, where they found two large, red fires already burning to the east of the docks. They delivered their loads from between 10,000 and 13,500 feet, and observed them falling onto or near the aiming-point, where they caused further fires. P/O Trench and crew reported a long line of fires on the West Bank of the Maas with explosions emanating from them.

Operations were posted on the 6th, 8th and 9th, and then cancelled, and it was the 10th before one would actually take place. Essen and Cologne were the main targets selected, for which forces of seventy-eight and sixty-nine aircraft respectively were made ready, while a further eighty crews were briefed for targets on the occupied coast. 115 Squadron was ordered to provide eleven Wellingtons for the port of Bordeaux in south-western France, and they departed Marham between 21.19 and 22.07 with W/C Freeman and S/L Coleman the senior pilots on duty. Sgt Morton soon found X9909 to be misbehaving with the starboard wing flying low, and turned back from a position over the Channel ten miles south of Bridport in Dorset. Sgt Thompson and crew appear to be the only ones to positively locate the primary target, attacking it on a south-easterly heading from 10,000 feet at 03.10 and watching their bombs fall towards the junction of a river. The others reached the target area and stooged around for some time searching in vain for a gap in the clouds, and P/O Trench eventually jettisoned his bombs into the sea at

04.20 before returning to land at Hampton Norris. The recently-promoted F/L Duff and Sgt Dutton brought their bombs back, while Sgt Runagall and crew, after cruising over Bordeaux from 02.10 to 02.55 at between 11,000 and 6,000 feet, headed for St Nazaire as an alternative target. They were not alone, as S/L Coleman, W/O Snowden, F/Sgt Edwards and Sgt Prior and their crews had the same idea, and delivered their loads from between 3,000 and 11,500 feet without being able to assess the results. W/C Freeman attacked an unidentified French aerodrome from 8,000 feet, but could not determine the outcome. Weather conditions over western Germany were equally unhelpful, and neither of the operations taking place in that region produced more than the slightest damage.

A busy night of operations on the 12/13th brought a new record number of 373 sorties, 152 of them for the first major raid of the war on Nuremberg, the birthplace of Nazism, while a predominantly Wellington force of ninety-nine aircraft went to Bremen, and 5 Group targeted a chemicals factory at Hüls in the Ruhr. 115 Squadron briefed eleven crews for southern Germany with S/L Coleman to lead, and they took off between 19.12 and 19.36 carrying 500, and 250 pounders and SBCs of incendiaries. Sgt Morton and crew again failed to reach the target after being caught in a searchlight belt somewhere near the French or Belgian coast, and being forced to shed altitude to escape back out to sea. They then became involved in an engagement with a ME110, which was eventually shaken off after causing some damage. The others reached the target area, where they bombed from between 8,500 and 13,000 feet, and returning crews reported starting new fires and adding to those already burning. One large fire could be seen from some sixty miles into the return flight. X9751 was shot up by flak, which damaged the hydraulics and wounded the second pilot in the foot, but Sgt Edwards brought the Wellington back to a safe landing. The 3 Group ORB described this as a successful raid, but, in truth, few bombs fell where intended, and most were wasted on outlying communities north of the target, some even finding a village sixty-five miles away.

Düsseldorf and Cologne were the main targets on the following night, 3 Group providing aircraft for the former, but none from 115 Squadron. Eleven crews were called to briefing on the 14th to learn of a return to Nuremberg that night as part of an overall force of eighty aircraft of which fifty-two would represent 3 Group. They departed Marham between 22.14 and 22.58 on another night of adverse weather conditions, with F/L Duff the senior pilot on duty. All reached the general target area, despite encountering thick, ice-bearing cloud, and Sgts George and Thompson, F/O Paterson and P/O Trench bombed on e.t.a from between 8,000 and 15,000 feet without observing anything other than flashes and a glow. Sgt Leslie and crew experienced icing and engine problems, and thought that they had attacked the primary target, but, after plotting the return track, realized that they had actually bombed in the region of Regensburg, a further fifty miles to the south-east. P/O Wiley and Sgt Bruce attacked Mannheim as a secondary target, the former from a perilously low 4,000 feet, after which a fire was seen to develop and was burning furiously as they turned away. F/Sgt Edwards and crew bombed what they believed was Darmstadt from 9,000 feet, and F/L Duff, after cruising around at heights ranging from 12,000 down to 5,000 feet, eventually headed for home and bombed the estimated position of Trier close to the Luxembourg frontier. Sgt Runagall and crew dropped their load on the estimated position of Frankfurt from 12,500 feet, and had no clue as to the results. Z8844 failed to return with the crew of Sgt Browne RAAF after crashing in southern Germany without survivors. Local reports mentioned three areas of damage in Nuremberg, all of a minor nature, but a workshop was destroyed in a Siemens factory.

At around this time F/L Foster was handed the acting rank of squadron leader to enable him to succeed S/L Sindall as a flight commander. On the 16th Duisburg was posted as the target for eight 115 Squadron crews in company with seventy-five others, while three freshmen were briefed for the docks at Dunkerque. P/Os Smith, Sword and Sgt Davie and their crews took off for the French coast at 18.45, and attacked the docks and a marshalling yard from between 11,000 and 13,500 feet. They had all returned home and were probably in bed when the Duisburg-bound element took off between 00.15 and

00.50 with no senior pilots on duty. All eight aircraft reached the target area, where they bombed on estimated positions through complete cloud cover from between 9,500 and 14,000 feet. Bremen was the main target on the night of the 20/21st, for which a force of 153 aircraft was assembled, sixty-two of them provided by 3 Group. The group also detailed seventeen Wellingtons to attack the docks at Antwerp, and 115 Squadron was represented by W/C Freeman, who had the station commander, G/C Macdonald, flying with him as second pilot. They took off at 19.00 carrying five 500 pounders and two SBCs of incendiaries, which they brought home after failing to locate the target beneath cloud.

Bremen's shipyards were offered as aiming-points for a force of 136 mixed aircraft on the night of the 21/22nd. Marham and Stradishall provided twenty-eight Wellingtons of which nine represented 115 Squadron, and they took off between 18.00 and 18.11 with S/L Coleman the senior pilot on duty. Eight crews managed to find the target, which was largely hidden beneath cloud, and bombed it from between 9,000 and 16,000 feet. Only F/O Paterson seemed to catch a clear glimpse of the ground silhouetted against the flak in the north-west of the city, but his bombs hung up on the first pass, and then overshot the aiming-point to fall into what the ORB refers to as the Freihafen. Sgt George and crew failed to locate the target, and returned their bombs to store. The squadron sat out an ineffective raid on Mannheim on the following night, before making ready nine Wellingtons for an operation against Kiel on the 23rd, for which S/L Coleman was to be the senior pilot. They took off between 17.30 and 18.06 in the first of two widely separated waves, and headed for the west coast of Denmark to cross the Schleswig-Holstein peninsular. It was here that P/O Trench turned back with heating system failure, and brought his bombs home. W/O Snowden was also forced to abandon his sortie after the rear gunner was found to be unconscious, probably as the result of oxygen starvation. The others pressed on to reach the target and bomb on estimated positions from between 13,000 and 18,000 feet, and returned safely with nothing of value to report. Local reports revealed that some bombs from the second wave had, at least, fallen into the Deutsche Werke U-Boot yard and the naval base, and had caused some damage.

The month ended as it had begun, with adverse weather conditions impeding the ability of crews to effectively carry out their work. The main target on the night of the 31st was Hamburg, while forty Wellingtons and eight Stirlings of 3 Group tried again at Bremen. S/Ls Coleman and Foster were the senior pilots on duty as the fourteen 115 Squadron participants departed Marham for the latter between 17.30 and 18.20, and set course for the North Sea and north-western Germany. S/L Coleman turned back early with a dead starboard engine, leaving the others to try to locate the primary target, and F/O Sword also experienced engine trouble and bombed De Kooy aerodrome from 6,000 feet. On return he and his crew reported observing fires that resembled burning aircraft, and also fires on both sides of the flare-path and near hangars on the south-eastern side of the airfield. F/O Paterson and Sgt Leslie also attacked this target from 8,500 feet and 14,000 feet respectively, but the former felt his bombs were too wide to hit dispersed aircraft. P/O Wiley bombed Borkum island from 16,000 feet, and started fires close to flak and searchlight installations. S/L Foster, P/O Smith and F/Sgt Edwards were the only ones to reach the target area, and they delivered all or part of their loads from between 13,000 and 15,000 feet without observing results. F/Sgt Edwards had dropped only his incendiaries, and dumped the high explosives onto a searchlight and flak concentration at Groningen in Holland on the way home. Sgt Soames attacked Emden from 13,000 feet on e.t.a, and Sgt George followed suit from a little higher, but neither crew saw anything of value to report. X9873 failed to return home after being attacked and damaged by the night-fighter of Ofw Paul Gildner of 4/NJG.I. W/O Snowdon carried out a crash-landing on the Dutch Frisian island of Schiermonnikoog, where he and his crew were captured. During the course of the month the squadron operated on nine nights and dispatched eighty-nine sorties for the loss of two Wellingtons and crews.

Wellington X9873 31/1 November 1941. Attacked 19.30 by night fighter Ofw Paul Gildner 4./NJG 1, his 20th victory. Crash landed onto tidal flats on the Dutch island of Schiermonnikoog. The crew were taken captive and became prisoners of war in various camps. This Wellington was the only aircraft lost.

November 1941

November began with a major attack on Kiel on the night of the 1/2nd, although only a little over half of the 134 participating crews reached the target area, and none managed to locate the port through thick cloud. 115 Squadron remained at home, and began the new month in low-key style by sending the freshman crews of Sgt Buckingham and Horsley to Boulogne along with six others from the Group. They took off at 18.39, only for the former to turn back with engine issues and land at 20.55 with their bombs still on board. The latter were unable to locate the primary target through thick cloud, and dropped their bombs through total cloud cover onto what was probably Le Touquet in northern Belgium. On return X9616 crashed on landing at Manston, but was not seriously damaged, and the crew walked away unscathed.

Thereafter, there would be little activity for the Command generally, largely because of the weather, but 3 Group detailed thirty Wellingtons on the 4th to carry out a nuisance raid that night over the Ruhr. The order was changed later in the day to specify the Krupp works at Essen as the main target, while ten freshmen targeted the docks at Ostend. 115 Squadron was originally ordered to provide eight aircraft for Essen and a singleton for Ostend, but when the time to take off at 18.00 arrived, only seven were lined up at the threshold, Sgt Buckingham destined for Ostend and the others for Essen. S/L Coleman was the senior pilot on duty and was last away at 18.35, and set course for the North Sea to enter enemy territory via the Rotterdam area and approach the Ruhr from the north. F/Sgt Edwards and crew were caught in the Rotterdam flak at 15,000 feet, and had to dive to 5,000 feet and jettison their bombs in order to escape. F/L Paterson's X9871 developed engine problems, which persuaded him to divert from the main target and head for Ostend, which he bombed from 7,000 feet and observed a reddish-yellow fire in the docks area. Sgt Buckingham and crew had reached the Belgian coast earlier to bomb from 11,000 feet, and, although they failed to observe the burst of their bombs, a red glow was seen to the east of the docks immediately afterwards. This left four crews to bomb at Essen through cloud from between 11,000 and 15,000 feet, and none was able to offer an assessment. F/L Hogg was posted to the squadron from 15 O.T.U on the 6th as a flight commander in waiting.

Undoubtedly frustrated by his inability to strike effectively at Germany, and eager to erase the stinging criticisms of the Command arising out of the Butt Report, C-in-C Pierse planned a record-breaking night of operations on the 7/8th. He intended to send over two hundred aircraft to Berlin, and persisted with the idea despite a late forecast of storms, thick cloud, hail and icing conditions through which the force would have to fly to reach their destination. The 5 Group A-O-C, AVM Slessor, questioned the plan, and was allowed to withdraw his contribution of seventy-five aircraft and send them to Cologne instead. 115 Squadron made ready nine Wellingtons, seven for Berlin and two for freshman crews to take to Ostend. 169 aircraft ultimately took off for the capital, while a third force of fifty-three 1 and 3 Group Wellingtons and two Stirlings headed for southern Germany to hit Mannheim. Together with the night's minor operations, a record total of 392 sorties was committed to the fray on this night. The 115 Squadron element departed Marham either side of 18.00 with S/L Coleman the senior pilot on duty. X9733 became a victim of the Rotterdam flak, and sustained damage to its starboard propeller, which persuaded P/O Wiley to turn back and drop his bombs from 12,000 feet onto the Waalhaven district of the offending city. Sgt Leslie and crew consumed too much fuel while taking evasive action, possibly also at the Dutch coast, and, realising they couldn't reach Germany's Capital, dumped their bombs live over the Ruhr, only to set off a hornet's nest of flak that chased them out of the area. Sgts Bruce, Dutton and Runagall, P/O Trench, and S/L Coleman bombed on e.t.a through complete cloud cover from between 14,000 and 15,000 feet, and returned safely with nothing to report. Sgt Horsley and P/O Stock attacked Ostend from 12,000 and 13,000 feet respectively, and both claimed to have started fires in docks 10, 14 and 16. At debriefing only seventy-three crews claimed to have reached Berlin, and local reports would reveal damage to be limited to a few dozen buildings. Twenty-one crews failed to make it to debriefing, and their loss was a new record for a single target. 5 Group fared better in terms of losses, coming through unscathed, but unfortunately, so did Cologne. It was a similar story at Mannheim, where no bombs were reported by the city authorities, and seven Wellingtons were missing. The minor operations cost a further nine aircraft, to bring the overall losses to thirty-seven, more than twice the previous highest number in a single night. It was a disaster, and Peirse was summoned to an uncomfortable meeting with Churchill at Chequers on the evening of the 8th to make his explanations. Earlier in the day P/O Trench had been posted to HQ 6 Group (Training) at the conclusion of his tour.

Pierse's time at the helm of Bomber Command was effectively over, although he would remain in post until the end of the year, but under orders from the 13th to restrict further operations, while the future of the Command was considered at the highest level. On the 11th, Sgt Dutton took off in X3394 in the late morning for a fuel consumption test and cross-country training flight with F/L Mellows, the squadron medical officer, among six others on board. At 12.03 the Wellington crashed at Carol House Farm near Swaffham in Norfolk, killing all on board. Acting S/L (F/O) Foster was posted to 29 O.T.U on the following day, and would, no doubt, have to shed at least one rank. On the 15th, forty-nine and forty-seven aircraft respectively were made ready to attack the naval ports of Emden and Kiel that night. 115 Squadron briefed seven crews for the latter, but it was Sgt Horsley and crew who took off first for Emden, at 17.32, some two hours ahead of the main element. X9888 and its crew would never be seen again, and it must be assumed that the Wellington found its end somewhere in the cold North Sea. Those bound for Kiel on the other side of the Schleswig-Holstein peninsular departed Marham between 21.30 and 21.51, and reached the target area only to be thwarted by complete cloud cover. Bombing was carried out from between 13,000 and 16,300 feet on estimated positions, but Sgt Davie and F/Sgt Edwards intentionally flew a further fifty miles to the north-west to attack the naval port of Flensburg, situated on the frontier with Denmark. Sgt Leslie was unable to locate the target, and reported bombing a location from 15,000 feet referred to in the ORB as Sciverin, which was possibly a misspelling for Scheveningen, situated on the Dutch coast north of Rotterdam. Where all of the night's bombs fell is not known, but they certainly did not land in Kiel, and the cost of this failure was another four Wellingtons. The squadron's Z8848 ditched ten miles off Whitby on the Yorkshire coast, but P/O Stock and his crew were rescued by a Norwegian-crewed destroyer and returned safely to base.

S/L Grant was posted to the squadron from 15 O.T.U on the 16th, as the successor to the soon-to-depart S/L Coleman, while the newly-promoted S/L Hogg would fill the other flight commander post recently vacated by S/L Foster. They carried out training flights until being handed their first opportunity to fly operationally with the squadron, which occurred on the night of the 23/24th, when Dunkerque was the target for a 3 Group force of thirty-six Wellingtons and a single Stirling. 115 Squadron put up four aircraft, with W/C Freeman the senor pilot on duty and S/L Grant flying as his second pilot. S/L Hogg was also on the Order of Battle, and they took off in a four-minute slot from 17.10 on another night of heavy cloud. W/C Freeman searched the enemy coast from the Dunkerque area as far north as the Scheldt Estuary, but saw nothing of the ground and returned with his bomb load intact. S/L Hogg bombed from 6,500 feet and observed bursts but no detail, while freshmen Sgts Anderson and Holder dropped their five 500 pounders and two SBCs of incendiaries each from 12,500 and 13,500 feet respectively, and also saw bursts but nothing else. The month's second tragic accident took place on the 24th, when Sgt Bruce took his aircrew and three members of ground crew for a Lorenz system training flight in Z8863. While engaged in a spot of low flying over Cambridgeshire, the Wellington collided with a line of railway trucks on the March to Spalding line two miles north-west of March, possibly after hitting telephone wires. The crash, in which all nine occupants perished, ripped up track, and one engine lodged beneath a coal truck, which became engulfed in flames in the ensuing fire that consumed a further four trucks. This would prove to be the squadron's final casualty of the year, although it would continue to participate in the reduced operational activity.

Coastal targets provided a relatively simple option for maintaining an offensive posture without penetrating deep into enemy territory at what was a dark time for the Command. Emden, as an important naval base located on the Ems Estuary that separated Germany from Holland at its north-western extremity, was a regular destination for bombers, particularly those crewed by freshmen during the early war years, although its attraction would decline. On the night of the 26/27th, eighty Wellingtons and twenty Hampdens set out to attack it on yet another cloudy night, and among them were four of the former belonging to 115 Squadron, all captained by sergeant pilots. They were part of a 3 Group effort of fifty-one Wellingtons, and took off in a six-minute slot from 17.18. Sgt Holder and crew were back on the ground within ninety minutes after Z1070 refused to climb to a respectable height. Sgt Anderson navigated by the flak coming up from the Frisian Islands, and reached the target area to deliver his load from 11,500 feet. Sgt Buckingham bombed from 500 feet lower and Sgt Hyde from 1,000 feet higher, but none was able to assess what happened to their hardware after it disappeared into the cloud tops.

Despite the risks of venturing to the Ruhr with the current restriction in force, Pierse decided to send a force of eighty-six aircraft to Düsseldorf, the mighty industrial city situated between Duisburg to the north and Cologne to the south. 115 Squadron made ready ten Wellingtons, which departed Marham between 17.07 and 17.36 with S/L Hogg the senior pilot on duty. Seven claimed to have reached the target area to bomb from between 12,000 and 15,000 feet without observing any results. Sgt Holder was unable to find the primary target, as, despite their claims, were most of the others, and flew further south to attack Bonn on DR (dead-reckoning) from 15,000 feet. F/L Paterson bombed Cologne from 15,000 feet and might have been among a few to hit it, as damage in the Rhineland Capital was greater than that at the intended target. Sgt Leslie admitted defeat and dropped his load on Eindhoven aerodrome from 10,000 feet on the way home. At debriefing F/Sgt Edwards reported identifying the primary target by the marshalling yards by the Rhine and the distinctive forked docks south-east of the city centre. He was sure his bombs had set off a large, red fire, and F/O Sword also referred to numerous fires, some of which were large. The Düsseldorf authorities reported just two high explosive bombs and two hundred incendiaries. On the credit side, just one aircraft was missing from the night's activities.

The final operation of the month was directed at Hamburg on the night of the 30th, and did not involve 115 Squadron 181 aircraft took off, and 122 returning crews claimed good bombing results, which were modestly confirmed by local reports of twenty-two fires and 2,500 people bombed out of their homes. During the course of the month the squadron operated on just seven nights, and dispatched forty-four sorties for the loss of four Wellingtons and three crews.

December 1941

The next two months were to be dominated by the campaign against the German warships at Brest, and no fewer than twelve raids of varying sizes would be mounted against the port during the course of December. There were no operations at all until the night of the 7/8th, when the Nazi Party HQ in Aachen was selected somewhat optimistically as the aiming-point for the main raid employing 130 aircraft. 3 Group would support this operation with aircraft from Honington, Waterbeach and Wyton, while sending a force of twenty-three Wellingtons and seven Stirlings to Brest for what would be a significant occasion in the development of bombing techniques. Six of the Stirlings were equipped with the highly-secret Oboe blind-bombing device for its very first live trial. Sixteen months hence Oboe would transform the accuracy of bombing, particularly over the Ruhr, and signal the end for the Ruhr industrial power house. Other raids on this night involved mostly freshman crews attacking dock installations at Calais, Boulogne, Dunkerque and Ostend. 115 Squadron prepared eleven Wellingtons for Brest and two for Boulogne, with take-offs spread over almost two hours between 15.40 and 17.35. S/L Hogg was the senior pilot on duty of the Brest-bound element, and he was one of ten from the squadron to report bombing in the target area from between 9,500 and 15,000 feet. The presence of cloud and the usual effective smoke-screen ensured that no results were observed other than bomb bursts. Sgt Anderson and crew failed to locate Brest, and attacked Dunkerque from 12,000 feet as a secondary target. S/L Grant and Sgt Harris were among the last to depart Marham, at 17.20, and they found more favourable conditions at Boulogne, which enabled them to identify ground detail. They delivered their loads from 12,500 and 10,500 feet respectively, and watched some of their bombs strike home across docks 6 and 7. Poor conditions contributed to the failure of the Aachen operation, after just half of the force reached the target area, and all but a handful deposited their bombs in open country.

There was an early start for the eleven crews of 115 Squadron selected to carry out the next assault on Brest, a small-scale 3 Group affair on the 11th. W/C Freeman and S/Ls Hogg and Coleman were the senior pilots on duty as they took to the air between 15.30 and 16.45, and those reaching the French coast were confronted by cloudy conditions. P/O Stock turned back with technical failures, while F/L Sword brought his bombs home after failing to locate the target. The freshman crew of Sgt Beattie also failed to find the primary target, and dropped their bombs from 9,000 feet onto a flak position on the outskirts of Rouen. Sgt Faith and crew released two 500 pounders on their first pass across the target, and then were unable to relocate it and brought the rest of their load home. W/C Freeman attacked on estimated position from 8,700 feet, and watched his 2,000 pounder fall in the light provided by flares from Stirlings. The others attacked from between 10,000 and 12,000 feet without observing results, and all were safely back on the ground by 23.00. The main target on this night had been Cologne, which was reached by less than half of the sixty-strong force, and, according to local reports, no bombs fell within the city.

It was Brest again for seven 115 Squadron crews on the 16th, while the two freshman crews of Sgts Perry and Slade cut their teeth on Ostend. They took off at 17.20, to join up with thirty other aircraft, seven of them representing 3 Group. Sgt Slade went in at 12,000 feet and dropped his bombs in a single stick from east to west through a break in the cloud, but was unable to observe results. Sgt Perry bombed from 500 feet higher and saw bursts across docks 11 and 12 and a small fire, but reported a large fire caused by another aircraft to the east of dock 16. The main element departed Marham between 17.50 and 18.45 with S/Ls Grant and Hogg the senior pilots on duty, and all reached the target to be greeted by cloud and the smoke-screen through which they bombed from between 9,800 and 14,500 feet. Sgt Soames and crew arrived fifteen minutes early, and cruised down to Quimper to kill some time, but could not locate Brest when they returned and brought their bombs home. A number of operations were posted at Marham and cancelled over the ensuing week-and-a-half, and raids were carried out on Cologne on the 23/24th and Düsseldorf on the 27/28th which did not involve 115 Squadron.

Having celebrated the third wartime Christmas in traditional fashion, fourteen crews were called to briefing on the 28th, thirteen to learn that the naval port of Wilhelmshaven was to be their target that night, while the freshman crew of Sgt Reynolds would try their hand at the less-demanding Emden situated some thirty-five miles to the west. The last-mentioned took off first at 16.55, and reached the target to deliver their bombs across dock 7 from 11,000 feet on a north-westerly heading. One white and three red fires were started that could be seen burning for at least fifteen minutes, and an aircraft was seen to fall in flames in the region of the Leeuwarden Luftwaffe fighter airfield known as the Wespennest (Wasps' nest). The main element departed Marham between 17.40 and 18.46 with S/Ls Grant and Hogg the senior pilots on duty, and all but Sgt Morton and crew, who turned back early on with engine issues, reached the target area to encounter unusually clear vertical visibility. Bombing took place from between 9,000 and 14,700 feet, and S/L Hogg saw his hardware straddle the narrow Zwischenhaven at the eastern end of Lake Brant on the southern side of the port, while Sgt Perry specified the entrance to the Bauhaven as the point of impact of his load. The eighty-six-strong all-Wellington force took advantage of the conditions to deliver an effective raid and cause widespread damage, particularly in the town. This was the final operation of the year for 115 Squadron and, indeed, most of the Command. During the course of the month the squadron operated on just four nights and dispatched forty-seven sorties without loss.

The year ended with the Command still under the black cloud cast by the Butt Report, and the future of an independent bomber force in question. It had been a disappointing year all round, with little discernible advance on the performance of 1940. The three new aircraft types, the Stirling, Halifax and Manchester, introduced into squadron service early in the year, had all failed to meet expectations, and all had been grounded for protracted periods, while essential modifications were put in hand. As a result, production was slow, and the trusty Wellington would continue to be the backbone of the Command throughout the coming year. Peirse had done his best to fulfil the often-unrealistic demands of his superiors, but the frequently changing priorities, and ever-growing list of targets had forced him to spread his resources too thinly. The policy of dispatching small numbers of aircraft to multiple targets simultaneously had produced negligible results, and had had almost no effect on the enemy's capacity to wage war. The crews, as always, had exerted themselves magnificently for the cause, and many of the finest pre-war airmen had been sacrificed in the process. As far as the hard-pressed crews were

An unidentified airman poses next to a 115 Sqn Wellington. The wing is wrapped in cloth, in order to protect the delicate wing fabric against damage from frost and ice.

concerned, the new year promised more of the same, although the first quarter would see the advent of two crucial components, which would herald the first foot on the road to recovery. The Lancaster was already in the hands of 44 Squadron, and in March would make its operational debut, while in February, a new Commander-in-Chief would arrive at the helm to lead by force of purpose and character.

January 1942

The New Year began as the old one had ended, with the continuing obsession with Brest and its lodgers. Seven raids would be sent against the port in the first ten nights of January, and in all, ten operations would be mounted during the month. A number of operations were posted on the board at Marham only to be cancelled, and it was not until the early hours of the 6th that 115 Squadron stirred itself for the year's maiden outing, which involved just two crews. Sgts Harris and Beattie took off at 03.18 and 03.28 respectively, and headed for north-western France where they were confronted by six to nine-tenths cloud. The aiming-point was the port's arsenal power plant situated on the west bank of the Penfeld estuary to the west of the main docks area, which was a somewhat optimistic demand for freshman crews. Sgt Harris identified the Pte des Espagnon and the breakwater at Brest through a gap in the clouds, and bombed from 13,000 feet at the same time as two other aircraft. Sgt Beattie caught site of the docks through a break in the cloud, but it had closed by the time of bomb release from 9,500 feet, and he estimated that they fell to the north of the docks area, where he had observed a large yellow, orange fire. 1 Group returned to Brest twenty-four hours later, when a near miss holed Gneisenau's hull and flooded two compartments.

AM Sir Richard Pierse departed Bomber Command on the 8th, and he would eventually be appointed C-in-C Allied Air Forces in India and South-East Asia. The 3 Group A-O-C, AVM Baldwin, was put in temporary command until the appointment of a permanent successor. Small forces continued the assault on Brest for three more nights until the 10/11th, when attention switched to Wilhelmshaven, but 115 Squadron remained at home conducting training flights. The first of two raids on Hamburg on

Above left: The squadron's mascot 'Wimpey' in 1942. Right: Wellington A crewman in typical flying kit.

consecutive nights took place on the 14/15th, when, again, the services of 115 Squadron were not required, but a single freshman sortie involving Sgt Weller and crew was dispatched to Emden. They took off at 17.20 carrying a dozen 250 pounders and two SBCs of incendiaries, but returned within three hours after failing to gain sufficient height. The Hamburg operation produced fires, but no significant damage, and it would be a similar story for the second one on the following night. This time the squadron sent Sgts Beattie and Reynolds and their crews to the main target, and Sgt Weller and crew back to Emden, the trio departing Marham between 17.50 and 18.15. Sgt Weller's flight lasted just thirty minutes after the fuses blew twice, but the Hamburg-bound pair made it all the way to their target along with fifty others from the original force, and they bombed from 12,000 and 13,000 feet. Both crews observed their bombs falling towards the docks area, but were unable to provide an assessment of the results. Hamburg reported damage to the Altona railway station and seven large fires, but, again, no significant damage. While this operation was in progress, the challenging weather conditions, which had made life so difficult for crews during the final quarter of 1941, caused 115 Squadron's first casualties of the year. While approaching to land following a cross-country training exercise, Sgt Faith and his crew fell foul of icing conditions in the Marham circuit. The windscreen glazed over and this was a major factor in Z1563's crash on the edge of the airfield at 21.11 in which all occupants lost their lives.

A disappointing raid on Bremen followed on the night of the 17/18th in the absence of a contribution from 115 Squadron, when ten-tenths cloud led to bombing on estimated positions and Hamburg almost certainly received more bombs than the intended target. When Sgt Weller and crew took off at 18.05 on the 21st, they were probably anxious not to achieve a hat-trick of "boomerangs". They and Sgt Anderson and crew had been briefed to attack Soesterberg aerodrome, situated some twenty miles south-east of Amsterdam, and both succeeded in locating and attacking it from 7,500 and 6,500 feet respectively, in good but hazy conditions, before returning safely home to report explosions and fires. The main efforts on this night had been directed at Bremen and Emden involving fifty-four and thirty-eight aircraft respectively, and those returning from the Bremen force claimed good results, although there was no confirmation. There had been no raids on inland Germany since late December, and this period was brought to an end by an attack on Münster on the night of the 22/23rd, which was followed by Hannover on the 26/27th. Fires were reported at both locations and damage was claimed to the railway station at the former, but, again, no local confirmation was forthcoming. Münster was posted to host its second operation within a week on the night of the 28/29th, and this signalled a return to operational activity for 115 Squadron, albeit for just two crews, whose Wellingtons were each loaded with a 1,000 pounder and four 500 pounders. Sgt Harris and F/Sgt Soames took off 18.25, and both bombed from around 14,000 feet on e.t.a in very poor visibility through ten-tenths cloud, which prevented them from observing any results. Local authorities reported no bombs falling within the town. During the second half of the month six sergeant pilots were posted to 99 Squadron, which would shortly be leaving Bomber Command for duties in India. It had been a month of limited activity for 115 Squadron, which operated on just five nights and dispatched ten sorties for the non-operational loss of one Wellington and crew.

February 1942

A new aircraft type, the Stirling, had arrived at Marham during January to equip 218 Squadron, and, by mid-February, the conversion would be complete. One wonders whether the 115 Squadron crews looked longingly at their neighbours' gangly four-engine monsters, hoping, perhaps, also to convert soon. In the event, 115 Squadron would be the only long-serving 3 Group unit to not take on the flawed Stirling, and would persevere with the trusty Wellington for more than a year, benefitting from its reliability, sturdiness and ability to take punishment. There were no operations at all to occupy the crews until the 6th, when 5 Group sent almost fifty aircraft on daylight mining sorties, and, later that afternoon, sixty aircraft, including fourteen from 3 Group were dispatched to continue the tiresome campaign against Brest. Only a third of the crews located the target area in ten-tenths cloud, and the whole operation was another dismal failure. It was a similar story at Brest on the night of the 10/11th, when twenty crews tried again, while fifty-five others were sent against Bremen. On the following evening, eighteen Wellingtons followed the well-trodden path back to Brest and carried out another inconclusive attack in poor weather conditions. The crews were unaware as they headed homewards, that they had just been involved in the final attempt to catch the warships in their lair in the French port.

Vice-Admiral Otto Cilliax, the Brest Group commander, whose flag was on Scharnhorst, put Operation Cerberus into action shortly after the bombers had headed for home, Scharnhorst, Gneisenau and Prinz Eugen slipping anchor at 21.14, before heading into the English Channel under an escort of destroyers and E-Boats. It was an audacious bid for freedom, covered by bad weather, widespread jamming and meticulously planned support by the Kriegsmarine and the Luftwaffe, all of which had been practiced extensively during January. The planning, and a little good fortune, allowed the fleet to make undetected progress until spotted off Le Touquet by two Spitfires piloted by G/C Victor Beamish, the commanding officer of Kenley, and W/C Finlay Boyd, both of whom maintained radio silence, and did not report their find until landing at 10.42 on the morning of the 12th. 5 Group was standing by at four hours readiness when Operation Fuller, which had been planned well in advance for precisely this eventuality, ground slowly into action.

The first of a record number of 242 daylight sorties were dispatched at 13.30, and were followed by others throughout the day, but the squally conditions and low cloud prevented all but a few crews from catching sight of their quarry, and those attacks that did take place failed to find the mark. The original 3 Group intention had been to catch the enemy at a position some thirty miles west of the Hague between 16.00 and 16.30, and attack from high level under the protection of a fighter escort. This idea was abandoned, however, as it became clear that no sighting would be possible unless aircraft came down beneath the very low cloud base. The squally conditions made it almost impossible to catch a glimpse of the enemy, and harder still to carry out an attack. A number of ships were straddled by bombs, but no hits were scored before the fleet made good its escape into open sea. 3 Group dispatched sixty-five Wellingtons and Stirlings, including three of the former representing 115 Squadron. P/O Runagall took off first from Marham, while Sgts Reynolds and Slade departed from Lakenheath at 16.30. Reynolds and Runagall both failed to locate the enemy fleet and brought their bombs back, but Sgt Slade and crew carried out an attack from 2,000 feet, and observed their bombs to fall some distance ahead and to starboard of some escort ships. Both Scharnhorst and Gneisenau struck air laid mines, which slowed their progress to an extent, but by the following morning, all had arrived safely in home ports. The fact that enemy warships had been able to sail through England's "back yard" and get away with it, in what became known as the Channel Dash, was a major embarrassment to the government and the nation. However, this annoying eleven month-long itch had at least been scratched for the last time, and the Command could now concentrate its full resources on the business of strategic bombing, to which it was much better suited. Sadly, this final attempt to hit the warships cost a further fourteen crews on top of all those lost throughout the many months of the campaign.

On the 14th, a new Air Ministry directive opened the way to the blatant area bombing of Germany, and reaffirmed the assault on the morale of the civilian population, particularly the workers. This had, of course, been a fact of life for a very long time, despite the denials of the government, but it could now be prosecuted openly, without the former pretence that only military and industrial installations were being targeted. Waiting in the wings, and, in fact, already steaming from America's eastern seaboard in the armed merchantman SS Alcantara, was a new leader, who would not only pursue this policy with a will, but would also fight Bomber Command's corner against all-comers. That night, Mannheim was the destination for ninety-eight aircraft of which fifteen were provided by 3 Group. 115 Squadron was not invited to take part, but sent the crew of F/L Paterson to join others targeting the docks at Le Havre, although he and his crew were shown in the ORB as being briefed to attack an enemy aerodrome near Crepon further to the west. This he managed to locate after taking off at 18.30, and bombed it from 10,000 feet before returning safely home to report observing seven or eight bomb bursts. F/L Paterson and crew were the squadron's only operational crew again on the night of the 16/17, when taking off at 18.10 for a nickelling (leaflet-dropping) trip to Lille in north-eastern France. Unfortunately, a starboard engine issue curtailed their sortie and they were back on the ground within seventy minutes. The sortie was repeated on the night of the 18/19th with a take-off at 18.15, followed by another early return at 19.35 with starboard engine trouble.

ACM Sir Arthur Harris took up his appointment as C-in-C on the 22nd, with firm ideas already in place on how to win the war by bombing alone. He had spent the first year of the war as A-O-C 5 Group, before becoming second deputy to Sir Charles Portal in November 1940. In June 1941 he was sent to America as part of a mission to expedite war equipment and materials, and returned in February 1942 specifically to take over the reins of Bomber Command. He was a Bomber Baron to the core, having spent much of his time as a squadron commander oversees, developing the theory and practice of precision bombing by both day and night. In order to strike effectively at Germany, he knew he must concentrate his forces over a single target, in order to overwhelm the defences, and to prevent the emergency services from operating efficiently. Concentration in time and numbers was the key, and this meant pushing the maximum number of aircraft across the aiming-point in the shortest possible time. This would not only prevent the flak batteries from locking-on to individual aircraft, but would also create chaos on the ground. The cratering of streets, with the resultant rubble, fractured gas and water mains, and general communications breakdown, would hinder the arrival of fire crews, thus allowing conflagrations to flare out of control. Harris was aware, that urban areas are destroyed most efficiently by fire rather than blast, and it would not be long before the bomb loads carried in his aircraft reflected this thinking.

In the meantime, for the remainder of the month, Harris contented himself with a continuation of the small-scale attacks on German naval ports. F/L Paterson finally completed the leaflet drop on the evening of the 24th, when he and his crew departed Marham at 18.45, located the target despite thick haze, and delivered their bundles of what Harris referred to as "toilet paper" from 10,000 feet. It was during one of the raids on a German port, that the war threw up one of its great ironies. In the course of an attack on the floating dock at Kiel on the night of the 26/27th, one of a modest number of Wellingtons, Hampdens and Halifaxes landed a high explosive bomb on the bows of the Gneisenau, now supposedly at safe haven after enduring almost a year of constant bombardment at Brest. The damage was so severe, that her sea-going career was ended for good, and her main armament would ultimately be removed for coastal defence work. During the course of another low-key month, 115 Squadron operated on four nights and one day, and dispatched seven sorties without loss.

March 1942

Bomber Command's evolution to war-winning capability was to be long and gradual, but the first signs of a new hand on the tiller came early on in Harris's reign. In response to an Air Ministry request, Harris prepared a meticulous plan to attack the Renault lorry factory located in a loop of the Seine in the district of Billancourt to the south-west of the centre of Paris. The plant was capable of building 18,000 lorries per year, which was a massive boon to the German war effort. The operation would be conducted in three waves, led by experienced crews, and would involve extensive use of flares to provide illumination. A force of 235 aircraft, a new record for a single target, was assembled on the 3rd, 3 Group making ready a maximum effort of thirty-seven Wellingtons and twenty-nine Stirlings. Orders had excluded Gee-equipped aircraft from taking part, and this meant that 115 Squadron would have to stay at home on this momentous occasion. In the absence of a flak defence, crews were encouraged to attack from as low a level as possible, and 223 returning crews reported bombing the target during the one-hour-fifty-minute duration of the raid. The operation was an outstanding success, which destroyed 40% of the factory buildings, and halted production for a month, depriving the enemy of around 2,300 lorries. The Command lost just a single Wellington, but 367 French civilians were killed in adjacent residential districts, a figure that was twice the highest death toll at a German target thus far. The problem of collateral damage would never be satisfactorily addressed, and French civilians, in particular, of those populations under occupation, would pay a high price for their freedom right up to the time when liberation beckoned in the summer of 1944. It was somewhat ironic, that Harris, as a fierce advocate of area bombing, should gain his first major success by way of a precision attack.

The industrial city of Essen was to feature prominently in Harris's future plans, and become something of an obsession. He began his first campaign against it with the assembly on the 8th of a force of 211 aircraft, while their crews were briefed for what would be a three-wave operation using the Krupp works as the aiming-point. 3 Group was to provide the flare-force, drawn from the Gee-equipped Wellington squadrons at Feltwell, Honington, Marham and Oakington, which would carry flares and a few 250 pounders each and provide illumination for the following incendiary force consisting of aircraft from the same stations. The final wave was made up of aircraft from all groups carrying high explosives. 115 Squadron prepared a record seventeen Wellingtons, six for the flare-force and eleven for the incendiary force, and they took off between 23.30 and 00.50 led by W/C Freeman, who had S/L Cousens flying with him as navigator. S/Ls Grant and Hogg were also assigned to the vanguard, while S/L Coleman was the senior pilot among the squadron's incendiary force element. F/Sgt Hyde and crew were twenty miles from the Dutch coast when the oxygen supply to the rear turret failed, and Sgt Soames and crew were forty miles further east over Holland when low engine oil pressure and rising temperatures persuaded them to turn back, and both crews returned their bombs to store. The squadron ORB is confused in recording individual loads, but is clear that W/C Freeman delivered his flares from between 10,000 and 15,000 feet, S/L Hogg from 15,000 feet, S/L Grant from 16,000 feet and P/O George from 19,000 feet. The others bombed from between 15,000 and 19,000 feet, many of them employing Gee to fix their positions over the Ruhr on a fine night with thick industrial haze concealing ground detail. Some returning crews were adamant that their bombs had fallen close to the Krupp works or into the centre of the city, and bomb bursts and fires were reported. F/L Paterson claimed to be able to see the fires burning from a distance of 110 miles. Eight aircraft failed to return, and among them was the squadron's X3419, which disappeared without trace with the experienced crew of P/O Runagall DFC, whose navigator also wore the ribbon of a DFC and the rear gunner a DFM. The operation turned out to be a major disappointment, the first of many at this target, and succeeded in destroying only a few buildings. It demonstrated two things, firstly, that Gee was effective in terms of finding an approximate target area, but was insufficiently precise to use as a blind-bombing device, and, secondly, that it remained extremely difficult from high above to interpret what was happening on the ground.

187 aircraft were made ready for a return to Essen on the 9th, of which ten of the Wellingtons were provided by 115 Squadron, six of them in the twenty-three-strong Gee-equipped flare force and the remainder in the main force. The group put up twenty-seven Wellingtons and Stirlings for the incendiary force and thirty-six for the main force, but the squadron ORB does not distinguish the precise role of each crew. They took off between 19.15 and 19.38 with S/L Grant the senior pilot on duty, and only F/Sgt Davie and crew failed to reach the target area after the Gee equipment broke down. The others located Essen in good conditions with thick ground haze, and some crews would claim to have identified the Krupp works. Bombing took place from between 15,500 and 19,000 feet, F/L Sword claiming to have straddled the Krupp complex with his flares and bombs. P/O Perry reported a large, red fire with thick, black smoke on the south-east corner of the Krupp works, and the 3 Group ORB described the night's work as most successful. This was not borne out by local reports from Essen, which admitted to two buildings being destroyed and some seventy damaged, while twenty-four other Ruhr locations reported bombs falling. For the third night in a row, Harris persisted with Essen on the 10th, for which a reduced force of 126 aircraft was made ready. 115 Squadron briefed ten crews who would be led by S/L Hogg, and they took off between 19.00 and 19.15, after which all but Sgt Soames and crew, whose I.F.F system failed, reached the target area to find variable amounts of cloud with only moderate visibility. P/O Leslie and crew suffered the disappointment of reaching the target area only for their TR1335 (Gee box) to fail, and they brought their bombs home. Bombing by the others took place from between 13,500 and 20,000 feet, Sgt Holder and crew recognizing that they had attacked Bochum, some ten miles east of Essen, and S/L Hogg observed incendiaries falling around Schwerte, further east still. This time there was no confidence in the accuracy of the attack, which had been carried out largely on estimated positions based on a Gee-fix, and the pessimism was borne out by local reports.

There was some encouragement to be derived from an attack on Kiel on the night of the 12/13th, when the port area was successfully bombed and damage inflicted upon the naval port area and the Deutsche Werke and Germania Werft U-Boot construction yards. 3 Group supported the operation with aircraft from Feltwell, Honington and Stradishall, while it was their colleagues from Marham and Oakington that were detailed on the 13th for an operation that night against Cologne. Fourteen 115 Squadron Wellingtons were loaded with a total of 168 bundles of reconnaissance flares and fifty-six 250lb bombs and took off between 18.39 and 18.58 with S/L Grant the senior pilot on duty. P/O Leslie was forced to return within the hour because of an undercarriage malfunction, and his bombs were brought back, as were those of P/O Weller and crew, who were unable to locate the target on this moonless night. The others arrived in the target area to find a thin layer of five-tenths stratus cloud, and delivered their illumination and bombs from between 14,500 and 16,500 feet. A number of crews reported identifying major ground features, like the River Rhine and the Hohenzollern Bridge, and the general consensus at debriefing was of a successful operation. This confidence was borne out by local reports, which catalogued a number of war industry factories losing production and fifteen hundred houses suffering destruction or damage. This represented the first genuine success for Gee, and provided a glimpse of what the Command could achieve with the appropriate equipment.

The middle part of the month was devoted to minor operations, and 115 Squadron's next outing was a daylight "moling" operation to Essen, for which five crews set off on the afternoon of the 18th, before common sense prevailed and they were recalled because of a lack of cloud cover. Harris was drawn back to Essen on consecutive nights beginning on the 25/26th for which 115 Squadron made ready a record-equalling seventeen Wellingtons as part of an overall force of 254 aircraft. They departed Marham between 19.40 and 19.55 with S/L Grant the senior pilot on duty and carrying between them seventy-two three-flare bundles, thirty-six 250 pounders, a single 4,000 pounder and sixty-three SBCs of incendiaries. F/Sgt Hyde and crew were the only ones to turn back after their Gee and rear turret became unserviceable, and they dumped their cookie into the sea. The remaining sixteen all reached the target area in the vanguard of the attack, and delivered the contents of their bomb bays from between 15,000 and 18,000 feet based on either visual or TR-fix, some after identifying ground features that they recognized as belonging to Essen. There was less confidence about the effectiveness of this operation, and local reports confirmed it to have been a dismal failure. It had largely missed the city, partly through being drawn away by a decoy fire site at Rheinberg, eighteen miles to the west, and had cost nine aircraft, including 25% of the 5 Group Avro Manchester element.

The squadron prepared fifteen Wellingtons for the following night's return to Essen by a predominantly 3 Group force of 104 Wellingtons and eleven Stirlings, for what would be the fifth raid of the month on the Ruhr giant. S/L Grant was again the senior pilot on duty as they took off between 19.40 and 19.59 carrying the same loads as twenty-four hours earlier. Thirteen are known to have reached the target, which they found in outstandingly good weather conditions, with a reduced level of industrial haze, but an increase in flak and searchlight activity. Crews bombed visually or on TR-fix from between 14,000 and 18,000 feet, some claiming on return to have identified the Krupp works, which was usually the briefed aiming-point. Sadly, it turned out that only twenty-two high explosive bombs had fallen in the city, and just two houses had been destroyed to add to the single one destroyed in the previous night's raid, all at a cost of ten Wellingtons and a Stirling, 10% of those dispatched. Two of the missing Wellingtons were 115 Squadron's X3589, which crashed four miles east-south-east of Goch to the north of the Ruhr, and X3604, which came down close to the town of Dieren in eastern Holland. There were no survivors from the crews of Sgt Taylor and P/O Soames respectively.

The ineffectiveness of operations throughout the war to date had been caused largely by the inability of crews to navigate accurately over a blacked-out country, which was also frequently hidden by cloud. The electronic tools to transform navigation and bombing were still in the development stage, and, although Gee had proved itself to be a useful aid to preliminary navigation, its range was limited, and it was subject to jamming by the enemy. Too often were crews forced to rely on highly imprecise dead-reckoning (DR), and this was no formula for success. Harris understood the need to provide his crews with identifiable pinpoints on the ground, and for his next major operation, he selected a target on a coastline. Lübeck, the ancient and historic Hansastadt (free-trade city) situated on the Baltic, with narrow streets and half-timbered buildings in its centre, was ideally suited to an area attack, and was poorly equipped to defend itself. A force of 234 aircraft was assembled on the 28th, Palm Sunday, for an operation that night to be conducted along similar lines to those employed so successfully against the Renault lorry factory in Paris at the start of the month. 115 Squadron loaded fifteen Wellingtons with the usual war loads, and they took off for the three-wave attack between 19.30 and 20.50 with W/C Freeman and S/L Grant the senior pilots on duty. The latter took off at the head of the flare force, while the commanding officer put himself at the tail end of the raid to enable him to better assess the outcome.

The two-thirds incendiary bomb loads carried by the force reflected Harris's intention to destroy the target by fire, and, the lack of a credible defence would allow the crews to attack from as low a level as practicable to ensure accuracy. F/Sgt Hyde and crew were recalled because they had taken off too early, but the other 115 Squadron participants delivered their loads from between 3,500 and 16,000 feet, and it was clear by the end of the raid that fires had taken hold. Twelve aircraft failed to return home, eight of them representatives of 3 Group, and among them was 115 Squadron's X3341, in which P/O Weller and his crew lost their lives after crashing in northern Germany. The operation was an outstanding success, which laid waste to 190 acres of the Old Town and destroyed more than fourteen hundred buildings, most of them consumed by fire. Almost two thousand other buildings were seriously damaged, and the total destruction amounted to 30% of the city's built-up area. Thus was registered the first genuine success for the area bombing policy, but the principles put into operation on this night would form the basis of all similar operations in the future. There was an outcry following this unexpected attack on Lübeck, which was a vital port for the Red Cross, and an agreement was struck that ensured its future protection from bombing.

The only aircraft operating on the night of the 31st were four Wellingtons from 115 Squadron, captained by F/L Paterson, P/Os George and Perry and Sgt Holder, who had been standing-by all day and were dispatched to Essen eventually at intervals between 19.10 and 00.10. They flew into icing conditions and only P/O George and crew reached the target to bomb on TR-fix from 13,000 feet. Sgt Holder and crew were unable to locate the primary target, and dropped their bombs from 15,000 feet on Hamborn on the northern side of Duisburg. The other two crews were defeated by the conditions and jettisoned all or part of their bomb loads before returning safely home. This was the final operation of a month which had seen the squadron operate on eight nights and one day, and dispatch 197 sorties for the loss of four Wellingtons and crews.

April 1942

The first few nights of April would be occupied by small-scale operations, beginning on the 1/2nd, when 3 and 5 Groups joined forces to send thirty-five Wellingtons and fourteen Hampdens on Operation Lineshoot, an experiment to test the viability of attacking railway targets from low level. The targets were located in the Hanau to Lohr region of southern Germany to the east of Frankfurt, which required a deep penetration into hostile territory in what turned out to be poor weather conditions that made towns and railway tracks difficult to identify. While this was in progress 1, 3 and 5 Groups dispatched fifty-six mostly freshman crews to bomb the docks at Le Havre, for which 115 Squadron briefed four crews. They departed Marham between 20.10 and 20.22 with P/O Wood the senior pilot on duty and each carrying sixteen 250 pounders. P/O Wood and crew were back within three hours after experiencing engine issues, leaving the remaining three freshman crews to locate and bomb the target from between 12,000 and 15,000 feet. The Le Havre force posted missing a single Wellington, while, many miles away, disaster was befalling the Lineshoot force, which lost a dozen Wellingtons and a Hampden, both in the target area and homebound over France and Belgium. 3 Group received a mauling, which cost 214 Squadron seven of its fourteen aircraft and 57 Squadron five of its twelve, and all thoughts of further low-level forays were shelved for the time being.

3 Group supported two operations on the following night, when providing twenty-four aircraft in a force of fifty for an attack on the Matford Motor Works at Poissy, a north-western suburb of Paris, and a dozen Wellingtons with freshman crews for Le Havre. The Poissy operation had been attempted on the previous night by 4 Group, but photographic reconnaissance had revealed it to have failed in its purpose. 115 Squadron made ready six Wellingtons for Paris and three for Le Havre, and the latter took off first, shortly after 20.00, to be followed into the air between 20.15 and 20.25 by the main element with F/Ls

Sword and Paterson the senior pilots on duty. The freshman crews of Sgt Beckett, F/Sgt Loughead and P/O Wood carried out their attacks on the docks in good weather conditions from between 10,000 and 13,000 feet, and bomb bursts were observed. Conditions over Paris were also ideal for low-level bombing, which the Marham crews carried out from between 3,500 and 4,000 feet, sending a cookie, five 1,000 pounders and twenty-five 500 pounders to fall onto and around the factory. The squadron's aircraft were now almost all equipped with a camera, and five photographs taken by F/L Sword confirmed the attack as successful. At 10.35 on the 4th, Sgt Beckett and crew took off for a "moling" sortie to Essen, which they found by TR-fix and bombed from 13,000 feet, plotting the fall of their seven 500 pounders to be some ten miles north-west of Essen in the Sterkrade district of Oberhausen.

A new record force of 263 aircraft was assembled on the 5th for an operation to Cologne that night, and they were given the Humboldt works as the aiming-point. A major manufacturer of artillery pieces, the factory complex was located in the Deutz district on the East Bank of the Rhine near the city centre. 3 Group detailed 106 aircraft, which were spread between the flare force, the incendiary force and the main striking force, in what was now a standard format for large raids. 115 Squadron briefed sixteen crews, six of them for the flare-force element, which took off between 22.55 and 23.09 carrying twelve three-flare bundles each and four 250 pounders. F/L Sword was the senior pilot on duty and he was accompanied as second pilot by W/C "Ted" Olson, who was about to take command of 75(NZ) Squadron over at Feltwell. The remainder took to the air between 00.30 and 01.02 with F/L Paterson the senior pilot, three of the Wellingtons loaded with a 4,000lb cookie and seven with a 1,000 and five 500 pounders. F/Sgt Davie and crew returned early from the flare-force after the navigator became ill, and they brought their bombs and flares home, while F/Sgt Anderson and crew were forced back prematurely with flat batteries and jettisoned their load safe. P/O Leslie and crew had their oxygen system fail, and they also jettisoned the contents of their bomb bay. The others pressed on to the target, which they found in reasonable weather conditions of five-tenths cloud, and delivered their attacks from between 11,500 and 17,000 feet. Over two hundred crews claimed to have bombed in the target area to good effect, but returning 3 Group crews were divided in their opinions as to the success of the operation, those at Marham, Feltwell and Oakington expressing doubts, while those at Honington, Mildenhall, Stradishall and Wyton were confident that they had identified and bombed the target. Of the bombing photographs plotted, none proved to be within five miles of the intended aiming-point, and local reports described the bombing as scattered across the city. There was minimal industrial damage, and any gains were modest, indeed, in proportion to the effort expended.

Harris resumed his campaign against Essen on the 6th, for which a force of 157 aircraft was made ready. 115 Squadron contributed ten Wellingtons, which took off between 23.58 and 01.02 with W/C Freeman the senior pilot on duty. Weather conditions were not good over England, and ten-tenths ice-bearing cloud awaited the crews at the Dutch coast, persuading many of them to turn back. Among the crews returning early to Marham were those of W/C Freeman, F/L Paterson, P/O Patterson, P/O Leslie and P/O Wood. The remainder pressed on to bomb through cloud from between 14,000 and 16,000 feet based on a TR-fix, but had little idea of where their bombs fell. Only a third of the original force claimed to have reached the target, and local reports confirmed that the operation had failed. A forecast of similar weather conditions on the 8th did not dissuade the operations planners from scheduling a raid on Hamburg that night, for which a new record force of 272 aircraft was assembled. 3 Group detailed a hundred aircraft to take part, and thirteen of the Wellingtons were to be provided by 115 Squadron. Twelve took off between 22.30 and 23.15 with F/Ls Sword and Paterson the senior pilots on duty, but it was 23.42 before Sgt Harris and crew got away, presumably as part of the third wave. They encountered electrical storms and icing conditions which persuaded many crews to turn back, and among those were

On its way to Rostok, the Wellington was attacked and shot down by a nightfighter and crashed on a crossroads near Bevtoft, Denmark with the bomb load exploding killing all on board.

The German Wehrmacht and the Danish police closed the area off and not until Thursday April 30 did they arrive to retrieve the remains of the crew and the wreck. The body parts were due to be dropped in the bomb crater and not given a proper burial.

A Danish teacher Frederik Tychsen complained about this and managed to get permission to collect and bury the remains of the crew. Tychsen brought in a ship's chest and laid the body parts in it.

At sundown a grave was dug in P. Riss' plantation. The chest, the box was placed in the grave and Tychsen performed the graveside ceremony.

Crew: Sgt A T Fone (Pilot), Sgt I J Rollinson (Pilot), Sgt A Duncan (Observer), Sgt W G Smith (W.Op/AG), Sgt J S Grieve (W.Op/AG), Sgt A E Simmans (AG). All now buried in Aabenraa Cemetery Denmark Allied Military Plot.

115 Squadron's Sgt Slade, Sgt Butterworth and P/O Perry. The others battled the conditions to reach the target area, but were denied any sight of the ground and were forced to bomb from between 13,000 and 16,000 feet on TR-fix or e.t.a. The oxygen feed to the rear turret failed in Sgt Beckett's X3724, incapacitating the occupant, and it was decided to bomb Cuxhaven as a last resort target. They carried out the bombing-run at 13,000 feet, and observed six bursts as they turned away. F/Sgt Loughead and crew suffered the additional frustration of their bomb-release system failing, and they jettisoned their bombs safe. Returning crews reported observing bursts and a glow on the ground, but could offer no useful assessment at debriefing. Local reports estimated that about fourteen bomb loads had hit the city, causing eight fires but no significant damage, and some incendiaries also fell into the Vulkan U-Boot construction yards at Bremen some sixty miles to the south-west.

S/L Cousens, a navigator, was posted to the squadron from 3 Group HQ on the 10th, and would succeed S/L Hogg as a flight commander on the latter's posting to S.D.L next day. It should be noted that the 115 Squadron ORB refers to S/L Cousens as crew captain, suggesting that he was the pilot, and includes the name of a second pilot and a navigator in a five-man crew, at a time when most crews consisted of six men. This suggests that the scribe was unaware that S/L Cousens was not a pilot, and omitted the actual pilot's name.

The 10th was the day on which Harris ordered another assault on Essen, for which 254 aircraft were made ready. 115 Squadron loaded fifteen Wellingtons with sufficient fuel for the 550-mile round trip, and filled the six flare-force bomb bays with twelve three-flare bundles and four 250 pounders, eight of the others with nine SBCs of incendiaries, and one with a 4,000lb cookie. They departed Marham between 21.21 and 22.49 with S/L Grant the senior pilot on duty, and all reached the Ruhr expecting to meet clear skies, but, instead, found themselves separated from their target by five to ten-tenths cloud. S/L Grant let his 250 pounders go over Duisburg from 16,500 feet when some ten miles short of Essen, which suggests that he was in some kind of difficulty on a night of intense anti-aircraft fire. The remainder carried out their part in the raid from between 13,000 and 16,000 feet, before returning safely to report their impressions. Most were confident that their bombs had fallen within the built-up area of the city, but local reports of just twelve houses destroyed demonstrated again that the Command needed a technological breakthrough before accuracy could be achieved in the Ruhr Valley.

Two days later on the 12th, the teleprinters on bomber stations across eastern England churned out the day's instructions from HQ Bomber Command, informing them of the intention to return to Essen that night for what would be the eighth time since the first Gee-led operation of the 8/9th of March. Another sizeable force of 251 aircraft included a large contribution from 3 Group, including sixteen Wellingtons made ready by 115 Squadron. The six members of the flare force began to depart Marham at 21.35 led by W/C Freeman and S/L Grant, but the commanding officer was defeated by icing conditions outbound, and turned back with his bombs from a position over enemy territory. He found F/Sgt Davie and crew already on the ground after their X3591 and refused to climb to operational height, forcing them to jettison part of their bomb load. The others arrived in the target area to find fair weather conditions, and bombed either by visual reference or on TR-fix from between 14,000 and 16,500 feet. A spirited flak defence caused some difficulties, as did searchlight glare, and seven of the squadron's Wellingtons were damaged, including F/Sgt Anderson's X3412, in which the wireless operator sustained a leg wound. Returning crews reported bomb bursts and fires, and most were confident that they had hit a built-up area and caused some damage. Local reports suggested a slight improvement on recent performances, but bombs had again been sprayed liberally around the Ruhr, and damage in Essen was modest in the extreme. 115 Squadron's X3596, which was one of ten missing aircraft, had sent out an S.O.S signal, which two fixes had plotted in the Zuider Zee area, but nothing further was heard. It was established later, that the Wellington had fallen victim to a night-fighter over Holland while outbound, and had crashed at 01.00 into the Ijsselmeer, taking Sgt Holder and his crew to their deaths. Thus ended Harris's first concerted effort to destroy this industrial powerhouse. During eight operations 1,555 sorties had been launched, of which two-thirds had claimed attacking Essen and sixty-four aircraft had been lost. Of 212 photographs showing ground detail, only twenty-two had been plotted within five miles of the city, and, on only two occasions, had any minor industrial damage resulted. (Bomber Command War Diaries, Martin Middlebrook and Chris Everitt). Harris had lost the battle, and the Ruhr would continue to confound him for the remainder of the year until technology handed him a silver bullet.

The night of the 13/14th was devoted to minor operations including mining in the Frisians and the German Bight. Among the 3 Group participants were four 115 Squadron crews, who were undertaking the squadron's first "gardening" sorties of the war. They took off between 21.12 and 21.25 with F/L Sword the senior pilot on duty, and three of them delivered their two 1,500lb parachute mines each by TR-fix from between 600 and 800 feet. Sgt Butterworth and crew found their Gee equipment to be malfunctioning, and failed to locate their drop zone. Attention was now turned upon Essen's neighbour, Dortmund, for which the force of 208 aircraft assembled on the 14th was considerably larger than any previously sent to this target. 115 Squadron made ready a dozen Wellingtons, which took off between 21.40 and 23.05 with S/L Grant the senior pilot on duty and a member of the flare force. All reached the target area to find good visibility, and carried out their assigned tasks from between 15,000 and 16,000 feet, while Sgt Fone and crew, who were uncertain as to their precise position, opted to drop their six 500 pounders safe. Returning crews reported bomb bursts and fires, one conflagration described as particularly large near the city centre, and some commented on the intensity of the searchlight and flak defences and the presence of night-fighters, which accounted for nine bombers. Despite the belief that the operation had been reasonably successful, bombing photos were plotted over a forty-mile stretch of the Ruhr, and local reports listed isolated and insignificant damage.

The force prepared for the return to Dortmund twenty-four hours later was reduced to 152 aircraft, of which nine were provided by 115 Squadron. They took off between 22.29 and 23.52 with W/C Freeman the senior pilot on duty, and set course for the Belgian coast in good weather conditions, only to encounter icing on the outward leg and six-tenths cloud in the target area. Sgt Butterworth and crew suffered failure of the a.s.i, and jettisoned their bombs over southern Belgium from 12,800 feet, but the others found the target either by visual reference or TR-fix, and delivered their loads from between 15,000 and 16,000 feet. Some bomb bursts were observed, but few returning crews could offer any useful assessment of the outcome, although they commented again on the intensity of the searchlight and flak defences, and ground crews would be kept busy on the following day patching up holed Wellingtons. One crew reported an aircraft shot down near Ostend, and this would have been a 149 Squadron Stirling, one of just four failures to return, three of which belonged to 3 Group. Local reports described minor damage in Dortmund, caused by no more than eight bomb loads.

Crews were no doubt relieved when orders came through on the 17th which would not involve them running the gauntlet of searchlights, flak and night-fighters to and from the Ruhr. Instead, they could look forward to a North Sea crossing to Hamburg, where the opposition would be equally intense but less prolonged during a relatively shallow penetration into enemy territory. 115 Squadron contributed fourteen Wellingtons for the main event as part of an overall force of 173 aircraft, while Sgt Fone's X3662 was loaded with fifteen 250 pounders to take to Le Havre and took off first at 21.40. The remainder took off between 23.26 and 23.50 with S/L Grant the senior pilot on duty and nine of them carrying SBCs of incendiaries, while three had a 1,000 pounder and five 500 pounders on board and two a 4,000lb cookie each. Weather conditions were good as they set off, and Sgt Morton and crew were approaching Sylt when an overheating starboard engine curtailed their sortie. They dropped their bombs onto the island from 12,000 feet, and observed a large, red fire. F/Sgt Davie and crew were also thwarted by an overheating engine, which prevented them from climbing to operational height, and they jettisoned part of their load from 11,000 feet as they turned for home. P/O Patterson and crew were attacked by a night fighter, and were at 14,000 feet when they became the second crew to attack Sylt as a last-resort target, observing their bombs to fall harmlessly into muddy open country. S/L Grant experienced engine problems and was another to let his bombs go before reaching the target, in his case from 16,500 feet at 02.45, which must have put him somewhere over north-western Germany. Sgt Beckett and crew were defeated by an unserviceable a.s.i and decided to drop their bombs on the port of Emden, which they identified visually from 17,000 feet. The remaining crews located Hamburg either visually through the ground haze, or by TR-fix, and bombed from between 12,000 and 16,000 feet. Some returning crews reported observing bursts and fires, but it was difficult to make a meaningful assessment, and the 3 Group ORB described the operation as only moderately successful. Local reports described seventy-five fires, thirty-three of them classed as large, but attributed the damage to an estimated fifty aircraft.

On the 22nd 3 Group put together a Gee-equipped force of sixty-four Wellingtons and five Stirlings for an attempt to use Gee as a blind-bombing device, for which Cologne was selected as the objective. Before the main element of twelve 115 Squadron Wellingtons departed Marham between 21.32 and 22.15, the freshman crew of P/O Rohde took off at 21.28 for the docks at Le Havre. S/L Grant was the senior pilot on duty as the main element flew out towards the Belgian coast, and it was as they crossed into enemy territory that Sgt Morton and crew were compelled by a failed Gee-box to abandon their sortie. The others pressed on to find Cologne hidden beneath cloud and haze, which served the purpose of the trial, and bombing was carried out from between 13,000 and 15,000 feet. The explosion of a cookie lit up the clouds, and the glow of what appeared to be many fires suggested an effective attack, but an accurate assessment was impossible. Some photographs managed to capture ground detail, but this was up to ten miles from the target, and local reports confirmed that no more than about fifteen bomb loads had hit the city. Meanwhile, P/O Rohde and crew had attacked the docks at Le Havre from 12,500 feet, and observed bursts but no results.

Further Gee trials would take place, but, in the meantime, Harris returned to the Baltic coast, to try to repeat the success of Lübeck at Rostock, another ancient member of the Hanseatic League. A Heinkel aircraft factory on the southern outskirts of the town was an additional attraction, and a small element from 5 Group was directed specifically at this, while 143 crews were briefed to attack the town. 115 Squadron prepared ten Wellingtons, loading two of them with nine SBCs of incendiaries, and the rest with a 1,000 pounder and five 500 pounders each. For weeks now the squadron had been dispensing leaflets with their bombs, and this would continue at Rostock. They took off between 22.25 and 22.54, led away by W/C Freeman with S/L Grant in close support, and all reached the target area to find cloudless skies and good visibility. The opportunity was at hand to deliver a crushing blow, and returning crews reported bombing the town centre from between 9,000 and 12,500 feet, and observing bursts and fires. What went wrong is not clear, but photographic reconnaissance revealed the main weight of the attack to have fallen between two and six miles from the narrow streets of the Altstadt, and claims of heavy damage to the Heinkel works were shown to be completely false.

Fortunately, the destruction of Rostock had been planned as a series, and the second attack was mounted on the following night at the hands of a force of 125 aircraft, ninety-one for the town and thirty-four for the Heinkel works. This time 115 Squadron was required to provide four Wellingtons for the main raid and two freshman crews for the docks at Dunkerque, and they took off between 22.11 and 22.24 on another night of fine weather conditions and no senior pilots on duty. Dunkerque was located with ease by means of TR and a visual reference, and was bombed from 12,500 feet by both crews, who returned to report hitting the docks and starting large fires. Meanwhile, some five hundred miles to the north-east the 115 Squadron crews were attacking the centre of Rostock on Gee-fix and visual reference from between 9,500 and 13,000 feet, and observing their bombs to start many red fires. Sgt Slade and crew reported seeing an entire street on fire in the old town, and his confidence concerning the success of the raid would be confirmed by photographic reconnaissance. The Heinkel factory managed once more to evade the bombs, but its time was fast approaching.

For the third night in a row a force of aircraft, made up of six types, made its way across the North Sea to enter enemy territory over Denmark close to its frontier with Germany on the Schleswig-Holstein peninsular. 110 crews had been briefed to attack the town, while eighteen others, led by W/C Guy Gibson of 5 Group's 106 Squadron targeted the factory and, finally, scored some hits. 115 Squadron had dispatched a dozen Wellingtons between 22.13 and 22.29 led by F/Ls Paterson and Sword, and all but P/O Patterson made it to landfall over Denmark. It was on approach to the coast that X3750 lost the use of its port engine, which stopped the hydraulic pump to the rear turret, and P/O Patterson was forced to turn back, jettisoning part of the bomb load into the Wash before landing safely. X3633 was set upon by a night fighter over Denmark, and crashed at 02.00 near Over Jerstal with no survivors from the crew of Sgt Fone. The others reached the target area, where the weather conditions remained excellent, but the searchlight and flak defences had been strengthened since the last attack. Bombing by the 115 Squadron element took place from between 9,000 and 11,500 feet, and, at debriefing, they described the whole town as ablaze. The last of the four-raid series against Rostock took place on the night of the 26/27th, at the hands of an initial force of 106 aircraft, divided roughly equally between the town and the Heinkel factory. 3 Group provided aircraft from Mildenhall and Wyton only, allowing 115 Squadron to enjoy a night off. The operation was highly successful, and added substantially to the damage caused by the earlier attacks. An assessment of this mini-campaign revealed that 1,765 buildings had been destroyed and 513 seriously damaged, creating 130 acres of destruction, which amounted to around 60% of the main town area.

The month's busy schedule continued with the posting of Cologne as the target for the night of the 27/28th, for which 115 Squadron made ready a dozen Wellingtons plus another for a freshman sortie to Dunkerque. The squadron was not providing illumination on this operation, and ten of the aircraft were loaded with nine SBCs of incendiaries, while one carried a cookie and the other a 1,000 pounder and six 500 pounders. The main element took to the air between 21.33 and 21.44 as part of an overall force of ninety-seven aircraft, more than half of which had been provided by 3 Group. S/L Grant was the senior pilot on duty as they made their way south to cross into enemy territory by way of the Belgian coast, and, as they did so, Sgt Williams and crew departed Marham at 22.34 bound for Dunkerque with a bomb bay bearing fifteen 250 pounders. The Rhineland was reached by all 115 Squadron participants, and in weather conditions ideal for bombing. Sgt Butterworth's port propeller broke as he approached the target, and he was forced to jettison his bombs just south of the city when at 9,500 feet. The others ran across the target at heights ranging from 11,500 to 18,000 feet, and delivered their hardware into the city, a number of crews specifying the East Bank of the Rhine as receiving perhaps the main weight of the attack, and the Deutz area, in particular was seen to contain many fires. Six Wellingtons and a Halifax failed to return, and among the former was the squadron's X3639 containing the crew of Sgt Harris. New eventually came through via the Red Cross that the rear gunner had survived, and was safe in enemy hands. Remarkably, he was the first to prevail from eight missing or crashed 115 Squadron aircraft thus far during the year. An assessment of the raid revealed that more than fifteen hundred houses and nine industrial buildings had sustained varying degrees of damage, but a proportion of the bombing had also fallen wide of the city. While this operation was in progress, Sgt Williams and crew had been unable to locate Dunkerque docks through the cloud, and jettisoned their bombs into the sea.

Marham was not called upon for an operation to Kiel on the night of the 28/29th, but ground crews were kept busy on the 29th preparing sixteen Wellingtons for operations that night. A force of eighty-eight aircraft was assembled to attack the Gnome & Rhone aero-engine factory in the Gennevilliers district of Paris, and 115 Squadron was to provide fifteen of the Wellingtons along with another for Sgt Williams and crew to take to Ostend. S/L Cousens was on the Order of Battle for the first time since joining the squadron from 3 Group HQ, when S/L Grant was the senior pilot on duty. They took off between 21.14 and 21.47, six of them with all-incendiary loads, while eight carried a 1,000 pounder and six 500 pounders and one a 4,000lb cookie. At 22.21 Sgt Williams and crew departed Marham, and would reach the target only to be frustrated by the failure of their bomb-release system over Ostend, forcing them to bring back their sixteen 250 pounders. Weather conditions in the Paris area were conducive to accurate bombing, and the location of the factory complex in the Port de Paris, in a loop of the River Seine to the north of the city centre, provided a clear pin-point to guide the bombs to the mark. The 115 Squadron crews bombed from between 6,000 and 10,500 feet and observed many bomb bursts and developing fires before returning home to make their reports. Absent from debriefing was the crew of Sgt Reynolds, whose X3593 had crashed some seven miles south-east of Versailles, almost certainly after bombing, killing all on board. Despite the confidence of the crews, and an entry in the 3 Group ORB describing the raid as an undoubted success, the main factory buildings entirely escaped damage. During the course of the month the squadron operated on eighteen nights and one day, and dispatched a record 194 sorties for the loss of four Wellingtons and their crews.

May 1942

The May account opened for 115 Squadron with participation by ten of its Wellingtons in a major night of mining operations from northern Germany to the Brittany coast on the 2/3rd. A total of ninety-six aircraft from 3 and 5 Groups were involved, the 115 Squadron element taking off between 23.19 and 23.40 led by F/L Paterson. The ORBs are not specific concerning the particular "garden" to be serviced by the Marham units, but clues reveal it to be off the French coast, where the two 1,500lb mines (vegetables) each were sown from between 300 and 800 feet. Only F/Sgt Morton and crew were unable to locate their drop zone, and they jettisoned their mines "safe" into the sea. The main target for what turned out to be a modest force of eighty-one aircraft on the night of the 3/4th was Hamburg, while freshman crews attended to the docks at St-Nazaire. The original intention to send a larger force to north-western Germany had been modified in the face of a forecast of unfavourable weather conditions, and just twenty-seven 3 Group aircraft were involved. 115 Squadron was not invited to take part, but loaded a single Wellington with fourteen 250 pounders for Sgt Williams and crew to take to the Brittany coast. They took off at 00.25 and reached the target to find fair conditions that enabled them to bomb visually from 13,000 feet, observing two bursts. No other results were seen at first, but a red glow became visible when they were fifteen miles into the return journey. The Hamburg raid was remarkably effective despite the fact that only fifty-four crews reported bombing the target. More than a hundred fires were started, of which half were classed as large, and a single "cookie" destroyed eleven apartment blocks by blast.

Harris next turned his attention to southern Germany, selecting the industrial city of Stuttgart for a mini-campaign over three consecutive nights beginning on the 4th. A force of 121 aircraft was put together of which thirteen Wellingtons were provided by 115 Squadron. Eleven were loaded with nine SBCs each, and two others with a cookie, and they took off either side of 22.00 with S/L Grant the senior pilot on duty. Situated in a series of valleys, Stuttgart was rarely easy to locate, and complete cloud cover on this night would present the crews with almost insurmountable problems. The presence also of a decoy fire site at Lauffen fifteen miles to the north, which was cunningly defended by dozens of searchlights and flak guns, would attract many bomb loads and continue to do so for the remainder of the war. The aiming-point for this operation was to be the highly important Robert Bosch factory, which manufactured electrical components for the war effort, but there was little prospect of it being identified. There were no early returns among the squadron participants, which reached the target area to bomb from between 9,000 and 14,500 feet either visually or on a TR-fix. F/L Sword failed to locate the primary

W/O E Callander - Air Gnr.
He escaped from Stalag Luft VI on 5 March 1944
but was recaptured and taken to Mauthausen
concentration camp, where he was executed,
although the exact details and date are unknown.

P/O P H F W Leland RNZAF (Observer)

target, and bombed the city of Trier, situated close to the Luxembourg frontier, from 9,000 feet as an alternative. P/O George was also unable to identify the primary target, and, from 8,200 feet, attacked a last-resort alternative, described in the ORB as an unidentified built-up area. The raid scattered bombs across the city and surrounding countryside, and the only significant incident involved a cookie exploding in the northern districts of Zuffenhausen and killing twelve people. The force of seventy-

seven aircraft setting out for Stuttgart twenty-four hours later did not contain an element from 115 Squadron, which spent the night at home after a day of minimal activity involving just three training flights. The benefit of clear skies over southern Germany was lost through ground haze, and the Lauffen decoy fire site performed well to ensure that no bombs fell in the city.

Marham returned to a state of feverish activity on the 6th as both squadrons prepared aircraft for that night's third and final operation to Stuttgart. 115 Squadron loaded eleven of its Wellingtons with nine SBCs each of either 4lb or 30lb incendiaries, one with a 1,000 pounder and five 500 pounders and the last with a 4,000lb cookie. There were also to be some freshman sorties to Nantes in north-western France, with Sgt Fry and crew representing the squadron, and their aircraft was loaded with fourteen 250 pounders. They were the first to depart Marham, at 21.01, and made a visual identification of the target, which they attacked from 9,800 feet, only to watch the bombs fall short. S/L Cousens was the senior officer on duty as the main element took off between 21.41 and 22.18 to head for the south coast near Beachy Head. P/O George and crew had reached the Luxembourg/German frontier when engine failure curtailed their sortie, and the bombs were jettisoned some ten miles south-west of Trier. F/Sgt Davie and crew also experienced engine trouble shortly afterwards, and delivered their load from 13,000 feet onto

Saarbrücken as a last-resort target. Sgt Beckett and crew penetrated even deeper into Germany, but were still some fifty miles short of Stuttgart when they unloaded the contents of their bomb bay from 12,000 feet onto Karlsruhe. The remainder pressed on to the target, where, despite clear skies again, they were mostly unable to positively identify it, and bombed the general area from between 9,000 and 15,500 feet. P/O Patterson was certain that his bombs had fallen near the railway station, and a few bursts were observed, otherwise there was little useful intelligence to be imparted at debriefing. Two of the squadron's most experienced crews were absent from Marham, and it would be some time before news of their fate filtered through. X3466 contained the crew of F/L Paterson, who was a New Zealander serving in the RAF, and crashed near Laon in north-eastern France. The pilot and fellow Kiwi, P/O Leland, lost their lives, but the other three members of the crew survived to fall into enemy hands. Rear gunner, Sgt Callendar, had earned a coveted DFM while serving with 75(NZ) Squadron, and he would escape from Stalag Luft IV in January 1944, only to be recaptured and handed over to the Gestapo. He died in Dachau concentration camp two months later. F/L Sword DFC, AFC and his crew were in X3591, and, it is believed, all managed to parachute from the stricken Wellington somewhere over Germany. However, F/L Sword and his navigator, Sgt Batty, fell to their deaths, possibly through not fastening their harnesses correctly in the rush to get out. The four survivors were soon picked up by the enemy and joined their squadron colleagues in captivity. The loss of two such senior crews in one night would be keenly felt. *(The above information comes from Bill Chorley's RAF Bomber Command Losses 1942)*.

Thus far, operations to the Baltic coast had been profitable, and the next town to be targeted, on the night of the 8/9th, was Warnemünde, situated at the mouth of the Unterwarnow Estuary some eight miles north of Rostock. The Arado aircraft factory, referred to in most accounts as belonging to Heinkel, was probably the intended target for the force of 193 aircraft, which was drawn from all of the heavy groups, and contained all six types currently operating. 115 Squadron contributed thirteen Wellingtons, which took off between 21.30 and 22.21 with W/C Freeman and S/L Grant the senior pilots on duty. Three were carrying a cookie each, while the others were loaded with a 1,000 pounder and four or five 500 pounders. S/L Grant was preparing to start his bombing run when, for no obvious reason, his cookie fell out and into the sea six miles north-west of the target. The others managed to identify the target visually, and carried out their attacks from between 6,000 feet (W/C Freeman) and 13,000 feet and observed bomb bursts but no detail in the glare of searchlights. Returning crews were confident that the town and factory had received many bombs, but the operation was not successful, and cost a hefty nineteen aircraft, including four Lancasters of 44 Squadron, one of which contained the crew of the newly-appointed commanding officer, W/C Lynch-Blosse, who, it will be recalled, had served with distinction with 115 Squadron in 1940.

The squadron ORB entry for the 11th declares that "There were no operations today, and nothing of interest occurred." In fact, X3602 had taken off in the afternoon for local flying with just three occupants, all pilots, on board, and, while trying to establish their position in poor visibility, had collided with a 240 foot-high wooden radio mast and crashed at 16.00 three miles south-west of Sheringham in Norfolk. Sgts Batchen, Jones and Reynolds were all killed. There were no major operations between the 9th and the 19/20th, during which period a number of mining operations were mounted. On the night of the 17/18th, 3 Group briefed thirty-two Stirling and twenty-eight Wellington crews for gardening duties off the Frisians and Heligoland. 115 Squadron loaded ten Wellingtons with two 1,500lb mines each and another with sixteen 250 pounders to drop on the docks at Boulogne. The agricultural brigade got away first, between 22.29 and 22.40 with no senior pilots on duty, and P/O Stanford and crew were last off the ground at 22.42 for their freshman sortie to the French coast. Their Gee-box malfunctioned on the way south, which prevented them from identifying the target through seven to ten-tenths cloud, and they returned their bombs to store. The mining force found better conditions, and the 115 Squadron element located their drop zones without difficulty to deliver their vegetables from between 600 and 700 feet. A number of crews observed a combat taking place at 3,000 to 4,000 feet off the island of Pellworm a few miles to the west of the Schleswig-Holstein peninsular, and an aircraft crash at 00.45. Five Stirlings and two Wellingtons failed to return, among them 115 Squadron's X3644, and it is suggested that this was the aircraft seen falling out of control at 01.38 some one hundred miles off the west coast of Denmark. Sgt Butterworth and his four crew members lost their lives, and only one body was recovered from the west coast of Pellworm for eventual burial in Hamburg.

Preparations were put in hand on the 19th for an operation that night against Mannheim, for which eleven 115 Squadron crews were briefed. They were to be part of an overall force of 197 aircraft, and took off between 22.40 and 23.12 with the senior pilots all of pilot officer rank. As the last one faded into the night sky, Sgt Dunn and crew took off at 23.15 for their freshman sortie to St Nazaire, which they would identify visually and bomb from 11,000 feet. Those heading for southern Germany all claimed to have reached the target area, where most were able to make a visual identification and bomb from between 10,000 and 17,000 feet, observing many bursts and fires. P/O George and crew reported their bombs bursting in a built-up area, and a terrific fire developing which could be seen from a hundred miles into the return journey. This is one of many examples of crews witnessing what they believed to be a successful attack, which was, in fact, absolutely contrary to what actually occurred. The report from Mannheim mentions a long delay before the bombing began, as aircraft passed to and fro at greater altitude than normal as if searching for the aiming-point, and, then, only around ten loads found their way into the city to cause minor damage.

This unsuccessful operation preceded another lull in operations, as Harris prepared for his master stroke. At the time of the appointment of ACM Harris as C-in-C, the figure of four thousand bombers had been bandied about as the number required to wrap up the war. Whilst there was not the slightest chance of procuring them, Harris, with a dark cloud still hanging over the existence of an independent bomber force, needed to ensure that those earmarked for him were not spirited away to what he considered to be less deserving causes. The Command had not yet achieved sufficient success to silence the detractors, and the Admiralty was still calling for bomber aircraft to be diverted to the U-Boot campaign, while reverses in the Middle East also needed to be redressed. Harris was in need of a major victory, and, perhaps, a dose of symbolism to make his point, and out of this was born the Thousand Plan, Operation Millennium, the launching of a thousand aircraft in one night against a major German city, for which Hamburg had been pencilled in. Harris did not have a thousand front-line aircraft, and required the support of other Commands to make up the numbers. This was forthcoming from Coastal and Flying Training Commands, and, in the case of the former, a letter to Harris on the 22nd promised 250 aircraft. However, following an intervention from the Admiralty, the offer was withdrawn, and most of the Flying Training Command aircraft were found to be not up to the task, leaving the Millennium force well short of the magic figure. Undaunted, Harris, or more probably his able deputy, AM Sir Robert Saundby, scraped together every airframe capable of controlled flight, or something resembling it, and pulled in the screened crews from their instructional duties. He also pressed into service aircraft and crews from within the Command's own training establishment, 91 Group. Come the night, not only would the thousand mark be achieved, it would be comfortably surpassed.

Over the succeeding days, the arrival on bomber stations from Yorkshire to East Anglia of a motley collection of aircraft from a variety of training units gave rise to much speculation, but as usual, only the NAAFI staff and the local civilians knew what was afoot. The only remaining question was the weather, and, as the days ticked by inexorably towards the end of May, this was showing no signs of complying. Harris was aware of the genuine danger, that the giant force might draw attention to itself, and thereby compromise security, and the point was fast being reached when the operation would have to take place or be abandoned for the time being. Harris released some of the pressure by sanctioning operations on the night of the 29/30th, for which the Gnome & Rhone aero-engine factory was the main target. 115

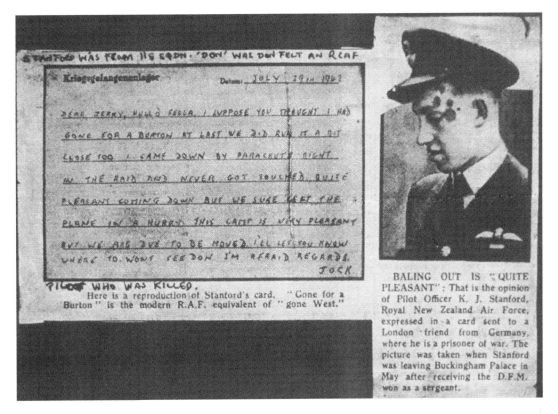

STANFORD WAS FROM 115 SQDN. 'DON' WAS DON FELT AN RCAF PILOT WHO WAS KILLED.

Here is a reproduction of Stanford's card. "Gone for a Burton" is the modern R.A.F. equivalent of "gone West."

BALING OUT IS "QUITE PLEASANT": That is the opinion of Pilot Officer K. J. Stanford, Royal New Zealand Air Force, expressed in a card sent to a London friend from Germany, where he is a prisoner of war. The picture was taken when Stanford was leaving Buckingham Palace in May after receiving the D.F.M. won as a sergeant.

A newspaper article featuring a POW postcard from P/O K J Stanford

Squadron made ready four Wellingtons for this and five for the docks at Cherbourg, and it was the freshman crews who took off first at 22.10, only for four of them to fail to locate their objective through nine to ten-tenths cloud and either jettison their bombs or bring them home. Only Sgt Edwards and crew managed to catch a glimpse of the ground, and dropped some of their bombs from 9,000 feet without observing any results. They jettisoned the rest and made it safely home with the others. The Paris-bound

element departed Marham between 00.18 and 00.23 with S/L Grant the senior pilot on duty, and all visually identified the aiming-point before bombing from between 5,500 and 7,000 feet. Drifting cloud and searchlight glare prevented an observation of results, and local reports revealed little damage to the factory, while the destruction of adjacent housing resulted in thirty-four French civilian fatalities.

It was in an atmosphere of frustration and hopeful expectation, that "morning prayers" began at Harris's High Wycombe HQ on the 30th, with all eyes turned upon the chief meteorological adviser, Magnus Spence. After careful deliberation, he was able to give a qualified assurance of clear skies over the Rhineland, while north-western Germany and Hamburg would be concealed under buckets of cloud. Thus, did the fates decree that Cologne would bear the dubious honour of hosting the first one thousand bomber raid in history. At briefings crews were told that the enormous force was to be pushed across the aiming-point in just ninety minutes. This was unprecedented and gave rise to the question of collisions as hundreds of aircraft funnelled towards the aiming-point. The answer, according to the experts, was to observe timings and flight levels, and they calculated also that just two aircraft would collide over the target. It is said, that a wag in every briefing room asked, "Do they know which two?"

Late that evening, the first of an eventual 1,047 aircraft took off to deliver the now familiar three-wave attack on the Rhineland Capital. Some of the older training hacks struggled somewhat reluctantly into the air, and were lifted more by the enthusiasm of their crews than by the power of their engines. Some of these, unable to climb to a respectable height, would fall easy prey to the defences, or would drop from the sky through mechanical breakdown. A total of 258 aircraft took off from 3 Group stations, and it was Marham that produced the group's best effort of the night, in despatching eighteen 115 Squadron Wellingtons, and nineteen Stirlings from 218 Squadron, all but two of which would complete the operation and return safely home. It took ninety minutes to launch the 115 Squadron element, with take-offs beginning at 22.50 and continuing until 00.21. S/Ls Grant and Cousens were the senior pilots on duty, and departed Marham in the first element with six other crews between 22.50 and 23.04, leaving the remainder to follow on between 23.59 and 00.21, eleven of them carrying nine SBCs of incendiaries and the others a selection of 4,000, 1,000 and 500 pounders.

There were no early returns, and, on reaching the target area, they found Spence's forecast to be accurate, the clouds parting to allow the moon to cast its light onto the magnificent city below. The 115 Squadron crews bombed from between 10,000 and 15,000 feet, and observed fires to develop, to the extent that, as the final wave departed the scene, the entire city appeared to be on fire. Despite early returns and outbound losses depleting the numbers, 868 aircraft delivered their bombs in what became the outstanding success of the war to date. Over 3,300 buildings were totally destroyed, and a further two thousand were seriously damaged, leaving 45,000 people without homes and a death toll of around 470. It was not an entirely one-sided affair, however, and, in conditions which favoured attackers and defenders alike, a new record number of forty-one aircraft failed to return. This represented 3.9% of those dispatched, which, when set against the scale of success, was acceptable and sustainable. The 115 Squadron casualty was Z1614, which was lost without trace with the crew of Sgt Edwards. During the course of the month the squadron dispatched 101 sorties on nine nights, losing five Wellingtons and their crews and three pilots while training.

June 1942

While the Thousand force was still assembled, Harris was keen to employ it again, and, after a night's rest, he ordered the old enemy, Essen, to be posted as the target for the night of the 1/2nd. The losses and necessary repairs resulting from Cologne had reduced the available force to 956 aircraft, and they would once more be led by the experienced 3 Group Wellington crews, whose first task was to dispense large numbers of flares over the target. 229 aircraft were launched from 3 Group stations, and among them were eighteen Wellingtons belonging to 115 Squadron, which took off from Marham between 22.55 and 00.13 with S/L Cousens the senior officer on duty. P/O Felt and crew reached Krefeld on the edge of the Ruhr only to suffer Gee and hydraulics failure, which forced them to jettison their bombs. Sgt McKee and crew dumped their bombs live over Rees on the German side of the Rhine north of the Ruhr, after X3351 demonstrated a reluctance to climb to operational altitude, while F/Sgt Hutchison and crew brought their bombs home after failing to identify the target or a suitable alternative. Target identification proved to be a problem for the remainder of the 115 Squadron participants also, who bombed on TR and DR-fixes from between 12,500 and 19,000 feet without ever catching a glimpse of the ground, and, like the rest of the force, scattered their bombs across the Ruhr, with just a few loads actually hitting Essen. Damage was no greater than that inflicted in the recent series by much smaller numbers, and it was clear that there would have to be major advances in technology, before this most important of industrial cities could be pinpointed. The disappointment was compounded by the loss of thirty-one aircraft, a dozen of which were from the training units, which had also lost twenty-one on Operation Millennium, and the policy of employing instructors and students on major operations would continue to bleed the Command for much of the year. Among the missing was 115 Squadron's X3721, and no trace of it or the crew of F/O Williams was ever found.

The squadron was not involved in a follow-up raid on Essen by fewer than two hundred aircraft on the night of the 2/3rd, which again almost entirely missed the mark, and then it was the turn of Bremen to host a raid twenty-four hours later. 115 Squadron prepared fifteen Wellingtons for battle as part of an

Wellington KO-P X3662 at RAF Marham, Norfolk, June 1942.After 36 raids, the aircraft was retired to serve with No 20 OTU. She was lost in a ditching off Skye on 8 October 1943; all the trainee crew were killed.

overall force of 170 aircraft. S/L Grant was the senior pilot on duty as they took off between 22.51 and 23.24 and headed for north-western Germany in good weather conditions, which would hold firm to provide a clear sight of the target city. Thirteen of the squadron's aircraft are known to have reached the target, which was identified and bombed visually in good vertical visibility from between 10,000 and 16,000 feet, and crews were able to report many bomb bursts and fires. X3749 crashed at Marham on landing and burst into flames, but not before P/O A'Court and his crew had scrambled clear, and no casualties were reported. Although crews were unsure of the outcome of the raid, local reports suggested the most destructive attack of the war to date on this important port-city. Most of the damage occurred in residential districts and the harbour, although it seems that the U-Boot construction yards and the Focke-Wulf factory escaped relatively lightly. Eleven aircraft failed to return, and it became a bad night for 115 Squadron, when two of the missing Wellingtons were found to be its own X3635 and X3724. The former contained the crew of F/O Wood, and the precise details of their demise is unknown. The fact that one gunner survived to fall into enemy hands, while the pilot is buried at Becklingen Cemetery, south-east of Bremen, and four crew members are commemorated on the Runnymede Memorial, suggests that the Wellington went down in the target area or, perhaps in the Weser or off the coast. The latter Wellington is known to have crashed into the North Sea off the Dutch Frisians with total loss of life among the crew of F/Sgt Hutchison RCAF, who was washed ashore with one other crew member to be buried on Texel.

Dixon-Wright was posted to the squadron from HQ 3 Group w.e.f. the 5th, to succeed W/C Freeman as commanding officer. He was thirty-one years old and had previously served as the commanding officer of 99 Squadron between January and December 1941, proving to be the kind of commander who led from the front. Harris's stubborn, single-minded determination would not permit him to leave Essen alone, and he decided to mount further operations against it, beginning on the night of the 5/6th, for which a force of 180 aircraft was assembled. 115 Squadron was not invited to the party, but sent the single freshman crew of Sgt Norrington to join others on a mining sortie to the Nectarines region off the Frisians. They took off at 23.24 and returned a little over three hours later to report delivering their two 1,500lb parachute mines into the briefed location from 500 feet, and observing the splash as they hit the

111

water. A force of 233 aircraft was prepared for a raid on Emden on the 6th, of which 103 were provided by 3 Group with thirteen of the Wellingtons representing 115 Squadron. They took off between 23.28 and 23.56 with S/L Grant the senior pilot on duty, accompanied by acting S/L Parkin, who was flying as second pilot. Weather conditions outbound were good and held firm in the target area, where all of the 115 Squadron participants arrived to visually identify the aiming-point and deliver their bombs from between 13,000 and 16,000 feet, aided by the flares that they and other members of the flare force had carried. Returning crews were confident of an effective operation, which was confirmed by post-raid reconnaissance, and local reports of three hundred houses destroyed and a further two hundred seriously damaged.

Mining operations on the night of the 7/8th involved forty-three aircraft including eight Wellingtons provided by 115 Squadron. They took off between 23.38 and 23.48 for unspecified garden areas with W/C Dixon-Wright the senior pilot on duty for his first operation with the squadron. The flight duration of under four hours suggests that north-western France or the Frisians/north-western Germany were the likely target areas, which all crews located without difficulty to deliver their vegetables either visually or by TR-fix from between 600 and 800 feet. The squadron sat out Harris's next attempt to unsettle Essen, which took place on the night of the 8/9th and involved 170 aircraft, which largely failed to find the target area, and scattered bombs across the Ruhr, and, in so-doing, caused only minor damage at the intended target.

A period of minor operations would occupy the ensuing eight days, and another night of mine-laying on the 9/10th was supported by eleven Wellingtons from 115 Squadron. They took off for the Nectarines garden off the Frisians between 23.28 and 23.46 with the senior pilots on duty all of pilot officer rank. They and their NCO colleagues all found their allotted drop zones by TR or DR and delivered their stores from between 500 and 800 feet before returning safely. On the night of the 11/12th ninety-one aircraft set off for further mining duties off the Frisians and in the Baltic off Swinemünde, 115 Squadron contributing six Wellingtons for the former. They departed Marham between 23.42 and 23.51, again with pilots of pilot officer rank and a single flight sergeant, and all deposited their two 1,500lb mines each into their allotted locations from between 500 and 700 feet.

Harris returned to Essen on the night of the 16/17th with a force of 106 aircraft, which once more achieved a resounding lack of success, and thus was concluded Harris's second concerted effort against this city. As was the case in the March/April campaign, the balance sheet made discouraging reading, with more than sixteen hundred sorties despatched on five raids over a sixteen-night period, resulting in no industrial damage, a very limited amount of residential destruction, and the loss of eighty-four aircraft. 115 Squadron did not take part in the Essen failure, but was called to action on the following night to participated in a small-scale attack on the docks at St-Nazaire. Five freshman crews took off either side of 22.45 and headed towards the south-west on a night of unhelpful weather conditions, which prevented all from locating the target. Four crews jettisoned part of their load of fourteen 250 pounders each, but, because of engine failure, F/Sgt Mooney jettisoned the entire contents of his bomb bay and crash-landed Z1648 at Exeter without undue damage to either Wellington or crew. Sixty-five aircraft were sent mining off Lorient and the Frisians on the night of the 18/19th, among which were four B Flight Wellingtons belonging to 115 Squadron. They took off either side of 23.50, and, according to the sortie duration of around four hours, it is believed that they were bound for the Frisians, where they delivered their stores from between 400 and 800 feet.

Having enjoyed success at Emden early in the month, further attacks on the naval port were scheduled over a five-night period beginning on the 19/20th. A force of 194 aircraft was assembled, which did not include a contribution from 115 Squadron. The operation was a failure after part of the flare force illuminated Osnabrück, situated some eighty miles south of the target, and attracted a few bomb loads.

Five high-explosive bombs and a few hundred incendiaries fell in Emden, and damage was, consequently, very slight. 185 aircraft were made ready to return twenty-four hours later, and this number included thirteen 115 Squadron Wellingtons, six of which were assigned to the flare force. They departed Marham between 23.39 and 23.58, again with no senior pilots on duty. P/O Freegard and crew returned early after problems developed with a turret, but the remainder pressed on to be among about 60% of the force to actually identify the target and deliver their bombs in conditions of seven-tenths cloud and ground haze. The 115 Squadron element attacked from between 13,000 and 15,000 feet, but few observed any results to help the intelligence section to assess the raid, and it was a local report that mentioned that about a hundred houses had been damaged. 115 Squadron made ready fourteen Wellingtons on the 22nd to contribute to an overall force of 227 aircraft for the third and final operation to Emden that night. S/L Cousens was the senior officer on duty as they took off between 23.26 and 00.08 and headed for Germany's north-western coast in good weather conditions. P/O Freegard and crew turned back with engine failure, but couldn't keep X3555 in the air and ditched safely in the North Sea some sixty miles north-east of Cromer. They all made it into the dinghy, and were picked up later in the morning of the 23rd by a Walrus seaplane. P/O Croxton and crew were coned three times over the target, and decided to seek an alternative objective, ultimately dropping their bombs from 12,000 feet onto Borkum and setting off a large fire. The others all identified the primary target and attacked it from between 11,000 and 14,000 feet before returning safely. The operation brought to an end a disappointing series in which only around fifty houses had been destroyed.

3 Group contributed to a small-scale freshman raid on the docks at St-Nazaire on the night of the 23/24th, and Sgt Fletcher and crew represented 115 Squadron, taking off at 23.28 loaded with fourteen 250 pounders. Ten-tenths cloud in the target area led to just three of the fourteen participants locating the aiming-point and releasing their bombs, while Sgt Fletcher jettisoned half of his load from 7,000 feet and brought the rest home.

The Thousand force was brought together for the third and final time on the 25th, for a raid that night on Bremen, 3 Group offering 196 aircraft for what the 3 Group ORB called Millennium 2. Ordered by Churchill to take part, Coastal Command contributed 102 aircraft, in what was classed as a separate operation, but the combined total of 1,067 departing their stations in the late evening, surpassed the number going to Cologne a month earlier. 115 Squadron made ready eighteen Wellingtons, which departed Marham between 23.25 and 23.54 with F/L Sandes the senior pilot on duty, he having arrived from 22 O.T.U at Wellesbourne Mountford on the 15th. Nine of them were carrying a mixture of high-explosive bombs and the others nine SBCs of incendiaries each, and all reached the target area to be greeted by ten-tenths cloud. The 115 Squadron crews were able to use a TR-fix to establish their position for bombing, and most released their loads from between 13,000 and 15,000 feet without being able to observe the result. P/O Slade suffered the frustration of a total hang-up and had to bring his bombs home, as did F/Sgt Loughead and Sgts Fletcher and Williams after failing to locate the target. P/O A'Court and crew attacked Wilhelmshaven from 14,000 feet as an alternative, and all but one arrived safely home. A message was received from P/O Croxton and crew in X3554 to say that they were having to ditch in the North Sea, and nothing further was heard. A search was carried out to no avail, and only one body eventually came ashore in north-western Germany for burial. Despite the numbers employed against Bremen, only moderate success was achieved, although this was far in excess of that arising out of the Essen debacle. Over 570 houses and apartment blocks were destroyed, and more than six thousand others were damaged to some extent, while a number of important war industry factories were also hit. A new record loss of forty-eight aircraft included thirty-four from the training units with instructor/pupil crews on board.

S/L Grant was posted to 3 Group HQ on the 26th at the conclusion of his tour, and his experience would, therefore, be absent from the series of follow-up raids on Bremen beginning on the night of the 27/28th and spanning the turn of the month. 3 Group provided sixty-six aircraft in an overall force of 144, and 115 Squadron contributed fourteen of the Wellingtons. They took off between 23.19 and 00.01 with F/L Sandes the senior pilot on duty, nine of them carrying all-incendiary loads, while the bomb bays of the remainder were filled with a variety of high-explosives. They all reached the target area to encounter ten-tenths cloud, with good visibility above, and relied on a TR-fix to establish their position. BJ589 was attacked by a night-fighter over the target and badly shot up, persuading F/L Sandes to jettison his load from 13,000 feet before heading home. The rear gunner was found to have been fatally wounded, and damage to the Wellington led to the collapse of the undercarriage on landing. The others delivered their bombs from between 13,000 and 17,000 feet, observing bursts and the glow of fires but no detail to report at debriefing. Local reports confirmed some useful damage, including to the Atlas Werke and Korff refinery, which had been hit during the "Thousand" raid two nights earlier.

A force of 253 aircraft was assembled on the 29th for a return to Bremen that night, for which 115 Squadron made ready thirteen Wellingtons as part of 3 Group's contribution of 124 aircraft. They departed Marham between 23.22 and 23.34, seven containing captains of pilot officer rank, and the remainder NCOs. BJ796 was outbound over the North Sea with the crew of F/O Stanford DFM, RNZAF, when engine failure curtailed their sortie, and, despite jettisoning the bomb load, the Wellington could not maintain height. It eventually came down some forty miles east of Lowestoft, and sank with the front gunner still on board. The remaining four crew members were picked up by an air-sea rescue launch and returned safely to dry land for what, sadly, would prove to be only a temporary reprieve. *(The squadron ORB records a five-man crew, while Bill Chorley, in RAF Bomber Command Losses 1942 lists six names.)* The others from the squadron arrived over the target to find ten-tenths cloud, although this diminished to around five-tenths as the raid progressed, and this allowed some crews to identify ground detail. Bombing was carried out either by TR-fix or visual reference from between 11,000 and 16,000 feet, and contributed to further damage to five war materials producers including the Focke-Wulf aircraft factory and the A.G Weser U-Boot construction yards. During the course of the month the squadron operated on fifteen nights, dispatching 153 sorties for the loss of seven Wellingtons and four complete crews.

July 1942

A new record non-1,000 force of 325 aircraft was assembled on the 2nd to continue the assault on Bremen that night, for which 3 Group contributed 118 aircraft, including fourteen 115 Squadron Wellingtons. They took off between 23.16 and 23.44 with S/L Cousens the senior officer on duty and first off the ground, and all reached the target area to find good but hazy conditions. It was noticed that many bomb loads were falling between five and ten miles short of the city's southern fringe, and many of the offending aircraft had established their position by TR-fix. Those relying on a visual reference achieved greater accuracy, but bombs were still scattered across the built-up area and the harbour. The 115 Squadron crews bombed from between 12,000 and 16,400 feet, aiming for the docks, railway installations, bridges and concentrations of buildings. On the way home X3662 was damaged by flak and a night-fighter, and the sortie ended with a crash-landing at Horsham-St-Faith, from which P/O Slade and his crew walked away. Local reports eventually confirmed damage to a thousand houses, seven ships and port installations.

Mining and minor operations occupied the following few nights until Wilhelmshaven was posted as the destination for 285 aircraft on the 8th, of which 113 were provided by 3 Group. A dozen of the Wellingtons were made ready by 115 Squadron, and they departed Marham between 23.43 and 00.10 with no senior pilots on duty. The four members of the flare-force carried twelve bundles each, along with a little high-explosive, and, in all, the squadron carried three 4,000lb cookies, six 1,000 pounders, forty 500 pounders and nine SBCs of incendiaries. They all reached the target area, where the illumination was initially scattered and sparse, and this led to many bomb loads falling into open country to the west. The 115 Squadron participants carried out their attacks from between 13,000 and 15,000 feet, and managed to hit parts of the built-up area, causing damage to housing and a variety of buildings in the town and harbour areas. This was the last major operation until mid-month, and mining and small-scale operations filled the void. 115 Squadron contributed three crews to gardening duties on the 9th, P/Os Grimston and Slade assigned to Rosemary South, off Heligoland, and Sgt Norrington to Nectarines II off the Frisians. They took off either side of midnight to deliver their vegetables into the briefed locations from between 1,800 and 3,000 feet, employing either TR of DR to fix their positions, and all returned safely from uneventful sorties.

Thirty-nine 3 Group aircraft were loaded with 1,500lb mines on the 11th to deliver to the Quinces South, Nectarines III and Rosemary gardens. 115 Squadron launched five Wellingtons to Quinces, situated in the Great Belt in the Kiel Bay area, and seven to Rosemary and Nectarines III off the Frisians, and they were on their way by 22.20 with F/L Sandes the senior pilot on duty. F/Sgt Mooney turned back with his mines after his TR equipment failed, and F/L Sandes was unable to locate his briefed drop site in the face of poor visibility off the eastern Schleswig-Holstein coast, which defeated all but four of the fifteen crews assigned to it. Two 115 Squadron crews were among the four, and those failing to establish their position either flew to the alternative garden on the Hawthorne region in the approaches to Esbjerg or brought their mines home. P/O Freegard became totally lost, and, finding himself at 1,200 feet over Wilhelshaven, dropped his pair of mines onto land from 1,200 feet, observing a blinding, white flash when they exploded north of the Bauhafen. Conditions were equally unhelpful for those closer to home off the Frisians, but they managed to deliver their stores into the assigned locations from between 600 and 3,000 feet, either by guesswork or after establishing their positions by TR-fix.

Harris decided to turn his hand against Duisburg after failing spectacularly to nail its neighbour, Essen. Located at the western end of the Ruhr Valley on the East Bank of the Rhine, and within ten miles of Essen lying further to the east, Duisburg was another industrial giant supporting the German war effort, and would prove to be equally difficult to locate and hit. Harris planned a series of raids beginning on the night of the 13/14th, for which a force of 194 aircraft was made ready that included twelve 115 Squadron Wellingtons. They took off between 00.13 and 00.40 with F/L Sandes the senior pilot on duty, four of them carrying twelve bundles of flares and six 500 pounders, while three others had nine SBCs of 30lb incendiaries on board and the remainder were loaded with either a cookie or 1,000 pounders plus 500 pounders. They all arrived in the target area to encounter six to ten-tenths cloud, which allowed some to gain a visual reference, while the majority bombed on a TR-fix from between 13,400 and 15,000 feet, observing bursts and a number of fires but little detail. X3560 was hit by flak over the target, which knocked out its starboard engine, and F/Sgt Mooney pointed the nose towards the west and dived to escape the searchlights. The Wellington shed 9,000 feet before levelling out, but could not maintain height, and the decision was taken to abandon it to its fate. All five crew members arrived safely on the ground near Eindhoven in southern Holland, and eventually fell into enemy hands. F/Sgt Mooney RCAF and his crew had enjoyed an interesting start to their operational career after joining the squadron from an O.T.U. at the start of June. Mooney had flown his first operation as a second pilot on the night of the 6/7th, when Emden was the target. Less than a week later, the wireless operator was killed, when a German bomb flattened the pub he was frequenting in King's Lynn. The eventful first tour continued with a collapsed undercarriage at Exeter on return from an intended raid on St Nazaire on the night of the 17/18th, although, in the face of poor weather conditions, Brest had been bombed instead. Trips followed to Emden and Bremen three times, including the Thousand raid, before this fateful night that saw them posted missing. This first 115 Squadron failure to return in July would prove to be the prelude to a horrendously expensive second half of the month.

115

The squadron was not involved in any further operations until the night of the 21/22nd, which would turn out to be the first of three raids on Duisburg in the space of five nights. Sixteen Wellingtons were made ready at Marham, fourteen to take part in the main operation and two to carry out gardening duties off the Frisians. The newly-promoted S/L Sandes was the senior pilot on duty as all sixteen aircraft took to the air either side of midnight as part of an overall force of 291 aircraft. They made their way eastwards in good weather conditions, and it was during the North Sea crossing that P/O Fry was forced to turn back with an overheating starboard engine. Fifteen minutes after Z1624 landed back at Marham, P/O Grimston and crew also returned early with an electrical failure in the port propeller.

The remainder pressed on to the target on this moonless night to find the favourable conditions persisting, despite which, a proportion of the flare-force, guided by Gee (TR), illuminated an area to the west of the Rhine, causing some bomb loads to be wasted on open country. Sgt Glauser had to take evasive action over Duisburg, which threw him off course, and he decided to carry on towards the east, where he dropped his bombs from 15,000 feet on Dortmund. The others bombed from between 12,500 and 14,800 feet, some identifying ground detail through the industrial haze, and the consensus on return was that a successful operation had taken place. Twelve aircraft failed to return, and 25% of these were from 115 Squadron, two of them containing crews who had recently survived a ditching in the North Sea. X3561 was outbound at 14,000 feet, and within thirty miles of the target when it fell victim to a night-fighter and crashed at 01.55 near Roermond in south-eastern Holland. Three members of the crew lost their lives, while P/O Freegard and one of his crew managed to save themselves and were taken into captivity. They were joined by P/O Stanford DFM, RNZAF and all but one of his crew, after X3726 was hit by flak at 8,000 feet, causing the flares to ignite and burn out of control. This left the crew with no option but to abandon the Wellington to its fate, and it crashed close to the target, taking with it to his death the front gunner. The navigator, Sgt Darlington, landed in the Rhine and was fortunate not to drown. X3570 came down a mile east of Eindhoven in southern Holland, and there were no survivors from the crew of Sgt Fletcher. Meanwhile, Sgt Newman and F/Sgt Boutilier had delivered their mines into the allotted locations off the Frisians from 1,000 feet, the former reporting five ships steaming south at a moderate rate. The latter's Wellington sustained unspecified damage on landing, and further excitement awaited him and his crew two nights hence.

There was another late take-off for the eleven 115 Squadron crews detailed to be part of the 215-strong force returning to Duisburg on the night of the 23/24th. S/L Cousens was the senior officer on duty as they departed Marham between 00.41 and 00.59 on a night of heavy cloud over western Germany. F/Sgt Boutilier and crew were directly over the target and preparing to bomb when a flak shell exploded beneath them and stripped all of the fabric from the lower fuselage. The bombs were jettisoned before the crew attempted to nurse the badly damaged BJ595 back across the North Sea, and, had they pointed the nose more towards the west, they would have made landfall safely over Norfolk and been able to reach Marham. In the event, they passed within sight of the coast heading in a north-westerly direction, and eventually came down in the sea some ten miles out from Grimsby, from where they were picked up within minutes by a rescue launch. S/L Cousens bombed somewhere near Essen from 14,000 feet, while the others reported bombing the target on TR or by the light of flares from between 13,500 and 15,500 feet and observing little of the results. Local reports hinted at damage to residential areas, but the operation was a failure in the light of the size of the force sent to carry it out.

Bremen was posted as the target on the 25th, with Emden as an alternative, but new orders came through later in the day to inform the stations that Duisburg was "on" again for the assembled force of 313 aircraft. 3 Group provided ninety-one Wellingtons and forty-eight Stirlings, including twelve of the former belonging to 115 Squadron, which waddled their way to the threshold loaded with a mix of high-explosives and SBCs of 4lb and 30lb incendiaries. They took to the air between 23.57 and 00.22 with

S/L Sandes the senior pilot on duty, but Sgt Glauser and crew had to turn back with an overheating engine, leaving the others to press on to the target, which they found to be concealed beneath heavy cloud. Bombing was carried out from between 14,000 and 16,000 feet on a TR-fix, but no crew had any real idea where their bombs fell. Absent from debriefing was the crew of P/O Felt, who were all killed when Z1606 was brought down to crash near Krefeld, some ten miles south-west of the target. This loss and the others thus far during the month were about to be added to on a disastrous night twenty-four hours later, when a record non-1,000 force of 403 aircraft was prepared for what, by war's end, would be shown to be an annual event, a raid on Hamburg during the final week of July.

3 Group put together a contribution of 137 aircraft of which thirty-nine were Stirlings, and fourteen of the Wellingtons were provided by 115 Squadron. They took off between 22.53 and 23.27 with W/C Dixon-Wright the senior pilot on duty, supported by S/L Sandes, but soon lost Sgt Glauser and crew to an overheating engine, and they returned to Marham two hours and forty minutes after taking off. The others encountered patches of ice-bearing cloud while outbound, and it is not clear whether it was at this stage of the operation that matters began to go awry for 115 Squadron. What is known is that nine crews definitely reached the target to find clear skies, and, bombed from between 13,000 and 16,000 feet to contribute to one of the most effective raids of the war to date on Germany's Second City. Over five hundred of the resultant eight hundred fires were deemed by the city authorities to be large, and damage was widespread, particularly in residential districts, where 823 houses were destroyed and more than five thousand damaged to some extent. On the debit side, a massive twenty-nine aircraft failed to return, and 115 Squadron posted missing four crews, among which was that of the commanding officer, W/C

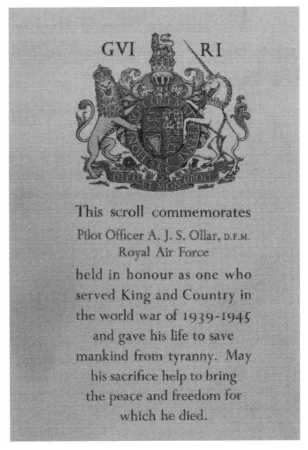

P/O A J S Ollar DFM was an Air Gunner in Wellington Mk III BJ615 KO-G piloted by W/C Dixon-Wright which was shot down and crashed into the sea near Hamburg on 26th July 1942. Five of the crew are commemorated on the Runnymede Memorial. (Ollar Collection).

Dixon-Wright DFC, who disappeared, presumably into the North Sea, in BJ615. The body of the navigator was eventually recovered for burial in Hamburg, and he was one of two members of this highly experienced crew to hold the coveted DFM. BJ670 also came down into the sea in a controlled ditching after being attacked by a night-fighter, and, although both gunners died, their bodies washing ashore later for burial on Texel and at Esbjerg, Sgt Feredey and two of his crew were picked up by the enemy to spend the rest of the war as PoWs. They were joined by Sgt Howell and Sgt Burtt-Smith and their crews, who had been forced to part company with X3412 and BJ723 respectively under undisclosed circumstances.

A return to Hansastadt Hamburg on the night of the 28/29th was intended to involve more than three hundred aircraft, of which 168 were to be provided by 3 Group. In the event, the poor weather conditions over the 1, 4 and 5 Group stations and on the proposed outward route caused their participation to be cancelled and the O.T.U element to be recalled. This effectively left 3 Group to go on alone, along with the O.T.U aircraft that failed to pick up the recall signal. 115 Squadron put up nine Wellingtons, which took off between 23.08 and 23.30 with S/L Sandes the senior pilot on duty, and headed into heavy cloud and icing, which would persist all the way to the target. Thirty-one 3 Group crews turned back, while many others were unable to locate the target and either brought their bombs home or jettisoned them. Five 115 Squadron crews were among these, leaving only P/O A'Court and crew to positively identify and attack the primary target from 13,000 feet. They observed their bombs to fall on the western edge of the city north of the Elbe and start fires, while S/L Sandes came upon Bremen and decided to unload his bombs there instead from 14,500 feet, but observed no results. 3 Group posted missing twenty-five aircraft, a shocking 15% of those dispatched, and this was in return for a scattered and only modestly damaging raid, which continued 115 Squadron's run of appalling luck. It was eventually established that Sgt Williamson RNZAF and his crew had perished in Z1605, which came down somewhere near Kiel. Z1624 was shot down by a night-fighter over Holland, and crashed into the Ijsselmeer after P/O Mason RNZAF and his crew had baled out. Reports suggest that two parachutes were seen to be on fire, and perhaps these were the ones supporting the pilot and wireless operator, who both failed to survive, while the three others soon found themselves in enemy hands.

The month's operations had not yet been concluded, and orders came through on the 29th to prepare for the first major raid of the war on the city of Saarbrücken, situated close to the French and Luxembourg frontiers. A force of 291 aircraft was assembled, of which six Wellingtons represented 115 Squadron, and they departed Marham between 23.44 and 23.57 with no senior pilots on duty. As the defences were expected to be light, crews were encouraged at briefing to bomb from lower than normal heights. All of the 115 Squadron participants reached the target to find favourable weather conditions, which enabled them to pick out ground detail, and bomb the area close to the marshalling yards from between 5,000 and 14,000 feet. Fires were observed and reported at debriefing after all aircraft, much to the relief of the station after so much recent sadness, returned safely. Local reports confirmed this as an effective attack, which caused severe damage in northern and western districts, where the majority of the 396 destroyed buildings were located.

As the month drew to a close on the 31st the station teleprinters sprang into life to churn out the day's instructions, which were to prepare for a major operation to the Ruhr city of Düsseldorf. This would be the first operation presided over by 115 Squadron's new commanding officer, W/C Cousens, who was promoted from his flight commander role to take up his appointment on the 30th. A new record non-1,000 force of 630 aircraft was made possible by the inclusion of aircraft from the training units, and this would also be the first time that a hundred Lancasters could be mustered for a single operation. 3 Group launched 133 aircraft of which ten Wellingtons represented 115 Squadron, and they departed Marham between 00.16 and 00.45 with S/L Sandes the senior pilot on duty. F/O Skelton and crew were soon back on the ground after experiencing port-engine issues, but the remainder pressed on to the target, where favourable weather conditions enabled some ground detail to be identified. Bombing took place from between 11,000 and 16,000 feet and many fires were observed, although some crews believed them to be somewhat scattered. For the second operation running there were no absentees from the 115 Squadron side of Marham, and thus was concluded a very busy and sobering month of operations. Post-raid reconnaissance revealed that a proportion of the nine hundred tons of bombs had fallen into open country, but local reports confirmed another highly destructive raid, which destroyed 453 buildings in Düsseldorf and neighbouring Neuss, and damaged to some extent, mostly lightly, some fifteen thousand others. During the course of the month the squadron operated on eleven nights and dispatched 120 sorties for the loss of twelve Wellingtons and eleven crews.

August 1942

There was a gentle start to the new month, and it was not until the 5th that an operation involving 115 Squadron was actually launched after a number of cancellations on previous days. Ten Wellingtons were loaded with two 1,500lb mines each and took off between 22.03 and 22.25 with S/L Sandes the senior pilot on duty. He was forced to turn back with generator problems, leaving the others to press on to the garden, which was not specified in the ORB. Mining operations were taking place off France, Holland and Germany on this night, and the flight time for the 115 Squadron crews of a little under five hours suggests that north-western France or north-western Germany were the likely regions. All reached their respective drop zones, where they delivered their vegetables from between 600 and 1,000 feet before returning safely.

Almost two weeks since his last crack at Duisburg, Harris decided to try once more, and issued orders on the 6th that would send 216 aircraft back there for the fifth time in three-and-a-half weeks. 3 Group's contribution of ninety aircraft included seven 115 Squadron Wellingtons, which were loaded with a total of thirty-six bundles of flares and an equal number of SBCs of 4lb incendiaries and eighteen 500 pounders, and launched from Marham between 00.44 and 01.02 with S/L Sandes the senior pilot on duty. P/O Berry and crew turned back an hour out with a turret issue, leaving the others to reach the target area, where low cloud and industrial haze made pinpointing something of a challenge. To add to the difficulties, all crews experienced problems with TR, and this led to another frustrating night of scattered bombing, much of which landed in open country to the west, and caused only minor housing damage. The 115 Squadron crews bombed visually from between 12,000 and 16,000 feet and observed bursts and fires, but could provide no detailed assessment. This night's operation brought the tally of sorties over the five raids to 1,229, from which forty-three aircraft had been lost in return for the destruction of 212 houses and a limited amount of industrial damage. Duisburg's apparently charmed life would continue until well into the following year.

In contrast, a similar number of houses would be destroyed in the garrison town of Osnabrück in just one attack on the night of the 9/10th, which 115 Squadron supported with seven Wellingtons, while four freshman crews joined in a small-scale 3 Group raid on the docks at Le Havre. The latter element got away first in a four-minute slot from 21.17, and found sufficient breaks in the cloud to deliver their bombs visually from between 7,000 and 11,000 feet, and observe bursts and fires. Meanwhile, the main section, which included no pilots above pilot officer rank, remained on the ground at Marham until a minute after midnight, when Sgt Glauser was first away to be followed over the ensuing sixteen minutes by the others. The target lay roughly due east of Marham some three hundred and twenty miles away, and, by the time the force had passed over the Ijsselmeer, TR had failed completely. Fortunately, visibility was good, but the absence of TR caused the flare force to deliver illumination over a wide area, and this led to scattered bombing across the town. The 115 Squadron crews bombed from between 7,000 and 12,000 feet, and W/O Smith and crew, who were down at 7,500 feet, were able to observe theirs bursting near the marshalling yards and saw two large warehouses surrounded by fires. Local reports confirmed that more than two hundred houses had been destroyed and four thousand others damaged to some extent. There was also damage to industrial buildings and the docks, where ten canal barges were hit.

Preparations were put in hand on the 11th for the first large-scale raid of the war on Mainz, a culturally rich city located within twenty miles of Frankfurt in south-western Germany. A force of 154 aircraft was assembled of which eight Wellingtons represented 115 Squadron, and they took off between 22.32 and 22.56 with S/L Sandes the senior pilot on duty and S/L Herd flying with him as second pilot. All reached the target to carry out their attacks in apparently good visibility and from the comparatively low altitude of 7,000 to 9,000 feet, observing many bursts and fires that encouraged them to report a highly successful operation. Local reports confirmed much damage in the city centre, with many historic buildings affected, including the castle and its museum, which were destroyed by fire. As the crews were homebound at 01.42, P/O Friend and crew departed Marham for a freshman trip to Le Havre, where a flak burst beneath the Wellington caused a sudden loss of height and persuaded them to jettison their bombs live from 2,500 feet onto the target. 130 aircraft set off to return to Mainz on the evening of the 12th, and among them were a dozen Wellingtons belonging to 115 Squadron. They departed Marham between 22.15 and 22.44 with S/L Sandes the senior pilot on duty, but P/Os Owen and Shires returned within a little over two hours, the former with a turret problem and the latter, according to the ORB, having lost its navigator. The others pressed on over ten-tenths cloud, which made target location a challenge, and delivered their bombs from between 6,000 (P/O A'Court) and 13,500 feet, observing a scattering of bursts and fires, which left them unconvinced about the effectiveness of the raid. In fact, further extensive destruction had been caused in the city centre and also in industrial areas, and the main railway station sustained substantial damage. BJ706 was crash-landed at Gooderstone by P/O Duffy, but both Wellington and crew were returned to active duty. Bomber Command assessed that 135 acres of the city had been destroyed over the two raids, but the latter one also hit two outlying communities.

A new era for Bomber Command began on the 15th, with the formation of the Pathfinder Force, although it was two days later before the four founder heavy squadrons arrived on their stations in Huntingdonshire and Cambridgeshire. 3 Group was represented by the Stirling-equipped 7 Squadron at Oakington, and it would be up to 115 Squadron and the other 3 Group squadrons of the line to provide a steady supply of crews. 35 Squadron moved into Graveley with its Halifaxes to represent 4 Group, while 83 Squadron took up residence at Wyton, the Pathfinder HQ, as the 5 Group representative operating Lancasters. 156 Squadron retained its Wellingtons for the time being at Warboys, and would draw fresh crews from 1 Group. The new force would occupy 3 Group stations, falling nominally under 3 Group administrative control and receiving its orders through the group, which was commanded by AVM Baldwin, whose tenure, which had lasted since just before the outbreak of war, was shortly to come to an end. Although opposed in principle to the idea of an elite target-finding and marking force, a view shared by the other group commanders with the exception of AVM Roddy Carr of 4 Group, Harris, once overruled by higher authority, gave it his unstinting support. His choice of the junior G/C Don Bennet as its commander was both controversial and inspired, and ruffled more than a few feathers among senior officers. Bennett, a humourless Australian, was among the most experienced aviators in the RAF, and a Master Navigator of unparalleled experience, with many thousands of hours to his credit. He also had recent and relevant experience as a bomber pilot, having commanded 4 Group's 77 and 10 Squadrons, and had recently returned home from Norway after being shot down while attacking the Tirpitz and evading capture. Despite his reserve, he would inspire in his men great affection and loyalty, along with an enormous pride in wearing the Pathfinder badge.

Harris was eager to send his new force into battle at the earliest opportunity, and had intended its debut to take place on the night of the 17/18th, when Osnabrück was the objective, but the weather conditions were not ideal, and the operation went ahead without the Pathfinders or a contribution from 115 Squadron. There was just a twenty-four hour wait before thirty-one Pathfinder aircraft joined forces with eighty-seven others representing the main force to attack the supposedly easy-to-locate port of Flensburg, situated on the Baltic coast of the Schleswig-Holstein peninsular, close to the border with Denmark. Thirteen 115 Squadron Wellingtons took off between 20.45 and 20.52 with S/L Sandes the senior pilot on duty, but the early return of P/O Murphy and Sgt Allan with engine problems and Sgt Edwards with a rear turret issue, left ten to wing their way towards landfall on Denmark's western coast. In an inauspicious beginning to what would become an illustrious career, the fledgling Pathfinder force failed to identify the target in conditions of haze, and the only bombs to fall were recorded in a number of Danish towns. The 115 Squadron crews bombed from between 7,000 and 11,500 feet, and reported observing bursts and fires, but, in truth, had no real clue as to where their bombs fell.

Ten 115 Squadron Wellingtons were loaded with two 1,500lb mines each on the 20th, and took off for an unspecified garden between 21.46 and 22.06 with S/L Sandes the senior pilot on duty. Bomber Command was planting vegetables in a number of gardens on this night from the north-western coast of France to the eastern Baltic, and the flight duration of seven to eight hours of some crews suggested that the waters off Danzig were their destination. The weather was less kind than had been forecast, and enemy opposition greater than expected, but the eight crews returning to Marham reported delivering their mines into the allocated positions from between 700 and 1,000 feet. BJ660 had clearly been to the French coast and crash-landed at Exeter after being shot up, but P/O Grimston and crew walked away, and the Wellington was eventually returned to active duty. X3989 failed to return and was lost without trace with the crew of F/Sgt Newman.

The Pathfinders returned to the fray on the night of the 24/25th with a raid on Frankfurt, for which a force of 226 aircraft was dispatched. 115 Squadron made ready a dozen Wellingtons for the main operation and three others for mining duties off the Frisians. P/O Duffy and Sgts Crimmin and Pate took off shortly before 21.00, and were heading westwards by the time that the bombers got away between 21.07 and 21.32 with F/L Moore, a recent arrival from 9 Squadron, the senior pilot on duty.

They pointed their snouts towards the south to cross the Sussex coast near Beachy Head and enter Fortress Europe via the French coast, before hugging the Belgian frontier and crossing into Germany south of Luxembourg. F/Sgt Glauser and crew failed to get that far because of an issue with the starboard engine, but managed to return their bombs to store. The others pressed on, but difficulty in identifying the target in the presence of cloud led to another inadequate performance by the Pathfinders, which led to most of the bombs falling into open country, although sufficient fell within the city to cause seventeen large fires and more than fifty smaller ones. The 115 Squadron crews attacked from between 6,000 and 13,000 feet, and were confident at debriefing to report their high explosives and incendiaries bursting on the aiming-point and across the city. The mining trio also returned safely to confirm that they had delivered their mines into the briefed locations from between 1,000 and 2,500 feet.

On the 27th the teleprinters announced the city of Kassel as the target for a force of 306 aircraft for what would be the third outing of the Pathfinders. 3 Group stations ground into action to prepare almost 130 aircraft, of which thirty-three were Pathfinders and fifteen of the Wellingtons belonged to 115 Squadron. The latter took off between 20.38 and 20.58 with S/L Sandes the senior pilot on duty, and only Sgt Pate and crew had to turn back early because of a port engine issue. The others made their way across the North Sea towards the Frisians, which threatened an attack on a Ruhr city, but continued on for a further eighty miles beyond Germany's industrial heartland to reach the city that housed a subcamp of the Dachau concentration camp, from where the three Henschel aircraft and tank manufacturing sites drew slave labour. The Pathfinder element arrived to find relatively clear conditions, which, for the first time, allowed them to identify ground detail and provide the necessary illumination for the main force crews.

Above (left) W/C A G S Cousens and (right) Sgt Harry Clay (extreme right of group). On 27/28th August 1942, W/C Cousens was captain of Wellington X3351, on an op to Nuremberg, when the aircraft was attacked by an enemy fighter. Sgt. Clay was fatally wounded.

The 115 Squadron crews bombed from the remarkably low altitude of between 5,500 and 8,500 feet, and contributed to an effective attack, which caused extensive damage, particularly in south-western districts. 144 buildings were destroyed, and all of the Henschel factories sustained severe damage, as did a number of military establishments. It was not a one-sided affair, however, and the defenders fought

back to claim thirty-one aircraft, eleven of which belonged to 3 Group main force squadrons. BJ710 was missing from its Marham dispersal on the following morning, and it was learned later that only the front gunner had survived from the crew of F/O Skelton.

115 Squadron received orders on the 28th to prepare aircraft for two targets that night, ten to join 149 others at Nuremberg and five for an experimental attack on Saarbrücken by a force of 113. The latter was to employ 4 Group Halifaxes, which had been temporarily withdrawn from operations while design faults were rectified, 5 Group Hampdens, whose operational career was about to come to an end, and less-experienced or freshman crews in Wellingtons. The 115 Squadron elements departed Marham together between 20.26 and 20.48 with W/C Cousens the senior officer on duty supported by S/L Sandes, and headed for the Sussex coast and the Channel crossing. The two forces would follow parallel routes as far as Saarbrücken under an almost full moon, and it was hoped that the Nuremberg-bound force would draw attention away from the Saarland capital and allow the bombers there to sneak in, carry out their work, and sneak back out again. The squadron participants at Saarbrücken bombed from between 8,000 and 12,000 feet, and among them was F/L Moore from the Nuremberg force, who joined in when BJ842 began to experience engine problems. Bomb bursts and fires were observed in the town area and the marshalling yards, and all of the 115 Squadron crews returned to report what appeared to be a successful operation, but was, in fact, a scattered failure that destroyed just fifteen houses.

The Nuremberg element became depleted early on after S/L Sandes was forced to jettison his load and return with a port engine problem, and his unscheduled arrival at Marham was followed some forty-five minutes later by that of P/O Shires with an airscrew issue. W/C Cousens reached the target at 11,000 feet, but was attacked by a night-fighter before he was able to bomb, and was forced to jettison all but one can of incendiaries and turn back with a fatally wounded wireless operator. P/O A'Court attacked from 10,000 feet and observed his bombs and incendiaries burst among buildings, but P/O Berry saw nothing after he released his from 12,000 feet. The latter was running perilously short of fuel as he approached base, a problem caused by a faulty propeller pitch control, and he crash-landed Z1607 at 04.38 at Barton Bendish, seven miles west-south-west of Swaffham in Norfolk. The crew walked away, but the Wellington was written off. These were the fortunate ones on a sad night for the squadron, just one month since the disaster of Hamburg had cost it four crews. Only around a third of the force had bombed in the target area, causing modest damage, and twenty-three aircraft had failed to return, a massive 14.5% of those despatched. It was a particularly sobering night for the Wellington brigade, which lost fourteen of its number, a staggering 34%, and four of them were 115 Squadron aircraft. Shortly after crossing the Belgian/German frontier X3464 was hit by flak while flying at 10,000 feet over Prüm, and had to be force-landed by P/O Duffy, who, with his crew, managed to destroy any secret equipment on board before being captured. X3647 crashed near Rethel, north-east of Reims, probably while outbound, and only the front gunner survived as a PoW from the crew of Sgt Allen. X3675 was shot down outbound by a night-fighter flown by Hptm Bietmann of II/NJG.1, and crashed at 23.03 at Grand-Hallet in Belgium, killing W/O Smith and two of his crew. The navigator and wireless operator survived, and the former, Sgt Cope, ultimately evaded capture. There were no survivors from the crew of P/O Pafford RCAF in BJ688, which fell to a night-fighter flown by Lt Ludwig Meister of NJG.4 and crashed eight miles north-east of Worms. During the course of the month the squadron operated on ten nights and dispatched 117 sorties for the loss of seven Wellingtons and six crews.

September 1942

September began with an opportunity to rectify the recent failure at Saarbrücken with another operation on the night of the 1/2nd. A force of 231 aircraft included seven 115 Squadron Wellingtons, which took off between 23.29 and 23.41 with no senior pilots on duty. Five were carrying nine SBCs of incendiaries each and two a 4,000lb cookie, and it was one of the latter that was forced to return early with the crew of P/O Owen after the rear turret became unserviceable. The remainder reached a built-up area illuminated by the Pathfinder element, and bombed it from between 8,000 and 10,000 feet before heading for home convinced that an effective raid had taken place. BJ893 failed to arrive back at Marham after crashing in France, probably after an encounter with a night-fighter on the way home, and there were no survivors from the crew of P/O Shires RCAF, which included two other Canadians. An analysis of the operation soon revealed that the Pathfinders had "posted a black", and that the object of the attack had been the non-industrial town of Saarlouis, situated thirteen miles to the north-west of its more illustrious neighbour. Much to the chagrin of the inhabitants, and those of the surrounding hamlets, the main force crews had bombed with unaccustomed accuracy, and had inflicted extensive damage and casualties. The failure to identify the correct target could have been an ill-omen for the remainder of September, but, in fact, from the following night, the Command would embark on an unprecedented series of effective operations, which would see it through to mid-month.

This encouraging phase of operations began on the night of the 2/3rd, when the southern city of Karlsruhe was the target for a force of two hundred aircraft including 4 Group Halifaxes, which had now been returned to main force operations. 115 Squadron made ready six Wellingtons for the main operation and two others for mining duties, and it was the latter which took off first at 20.20, bound for the Frisians and carrying the crews of P/O Davies and F/Sgt Lanceley. These had reached their target area before the bombing element departed Marham between 22.35 and 22.47, but Sgt Edwards was back on the ground within half an hour after experiencing engine trouble, and he was followed an hour later by Sgt Pate for

Wellington III (X3464 KO-B) was lost on a mission to Nuremberg on 29th August 1942. Pilot P/O J H Duffy managed a near perfect crash landing so that all the crew survived and became POWs (Aircrew Remembered).

a similar reason. By this time the gardening duo had returned home safely to report delivering their vegetables into the allotted locations from 2,500 feet by means of a TR-fix. Sgt Crimmin and crew became the third early return on a night of poor serviceability for the squadron, and a faulty compass was the cause of their curtailed sortie. This left just Sgts Keith and Boaden and P/O Owen to reach and bomb the target from 11,000 feet and return to report extensive fires spreading across the built-up area. Photographic reconnaissance confirmed the effectiveness of the raid, revealing much housing and some industrial damage.

Bremen was posted as the target on the 4th, for which a force of 251 aircraft was made ready, among them a dozen Wellingtons representing 115 Squadron. Pathfinder tactics were constantly evolving, and this night would bring the introduction of the three-phase system of illumination, visual marking and backing-up, which would become standard practice for the remainder of the war. The 115 Squadron element took off between 23.59 and 00.30 with F/L Moore the senior pilot on duty, nine of the Wellingtons carrying nine SBCs of incendiaries and three a cookie each. There were no early returns, and it is believed that all reached the target area to deliver their bombs from between 10,800 and 14,000 feet into the built-up area, where some ground detail could be identified. Many bomb bursts were observed and fires were seen to be spreading across the city, confirming the attack in the minds of the crews as successful. Photo-reconnaissance and local reports revealed that 480 buildings, mostly houses, had been destroyed and almost fourteen hundred others seriously damaged, including some important war industry factories. The differing fortunes of war were evident from the fate of the two crews missing from 115 Squadron's ranks. P/O Davies and his crew were all killed, when BJ663 was shot down by the night-fighter of Oblt Herbert Lütje of III/NJG.1 while homebound near Rheine, but Sgt Keith and his crew all survived the demise of BJ771, and were taken into captivity.

Perhaps encouraged by these successes, Harris called for another shot at Duisburg, and a force of 207 aircraft was made ready on the 6th. 115 Squadron bombed-up eight Wellingtons, and loaded another with two 1,500lb mines, and it was the latter, Sgt Barker and crew, who departed Marham first at 20.14 bound for the shipping lanes off north-western Germany. They delivered their mines into the allotted location from 2,800 feet and returned home as the bombing brigade was taking off between 00.59 and 01.22 with F/L Moore the senior pilot on duty. There were no early returns among the 115 Squadron element, and they bombed the target from between 12,000 and 15,000 feet to contribute to the destruction of more than a hundred buildings, and, whilst this was a modest haul, it still represented something of a victory at this notoriously elusive target. BJ724 was homebound over Norfolk when it exploded in the air, possibly through the ignition of the photo-flash, and crashed six miles east of Norwich, killing three members of the crew and seriously injuring Sgt Lanceley, who would succumb two days later. The rear gunner was the sole member of the RAF on board and survived with injuries from which he would recover, while all four fatalities were members of the RCAF.

The night of the 7/8th was devoted to minor operations, and just three 115 Squadron Wellingtons took to the air either side of 20.00 on gardening sorties. Weather conditions were poor, leading to the recall of a small force sent to bomb the Heinkel works at Warnemünde, and the signal was picked up by P/O Friend and crew, who responded in error and came home early. Sgts Barker and Crimmin and their crews continued on, it is believed to the Biscay coast, and delivered their mines into the allocated locations from 2,500 feet. Frankfurt was the target selected for the night of the 8/9th, for which a force of 249 aircraft was assembled. 115 Squadron contributed eight Wellingtons, which took off between 20.34 and 20.54 with S/Ls Sandes and Parsons the senior pilots on duty, the latter having arrived on the 1st from 20 O.T.U to fill the vacant flight commander post created by the promotion of W/C Cousens. F/Sgt Edwards and Sgt Pate returned early with a turret and engine issue respectively, leaving the others to press on to the target, where the twenty-nine Pathfinders were unable to locate the aiming-point, and scattered illumination across the general area and over Rüsselsheim situated fifteen miles to the south-west. The 115 Squadron participants delivered their payloads from between 11,000 and 14,000 feet in conditions which enabled some of them to make out ground detail, and they reported bomb bursts and fires in the built-up area. This operation brought the recent run of successes to a temporary halt.

Training aircraft from 91, 92 and 93 Groups were drafted in on the 10th to add weight and numbers for an attack on Düsseldorf that night. A force of 479 aircraft included a contribution from 3 Group of sixty-six Wellingtons and Stirlings for the main force and thirty-nine Pathfinders, the latter employing for the first time rudimentary target markers called "Pink Pansies" in converted 4,000lb bomb casings. 115 Squadron launched ten Wellingtons between 21.09 and 21.35 with S/L Sandes the senior pilot on duty, and they all reached the target to bomb from between 11,500 and 13,000 feet and share in the destruction of over nine hundred houses in Düsseldorf and neighbouring Neuss. Dozens of war industry factories were also damaged sufficiently to lose production for varying periods, and this was the most successful raid since the Thousand effort against Cologne at the end of May, albeit at the high cost of thirty-three aircraft, sixteen of which were from training units. The training units were called upon again to bolster an operation to Bremen, for which preparations were put in hand on the 13th to assemble a force of 446 aircraft. 115 Squadron made ready eight Wellingtons, which took off between 00.33 and 00.48 with S/Ls Sandes and Parsons the senior pilots on duty. There were no early returns, and the city was located without difficulty, but haze prevented most crews from identifying ground detail. The 115 Squadron crews bombed from between 12,000 and 14,500 feet, before returning to report numerous fires burning across the city, and the success of the operation was confirmed by local reports, which mentioned 848 houses destroyed, the Lloyd dynamo factory out of action for two weeks and various sections of the Focke-Wulf works losing production for up to eight days. This surpassed the performance of the Thousand force in late June, and was achieved at a cost of twenty-one aircraft, fifteen of which belonged to training units.

A force of 202 aircraft made ready for a raid on Wilhelmshaven on the 14th included the last Hampdens to operate in Bomber Command front-line service. 115 Squadron dispatched eight Wellingtons either side of 20.00 with S/Ls Sandes and Parsons the senior pilots on duty. A comment in the 3 Group ORB suggests that P/O Boaden and crew had signalled that they were returning early, but nothing more was heard, and the recovery later in the year of three bodies, two on the Danish coast and one on German territory, leads to the conclusion that BJ693 had gone down in the sea. The others reached the target area, where accurate Pathfinder marking preceded the most destructive attack yet on this important naval port. The 115 Squadron crews bombed from between 11,500 and 14,700 feet, and, on return, reported many scattered fires and a number close to the aiming-point. 1 and 3 Groups joined forces to send forty aircraft mining on the night of the 15/16th, for which 115 Squadron contributed five Wellingtons, taking off a few minutes before 20.00 with P/Os Friend and Owen the senior pilots on duty. X3924 suffered engine trouble immediately after take-off, and P/O Friend jettisoned the pair of mines close to the airfield before landing safely. The others pushed on to the Frisians, where they delivered their stores into the allocated locations from between 1,800 and 2,800 feet. Among pilots arriving on posting from 25 O.T.U at this time was P/O Ian Willoughby Bazalgette, who had been born in Canada of English/Irish parents, and had served in the Army until transferring to the RAFVR in 1941. He would enjoy a successful career, which would end with an untimely death and the posthumous award of the Victoria Cross.

This was clearly the moment for Harris to strike again at the old enemy, Essen, and the assembly of a large force of 369 aircraft on the 16th reflected his intent. 115 Squadron bombed up eleven Wellingtons and launched them into the air between 20.16 and 20.35 with S/Ls Sandes and Parsons the senior pilots on duty. P/O Berry returned with his bombs after wireless failure curtailed his sortie, and Sgt Barker and crew landed only minutes later with an empty bomb bay after surviving an encounter with a night-fighter. The others reached the target and delivered their bombs from between 9,500 and 18,000 feet,

Sqn Ldr Ian Bazalgette VC   *Group Captain Blanchard Sims*

contributing to a scattered but effective raid, which started many fires, including thirty-three large ones and eighty classed as medium. The Krupp works was hit by fifteen high-explosive bombs and a crashing bomber, but it was housing that sustained the most damage. As usual at this target, bombing was scattered liberally around the region, and the Ruhr continued to be a dangerous place to be as the defenders fought back to claim a massive thirty-nine bombers, nineteen of them from the training units, and this represented the heaviest loss to date from a non-1,000 raid. Never the less, it had been an outstanding two weeks for the Command, and it can be no coincidence that it came at a time when the Pathfinder crews were emerging from their uncertain start, and were beginning to come to terms with the requirements of their complex and demanding role. There would be no overnight transformation from this point, and failures would continue to outnumber success for some considerable time, but the encouraging signs were there, and that boded ill for Germany in the years ahead.

A wide-ranging mining effort by 115 aircraft took place on the night of the 18/19th, covering gardens from Lorient in north-western France to Danzig on Germany's north-eastern coast. 3 Group contributed twenty Stirlings and seven Wellingtons, two of the latter representing 115 Squadron. P/O Owen and S/L Parsons and their crews took off at 19.41, and, once airborne, it is believed that they set course for the eastern Baltic. A message was received at some point from the squadron's X3718 to notify base that an engine had failed, and then the W/T key was clamped down to send a continuous signal to rescuers. Sadly, no trace of the Wellington and the crew of P/O Owen was found, and the conclusion has to be that they were claimed by the North Sea. S/L Parsons and crew located their drop zone after making a timed run from visually identified pinpoints, and delivered their mines from 500 feet before returning safely after more than seven hours aloft.

Saarbrücken and Munich were posted as the targets for the night of the 19/20th, and 3 Group supported both, sending a Stirling element to the latter and Wellingtons of 75(NZ), 101 and 115 Squadrons and Stirlings of 218 Squadron to the former. The five Marham Wellingtons took off between 20.09 and 20.20

all captained by sergeant pilots, and each carrying nine SBCs of 4lb incendiaries. Sgt Pate and crew returned after two-and-a-half hours with most of their load still on board, and reported an encounter with a night-fighter, which had delayed them sufficiently to prevent them from reaching the target in time. The others pressed on to the target, where ground haze hampered the Pathfinders in their attempt to mark the aiming-point, and bombs were scattered to the west of the town. The 115 Squadron crews bombed from between 6,000 and 12,000 feet, and it was not possible to accurately assess the results of their efforts. Sgt Pate reported fires about four miles to the west of the town, while Sgt Gill could only say that fires were observed in the target area. Local reports confirmed that the operation was a failure and that only thirteen houses had been destroyed.

A return to gardening duties on the night of the 21/22nd involved seven 115 Squadron Wellingtons, which departed Marham for the western Baltic between 19.29 and 19.43 with S/Ls Sandes and Parsons the senior pilots on duty. Sgt Gill and crew experienced an eventful night, which included intercom failure and the temporary loss of both engines at 2,000 feet in an electrical storm, and their return to working order at 1,000 feet, by which time the mines had been jettisoned and the sortie abandoned. S/L Sandes delivered one mine from 900 feet, but the other one hung up until dropping out five miles north of the aiming-point. Sgt Crimmin and crew lost their intercom, and decided to find an alternative location for their stores, ultimately dropping them between the island of Terschelling and the Dutch mainland from 1,000 feet. S/L Parsons delivered his mines into the allotted location from 500 feet, as did Sgt Marker and crew from 750 feet. Sgt McCrea and crew were also successful from 500 feet, but X3924 was hit by flak which knocked out the front turret and wounded the occupant. The Wellington crash-landed on return to Marham, but there were no further casualties and the aircraft was ultimately returned to service. BJ962 failed to return, and no clue to the fate of Sgt Evans and his crew has ever been found.

Jack Williamson, his crew and VIPs

128

On the 24th, the squadron concluded its long association with Marham, and took up residence at Mildenhall, where it would share the facilities with 75(NZ) Squadron, but remain only briefly. The first operation to be launched from the squadron's new home was a gardening effort involving ten Wellingtons as part of an overall force of fifty-two Wellingtons and nineteen Stirlings. Two gardens were allotted, around the Frisians and off Denmark, and four crews took off for the former between 19.12 and 19.17, while six others remained on the ground until 21.02, when S/L Parsons led them away with S/L Sandes bringing up the rear. This section was recalled, and S/L Parsons and Sgt McCrea jettisoned their mines live into the North Sea some fifty miles north of the Dutch mainland and 120 miles west of the Danish coast. The Frisians section delivered their mines as briefed from between 650 and 800 feet before returning safely to make their reports. The madness of "moling" cost the squadron an experienced crew on the afternoon of the 28th, when Mildenhall was ordered to provide six Wellingtons, three from each resident squadron, to attack the Dortmund-Ems Canal at Lingen in the Münsterland region of north-western Germany. S/Ls Sandes and Parsons and Sgt Crimmin took off shortly after 13.30, hoping to sneak over the enemy coast under cover of cloud to drop their nine 500 pounders each. Five aircraft turned back on finding insufficient cloud, but S/L Parsons and crew pressed on to carry out an attack on shipping, which failed to find the mark. On the way home over Holland the Wellington was attacked from the beam by a FW190 flown by Uffz Kurt Knespel of 10/JG.1. The wireless operator was killed in the engagement and the navigator was last seen with an extinguisher fighting the fire raging in the fuselage. Z1663 crashed into the Ijsselmeer at 18.02 after the two gunners, both members of the RCAF, had parachuted to safety, but also into the hands of the enemy.

The final operation of the month involved six 115 Squadron aircraft joining others to mine the waters off the Frisians. They took off either side of 19.30 with three pilots of pilot officer rank and three sergeants, and all reached the target area to deliver their mines by TR-fix from between 600 and 1,500

Some of the men who bombed Germany (Ollar Collection)

129

Some of the crew of Wellington Mk III - X3675 KO-D. Above: (left) Service photo of Sgt Jack Edward Cope DFM; (right) Photo from the Belgian State Security Archive file, taken at Antwerp by the Belgian escape line Comet for his fake documentation. Left: Sgt WJ Sharpe (Front Gunner).

The aircraft took off from Marham at 20.30 and was shot down by a night fighter on 28/29 August 1942 after a raid on Nuremberg and crashed near Luik, Belgium. Pilot W/O J G Smith, along with air gunners Sgt W Sharpe and Sgt L. Carr, lost their lives. Sgt. Cope parachuted safely and was eventually picked up by the Comet Line. He stayed in various safe houses before making his way by train to the south of France where he is guided by several across the Pyrenees to Spain. On the 24th September they were allowed to go to Madrid and then Gibraltar, from where they returned to the UK.

feet. During the course of the month the squadron undertook operations on sixteen nights and one day, and dispatched 122 sorties for the loss of eight Wellingtons and crews.

October 1942

The Ruhr city of Krefeld was posted as the first target for the new month, and a force of 188 aircraft was assembled, among which were thirteen 115 Squadron Wellingtons. Ten were loaded with nine SBCs of incendiaries and three with a cookie, while three others had two 1,500lb parachute mines winched into their bomb bays for delivery to the waters around the Frisians. The bombers took off first between 18.45 and 18.57 with S/L Sandes the senior pilot on duty, and the miners followed in their wake at 19.00, however, the Ruhr-bound Sgt Baldwin and crew were back on the ground within ninety minutes with an unserviceable rear turret. Sgt McCrea and crew must have been close to the target when evasive action became necessary and the bombs were jettisoned live. Severely hit by flak, BJ833 was down to 100 feet by the time it reached home airspace, but Sgt McCrea carried out a successful belly-landing at Mildenhall without crew casualties. The others were able to locate the general area of Krefeld to deliver their bombs from between 8,000 and 10,500 feet in poor visibility that prevented any observation of results. Numerous scattered fires gave hope of a successful operation, but a local report stated that just three streets in the north of the city had sustained damage. 115 Squadron registered its first loss of the month, when BK271 failed to return, and there was total loss of life among the crew of Sgt Adsett RCAF, three of whom were members of the RNZAF. The three gardeners returned home safely to report fulfilling their briefs from between 700 and 900 feet.

The city of Aachen is Germany's most westerly city and perches on the border with Holland to the north-west and Belgium to the south-west some thirty-eight miles south-west of Cologne. It was a major railway hub with two marshalling yards, and these may have been the aiming-points for the attack for which a force of 257 aircraft was made ready on the 5th. 115 Squadron loaded six Wellingtons with nine SBCs of 4lb incendiaries, a further six with nine SBCs of 30lb incendiaries and a singleton with a 4,000lb cookie. They took off between 19.10 and 19.25 with S/L Sandes the senior pilot on duty, and headed out in poor weather conditions which would persist throughout the operation. Sgt McCrea and crew returned early to Mildenhall with an electrical issue, and Sgt Pate and crew were also forced to abandon their sortie after experiencing a problem with an engine and propeller, and they crash-landed X3393 at Wattisham. The Pathfinders were unable to positively locate the target, and marking was spread over a wide area. The 115 Squadron crews dropped their hardware from between 6,000 and 11,000 feet, and, on return, reported many fires in various parts of the built-up area and expressed confidence that the operation had been effective. Sgt Baldwin and crew specified the southern outskirts of the city as the recipient of their incendiaries, and described fires in the centre. They arrived home with empty petrol tanks and successfully belly-landed BK272. Local reports suggested an attack by no more than ten aircraft, and confirmed five large fires among a total of thirty-four, a moderate amount of housing damage, and listed twenty-two industrial buildings as being hit.

The garrison town of Osnabrück was posted as the target on the 6th, and a force of 237 aircraft made ready. 115 Squadron contributed a dozen Wellingtons, led as usual by S/L Sandes, and they departed Mildenhall between 19.01 and 19.50 before setting course for the North Sea. Sgt Barker and crew returned early with a port engine problem, leaving the others to press on to north-western Germany which lay under broken cloud and haze. The Pathfinders illuminated the Dümmer See, a large lake some eighteen miles north-east of the target, and this enabled the main force crews to use it as a pinpoint for the run-in. P/O Wallace experienced problems with the bomb doors, and had to jettison six SBCs of incendiaries over the target and bring the rest home. The other 115 Squadron crews attacked from between 9,000 and 12,000 feet, and all reported fires taking hold in the built-up area, Sgt Crimmin and crew claiming that the glow was perceptible from the Dutch coast on the way home. BJ879 was carrying the single cookie, which was seen to burst among existing fires, but the Wellington was attacked by a night-fighter while homebound, and the rear end damaged. Sgt Pate landed at Oulton, where the rear gunner was found to be dead. Local reports confirmed that 149 houses and six industrial premises had been reduced to rubble, and that more than five hundred houses had sustained serious damage. Six aircraft failed to return, and among them was the squadron's BK313, which crashed in Germany with fatal results for the crew of F/O Smith RCAF.

S/L Wright arrived on posting from 23 O.T.U on the 7th to succeed the missing S/L Parsons as flight commander, but his time with the squadron would be all too brief. Mining operations dominated the following week, and fifty-seven aircraft were dispatched on the night of the 8/9th to sow vegetables in the coastal waters from north-western France to the Frisians. 115 Squadron dispatched five Wellingtons between 18.13 and 21.46, and the flight times of P/O Wallace and Sgt Ross, who took off first, point to St-Nazaire as their destination. They delivered their stores into the briefed locations from 2,000 and 700 feet respectively employing TR and DR-fixes to establish their positions. P/O Bazalgette and Sgts Baldwin and Gordon departed Mildenhall at 21.45, and the very short duration of their flights suggest that Ostend was their target area, where they delivered their mines into the briefed locations from 800 to 900 feet. Twenty-four hours later Mildenhall was the only station to operate, and sent seven Wellingtons each from 115 and 75(NZ) Squadrons to mine the waters around the Frisians. The 115 Squadron element got away either side of 18.30 and located their drop zones either visually or by TR/DR-fix, before dropping their mines from between 800 and 900 feet. Forty-seven aircraft were made ready on the 10th to continue the mining programme, and this time 115 Squadron dispatched ten Wellingtons between 18.15 and 18.45 with S/L Sandes the senior pilot on duty. The destination for the five most experienced crews was the Biscay coast, while the others headed for the Frisians, and all carried out their briefs by visual or TR/DR-fix from between 600 and 900 feet before returning safely. After a night's rest the squadron prepared ten Wellingtons for the next round of mining operations on the night of the 12/13th, and they took off either side of 18.00 with F/L Moore the senior pilot on duty. The ORBs provide no clue as to the gardens involved, but it is believed that the Hawthorne area, the southern approaches to Esbjerg, may have been the destination. All reached the drop zone and delivered their mines by visual or TR/DR-fix from between 500 and 900 feet.

The naval port of Kiel provided an opportunity to return to bombing operations on the night of the 13/14th for which a force of 288 aircraft included fourteen Wellingtons representing 115 Squadron. W/C Cousens was the senior officer on duty, backed up by S/L Sandes and F/Ls Moore and Fox, the last-mentioned having arrived on posting from 12 O.T.U on the 10th. They took off between 18.15 and 18.34, ten of them carrying nine SBCs of 4lb incendiaries, three with a single 1,000 pounder, six 500 pounders and two 250 pounders on board and one with a 4,000lb cookie. S/L Sandes was back on the ground within twenty minutes after experiencing engine trouble, but the remainder all reached the target area, where a decoy fire site was operating that would lure away half of the bomb loads. The 115 Squadron participants carried out their attacks from between 9,000 and 14,000 feet in good weather conditions and observed many large and concentrated fires along with others that were scattered. They also claimed that the glow from the burning town was visible from a hundred miles into the return journey. Local reports detailed a moderate amount of damage within the town, particularly in south-eastern suburbs, but half of the bomb loads found open country or other built-up areas as far away as Hamburg.

Preparations were put in hand on the 15th to make ready a force of 289 aircraft for an attack on Cologne that night, for which 115 Squadron was to contribute fifteen Wellingtons. They departed Mildenhall between 18.45 and 19.25 with S/L Sandes the senior pilot on duty, two of them carrying a cookie each and the others nine SBCs of 4lb incendiaries. The winds proved to be not as forecast, and this led to sparse Pathfinder marking, which failed to attract the main force away from another large decoy fire site, where most unloaded their bomb bays. The 115 Squadron crews dropped their loads from between 7,000 and 13,500 feet, believing them to have hit the target, where one large and numerous scattered fires were reported. The local authorities reported that just one of the seventy-one cookies dropped had fallen within the city, and only two houses were classed as seriously damaged. The failure cost the Command eighteen aircraft, but none from 115 Squadron, although there were some injuries in Sgt Gill's crew, who landed at Wattisham short of fuel. On the following night, thirty-four Wellingtons and Stirlings were made ready for gardening duties around the Biscay ports, eleven of the former provided by 115 Squadron. This night would allow S/L Wright the opportunity for a relatively gentle introduction to operations with the squadron nine days after his arrival, and he took off with the others between 18.00 and 19.15 before setting course towards the south-west. Each carried two 1,500lb parachute mines, and six had also been loaded with three 500 pounders for use against targets of opportunity. They found their allotted drop zones by means of a TR/DR-fix and made timed-runs from identified pinpoints to deliver their stores from between 700 and 800 feet. Sgt McCrea and crew attempted to bomb a river bridge near Nantes from 8,000 feet, but observed no results, while P/O Larkins dropped his 500 pounders on a searchlight concentration at St-Aubin-sur-Mer from 7,000 feet, and watched the beams become extinguished. Both missing Wellingtons belonged to 115 Squadron, BK312 containing the crew of flight commander S/L Wright, and X3946 with the crew of Sgt Gordon on board. Both are presumed to have gone down into the sea without survivors, Bill Chorley recording that four of S/L Wright's crew are buried in Sage war cemetery, which suggests that they were operating in northern waters, although this is purely speculation.

S/L Chilton arrived on posting from 20 O.T.U on the 20th to step into the shoes of S/L Sandes, who was posted to 20 O.T.U on the same day at the conclusion of his outstanding tour as a flight commander. This still left a vacancy for a flight commander after the loss of S/L Wright. The foolhardiness of daylight moling operations was brought home on the 22nd, when eight 115 Squadron Wellingtons were dispatched between 12.20 and 12.45, some to attack the town of Lingen and some the heavily defended Ruhr city of Essen. F/L Fox was the senior pilot on duty, and he had with him as second pilot W/C Sisley, an Australian who had joined the RAF in the mid-thirties and was currently on the staff of 3 Group HQ. He would eventually succeed W/C Cousens as commanding officer of 115 Squadron. They were close to Lingen when attacked by a fighter and badly shot-up, compelling them to jettison their bombs, and they were fortunate to be able to scuttle away and reach home safely. F/Sgt Crimmin and crew reached Lingen to attack the railway station from 400 feet, and observed it to be enveloped in smoke and debris. Sgt Baldwin and crew also arrived on the scene at the same height and bombed an engine shed, causing a corner of it to collapse. Both crews then machine-gunned trains before retreating towards the west and arriving home without incident. Sgt Pudsey and crew bombed Essen through cloud from 2,500 feet, and bursts were heard but not seen. The others either returned early through technical issues or abandoned their sorties in the face of insufficient cloud cover.

A new campaign was opened by 5 Group that night against Italian cities in support of Operation Torch, the Allied landings in North Africa, which would ultimately lead to Montgomery's victory over Rommel at El Alamein. Genoa was the target for this and a second attack twenty-four hours later, when 3 and 4 Groups intended to build on 5 Group's success. 115 Squadron made ready ten Wellingtons, which departed Mildenhall between 18.10 and 18.40 with F/L Fox the senior pilot on duty and accompanied again by W/C Sisley. Sgt Tuma and crew were forced to return early with wireless failure, and they brought their incendiaries home. Having crossed the Alps F/Sgt Hickman found that ice had built up on his wings, and he decided to bomb Turin as an alternative, which he did from 15,000 feet and watched his payload burst and set off fires in the city centre. The others attacked the primary target from between 5,000 and 15,000 feet, although the lower altitude may be a typing error. It belonged to Sgt Crimmin and crew, who reported hitting a built-up area north-west of the docks. F/L Fox crash-landed X3351 on return to base, but both Wellington and crew were returned to active duty. Z1574 came home to

Mildenhall in the hands of Sgt Pudsey and his crew displaying the scars of battle, and, after an inspection, was deemed to be beyond economical repair. Crews were enthusiastic as to the outcome of the operation, until it became clear that the cloudy conditions had led to the bombing of the coastal town of Savona situated some thirty miles west of Genoa.

5 Group turned its attention successfully upon Milan by daylight on the 24th, to be followed that night by elements of 1 and 3 Groups. 115 Squadron made ready six Wellingtons as part of an overall force of seventy-one aircraft, and they took off either side of 19.00 with W/C Cousens the senior officer on duty. Between 19.40 and 23.15 five aircraft returned with technical failures, leaving just one unaccounted for. This was BK306, which crashed into the sea off the Dutch coast, and took with it to their deaths the crew of Sgt Oldridge RNZAF, which contained two other Kiwis. The conclusion must be that they were homebound at the time, and seriously off course, possibly also having exhausted their reserves of fuel. It transpired that only half of the force had reached the target to find ten-tenths cloud, and little further damage was achieved for the loss of six aircraft. Only 3 Group operated on the night of the 26/27th, sending Wellingtons and Stirlings from Mildenhall and Downham Market to mine the waters off the Biscay coast and the Frisians. 115 Squadron made ready eight Wellingtons, and, according to the squadron ORB, dispatched the first, captained by W/C Sisley, at 21.15. His landing time, more than eleven hours later, shows the entry to be an error, and his actual departure time must have been between 02.45 and 03.05. The ORB does not specify the gardens involved, but all eight crews arrived home safely between 06.40 and 08.30 to report delivering their stores into the briefed locations from between 300 (W/C Sisley) and 900 feet.

A moling operation on the 29th finally demonstrated the insanity of the policy of sending inadequately armed, slow-moving bombers in broad daylight to the Ruhr with only cloud to protect them. 115 Squadron was ordered to provide six Wellingtons to attack Essen or alternative targets of opportunity, and they were dispatched between 13.49 and 14.00 carrying between them two 4,000lb cookies and thirty-six 500 pounders. P/Os Bazalgette and Wallace returned early because of icing and lack of cloud cover, and jettisoned their loads. Sgt McCrea stopped short of the Ruhr and attacked Wesel from 13,000 feet before turning for home and landing at 17.40 to make his report. The wait for the remaining three to come home continued until it became clear that they could no longer be airborne. Z1738 and BJ660 disappeared without trace, presumably into the sea, with the crews of F/O Rawlings and Sgt Barker respectively, and the recovery of the body of F/Sgt Urwin RNZAF at Flushing (Vlissingen) on the island of Walcheren shows that X3540 also crashed into the sea without survivors. What was achieved by sacrificing these crews to a highly dangerous daylight operation is hard to fathom. The final operation of the month involved nine 115 Squadron Wellingtons joining others to deliver mines to the shipping lanes serving the Biscay ports. W/C Sisley was the senior pilot on duty as they took off between 17.10 and 17.25, and all reached and identified their allotted gardens by means of DR-fix or visual reference to release their stores from between 800 and 1,000 feet. During the course of the month the squadron operated on fourteen nights and two days, and dispatched 157 sorties for the loss of nine Wellingtons and eight crews.

November 1942

The first week of November brought little activity for the Wellington squadrons of 3 Group. F/L Barrett arrived at 115 Squadron on posting from 1483 Target Towing and Gunnery Flight on the 3rd to compensate for the imminent departure of F/L Moore on the 8th, the day on which 115 Squadron would move to East Wretham after its brief period of residence at Mildenhall. It was back to work on the 3rd, when eleven of the squadron's Wellingtons were loaded with two 1,500lb mines each for delivery to waters off the Biscay ports. They took off between 17.15 and 17.30 with no senior pilots on duty, but

P/O Farquharson and crew were back on the ground within an hour and twenty minutes after a navigational error compromised their timing. Sgt Pudsey and crew joined them an hour later with a malfunctioning starboard engine, leaving the rest to push on to their respective gardens, where they dropped their stores from between 500 and 900 feet by visual reference or TR-fix. The squadron detailed ten crews for further mining duties on the 6th, and they were led away by W/C Sisley at 17.00 bound for the western coast of France. This time there were no early returns, and all delivered their mines according to brief in good weather conditions from between 600 and 1,000 feet before returning safely from what was their final operation from Mildenhall.

The move to East Wretham, located some fifteen miles to the north-east of Mildenhall with the town of Thetford between them, began on the 8th. It had been an operational station since 1940, boasting permanent buildings and facilities, and its association with bombers had begun in July 1940 as a satellite and dispersal site for 311 (Czech) Squadron based at Honington. A change of address rarely interfered with operations, but 115 Squadron was not invited to participate in a major raid on Hamburg on the night of the 9/10th, which was hampered by heavy cloud and icing conditions and resulted in a scattered and relatively ineffective attack. The abundance of four-engine types with their greater bomb-carrying capacity was beginning to see Wellingtons excluded from some of the larger operations, and they were increasingly put to work on mining. The first operation launched from its new home involved six 115 Squadron Wellingtons taking off from 17.00 bound for north-western France with S/L Chilton the senior pilot on duty for the first time. All reached the target area to deliver their mines visually or by DR-fix from between 600 and 900 feet, before returning safely home by shortly after midnight. Seven of the more junior 115 Squadron crews returned to French waters on the night of the 16/17th to continue the important and effective mining campaign. They departed East Wretham either side of 17.00, and six of them returned between 23.02 and 00.30, five to report dropping their mines as briefed from 500 to 900 feet, while P/O Thomas brought his back after encountering poor visibility. Sgt Gill and crew, whose garden had been off Bayonne, deep in south-western France, were absent from debriefing, and the washing up on the French coast later of four bodies confirmed that X3597 had gone into the sea without survivors. Sgt Ross and crew returned from the same Furse garden with flak damage, and crash-landed at base, suggesting that the loss of the Gill crew was probably also brought about by flak. The squadron

Wellington BK357 at RAF Mildenhall, November 1942

135

armourers found themselves loading bombs into 115 Squadron Wellingtons for the first time at East Wretham on the 18th. Five Wellingtons had one 1,000, four 500 and two 250 pounders winched into their bomb bays for a trip across the Alps to Turin, and they took off between 18.30 and 19.03 with W/C Cousens the senior officer on duty, supported by S/L Chilton and the newly-promoted F/L Ian Bazalgette. Sgt Pudsey and crew turned back when deep into France after ice-accretion prevented them from gaining sufficient altitude to traverse the mountain range, leaving the others to press on to deliver their payloads from between 9,000 and 13,500 feet. Many explosions and fires were observed in and around the city centre, no losses were incurred from the original force of seventy-seven aircraft, and the operation was declared to be successful, photo-reconnaissance revealing that the Fiat works was among buildings sustaining damage. A force of 232 aircraft was assembled for a return to Turin on the 22nd, and this represented the largest raid on an Italian city during this mini-campaign. 115 Squadron bombed up nine Wellingtons, and sent them skyward between 18.05 and 18.40 with F/O Larkins the senior pilot on duty. Sgts Baldwin and Robertson returned early with technical issues to do with engines, while the remainder pressed on to reach the target and bomb from between 7,000 and 12,000 feet. Bomb bursts were reported near the Fiat works and the marshalling yards, and fires were observed across the city before drifting smoke obscured the ground from view. Local reports of a death toll of 117 people confirmed the accuracy of the raid.

On the following night 115 Squadron contributed six Wellingtons to the thirty aircraft sent mining off the west coast of France from Lorient to Bayonne. They departed East Wretham between 17.49 and 18.39 and pointed their noses towards Land's End, but P/O Thomas turned back when over the Channel after the rear turret became unserviceable. The others reached their respective gardens and delivered their mines according to brief by visual reference or DR-fix from between 700 and 1,000 feet. Stuttgart was posted as the target on the 22nd for which a force of 222 aircraft was made ready. The 115 Squadron element of twelve took off between 18.40 and 19.01 with S/L Chilton and F/L Bazalgette the senior pilots on duty, half carrying incendiaries and the remainder a mixture of high-explosive bombs. The overhead escape hatch of BJ756 flew open during the outward flight over France, and all efforts to close it failed, forcing Sgt Rodgers and crew to turn back. Ground haze and a thin layer of cloud prevented the Pathfinders from accurately identifying and marking the target, and the bombing became focussed on the southern and south-western fringes of the city and outlying communities. The 115 Squadron crews attacked from the unusually low level for an urban target of between 6,000 and 9,500 feet, and returning crews were confident that they had hit the city centre, reporting hits on a factory in the north and the marshalling yards and claiming that fires were burning all over the town. F/L Bazalgette confirmed the official view by remarking on fires in a sparsely built-up area south of the city. The local authorities described two aircraft attacking the railway station from low level and causing extensive damage. Ten aircraft failed to return, and among them were two 115 Squadron Wellingtons, both of which came down in France. Sgt Coates RAAF and crew were in BJ842, which failed to survive an encounter with a JU88 night-fighter, and crashed some twenty miles east-north-east of Paris killing the two Canadians on board. Sgt Coates ultimately evaded capture, while his three surviving crew mates were taken into captivity. BK206 crashed nine miles north of Laon in north-eastern France, killing Sgt Robertson and three of his crew, leaving just the wireless operator to fall into enemy hands.

The Italian campaign continued at Turin on the night of the 28/29th when a force of 228 aircraft included just nineteen Wellingtons, of which eleven were provided by 115 Squadron. Until relatively recently, the Wellington had been the backbone of the Command and had always been the most populous type on major operations. The small number of the type employed on this night reflected its diminishing role in a predominantly four-engine heavy force, although an expansion during this period of Canadian squadrons would ensure its presence in front-line service until well into the second half of 1943. The East Wretham element was airborne by 18.05 with S/L Fox, now officially the successor to S/L Wright, the senior pilot on duty. All reached the target, where the first bombing took place before the Pathfinders had started marking, but, once under way, the attack proceeded according to plan. The 115 Squadron crews again went in low, between 1,700 and 9,000 feet, and many bomb bursts were seen in the city centre and near the Fiat works and marshalling yards. After dropping his bombs onto or near the Fiat factory from 6,000 feet, Sgt Pudsey machine-gunned the streets before turning for home. Z1653 overshot the runway on return in the hands of F/Sgt Hickman, and ended up crash-landing, but both aircraft and crew were soon returned to active service. It was on this operation that 149 Squadron's F/Sgt Middleton RAAF earned the posthumous award of the Victoria Cross.

The only operation on the last night of the month was a mining effort by six 115 Squadron Wellingtons off La Pallice. They took off either side of 17.00 with F/O Larkins the only officer pilot, and proceeded without incident to the target area, where they delivered their mines into the briefed locations either visually or by DR-fix from between 600 and 900 feet. During the course of the month the squadron operated on ten nights and dispatched eighty-three sorties for the loss of three Wellingtons and crews.

December 1942

Frankfurt was selected to open the new month's account, and a force of 112 aircraft was made ready which included fifteen Wellingtons, ten of them belonging to 115 Squadron. S/Ls Chilton and Fox were the senior pilots on duty as they took off between 01.41 and 02.07 with a three-hour outward flight across France ahead of them. Sgt Prager and crew returned early with intercom problems and jettisoned the bombs safe, despite which, they exploded on impact. The others pressed on to reach the target, where thick haze hid ground detail and prevented the Pathfinders from establishing their position. They delivered their loads of predominantly 1,000 and 500 pounders from between 8,000 and 10,000 feet, and all but one returned safely to report scattered fires but no detailed assessment of the outcome. Six aircraft failed to return, among them 115 Squadron's BK338, which, it is believed, came down in Germany on the way home, with no survivors from the all RCAF/RNZAF crew of W/O McCrae RCAF. Five crews were called to briefing on the 4th to be told that they would join others that night to mine the waters around the Frisians. They took off in a ten-minute slot from 21.30 with F/L Barrett the senior pilot on duty, and all reached their allotted drop zones to deliver their stores from between 800 and 1,000 feet.

The city of Mannheim brought a return to southern Germany on the night of the 6/7th, for which a force of 272 aircraft had been prepared. 115 Squadron put up six Wellingtons, which departed East Wretham at 17.30 with S/L Chilton the senior pilot on duty, one carrying a cookie and the others a 1,000 pounder and seven 500 pounders each. Those reaching the target found it completely obscured by cloud, which persuaded most of the Pathfinder element to withhold their flares. The main force crews bombed on DR, those from 115 Squadron doing so from 9,000 feet, and four of them returned home to report an inconclusive attack, which local reports would confirm as largely ineffective and causing only superficial damage. Ten aircraft failed to return, half of them Wellingtons from a total of fifty-seven of the type dispatched. 115 Squadron was represented by two of them, BK513, which crashed some twenty miles north-east of Laon, it is believed, while outbound, killing F/O Dixon RNZAF and his crew, and BJ898, which crashed ten miles north-north-west of Worms, probably on the way out of the target area, and there were no survivors either from the crew of F/O Larkins. The squadron detailed five all-NCO crews and S/L Chilton for mining duties on the 7th, Sgts Finnerty and Plum taking off at 15.20 for south-western France, leaving the remainder at home until their departure between 17.00 and 17.40 for the waters further north off western France. Sgt Finnerty returned early for an unspecified reason, but the others completed their assigned tasks before returning safely home between 23.35 and 00.10 to report delivering their mines from between 800 and 900 feet. F/L Moore was posted to 22 O.T.U on the 8th, and his valuable experience would be missed in the squadron.

The final three operations of the Italian campaign were directed at Turin, beginning on the night of the 8/9th, when 5 Group and a Pathfinder element delivered an accurate and destructive attack, which killed more than two hundred people and left fires burning so fiercely that they would act as a beacon for the larger force approaching twenty-four hours later. 115 Squadron contributed seven Wellingtons to this second raid, and they were airborne by 17.30 with W/C Sisley and S/L Chilton the senior pilots on duty. The former returned after thirty minutes when Z1696 demonstrated a reticence to climb to operational altitude, leaving the others to press on to the target, where drifting smoke from the previous night hampered Pathfinder efforts to mark the aiming-point. The 115 Squadron crews bombed from between 8,500 and 15,000 feet, and five of them returned safely to report being unable to pick out detail because of haze. X3393 failed to return home with the rest of the squadron participants, but at least there was good news concerning its predominantly Canadian occupants. Sgt Smith RCAF and his RAF navigator evaded capture, while the three remaining crew members, all RCAF, were taken into captivity.

The squadron was not involved in the final attack on Turin on the night of the 11/12th, but dispatched six Wellingtons either side of 17.00 to mine the waters off the French coast south of La Rochelle. All reached the target area, where Pointe de Aiguille and the Ile d'Aix were employed as pinpoints from which to make timed runs to the drop zones. The mines were delivered into the assigned locations from between 800 and 900 feet, and all returned safely home to make their reports. S/L Chilton was the senior

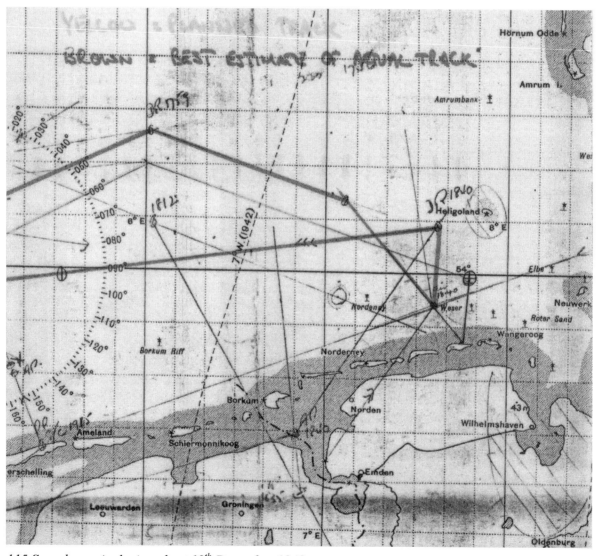

115 Squadron minelaying chart 12th December 1942

138

pilot on duty twenty-four hours later when six of the squadron's Wellingtons departed East Wretham either side of 16.30 to mine the sea-lanes off the Frisians. They fulfilled their briefs by pinpointing on Ameland and Terschelling and making timed runs to the gardens to deliver their mines from between 600 and 1,000 feet. The only incident of note involved P/O Campbell and crew silencing a flak battery on Langeoog with machine-gun fire. Mining continued to be the only activity for the heavy squadrons during this period of unfavourable weather conditions, and 115 Squadron briefed five crews on the 15th to ply their trade in Quiberon Bay on France's western coast between Lorient and St-Nazaire. They took off between 16.39 and 16.46, and delivered their two mines each from between 700 and 900 feet before returning safely. W/C Cousens was posted to Pathfinder HQ on the 16th, allowing W/C Sisley to succeed him on the same day as 115 Squadron's commanding officer. W/C Cousens would be appointed to command the newly-formed 635 Squadron in March 1944, and lose his life a month later during an attack on the marshalling yards at Laon while flying as one of the assigned Master Bombers in a Lancaster captained by P/O Courtney. At the time of his death he held the DSO, DFC and Czech MC.

Orders came through on the 17th for 3 Group to make ready sixteen Stirlings and six 115 Squadron Wellingtons for an operation against the Opel works at Fallersleben, a town situated some thirty-five miles east of Hannover, which would be renamed Wolfsburg after the war. In fact, a giant Volkswagen factory complex had been built there during the mid to late thirties, where the VW "Beetle" had been born, and was currently in production along with military vehicles. While this operation was in progress twenty-seven 5 Group Lancasters would be roaming far and wide across Germany to attack eight small German towns. The 115 Squadron aircraft were loaded with a single 1,000 and five 500 pounders, before being dispatched between 17.30 and 17.45 with S/L Chilton the senior pilot on duty. P/O Farquharson alone managed to locate the VW factory complex and dropped his bombs from 3,000 feet in its vicinity. S/L Chilton failed to locate the primary target and dropped his bombs from 2,000 feet onto a built-up area before shooting up searchlights. Sgt Plum found the town of Nienburg, situated twenty-five miles north-west of Hannover, which was one of the targets assigned to 5 Group, and bombed it from 2,000 feet without observing any results. He brought BK275 safely home, where the ground crew set about repairing the holes in the port wing and propeller courtesy of flak or a night-fighter. Sgt Finnerty dropped his bombs from 4,000 feet in the Uetze area, some twenty miles short of the primary target, and observed five bursts. His Wellington, BJ756, also returned with damage, some caused by flak and the rest by striking trees during the landing approach. BK274 was shot down at Wunstorf on the north-western approaches to Hannover, and there were no survivors from the crew of F/O Campbell RCAF. BK336 came down nine miles west of Quakenbrück, shortly after crossing the Dutch/German frontier, and Sgt Crisp and crew lost their lives. 3 Group also lost six Stirlings on this operation, four of them belonging to 75(NZ) Squadron, while nine 5 Group Lancasters failed to return, a third of those dispatched.

The night of the 20/21st was one of great significance for the Command, although the events would pass unnoticed by all but those participating. A force of 232 aircraft was prepared for an operation against Duisburg, for which 115 Squadron put up four Wellingtons. They took off between 18.10 and 18.27 with F/O Thomas the senior pilot on duty, each carrying two 1,000 pounders and five 500 pounders. They found the city under clear skies, but ground haze caused the usual problems, and, after bombing from between 12,000 and 13,500 feet, little could be seen other than bomb bursts and scattered fires. While this operation was in progress, six Mosquitos of 109 Squadron set off for a power station at Lutterade in Holland, to deliver their first Oboe-aimed bombs. Since becoming a founder member of the Pathfinders in August, 109 Squadron had been fully engaged in marrying the device to the Mosquito, and conducting exhaustive trials under its commanding officer, W/C Hal Bufton. This night's operation was a calibration test to check the margin of error, for which the surrounding terrain needed to be free from damage. In the event, reconnaissance photographs showed many craters from misdirected bombs intended for nearby Aachen in October, and the three successful releases could not be identified. Further tests would be carried out in the New Year, however, and the device would be ready, if not yet fully efficient, in time for the spring offensive.

3 Group's year was now effectively over, and it was not called upon to operate against Munich on the night of the 21/22nd. After celebrating the fourth wartime Christmas in traditional RAF style, five 115 Squadron crews were called to briefing on the 28th to learn that they had been detailed to mine the waters around the Frisians in the early hours of the 29th. They took off at 03.45, and three located their assigned gardens by pinpointing on Spiekeroog and making timed runs to release their mines from 500 to 600 feet. Two crews failed to locate their allocated gardens and found alternatives, P/O Thomas delivering his mines from 1,000 feet after establishing his position by Gee (TR), and Sgt Minnis from 500 feet after pinpointing on Terschelling. New Year's Eve dawned fair and clear with snow lying across East Wretham, and, later in the day, the teleprinter spawned orders to prepare six Wellingtons for mining sorties off the Biscay coast in company with twenty-three other aircraft. P/Os Farquharson and Hickman were the senior pilots on duty as they took off in a five-minute slot from 17.10 and headed for the south-west. Sgt Thurston and crew were more than an hour out when the navigator became ill and needed to be brought home, leaving the others to press on to the Cinnamon garden located around the ports of La Rochelle and La Pallice. The crews pinpointed on the Ile de Re, Ile d'Aix and Ile d'Oleron before making timed runs to deliver their stores from between 600 and 1,000 feet, and four of the East Wretham element returned safely. X3351 failed to return from this final mining operation of the year, but, happily, P/O Hickman and crew survived to see in the New Year, albeit as PoWs.

During the course of the month the squadron operated on twelve nights and dispatched seventy-two sorties for the loss of seven Wellingtons. It had been an expensive year for 115 Squadron, in which sixty-five aircraft had been lost as a result of operations, the highest number in the whole of Bomber Command. It had also been a year in which the gallantry of the squadron's airmen had been recognized by the award of nineteen DFCs and nine DFMs. The coming year would bring changes, and a gruelling round of operational activity, which would test the mettle of squadron morale. Another event bearing future significance for 115 Squadron at this time was the delivery to 5 Group's 61 Squadron of a complement of Hercules-powered Mk II Lancasters, which would be used for operational trials from mid January.

January 1943

New Year's Day brought with it the formation of the Canadian 6 Group, which would operate under the control of Bomber Command but be financed by Canada. It would be stationed in north Yorkshire and County Durham on former 4 Group stations, and the majority of the RCAF squadrons were transferred immediately, the remainder following on over the ensuing months. The year's operations began with the continuation of the Oboe trials programme, in which 109 Squadron Mosquitos marked for small forces of Lancasters from 1 and 5 Groups. The old enemy, Essen, was the principal objective, receiving no fewer than seven visits during the first two weeks of January, while Duisburg would be attacked once. For 115 Squadron the New Year began as the old one had ended, with a mining expedition by six Wellingtons to the waters off La Rochelle on the night of the 2/3rd. They took off between 21.10 and 21.30 with F/O Thomas the senior pilot on duty, but F/Sgt Aldwin's BK166 was soon in trouble with generator failure and turned back after fifteen minutes, only to collide with trees on approach to land, causing injury to the bomb-aimer and rear gunner. The others found the weather in the garden area to be clear with good visibility, and they were able to pinpoint on the northern tips of the Ile de Re and Ile d'Oleron before delivering their mines as briefed from between 600 and 1,000 feet. P/O Tuma and Sgt Rodgers departed East Wretham shortly after 17.00 on the 3rd to return to the waters off La Rochelle, and fulfilled their orders by delivering two mines each from between 600 and 1,000 feet into the allocated positions. The Pathfinders were granted group status as 8 Group on the 8th, and both terms will be employed for the purpose of this book.

The squadron made ready four Wellingtons on the 9th for the next round of mining operations, this time in the northern waters of the Yams garden on the approaches to Heligoland. They took off either side of 17.00 captained by NCO pilots, and made their way out in excellent conditions of three-tenths cloud at 2,000 to 3,000 feet and good visibility. F/Sgt Thurston and crew had almost reached the target area when they were attacked by a JU88, which forced them to jettison their two mines live and head for home with damage to the port tail-plane. The others delivered their mines from between 2,000 and 3,000 feet after making timed runs from well-defined pinpoints, although one of Sgt Rodgers' mines had to be jettisoned live after hanging up, and he returned home with BK275 displaying a hole in its fuselage courtesy of flak. Six crews were briefed on the 12th for a return to the La Rochelle region that night, and it was 01.00 before they began to take off with F/O Thomas the senior pilot on duty. They all reached the target area to find favourable weather conditions, and delivered their mines into the allocated positions from between 600 and 1,500 feet by using the usual pinpoints.

On the 14th, a new Air Ministry directive was issued in response to increasing Allied shipping losses in the Atlantic, and called for the area bombing of those French ports containing U-Boot bases and support facilities. A list of targets was drawn up accordingly, headed by Lorient, and preparations were put in hand that very day for the first of what would become a series of nine attacks over the ensuing four weeks. 122 aircraft were made ready, including four Wellingtons belonging to 115 Squadron, which each had a 4,000lb cookie loaded into its bomb bay. At the same time four others were prepared to return to the La Rochelle region to continue the mining programme, and they would take off first at 17.00 with P/O Tuma the senior pilot among them. They were on the way home by the time the bombers took off at 22.30 with S/L Chilton the senior pilot on duty, and, at debriefing could report delivering their mines according to instructions from between 300 and 1,000 feet. S/L Chilton had to turn back after ice built up on the wings of BK168 and affected his ability to control the Wellington, and he landed at Exeter after jettisoning the cookie. Sgt Minnis also came home early after the intercom system froze, and this left just Sgt Ross and F/O Thomas to carry out an attack from 9,000 and 11,000 feet respectively and contribute to what was, at best, only a modestly effective raid.

Twenty-four hours later, a force of 157 aircraft set off to return to Lorient with Wellingtons representing over a third of the numbers. 115 Squadron contributed ten of the type, which departed East Wretham either side of 17.30 with F/O Thomas the senior pilot on duty. They flew out in good weather conditions, and all reached the target to find varying amounts of cloud reported as being from nil to nine-tenths. The squadron crews carried out their attacks from between 6,000 (Sgt Pudsey) and 12,000 feet, and some observed numerous fires and two large ones in the town. Sgt Pudsey and crew paid the penalty of going in so low and were coned by searchlights and assaulted by flak, which caused some damage. The gunners fired down the beams and the Wellington came out the other side still in one piece and able to make it safely home. This raid was much more concentrated than the previous one, and left eight hundred buildings in ruins, fortunately, after most of the inhabitants had evacuated the town during the day.

Lancasters provided the main force on the 16th for the first of two disappointing raids on Berlin on consecutive nights. It cost just one aircraft, and, apart from the destruction of the ten-thousand-seat Deutschlandhalle, the largest covered arena in Europe, which was hosting the annual performance of the circus as the raid took place, damage was slight and superficial, and, amazingly, there were no casualties among the circus audience. The follow-up operation cost twenty-two aircraft, almost 12% of those dispatched, and the results were disappointing in the extreme, although this was not apparent to the BBC broadcaster, Richard Dimbleby, who observed the raid from a Lancaster of 106 Squadron flown by the soon-to-be-famous W/C Guy Gibson. 115 Squadron remained at home on these nights, but dispatched seven Wellingtons between 17.30 and 17.45 on the 18th to mine the waters around the Frisians. They flew out in poor visibility, but broken cloud of two-tenths at 1,000 feet in the garden area provided good conditions for the job in hand and all returned safely after delivering their mines by visual reference or by TR/DR-fix from between 200 and 1,000 feet. The squadron provided eight Wellingtons for a return to the Frisians on the 20th, for which they took off between 17.20 and 17.50 with P/O Tuma the senior pilot on duty for the second operation running. They all reached the target area to find ten-tenths cloud between 4,000 and 5,000 feet, but good visibility below, and delivered their stores according to brief from between 500 and 2,000 feet by pinpointing on Schiermonnikoog.

A predominantly four-engine heavy force attacked Lorient with accuracy on the night of the 23/24th, but it was a predominantly Wellington force of 157 aircraft that followed up on the 26th, for which 115 Squadron contributed a dozen of the type. They took off either side of 17.30 with S/L Chilton the senior pilot on duty, and only Sgt Thurston and crew returned early with intercom failure. The remainder reached the target, where visibility was found to be poor, and dropped their high explosives and incendiaries onto the town and docks from between 6,000 and 10,000 feet after making timed runs from a pinpoint on the coast. The main operation on the night of the 27/28th was carried out by an initial force of 162 aircraft in the absence of Wellingtons, and was directed at Düsseldorf, where Oboe Mosquitos carried out the first ground marking ahead of the Pathfinder heavy brigade. The raid was a major success, which resulted in the substantial destruction of industrial, public and residential buildings. It was back to mining duties for six 115 Squadron crews on this night, which took off either side of 17.30 led by F/O Thomas, five of them to make their way over ten-tenths cloud to the waters off La Rochelle, while Sgt Rhys and crew flew in the opposite direction towards the Frisians. The last-mentioned encountered five to seven-tenths cloud with a base at around 2,000 feet, and the presence of haze below that level persuaded them to deliver their mines into the briefed location by Gee-fix from 5,300 feet, before returning home safely at 20.50. Four of the crews assigned to the Biscay coast delivered their mines from between 800 and 1,000 feet after pinpointing on the usual landmarks, but Sgt Plum and crew were thrown off course by a faulty compass. They abandoned their sortie and headed home, and had reached the Chepstow area when the fuel state became critical. The mines were jettisoned safe and the crew took to their parachutes, leaving X3936 to crash at 01.15 into the River Wye near Bigsweir Bridge on the Gloucestershire border with Monmouthshire.

It had been planned to send six 115 Squadron Wellingtons to Lorient on the 29th, but their participation was cancelled, leaving elements of 1, 4 and 6 Groups to carry out the operation. The 115 Squadron crews were not given the night off, however, and took off instead between 17.30 and 17.40 to mine the waters off St-Nazaire with F/O Farquharson the senior pilot on duty. Adverse weather conditions persuaded four crews to turn back and bring their mines home, while F/O Farquharson and Sgt Ross delivered theirs from 600 and 800 feet respectively after pinpointing on Croisic Point. The month closed with the first H2S (ground-mapping radar) attack of the war on the night of the 30/31st, for which Hamburg was the target. Ultimately, the device would make a major contribution to the Command's success, but this night's effort produced widely scattered bombing, with fairly modest results despite setting off seventy large fires. During the course of the month the squadron operated on eleven nights, and dispatched seventy-five sorties for the loss of a single Wellington.

February 1943

The first major operation of the new month was directed at Cologne, for which a force of 161 aircraft was made ready on the 2nd. There were no Wellingtons among the heavy brigade, reflecting the type's gradual decline from front line duties. A combination of Oboe and H2S was employed at the Rhineland Capital, as the search for a reliable and effective target marking method continued. It again brought disappointing results in the form of scattered bombing, and, in the absence of concentration, most of the afflicted buildings were victims of blast, rather than the more destructive fire. A return to Hamburg was planned for the night of the 3/4th, for which 115 Squadron made ready seven Wellingtons, along with five more for a mining operation off St-Nazaire. It was the latter element that departed East Wretham first, between 17.30 and 17.40 with F/O Andrews the senior pilot, and all reached the target area to encounter a layer of cloud. Sgt Rodgers descended to 400 feet over Pointe-de-la-Percee in a vain attempt to come below the cloud base, but then found the Wellington to be incapable of climbing back up above it. Heavy flak opened up at this juncture, and the decision was taken to abandon the sortie. Sgt Rhys found a pinpoint at Pornichet and delivered his mines from 650 feet into the planned location, while Sgts Plum and Finnerty selected St-Gildas Point as their reference and dropped their mines from 1,000 feet F/O Andrews timed his run from Pointe-du-Pain Chateau, and watched his stores drift down on their parachutes from 900 feet. He landed at Harrowbeer through lack of fuel, but ran off the runway, tipped up and damaged BJ756's nose and both propellers. Meanwhile, the seven Hamburg-bound Wellingtons took off between 18.30 and 18.55 with F/Os Farquharson and Thomas the senior pilots, and six of them reached the enemy coast. Sgt Thurston jettisoned his load twenty miles west of the Frisian island of Overflakee after his starboard engine began to fail, while icing and an overheating engine persuaded F/O Farquharson to bomb Gilze-Rijen aerodrome from 11,000 feet as a last resort target. P/O Aldwin experienced similar engine problems when between Nienburg and Bremen, and unloaded his bomb bay on the town of Hoya from 13,000 feet. Sgts Minnis and Ross and F/O Thomas observed marker flares going down over the primary target, and aimed their bombs at them from between 12,000 and 13,000 feet without being able to determine their fall. BK166 was attacked three times by a ME110, but Sgt Ross and crew shook it off and returned with the starboard aileron partly shot away. 115 Squadron's BK127 disappeared into the sea on the return journey, taking with it the now experienced crew of P/O Tuma. The operation was no more successful than the one by a smaller force four nights earlier, but set off forty-five large fires.

103 Wellingtons made up the bulk of the force to continue the assault on Lorient on the night of the 4/5th, while a predominantly four-engine force was made ready for a trip across the Alps to Turin. Six Wellingtons were detailed to support the latter operation, and they were from 115 Squadron, while a single crew from the squadron carried out a mining sortie off Lorient. Sgt Rhys and crew took off first, at 17.35, and flew out over ten-tenths cloud to reach the target area, where the fires from the on-going attack on Lorient were of assistance. They were able to pinpoint on the Ile-de-Groix from which to make a timed run, and delivered their mines as briefed from 600 feet. Meanwhile, having taken off at 18.00 with S/L Chilton the senior pilot on duty, the Turin-bound 115 Squadron element encountered the same ten-tenths cloud until south of Paris, when it began to break up. By this time Sgt Thurston and crew had already turned back with restricted petrol flow from the overload tank, and F/O Thomas and crew would be forced by oil-pump failure to turn back also, just as the clouds were reforming to cover the Alps with tops at 17,000 feet. As often happened, the skies cleared east of the mountain range and provided clear visibility for the attack, but, as F/O Farquharson crested the peaks, the starboard engine failed and he dropped his bombs from 15,000 feet onto the town of Molaretto nestling in the foothills. Sgt Rodgers jettisoned a single 500 pounder to gain height when crossing Mont Cenis Pass, and eventually bombed what was believed to be the primary target on e.t.a. from 19,000 feet. S/L Chilton was at 14,500 when he aimed his bombs at marker flares, and Sgt Plum attempted to drop his from 13,000 feet, but suffered the frustration of a hang-up and had to bring them back, landing at Tangmere because of diminishing fuel reserves.

The night of the 6/7th was devoted to mining operations from north-western France to Texel, and five 115 Squadron Wellingtons were made ready to send to the shipping lanes off La Rochelle. They departed East Wretham between 02.05 and 02.15 with F/Os Andrews and Thomas the senior pilots on duty, but the former returned within minutes with an engine problem, and damaged the starboard undercarriage

Sgt D Rhys and Crew, East Wretham 1943

and propeller on landing. F/O Thomas and F/Sgt Thurston were defeated by the icing conditions over the French coast, and also returned early, leaving only Sgts Plum and Rhys to fulfil their briefs from 600 and 700 feet respectively. 323 aircraft were assembled later on the 7th for a two-wave assault that night on Lorient, and among them were five Wellingtons belonging to 115 Squadron. They took off at 19.00 led by S/L Chilton, but their numbers again became depleted when F/O Andrews and crew turned back after two hours through the failure of the oxygen system. The others pressed on to the target, where accurate Pathfinder marking led to a devastating attack. The 115 Squadron crews bombed from between 7,500 and 10,000 feet before returning safely to report explosions on and around the aiming-point. The squadron detailed three crews for mining duties off the Dutch coast on the night of the 9/10th, and dispatched them at 23.00 for what would be a trip of no more than three hours. The six mines were duly delivered within sight of the Dutch coast from between 700 and 800 feet, and all were safely back home by 02.00.

A force of 177 Lancasters, Halifaxes and Stirlings was made ready for a raid on the naval port of Wilhelmshaven on the 11th, and those reaching the target found complete cloud cover, which forced the Pathfinders to employ skymarking based on H2S, the least reliable of all marking methods. Despite that, the marking and bombing were highly accurate, and caused a naval ammunition dump at Mariensiel to explode with devastating results for 120 acres of the built-up area. Meanwhile, 115 Squadron dispatched P/O Baldwin and Sgt Plum and their crews at 18.10 to mine the sea lanes off La Rochelle. The former pinpointed on the northern tips of the Ile-de-Re and Ile-d'Oleron before releasing their two mines from 100 feet. The latter used the Pointe-du-Clie as the ground reference, and dropped their mines into the briefed location from 700 feet. The penultimate raid of the series on Lorient was scheduled for the night of the 13/14th, for which a force of 466 aircraft was made ready, 140 of them Wellingtons. 115 Squadron contributed just five, which took off shortly before 17.30 with S/L Chilton the senior pilot on duty, and flew out in perfect weather conditions which provided excellent visibility. Four of the 115 Squadron

144

crews made timed runs from the Ile-de-Groix, and flew up the Blavet Estuary to deliver their bombs from between 7,000 and 12,000 feet, observing them to burst in the docks and on the Keroman peninsular, where the enormous and impregnable U-Boot pens had been built. Seven aircraft failed to return, and among them was BK166 containing the crew of Sgt Rait, from which only the front gunner survived as a PoW.

There was something of a resurgence of the Wellington force during this period, as its continuing importance to the Command saw it employed in large numbers again. Eighty-five of the type were detailed to take part in an operation against Cologne by an overall force of 243 aircraft on the 14th, although only three of them were provided by 115 Squadron. P/Os Aldwin and Shott and Sgt Plum took off in the minutes leading to 19.00, and reached the target to find complete cloud cover. They bombed from between 13,000 and 14,000 feet on the release-point flares dispensed by the Pathfinder element, and returned safely with little to report other than the possible destruction of a ME110 night-fighter by the Plum crew. The raid was shown later to have been only modestly successful, with damage mostly in western districts. A simultaneous attack by Lancasters of 1, 5 and 8 Groups on Milan created fires visible from a hundred miles into the return flight. The final raid of the campaign against Lorient was scheduled for the night of the 16/17th, for which a force of 377 aircraft was made ready, including ninety-nine Wellingtons. Six of these were provided by 115 Squadron, and four of them were loaded with a cookie each plus incendiaries, while two others would carry only 4lb incendiaries. They took off at 18.30 with S/L Chilton the senior pilot on duty, and flew to the French coast over four-tenths cloud with tops at 6,000 feet, before identifying the target visually. They entered the Blave estuary with the Keroman U-Boot pens clearly visible, and delivered the contents of their bomb bays from between 8,500 and 11,000 feet. Explosions were observed on Keroman and in the town of Lorient, and a particularly large one was reported in the Port Militaire. By the time that the bombers withdrew, there was little left of the town other than a deserted ruin.

A three-raid series of attacks on Wilhelmshaven would begin on the night of the 18/19th in the absence of a Wellington contingent, while 115 Squadron contributed four Wellingtons to extensive mining operations from St-Nazaire to the Frisians. They were all safely airborne by 18.30 and set course for Beachy Head en-route to the sea lanes off La Rochelle. P/O Thurston and crew lost their port engine when twenty miles out over the Channel, and they landed at Tangmere with their mines still on board. The others pinpointed on the Ile-de-Re and delivered their stores into the briefed locations from between 600 and 1,000 feet. Three of the crews operating on this night were back on the Order of Battle twenty-four hours later as part of a force of 338 aircraft detailed to return to Wilhelmshaven, after a poor effort the night before had deposited most of the bombs in open country. 120 Wellingtons were on duty as the most populous type, and P/O Baldwin replaced P/O Thurston in the 115 Squadron quartet as they took off either side of 18.00. There was six-tenths medium cloud as they flew out over the North Sea, but the target area was found to be hidden by thick haze. A pinpoint was taken on the East Frisian island of Spiekeroog or the island of Mellum in the entrance to Jade Bay, and bombs were aimed at red target indicators (TIs) from between 11,000 and 14,000 feet. Unfortunately, the Pathfinders had used outdated maps, and had marked an area to the north of the town, rendering the raid ineffective. One particularly worrying aspect of this operation was the loss of five out of twelve Stirlings, and this trend of a disproportionately high casualty rate would, ultimately, lead to the withdrawal of the type from operations over Germany before the year was out.

The 3 Group A-O-C, AVM Sir Ralph Cochrane, was about to be appointed A-O-C 5 Group, where he would continue his distinguished career, and visited East Wretham on the 23rd with his successor, Air Commodore Harrison. 6 and 8 Groups completed the campaign against Wilhelmshaven on the night of the 24/25th, and achieved no greater success than in the earlier attempts. This would be the last major raid on the port until late in 1944. While a force of more than three hundred aircraft failed to make an impact at Nuremberg on the night of the 25/26th, five 115 Squadron Wellingtons took off at 18.55 to return to the shipping lanes off La Rochelle. Sgt Rodgers turned back because of ice accretion, P/O Baldwin with intercom failure and F/O Andrews through an inability to locate the drop zone in the hazy conditions, despite searching at 100 feet. Sgt Plum and P/O Shott delivered their mines into the briefed locations from 1,000 feet after pinpointing on the Pointe-du-Che and the Ile-de-Re respectively.

Although Wellingtons were being excluded now from the more distant targets, Cologne was well within range with a reasonable bomb load, and 126 of the type were included in a force of 427 aircraft made ready on the 26th for an operation that night. 115 Squadron contributed five of them, and they took off at 19.15 with F/O Andrews the senior pilot on duty. Sgt Pudsey and crew were an hour out when port engine failure curtailed their sortie, while Sgt Rodgers and crew gave up because of oxygen failure and bombed the aerodrome at Woerden, situated east of the Hague and some eighteen miles inland from the Dutch coast. The others located the target by means of red and green TIs and bombed from between 11,200 and 14,000 feet before returning safely home. Local reports suggested that only a quarter of the bomb loads had found the mark, mostly hitting the south-western corner and causing a moderate amount of damage, and this in exchange for the loss of ten aircraft.

Now that Lorient had been reduced to rubble, attention was turned upon St Nazaire, and a force of 437 aircraft was assembled which included 119 Wellingtons. 115 Squadron contributed just four of these, and they took off at 18.20 with S/L Chilton the senior pilot on duty. They flew out in favourable weather conditions, and all reached the target, which was clearly identified by the River Loire and plentiful Pathfinder marker flares. They delivered their bombs onto the aiming-point from between 8,000 and 11,000 feet, and returned to report large and concentrated fires. Photo-reconnaissance confirmed the accuracy of the raid, which destroyed an estimated 60% of the town's built-up area. During the course of the month the squadron operated on fourteen occasions, dispatching seventy sorties for the loss of two Wellingtons and crews.

March 1943

A new era began for 115 Squadron on the 1st of March, with the arrival on charge from 61 Squadron of Lancaster Mk II DS612. 61 Squadron had formed a third flight to conduct operational trials, but now reverted to standard Mk Is and IIIs, leaving 115 Squadron to become the first to be fully equipped with the Hercules-powered version. The power plant offered a higher rate of climb than the Merlin, but, above 18,000 feet, the performance dropped off, and this ensured that 115 Squadron crews would generally bomb from below their Merlin-powered Lancaster cousins, although still well above the Stirling fraternity. Conversion began immediately, but until operational status was achieved, the squadron would continue to go to war in the trusty old Wellington. The squadron was not involved in the operation against Berlin on the night of the 1/2nd, which was the most effective of the war to date on the Capital, despite the inability of the Pathfinders to focus the marking on the city centre. It demonstrated the difficulty of interpreting the image of a massive urban sprawl on the cathode ray tube display screen provided by the early version of H2S. Even so, almost nine hundred buildings were destroyed, and significant damage was inflicted upon industrial premises and railway workshops. 115 Squadron opened its March account on this night by sending four NCO-captained crews to mine the waters off the Dutch Frisians. They departed East Wretham between 19.00 and 19.21, and three returned safely to report pinpointing on the island of Terschelling and delivering their mines into the briefed locations from between 900 and 1,500 feet. BK495 was shot down at 20.42 off Ameland by the night-fighter of Lt Heinz Grimm of IV/NJG.1, and there were no survivors from the crew of Sgt Hunt, four of which are commemorated on the Runnymede Memorial. *(In Bomber Command Losses for 1943, Bill Chorley records this event occurring on the night of the 2/3rd.)*

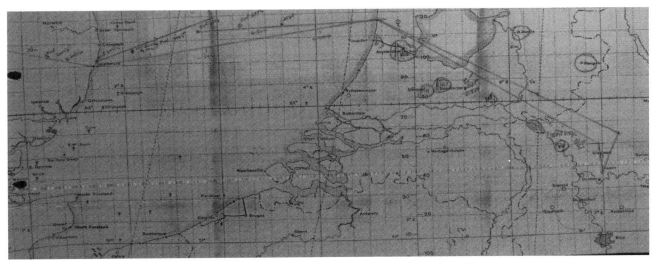

Chart for a 115 Sqn Lancaster operation against Essen

Now armed with the increasingly effective Oboe blind-bombing device, Harris was about to launch Bomber Command's most concerted campaign of the war against the towns and cities of the Ruhr. First, however, 417 crews had to negotiate a raid on Hamburg on the night of the 3/4th, in which 123 Wellingtons were included. 115 Squadron briefed six crews and sent them into the air between 18.30 and 18.45 with F/O Andrews the senior pilot on duty, but he returned in under two hours with an overheating port engine and defective oxygen supply system. Visibility was good in the target area, but reliance on H2S may have been responsible for some of the Pathfinders marking the town of Wedel, situated thirteen miles downstream of the intended victim, which then received many bomb loads. Four of the 115 Squadron participants bombed on Pathfinder marker flares from between 12,000 and 13,000 feet, and observed many fires and thick, black smoke rising to 1,500 by the time they turned away. Z1620 was missing from its dispersal after the raid, one of ten failures to return, and Sgt Laidlaw and his crew all lost their lives. Post-raid reconnaissance revealed that some of the bombing had fallen in Hamburg, where a hundred fires had to be dealt with before assistance could be rendered to Wedel.

Despite a huge effort in the past, success at Essen had eluded Harris, and it was appropriate, therefore, that this giant industrial city be selected to host the opening round of the Ruhr offensive, which was the first campaign for which the Command was adequately equipped and prepared. The operation was planned as a three-wave attack, in which 131 Wellingtons were to take part, including four from 115 Squadron. The aircraft and crew captains for this auspicious occasion were; Z1694 F/O Andrews, Z1657 W/O Noxon, BJ832 Sgt Small and Z1648 Sgt Fleming. They contributed to an overall force of 442 aircraft, which began to depart their stations shortly before 19.00 hours, to be overtaken on the outward flight by the eight high-flying Oboe Mosquitos of 109 Squadron. The 115 Squadron quartet took off at 19.30, but F/O Andrews was among the unusually high number of fifty-six early returns, in his case because of suspected icing, and he aimed his incendiaries at Alkmaar aerodrome from 10,000 feet and watched them fall short. The original force had been depleted to 362 by the time the target was reached, but these were able to exploit the accurate Oboe marking of the city centre, to wreak havoc on Essen for the first time. The three remaining 115 Squadron crews bombed from between 11,000 and 13,000 feet and contributed to the destruction of more than three thousand houses, and the serious damage to a further two thousand. The aiming-point for raids on Essen was always the Krupp works, and fifty-three buildings within its complex sustained damage. Returning crews described the glow of fires still visible from as far away as the Dutch coast, and this outstanding success, gained for the relatively modest loss of fourteen aircraft, provided the perfect start to what would be a five-month-long offensive. It would also send a chilling message to the enemy and shift the balance of failed versus successful operations firmly in the Command's favour.

Before returning to the Ruhr in a week's time, Harris turned his attention upon southern Germany, beginning with a major operation against Nuremberg, for which an all-four-engine force of 335 aircraft was made ready on the 8th. It was a clear but dark night, and the accuracy of the attack relied upon H2S, which failed to provide the hoped-for precision, and bombing was spread back for ten miles along the line of approach. Never the less, six hundred buildings were destroyed and a further 1,400 damaged to some extent. 115 Squadron remained at home on this night, and would not participate in the Munich operation planned for the following night, for which 264 four-engine aircraft were prepared. However, there was still an urgent need to keep the shipping lanes well-stocked with mines, and four 115 Squadron crews took off for La Rochelle at 19.20, and all reached the target area to pick up the usual pinpoints and deliver their mines into the briefed locations from between 650 and 900 feet. Stuttgart was posted as the target for 314 aircraft on the 11th, a night on which the 115 Squadron crews probably relaxed in the local watering holes. The Stuttgart operation was not successful, possibly as a result of dummy target indicators being employed by the enemy for the first time. Some damage was caused in south-western suburbs, but it was a poor return for the effort expended.

Preparations were put in hand on the 12th to resume the Ruhr offensive that night, and a force of 457 aircraft was assembled and their crews briefed to attack Essen. Four 115 Squadron Wellingtons were loaded with four 500 and two 250 pounders each plus incendiaries, and launched for the last time from East Wretham between 20.00 and 20.12, all captained by sergeant pilots. BJ756 did not make it as far as the target after crossing paths with the night-fighter of Lt Oskar Köstler of IV/NJG.1 and crashing into the Ijsselmeer at 21.35 with fatal consequences for Sgt Fallon and his crew. They were, therefore, the last to have their names added to the squadron Roll of Honour during the Wellington era. The others pressed on to the aiming-point, which, as usual at this target, was the Krupp complex to the west of the city centre, and Oboe initial marking allowed the Pathfinders to identify it and the main force to follow up with accurate bombing. The 115 Squadron trio bombed from between 9,000 and 14,000 feet before returning home to report a large concentration of fires, which were still visible at the Dutch coast. Post-raid reconnaissance revealed that the Krupp works had sustained even greater damage than a week earlier. Substantially fewer buildings were destroyed on this night, the tally standing at around five hundred houses, but it was another highly successful outcome, and a further step along the road to the elimination of one of Germany's most important industrial centres. This successful operation cost a total of twenty-three aircraft, and the above-detailed 115 Squadron casualty was the final one of ninety-eight Wellingtons to be lost by the squadron as a result of operations. No other squadron had suffered higher casualties on the type, but then, none had undertaken as many Wellington operations and dispatched as many sorties.

The squadron was declared operational on Lancasters on the 15th and conversion training proceeded at pace as the increased crew complement of the new type brought in an influx of fresh faces from the training units. There were no major operations during the middle part of the month, and so it was on the night of the 20/21st that 115 Squadron ventured forth in Lancasters for the first time. The only operational activity on this night was a mining effort off the Biscay ports, for which twelve Wellingtons and four 115 Squadron Lancasters were detailed. The Wellingtons were recalled, but the Lancasters, DS612, DS622, DS623 and DS625, took off between 19.20 and 19.30 with W/C Sisley the senior pilot on duty, and P/Os Ross and Minnis and Sgt Rhys and their crews sharing the honour to be the first to go to war in Lancasters. They pointed their snouts towards the south-west, and all reached their drop zone off La Pallice to deliver their six mines each from between 800 and 1,000 feet. Two days later, a force of 357 aircraft was made ready to continue the assault on St-Nazaire, among which seven 115 Squadron

Lancaster II KO-C East Wretham March 1943 Flt Lt Norman Plum DFC

Lancasters were detailed to carry out the unit's first bombing operation with the type. DS612, DS613, DS614, DS615, DS621, DS623 and DS624 took off at 19.10 with W/C Sisley again the senior pilot on duty, supported by F/Ls Avant, Bazalgette and Farquharson, P/Os Minnis and Prager and Sgt Rhys. Each Lancaster was carrying 1,250 4lb incendiaries, but bad weather over 3 Group stations caused a recall signal to be sent to all 3 Group aircraft at 21.00, and this would mean that only one load from East Wretham would reach the target. Sgt Rhys and crew failed to pick up the message, and went on to bomb the target on red Pathfinder markers from 10,000 feet. A total of 283 returning crews reported bombing the town and its port, and post-raid reconnaissance revealed an accurate and highly destructive operation.

Sgts Eggleston and Coles took off at 19.10 on the 23rd for mining duties off the Frisians, and delivered their mines according to brief from 650 and 800 feet respectively after pinpointing on the northern tip of Schiermonnikoog island. Duisburg was selected as the target for the third operation of the Ruhr campaign, and seven 115 Squadron Lancasters were among 455 aircraft made ready on the 26th. They took off either side of 20.30 with W/C Sims leading the squadron for the first time since his arrival as commanding officer-elect from 1657 Conversion Unit. Equipment failure afflicted five of the nine Oboe Mosquitos and a sixth was lost in the North Sea outbound, which meant that the initial marking as a reference for the Pathfinders was sparse. On a cloudy night requiring the least reliable sky-marking method, the 115 Squadron crews bombed on the Pathfinder parachute flares from between 14,000 and 19,000 feet and observed the red glow of fires reflected in the clouds. On return, F/L Bazalgette struck superficial damage, and Duisburg would continue to enjoy something of a charmed life for a further six weeks.

Sgt Eggleston and crew

trees, damaging DS615's undercarriage and propellers, but pulled off a successful belly landing without injury to the occupants. The operation was a scattered and disappointing failure which caused only

It was shortly before 20.00 on the 27th when Sgt Eggleston and crew departed East Wretham to lay mines off the Frisians, and they would fulfil their brief from 800 feet after pinpointing on the centre of Ameland. They were still outbound when six other 115 Squadron Lancasters took off between 20.20 and 20.30 bound for Berlin with F/Ls Avant, Bazalgette and Farquharson the senior pilots on duty. They were part of an overall force of 396 aircraft which had the centre of Germany's capital city as their aiming-point, but F/O Thomas turned back after an hour with an unserviceable compass, and F/L Farquharson jettisoned his load of two 1,000 pounders and incendiaries after stumbling into a heavy flak barrage in the Hannover area and being forced to dive down to 3,000 feet to escape. The others pressed on to bomb on red and green TIs from between 14,000 and 16,000 feet, before returning to report concentrated fires. Berlin lay beyond the range of Oboe, and the marking relied upon the interpretation of H2S operators staring at the image of the massive built-up area sliding indistinctly across their screens and trying to identify some recognisable feature to establish their position. Matters would improve in time, but, on this night, it led to the marking of two distinct areas, both well short of the planned aiming-point. Bombing photos would reveal that most of the attack had fallen between seven and seventeen miles short of the city centre to the south-west, and that no significant damage had resulted.

St-Nazaire was targeted again on the night of the 28/29th in an operation involving 323 aircraft, which 3 Group supported with Stirlings, leaving 115 Squadron at home. Berlin was posted as the target once more on the 29th, and 115 Squadron made ready eight Lancasters to contribute to an overall force of 329 aircraft, while 149 Wellingtons comprised the main force for an Oboe attack on Bochum in the Ruhr. The East Wretham gang took off between 21.45 and 22.15 with F/Ls Avant and Bazalgette the senior pilots on duty, but Sgt Finnerty returned within twenty minutes after jettisoning his bombs safe from an unstable aircraft. Sgt Minnis and crew were ninety minutes out when icing and a suspected problem with the starboard-outer engine curtailed their sortie, leaving the others to continue on in unfavourable weather conditions and wrongly forecast winds. The marking appeared to be concentrated, but, as would be discovered later, it was well to the south of the intended aiming-point. The main force element arrived a little later than scheduled, by which time the markers had disappeared and much of the effort was wasted in open country This disappointing performance cost twenty-one aircraft, and among them was the squadron's DS625, which disappeared without trace with the crew of Sgt Ross RCAF. This was the first Mk II Lancaster to be lost in Bomber Command service. W/C Sisley concluded his tour as commanding officer on the 30th, and was posted to Mildenhall pending a permanent appointment. He would return to the sharp end in mid July 1944, to assume command of 1 Group's 550 Squadron, on the death in action of W/C Connolly. Sadly, W/C Sisley's end would follow on the last day of August, during an attack on a V-2 site at Agenville in France. W/C Sims was installed as 115 Squadron's new commanding officer for what would be a relatively short term of office. During the course of the month the squadron operated on eleven nights, dispatching twenty-two Wellington and thirty-five Lancaster sorties for the loss of three Wellingtons and one Lancaster and their crews.

East Wretham 1943 Back row L-R: Keith Eggleston (Capt.); Bert Smith (B/A); Tony Graham (Nav); Len Fradgeley (RG); Ernie Black (M/UG) Taffy Lee (W.Op) Ted Albone ((Flt. Eng.)

April 1943

April would prove to be the least rewarding month of the Ruhr offensive, but this was born largely out of the proportion of operations directed at targets away from the region, and beyond the range of Oboe. 102 aircraft were detailed on the 2nd to be divided between Lorient and St Nazaire for what would be the final operations against French ports under the January Directive. 115 Squadron made ready one Lancaster for each of these, while six others were loaded with six mines each for delivery to the waters off La Rochelle. P/O Eggleston and crew took off at 20.00 bound for St-Nazaire, and they were followed into the air immediately over the ensuing ten minutes by the gardening element led by W/C Sims. It was a further hour before P/O Coles and crew departed for Lorient on a night on which all would reach their assigned destinations. The Ile de Re provided the main pinpoint for the mining brigade, and they delivered their loads accurately into the briefed locations from between 800 and 2,000 feet. P/O Eggleston dropped his bombs at St-Nazaire from 15,500 feet onto red and green TIs before being hit by heavy flak, which may have been responsible for two 1,000 pounders hanging up and having to be brought home. P/O Coles attacked Lorient from 14,000 feet, also on red and green TIs, and had three 1,000 pounders hang up.

Ted Smith (RG), George Edwards (Nav), Al Avant (Pilot) Fred Staines (W.Op/AG), Bill Hocking (M/UG), John Hargreaves (Flt. Eng.), Len Kennedy (BA).

The Ruhr offensive continued in promising fashion with another successful raid on Essen on the night of the 3/4th. A force of 348 aircraft included nine 115 Squadron Lancasters, which took off either side of 20.30 with S/L Fox the senior pilot on duty. F/L Bazalgette and Sgt Finnerty were recalled, and F/O Thomas turned back early because of communications problems between the cockpit and the rear turret, but the others pressed on to reach the target, where they bombed on red and green TIs from between 15,000 and 20,000 feet, observing large, orange explosions that emitted thick, black smoke rising to 1,000 feet. Post-raid reconnaissance revealed that central and western districts had been hardest hit by the well-concentrated pattern of bombing, and that over six hundred buildings had been destroyed. A new record non-1,000 force of 577 aircraft was assembled on the 4th for a major assault on Kiel that night. 115 Squadron dispatched seven Lancasters in a five-minute slot from 20.40 led by S/L Fox and each carrying ten 1,000 pounders. They all reached the target to find complete cloud cover, and delivered their loads onto red and green TIs from between 8,500 and 18,500 feet, before returning to report the glow of fires. S/L Fox returned in DS621 displaying the evidence of flak damage to the starboard wing between the engines. Strong winds, which caused the skymarkers to drift, and dummy fires were blamed for the failure of the operation, which, according to local reports, almost entirely missed the town.

Duisburg was posted as the primary target for attack on the 8th, for which 115 Squadron prepared seven Lancasters as part of an overall force of 392 aircraft. Three other Lancasters were loaded with six 1,500lb mines each, and they departed East Wretham first between 19.00 and 21.08 bound for the Gironde Estuary on the south-western coast of France. F/O Andrews and Sgt Small were well on their way to their target area when communications and compass problems respectively forced them to turn back and return their mines to store. This left just W/O Noxon and crew to press on to the drop zone, where the mines were delivered according to brief from 600 feet after pinpointing on Coubre Point. The Ruhr-

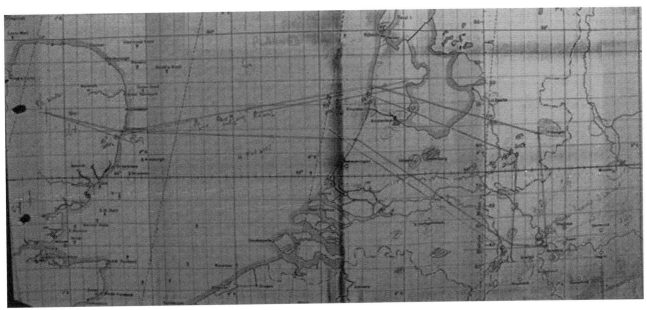

Chart for a 115 Sqn raid on Duisburg

bound element took off between 22.05 and 22.25 with S/L Fox the senior pilot on duty, and all reached the target area to find ten-tenths cloud, which, for an undisclosed reason, ruined the marking and led to scattered and inaccurate bombing. Sgt Rhys was unable to locate the target because of Gee failure, and brought his bombs home, while the remainder carried out their attacks from between 11,000 and 20,000 feet without observing any results. Local reports confirmed another failure at this important target, where only forty buildings were destroyed and its apparently untouchability continued. It was decided to try again twenty-four hours later employing an all-Lancaster heavy force of 104, which did not involve 115 Squadron. The outcome was the same, however, with just fifty houses destroyed and bombs sprayed across the Ruhr.

A force of 502 aircraft was made ready on the 10th to attack Frankfurt that night, and, this time, 115 Squadron contributed eight Lancasters, which took off in a fifteen-minute slot to 00.55 with F/L Farquharson the senior pilot on duty and last off the ground. Frankfurt was another city that had always proved difficult to hit effectively, and this night would bring no improvement in the Command's fortunes. DS604 failed to reach the target after crashing at 02.29 near Rethel in the Ardennes region of north-western France while outbound, and there were no survivors from the crew of Sgt Thomas. The others pushed on to southern Germany, where the persistent cloud cover concealed the city and was largely responsible for another wasted effort. The 115 Squadron crews bombed from between 16,000 and 19,000 feet on red TIs or the glow of fires reflecting in the clouds, but saw nothing of what was happening on the ground, and all bombing photos showed nothing but cloud. The local authorities reported only a few bombs falling into southern suburbs, and this disappointment for the Command was compounded by the loss of twenty-one aircraft. Six 115 Squadron crews were briefed for mining duties on the 11th, and departed East Wretham between 20.50 and 21.00 that night bound for the Gironde Estuary with S/L Fox the senior pilot on duty. They reached the target area and pinpointed on Coubre Point before delivering their six mines each into the allotted positions from between 600 and 1,000 feet.

Unusually for this stage of the war, Wellingtons were the most populous type and represented almost a third of the force of 462 aircraft assembled on the 14th to attack the southern city of Stuttgart. The first of eight 115 Squadron Lancasters took off at 22.00, and all were on their way towards Beachy Head within ten minutes for what would be an outward flight of around two-and-three-quarter hours. F/Os Andrews and Thomas were the senior pilots on duty, and each Lancaster carried a 4,000lb cookie, four

1,000 pounders and two 500 pounders to drop onto the important and highly industrialized target. Sgt Plum and crew were tracking south-east across France when the starboard-inner engine failed and forced them to turn back. They had intended to bring the bombs home, but the approach of an enemy night-fighter prompted an immediate dumping of the 9,000lb load some ten miles south of Arras, and they were able to make it safely home to land at 01.49. The weather was kind throughout the operation, and the others reached the target area, which they identified by means of the green Pathfinder TIs. Bombing took place from between 12,500 and 15,000 feet, and good fires were reported, which suggested a successful raid. Always a difficult target because of its location in a valley, the centre of Stuttgart, in fact, was again spared the worst ravages of a Bomber Command attack. However, the operation was rescued by an extensive creep-back, a feature of most heavy raids, which would never entirely be eliminated, and resulted from the practice by some crews of bombing the first fires they encountered, rather than pressing on to the markers. On this night, the creep-back worked in the Command's favour by falling across a number of northern suburbs, and most of the four hundred destroyed buildings were situated here.

On the 15th, 3 Group called for crews who had not operated two nights running to carry out mining operations off the Biscay coast. 115 Squadron offered F/O Andrews and P/O Starky, who took off at 21.00 bound for the Gironde Estuary, where they delivered their six mines each from 5,100 and 5,500 feet respectively after pinpointing on Pointe-de-la-Negade, and returned safely to land either side of 03.00. Preparations were put in hand on the 16th for a major night of operations, which would see 327 Lancasters and Halifaxes head for the Skoda armaments works at Pilsen in Czechoslovakia, while a predominantly Wellington and Stirling force of 271 aircraft carried out a diversionary raid on Mannheim. The plan of attack for the former called for the Pathfinders to drop route markers at the final turning point, seven miles from the target, which the crews were to then locate visually in the anticipated bright moonlight, and bomb from as low a level as practicable. It was a complicated plan that invited confusion, and the outcome questions the quality of some of the briefings. 115 Squadron made ready eight Lancasters, loading them with a mixture of high explosives and incendiaries and launched them from East Wretham between 21.35 and 21.45 with S/L Fox the senior pilot on duty. DS622 was hit by light flak somewhere over France, forcing P/O Prager to jettison his load live and turn back. When the route markers went down, which happened to be over an asylum situated seven miles short of the factory, the inevitable happened and many crews bombed them. The 115 Squadron crews reported bombing from between 4,500 and 10,000 feet after identifying the target by means of ground features, like the railway and a bend in the river. They also reported fires taking hold as they withdrew, but post-raid reconnaissance revealed that the factory had escaped damage. The disappointment was compounded by the loss of thirty-six heavy bombers, divided equally between the two types, and when added to the eighteen missing from the reasonably effective raid on Mannheim, this brought the night's total to a new record of fifty-four.

173 Lancasters and five Halifaxes were made ready on the 18th for a raid on the dockyard at La Spezia, situated on the Italian coast south-east of Genoa. 115 Squadron loaded nine Lancasters with a cookie each and SBCs of 30lb and 4lb incendiaries, before launching them into the air shortly after 21.30 with S/L Fox the senior pilot on duty. P/O Prager and crew were back within two hours with engine problems and a rear turret oil leak, and were followed home ten minutes later by F/L Avant with an indisposed navigator. The others pushed on in favourable weather conditions and found the target by means of red TIs and white flares. An effective smoke screen blotted out some ground detail, and bombing was carried out, in part, on estimated positions from between 10,000 and 14,000 feet. A good concentration of fires was observed in the harbour area and some in the estuary, but post-raid reconnaissance would reveal that the marking had fallen to the north of the planned aiming-point, and the railway station and many public buildings had sustained damage.

The main operation on the night of the 20/21st was against Stettin, the large port situated at the southern end of the Oder estuary at the eastern end of Germany's Baltic coast. A force of 339 aircraft was put together, while eighty-six Stirlings were made ready for a simultaneous attack on the Heinkel aircraft works at Rostock further west along the coast. 115 Squadron made ready eleven Lancasters, which took off between 21.30 and 21.41 with S/L Fox the senior pilot on duty, and all reached the target to find good visibility that enabled them to identify the town and docks, the Dammscher Lake and the River Oder. They bombed on green TIs from between 11,000 and 14,200 feet, and observed a solid mass of flames in the town and a terrific explosion in the docks area, which emitted large flames and a pall of black smoke. Unlike many German cities, Stettin never once escaped serious damage at the hands of a major Bomber Command assault, and this night brought the destruction of an estimated one hundred acres, in which almost four hundred buildings, including many of an industrial nature, were destroyed, and 586 people lost their lives.

There was a late take-off for eleven 115 Squadron Lancasters on the night of the 26/27th when Duisburg was the primary target. S/L Fox was once more the senior pilot on duty as they departed East Wretham between 00.55 and 01.35, loaded with a cookie each and SBCs of 4lb incendiaries. They all located the target by means of red and green TIs, and bombed from between 15,000 and 20,000 feet, observing both concentrated and scattered fires. It is not known whether P/O Minnis DFC, RCAF and crew, which included two holders of the DFM, had delivered their bombs before the end came for DS609 a few miles south of the target, and none survived to provide us with an account. Post-raid reconnaissance revealed that Duisburg's elusiveness was, perhaps, coming to an end, and an indication of this was the three hundred buildings reduced to ruins, although six neighbouring towns were also afflicted to some extent.

The night of the 27/28th was devoted to a massive gardening effort employing a record 160 aircraft sowing their vegetables off the French coast and around the Frisians. 115 Squadron briefed three freshman crews and dispatched them at 01.24 for the German Frisians (East Frisians) carrying eighteen mines between them. They encountered poor visibility, which prevented Sgt Wolfson and crew from identifying the drop zone off Spiekeroog Island, but Sgts Fleming and Wilkinson used their last reliable Gee-fix as a guide, and delivered their mines from 1,000 and 700 feet respectively. The following night brought a new record mining effort involving 207 aircraft plying their trade off north-western Germany and the Baltic. 115 Squadron launched F/L Avant and Sgt Rodgers and their crews skyward at 21.00 bound for Kiel Bay, and both reached the target area to pinpoint on Langeland Island and Fehmarn Island and deliver their mines as briefed from 700 and 1,000 feet respectively. A record 593 mines were successfully planted in important shipping lanes on this night, but the loss of twenty-two aircraft was also the highest of the war from this type of operation.

Essen was selected to host the final operation of what had been a busy month. 115 Squadron prepared eleven Lancasters as part of an overall force of 305 aircraft, and they took off between 00.59 and 01.15 with F/L Bazalgette the senior pilot on duty. They flew into challenging weather conditions, which persuaded six of them to turn back, mostly because of severe icing, and this left just five to press on to the target. Heavy cloud had been forecast for the target area, and the marking was based solely on Oboe skymarking, which worked well. The 115 Squadron crews bombed from between 16,000 and 19,000 feet, but were prevented by the cloud from observing results. Post-raid reconnaissance revealed new damage across the city with 189 buildings destroyed and the Krupp works sustaining further damage. During the course of the month the squadron operated on fifteen nights and dispatched 113 sorties for the loss of two Lancasters and their crews.

May 1943

May would bring a return to winning ways, and a number of stunning successes would take place, one of which would make headline news around the globe and become the most celebrated feat of arms in military aviation history. The production of new aircraft was allowing a gradual expansion to take place, and many squadrons were able to add a third or C Flight to their strength, most of which would be hived off in the autumn to form the nucleus of new squadrons. A manifestation of the growth of the Command was to come later in the month, but, in the meantime, a new record non-1,000 force of 596 aircraft was prepared for an attack on the Ruhr city of Dortmund on the night of the 4/5th. 115 Squadron made ready a dozen Lancasters, which took off between 22.55 and 23.40 with S/L Fox the senior pilot on duty. The recently-commissioned P/O Plum and crew had the Dutch coast on the horizon when their Gee and compass failed, and turned back after dumping their cookie live into the sea five miles from the shoreline. The remainder pressed on to approach the target from the north, identifying it by means of yellow release-point markers and red and green TIs, and dropped their bombs from between 16,000 and 19,500 feet. Large, concentrated fires were observed, as was a large explosion with orange flames rising to 6,000 feet and emitting thick, black smoke. There were other fires scattered over a wide area, and some of these may have resulted from a little errant backing-up on the part of the Pathfinders, and a decoy fire site. Despite these distractions, much of the bombing fell into central and northern districts of the city, and over twelve hundred buildings were destroyed, while a further two thousand sustained serious damage, among them a number of important war industry factories.

It was a week before the next major operation took place, after a number had been posted and then cancelled. W/C Sims is recorded as being posted on the 7th to Base HQ at Mildenhall for duties at East Wretham, possibly as station commander, and the likelihood is that he combined the roles of station and squadron commander until the appointment of his successor. This would occur officially on the 1st of June, but W/C Rainsford's name first appeared on the Order of Battle for the 21st of May, and we must assume, therefore, that he had arrived from 1657 Conversion Unit shortly before as commanding-officer-elect. His operational experience had been gained in the Middle-East in 1941 while serving as a flight commander and then commanding officer of 148 Squadron. Duisburg was the target for which 572 crews were briefed on the 12th, among them fifteen representing 115 Squadron, which would be setting a squadron record when they took to the air either side of 01.00 that night. F/Ls Avant and Bazalgette were the senior pilots on duty as they lifted heavily off the runway, five of them bearing the weight of an 8,000 pounder and incendiaries, and ten a cookie and SBCs of incendiaries, which would be used to good effect to finally bring an end to the hitherto charmed life of this city. All from East Wretham reached the target and delivered the contents of their bomb bays from between 16,000 and 19,000 feet onto accurate and concentrated red and green TIs, before returning safely to report many explosions and fires. The main force crews performed well, and Germany's largest inland port wilted under the onslaught, post-raid reconnaissance revealing that almost sixteen hundred buildings had been reduced to rubble, and sixty thousand tons of shipping had been sunk or severely damaged. It was not a one-sided affair, however, and the defenders fought back to bring down thirty-four bombers, the heaviest loss at a Ruhr target since the campaign began, exceeding the previous highest from the recent Dortmund raid by three.

On the following day 442 aircraft from all but 5 Group were made ready for a return to the Ruhr that night to attack Bochum. A simultaneous operation by 5 Group with 8 Group support would attempt to rectify the recent failure at Pilsen's Skoda works. 115 Squadron bombed up a dozen Lancasters for Bochum and winched six mines into the bomb bay of another for delivery to waters off the Dutch Frisians. The bombers departed first, between 00.35 and 00.46, with F/L Avant the senior pilot on duty,

156

and all reached the target area to identify it, partly by means of ground detail in the form of the River Ruhr, but mostly by the red and green TIs from the Pathfinder heavy brigade. They bombed from between 14,000 and 19,500 feet, and observed large explosions and concentrated fires with thick, brown smoke rising to 10,000 feet as they turned away. The opening fifteen minutes of the raid had been highly successful, until decoy markers succeeded in drawing away some of the effort, but, even so, almost four hundred buildings were destroyed and seven hundred others seriously damaged. Twenty-four aircraft failed to return, and nine were missing also from the unsuccessful attack on the Skoda works. While these operations were in progress, Sgt Giles and crew took off at 01.35 and delivered their mines into the briefed location from 700 feet after establishing their position by Gee-fix.

A nine-day break from major operations would now allow the crews to draw breath, and the squadrons to replenish, and it was during this period that 617 Squadron established its place in bomber folklore with its epic attack on the Möhne, Eder and Sorpe Dams to the east of the Ruhr Valley on the night of the 16/17th. Contrary to the impression given in the famous feature film of the operation, 617 Squadron was not the only unit over enemy territory on that night, and more than fifty aircraft were engaged in mining operations off the French and Dutch coasts. 115 Squadron dispatched F/Os Cammell and Anderson at 01.16 and 01.21 respectively to the Dutch Frisians, where they arrived about an hour after the third wave of 617 Squadron had made landfall a hundred miles to the south over the Scheldt Estuary. They delivered their mines into the briefed locations from 800 and 850 feet respectively and returned safely from uneventful sorties. On the following night F/O Cammell and crew took off at 20.40 for another mining sortie, this time off La Rochelle, and completed a timed run from Pointe du Payre to deliver six mines into the briefed location from 850 feet. F/O Cammell and crew were selected again on the 21st for their third mining operation in five nights, this one requiring a six-hour round-trip to the port of Bordeaux on the River Gironde. They took off at 22.25, and were followed into the air minutes later by W/C Rainsford and P/Os Barnes and Brown, who were bound for the Dutch Frisians. F/O Cammell identified the Pointe-de-la-Negade as his pinpoint, and delivered the mines from 800 feet, while those tending the Nectarines garden also planted their vegetables in the briefed locations from a similar height before returning from uneventful sorties. Earlier in the day F/L Edmonds had arrived on posting from 1657 Conversion Unit.

Fully rested, the Pathfinder and main force squadrons were prepared to return to the fray on the 23rd, and crews were informed at briefing that Dortmund was to be their target for the second time in the month. They were also told that they would be part of a new record non-1,000 force of 826 aircraft, and, such was the expansion that had taken place, this represented 230 aircraft more than for the previous record set less than three weeks earlier. 115 Squadron detailed its own record of sixteen Lancasters, and the four pilots recently engaged in mining sorties were to fly as second pilots to gain experience of a bombing operation. W/C Rainsford accompanied F/L Avant, P/O Brown was with S/L Fox, F/O Barnes with F/L Bazalgette and F/O Cammell with P/O Finnerty. They took off either side of midnight, half with an 8,000 pounder and incendiaries on board and half with a cookie and incendiaries, and all reached the target to find clear conditions, and bombed from between 16,000 and 20,000 feet onto either the red and green Pathfinder TIs or on the burgeoning fires around the aiming-point. Returning crews described large concentrations of fires emitting thick, black smoke, and other scattered fires to the north and north-east. Thirty-eight aircraft failed to return, a new record for the campaign, and the Halifaxes had suffered most, losing eighteen of their number. In return, the Command had delivered another stunning and devastating assault on a major Ruhr centre of production, leaving almost two thousand buildings in ruins, and severely damaging many war industry factories.

The long-serving S/L Chilton was officially posted to 1678 Conversion Unit on the 25th, and was now the holder of a DFC and AFC. This was the day on which Dortmund's neighbour, Düsseldorf, was selected to host the latest operation of the Ruhr offensive, and a force of 759 aircraft was assembled to carry out the task. During the afternoon the bomber stations of eastern England resounded to the noise of constant take-offs and landings as night-flying tests were carried out, and this was followed by the bombing-up, arming and fuelling process, while the crews attended briefings and ate their pre-operational supper of eggs and bacon. A late take-off meant that there was time to kill, and, with double summer time in operation, there were still streaks of light in the sky as they made their way to the dispersals to carry out final checks, smoke the last few cigarettes, urinate on the tail-wheel and settle into their crew positions. 115 Squadron was setting a new record of dispatching seventeen Lancasters on this night, and this took place between 00.27 and 00.50 with S/L Fox the senior pilot on duty. F/O Andrews was soon back in the circuit with starboard-inner engine failure, leaving the others to press on to the target, where eight-tenths cloud with tops at 8,000 feet awaited those at the head of the stream. This would reduce later to five-tenths, but the ground remained hidden by industrial haze and created problems for the Pathfinders, while decoy markers and fire sites added to the difficulties. Red and green TIs guided the main force crews to the aiming-point, and those from 115 Squadron bombed from between 15,000 and 20,000 feet, observing fires and explosions. Twenty-seven aircraft failed to return, but 115 Squadron was not represented among them, and, thus, it continued to enjoy a loss-free month. Post-raid reconnaissance revealed the raid to have failed, local reports claiming that fewer than one hundred buildings had been destroyed.

115 Squadron had a record eighteen Lancasters on stand-by for a raid on Cologne on the 26th, but this was cancelled. S/L The Hon. R A G Baird, the son of Viscount and Viscountess Stonehaven, arrived on posting from 4 Group's 10 Squadron on this day, which was a somewhat unusual move, and would require him to undergo Lancaster conversion training before he could fill the vacancy for a flight commander. The squadron detailed sixteen Lancasters on the 27th for an operation that night by 518 aircraft against Essen. This would be the fifth attack on Essen since the Ruhr campaign began, and, so far, all had been successful. The 115 Squadron element departed East Wretham between 23.09 and 23.25

F/L 'Al' Avant DFC in Lancaster DS624. The nose art was removed and is now in the Windsor & Eton Branch HQ of the RAFA. (Ted Smith)

with F/L Avant the senior pilot on duty, and all reached the target guided by route markers and release-point flares as they drifted into the cloud-tops on parachutes. It was at this point that DS655 blew up over the target after being hit by flak, flinging clear the pilot, F/O Cammell RNZAF, who, alone of his crew, survived, albeit in enemy hands, and was the first from the squadron to survive the loss of a Lancaster. The others bombed from between 15,000 and 20,000 feet, observing concentrated fires and two large explosions, one of which produced reddish smoke that ascended to 4,000 feet. Post-raid reconnaissance revealed that some of the bombing had undershot, but that almost five hundred buildings had been destroyed in central and northern districts, while ten other Ruhr towns had been hit. Twenty-three aircraft failed to return as "Happy Valley's" evil reputation became set for all time, and would continue to send chills coursing through the veins whenever it was mentioned as a target. This operation concluded the tour of F/L Avant DFC, and he stepped down to non-operational duties pending a posting to the 6 Group station at East Moor.

Mining operations occupied thirty-four aircraft on the night of the 28/29th, and just one of them represented 115 Squadron. The freshman crew of Sgt Ruff took off at 23.02 bound for the German Frisians, and delivered their six mines into the briefed location from 700 feet after pinpointing on Baltrum. 719 crews were briefed on the 29th for the final major raid of the month, which was to be directed against Barmen, one of the twin towns known jointly as Wuppertal, situated on the southern fringe of the Ruhr Valley. 115 Squadron made ready sixteen Lancasters, which took off between 23.25 and 00.05 with W/C Rainsford the senior pilot on duty, supported by S/L Fox, and headed via the southern route to the Ruhr over Belgium. It was here that DS627 crossed paths with the night-fighter of Ofw Fritz Schellwat of 5/NJG.1, who shot it down to crash at 02.18 some seven miles south-south-east of Lommel, killing Sgt Fleming and his crew. The others were guided to the aiming-point by yellow route-markers and red and green TIs, and delivered their bombs from between 15,500 and 20,000 feet before returning to report thick, black smoke rising to 10,000 feet. It was one of those rare occasions when all facets of the plan came together in perfect harmony, and the marking and bombing were both accurate and concentrated. Fire, possibly in the form of a firestorm, swept through the built-up area, reducing an estimated 80% of it to charred ruins, destroying in the process around four thousand houses, scores of industrial premises and most of the large factories. The death toll at 3,400 people was the greatest yet at a German urban target, and foreshadowed what was in store for the enemy civilian population for the remainder of the war. Thirty-three aircraft failed to return, and an eventful night for 115 Squadron saw DS616 barely survive an encounter with a night-fighter, but F/O Andrews brought it home with a mortally-wounded rear gunner, who would succumb to his wounds in hospital, and carried out a crash-landing at East Wretham without further injury to the occupants. Before coming to rest, however, the aircraft collided with P/O Coles's DS618, and this was also declared a write-off. Sgt Small's DS623 arrived back with damage to its fuselage, wings and fuel tanks courtesy of heavy flak ten miles west of Ostend. During the course of the month the squadron operated on eleven nights and dispatched 113 sorties for the loss of four Lancasters and two crews.

June 1943

As recorded earlier, W/C Sims officially concluded his brief period as commanding officer on the 1st of June, and was officially succeeded by W/C Rainsford on that day. There were no major operations during the first third of the new month, but F/Sgt Peate and crew took off at 23.11 on the 5th to carry out their maiden mining operation off the Frisians, and returned safely to report an uneventful sortie during which they fulfilled their brief from 800 feet. It was not until the night of the 11/12th, that the main force was called into action, and, after the long and probably boring period of inactivity, the crews were, no doubt,

P/O M. Coles' Crew and Ground Crew of P - Peter, East Wretham 1943. Photograph taken on completion of 25 ops.

overjoyed to receive the call to briefing. They learned that the target for that night was Düsseldorf, which had escaped relatively lightly less than three weeks earlier. Thirteen Lancasters were made ready at East Wretham as part of an overall force of 783 aircraft, but the crews had to wait until very late before setting out for the Ruhr. All got away without incident either side of 00.30 with S/L Fox the senior pilot on duty and S/L Baird undertaking his first sortie since arriving in May. P/O Eggleston and crew were back on the ground after an hour and twenty minutes after their starboard-inner engine failed, and S/L Fox and crew had the misfortune to be intercepted while outbound by German night-fighter ace, Major Werner Streib, of 1/NJG1. DS647 was shot down to crash at 02.16 some seven miles north-north-east of Uden in south-eastern Holland, killing all on board. The remaining eleven 115 Squadron participants pressed on to the target, where they were guided to the aiming-point by yellow route markers, release-point flares and red and green TIs, and bombed from between 17,500 and 22,000 feet. Returning crews reported a large concentration of fires with volumes of thick smoke rising to 16,000 feet, and a particularly large explosion was also observed as well as a few scattered fires. The plan worked perfectly until an Oboe Mosquito accidentally dropped some markers fourteen miles north-east of Düsseldorf, which caused some bomb loads to be wasted in open country. The damage was done, however, and post-raid reconnaissance revealed an area of fire measuring 8 x 5 kilometres in an around the city centre. Local reports mentioned more than 8,800 fires of which 1,444 were classed as large, 1,292 people losing their lives, while 140,000 others were bombed out of their homes. Many dozens of war-industry factories suffered a complete or temporary loss of production, and eight ships were sunk or damaged in the Rhine docks. The defenders fought back to claim thirty-eight aircraft, which equalled the highest casualty rate of the campaign to date.

Acting F/L Ian Bazalgette, whose substantive rank was flying officer, was promoted to the acting rank of squadron leader on the 12th to succeed S/L Fox DFC, whose vast experience would be missed. This promotion demonstrated how losses could catapult junior officers into positions of heavy responsibility, and a number of squadron commanders at this time had a substantive rank two or even three steps below their acting rank, and would lose their elevated status on posting at the conclusion of their tours. The Ruhr offensive continued at Bochum on the 12th for which a force of 503 aircraft was made ready. 115 Squadron contributed thirteen Lancasters, which took to the air between 23.59 and 00.10 with S/L Baird the senior pilot on duty, but he and his crew were forced to return early after the mid-upper gunner became ill. The recently-promoted F/L Starky's return had occurred ten minutes earlier, after DS629 became unstable at altitude because of a problem with an aileron. The others pushed on to the target area, which lay hidden beneath complete cloud cover, but located it by means of red and green TIs delivered with great accuracy by the Pathfinders. The squadron crews bombed from between 18,000 and 21,000 feet, and returned with an impression of a scattered attack, when, in fact, post-raid reconnaissance would reveal massive damage to the city centre in an area of 130 acres of devastation, and this demonstrated the huge benefits of Oboe. Local reports mentioned 449 buildings destroyed and more than nine hundred severely damaged. Among twenty-four missing aircraft was the squadron's DS652, which, it is believed, was shot down off the Dutch coast by a night-fighter, killing F/Sgt Ruff RNZAF and his crew, the bodies of the pilot and two others eventually washing ashore for local burial at the end of the month.

A modest force of under two hundred Lancasters pounded the Ruhr city of Oberhausen on the night of the 14/15th, and a similar force gained moderate success at Cologne two nights later, both without a contribution from 3 Group. It was the 19th before the 115 Squadron crews found themselves once more in the briefing room to learn that they would be mining that night off the French coast, while 107 of the group's Stirlings took part in a 3, 4, 6 and 8 Group attack on the Schneider armaments works at Le Creusot in central France. This target had been attacked famously by 5 Group in daylight in October of the previous year, but had escaped serious damage, and it would be a similar story this time also. Meanwhile, twelve 115 Squadron Lancasters departed East Wretham between 22.19 and 22.30, three to plant their vegetables off La Rochelle and the remainder in the mouth of the River Gironde, the waterway providing access to the port of Bordeaux. At La Rochelle F/Sgt Peate pinpointed on Pointe-de-la-Payre and delivered his mines according to brief from 600 feet, while F/O Barnes timed his run from the north-west tip of the Ile-de-Re and dropped from 500 feet. The third Lancaster assigned to this garden, DS668, failed to survive an encounter with a night-fighter while on the way home over France, and the crew was forced to abandon it to its fate. It ultimately crashed some twenty miles east of Angers, by which time, the pilot, F/O Brown, had landed in the River Loire and drowned, but his flight engineer and wireless operator managed to evade capture, while the remaining four members of the crew were apprehended. S/L Baird was the senior pilot among those heading further south to the Gironde Estuary, where the mines were delivered into the briefed locations from between 600 and 4,000 feet after pinpointing on Lake Hourtin.

A hectic round of four major operations in the space of five nights began at Krefeld on the 21/22nd. A force of 705 aircraft had been made ready, of which eleven Lancasters represented 115 Squadron. As always for operations over mainland Germany in mid-summer, take-off was late, and it was between 00.10 and 00.20 that the 115 Squadron element took to the air with W/C Rainsford and S/L Bazalgette the senior pilots on duty. F/O Anderson's sortie lasted just eighty minutes and was curtailed by the failure of the port-outer engine which necessitated the safe dumping of the 8,000 pounder. The remainder reached the target, where red and green TIs provided a clear and precise aiming-point to receive the 2,300 tons of bombs. The 115 Squadron crews attacked from between 16,500 and 21,000 feet and observed explosions at 01.35 and 01.38, and fires producing considerable amounts of smoke. Post-raid reconnaissance would reveal an unprecedented catalogue of damage, which amounted to over five and

161

a half thousand houses and apartment blocks destroyed. More than a thousand people lost their lives, and 72,000 others were bombed out of their homes, but the operation was far from a one-sided affair. It took place in bright moonlight, which enabled enemy night-fighters to infiltrate the bombers and contribute to heavy losses. The afflicted German civilians might have been cheered to know that forty-four of their tormentors would not be returning to England that night, a number representing more than three hundred individual airmen. This was the highest loss by far of the campaign to date, but 115 Squadron escaped the carnage, and came through unscathed.

On the following day Mülheim an der Ruhr was posted as the target for the first time, although it had almost certainly been hit by thousands of stray bombs intended for the neighbouring cities of Duisburg, Essen and Oberhausen. 557 aircraft were made ready, including nine Lancasters representing 115 Squadron, which also briefed the three freshman crews of Sgts Rashley and Jolly and F/Sgt Newton for mining sorties off the German Frisians. The mining trio departed a minute after midnight, to be followed within twenty-five minutes by the bombing brigade led by S/L Bazalgette. Sgt Wolfson and crew were well on their way to the target and had reached cruising altitude when the intercom and oxygen system failed, forcing them to turn back. The others were guided to the target by red and green TIs, and dropped their bombs from between 16,000 and 21,000 feet, observing a large concentration of fires on and around the aiming-point. Post-raid reconnaissance confirmed another highly accurate and destructive operation,

Lancaster DS669 KO-L of 115 Sqn after Cologne raid 28-29 June 1943. Piloted by Sgt Jolly, an attack by a nightfighter sheared off the rear turret. The rear gunner, Sgt Geoffrey White, was never found.

Lancaster KO-J from B-24

115 Sqn Lancaster DS652 KO-B First operation 4 May 1943 FTR Bochum 13 June 1943

which had reduced to rubble eleven hundred houses, while damaging many thousands more, including numerous public and industrial buildings. The heavy losses continued, however, and this night's casualty figure was thirty-five, although 115 Squadron again came through intact. A short time after the bombers' return the miners came home after delivering their stores into the briefed locations from between 600 and 1,000 feet after pinpointing on either Baltrum or Nordeney islands. Sgt Rashley's DS666 brought back a little damage to its port wing after hitting a balloon tethered to a ship in a convoy.

F/O Anderson and Sgt Wolfson and their crews departed East Wretham for the Frisians at 22.50 on the 23rd, and returned safely a little under six hours later having deposited their mines in the briefed locations from 1,500 and 2,000 feet respectively. After a night's rest for the main force, 630 aircraft prepared to set off on the evening of the 24th for Elberfeld, the other half of the Wuppertal conurbation. 115 Squadron contributed fourteen Lancasters, which took off either side of midnight with S/L Baird the senior pilot on duty, and, after F/Sgt Peate and crew had returned early with port-inner engine failure, the remainder reached the target to follow up on accurate Pathfinder marking. The usual red and green TIs marked out the aiming-point, and the squadron participants bombed from between 11,500 and 21.500 feet, observing concentrated fires and a pall of black smoke rising to 15,000 feet. Post-raid reconnaissance revealed a more extensive creep-back than of late, but the attack was equally as destructive as that which had wiped out the Barmen half a month earlier. An estimated 94% of the town's built-up area had been laid waste, with scores of industrial premises destroyed, along with three thousand houses, and local reports put the death toll at eighteen hundred people. The heavy losses of Bomber Command aircraft and crews continued, however, and thirty-four dispersals lay empty on the following morning.

The Ruhr city of Gelsenkirchen had been a regular destination for the Command during the oil campaigns earlier in the war, but had not been attacked in numbers since 1941. A force of 473 aircraft was put together on the 25th, and among them were a dozen Lancasters representing 115 Squadron.

Sgt. E.T.G. Hall (third from left) and Crew at Buckingham Palace after Investiture of C.G.M. (Air).
Sgt Hall was the mid upper gunner when Lancaster DS669 lost its rear turret
and he received the CGM for his actions.

Before they departed East Wretham, however, Sgts Bennett and Whitehead and their crews took off to mine the waters off La Rochelle. The bombing element took off either side of midnight with F/Ls Prager and Starky the senior pilots on duty, but, for the second operation running, F/Sgt Peate and crew were forced to turn back with engine failure, this time afflicting the starboard-outer. F/L Starky collided with what was believed to be another Lancaster over Enschede on the Dutch side of the frontier with Germany, and DS629 sustained damage to its starboard wing, which forced the abandonment of the sortie and the dumping live of the bomb load. The others reached the target to find it completely hidden beneath cloud, and, for once, the Oboe marking, having been depleted by equipment failure in five of the twelve Mosquitos, failed to provide a confirmed reference for the main force, and bombs were sprayed liberally around the Ruhr in an echo of the past. The 115 Squadron crews reported bombing on release-point flares from between 18,000 and 21,000 feet, and observing the glow of fires through the cloud, but few if any hit the intended target and the operation was a failure. DS666 was absent from its dispersal following this operation, and the fate of it and the crew of Sgt Rashley has never been established. Sgt Bennett and crew were the last to land, having delivered their mines to the briefed location from 700 feet after pinpointing on Pointe-de-la-Payre. The return of Sgt Whitehead and his crew in DS663 was awaited in vain, and news eventually came through that they had all died in a crash near Nantes in north-western France.

A series of three major attacks on Cologne would span the turn of the month, and preparations for the first one were put in hand on the 28th. 115 Squadron loaded thirteen Lancasters with either 8,000 or 4,000 pounders, and filled up the spaces in the bomb bays with incendiaries. They were part of an overall force of 608 aircraft, and took off between 00.10 and 00.30 with F/L Prager the senior pilot on duty. Between 02.15 and 02.30 Sgt Wolfson, Sgt Bennett and P/O Small arrived back at East Wrethem with starboard engine trouble, intercom failure to a number of crew stations and shuddering controls respectively. The others pressed on and were greeted by ten-tenths cloud over the target, necessitating the employment of skymarking, the least reliable of all the marking methods. To add to the difficulties, only six of the twelve Oboe Mosquitos were able to deliver their markers as a reference to the Pathfinder heavy brigade, and the marking was six minutes late. The 115 Squadron crews bombed from between 16,500 and 21,500 feet on release-point flares, and the glow of fires beneath the cloud combined with black smoke rising up through it were the only indications of what was happening on the ground. Two large explosions were witnessed from eighty miles into the return journey at 02.25 by Sgt Jolly and crew, whose DS669 was then attacked by a night-fighter, and sustained damage to the rear turret and rudders. When other crew members reached the rear of the aircraft, the turret was no longer attached and its occupant, Sgt White, was, ultimately, declared missing believed killed. Despite the difficulties, Cologne had undergone its most terrifying ordeal of the war, and suffered a degree of destruction unprecedented thus far. More than 6,400 buildings were left in ruins, including dozens of an industrial nature, a further fifteen thousand were damaged to some extent, and the death toll was put at 4,377 people, all at a cost to the Command of twenty-five aircraft. During the course of the month the squadron operated on ten nights and dispatched 105 sorties for the loss of five Lancasters and crews.

July 1943

Having ended June's operations, it fell to Cologne to open the July account, and a force of 653 aircraft was made ready on the 3rd of which fourteen Lancasters belonged to 115 Squadron. They took off either side of midnight with F/Os Barnes and Larson the senior pilots on duty, six of them carrying an 8,000 pounder and incendiaries and eight a cookie and incendiaries. Sgt Sutton and crew returned at 01.40 with their bombs on board after starboard-inner engine failure forced them to abandon their sortie, but the others pressed on in good conditions to find the aiming-point on the eastern bank of the Rhine clearly identified by release-point flares and red and green TIs. The 115 Squadron crews bombed from between

17,500 and 21,000 feet, and observed two very bright explosions, concentrated fires and smoke rising to 10,000 feet. It was on this night that the Luftwaffe introduced a new system of night-fighting, which they named Wilde Sau or Wild Boar, and relied on standard single-engine day fighters flying over the cauldron of a burning city and attacking bombers silhouetted against the fiery backdrop. JG300 was led by the charismatic Major Hans-Joachim (Hajo) Hermann, who, along with his pilots, would have to expose themselves to the dangers posed by their own flak, although, when they were operating, the flak could be restricted to a predetermined height. Thirty aircraft were claimed by the defenders on this night, and some, inevitably fell victim to JG300, although, until this new threat was recognised, many crews, unused to being attacked over the target, would ascribe damage to friendly-fire incidents. W/O Boutilier and crew returned with flak damage to the underside of the rear turret of DS683 and a hole in the starboard rudder, which they credited to friendly fire. DS662 went down somewhere between the Dutch/German border and the target, and only the bomb-aimer from the crew of Sgt Stokes-Roberts survived to fall into enemy hands. Post-raid reconnaissance revealed another stunningly successful raid, which laid waste to a large area of the city east of the Rhine, destroying a further 2,200 houses and twenty industrial premises.

It was left to an all-Lancaster force to conclude the series against Cologne on the night of the 8/9th, again with stunning success, which left more 2,300 residential buildings in ruins in hitherto less afflicted districts of the city. Eventually, the Cologne authorities were able to compile statistics on the effects of the three raids, and assessed that eleven thousand buildings had been destroyed, five and a half thousand people had been killed, and a further 350,000 had been rendered homeless. 115 Squadron had not been called into action for the final Cologne raid, but detailed fifteen Lancasters on the 9th for another attempt that night on Gelsenkirchen's oil-production sites, for which a force of 418 aircraft was made ready. The 115 Squadron participants departed East Wretham either side of 23.30 with F/Ls Prager and Starky the senior pilots on duty. Also on the Order of Battle was Lt Andrews, who was on attachment from the USAAF 8th Air Force. Sgt Sutton and crew turned back ninety minutes after their departure when the rear gunner became ill through oxygen starvation. The others reached the target to find complete cloud cover, and bombed on release-point flares from between 18,500 and 22,500 feet in the belief that they were over the intended aiming-point. In fact, half of the Oboe Mosquitos had suffered equipment failure, and a sixth had dropped skymarkers ten miles to the north in error. Despite this, much of the bombing fell into the southern districts of Gelsenkirchen and into Bochum and Wattenscheid further south still, and damage to the intended target was slight. Although two more operations to the region would take place in the final week of the month, the Ruhr offensive had now effectively run its course. Harris could look back over the past five months with genuine satisfaction at the performance of his squadrons, and, as a champion of new technology, take particular pleasure from the success of Oboe, without which, many of the raids would have produced scant reward in the face of cloud and industrial haze. It was true that losses had been grievously high, but much of Germany's industrial heartland now lay in ruins, while the factories at home and the Empire Training Scheme were easily able to keep pace with the rate of attrition and feed fresh aircraft and men to the squadrons.

With confidence high, Harris now sought an opportunity to deliver a knock-out blow against a major German city, and thereby to rock the very foundations of enemy morale. The intention was to mount a short, sharp campaign until the job was done, and to expend around ten thousand tons of bombs. In each year of the war to date, the Command had gone to Hamburg during the final week of July, and it was this city, spared by the weather from hosting the first thousand bomber raid a year earlier, that Harris selected for the aptly named Operation Gomorrah. As Germany's Second City, it possessed the necessary political status, while also being a major producer of war materials, particularly with regard to U-Boots and shipbuilding generally. However, it also offered advantages in terms of operational considerations,

An unidentified 115 Sqn Lancaster after what appears to be an overrun.

W/O E Boutilier with air- and groundcrew

being approachable from the sea, without the need to traverse large tracts of hostile territory, and was close enough to the bomber stations to allow a large force to approach and withdraw in the few hours of darkness afforded by mid-summer. Perhaps most importantly of all, lying beyond the range of Oboe, which had proved so decisive at the Ruhr, Hamburg boasted the wide River Elbe to provide a strong H2S signature for the navigators high above.

As planning for the destruction of Hamburg went ahead, a force of 1, 5 and 8 Group Lancasters delivered a highly destructive attack on Turin on the night of the 12/13th, which cost the life of the 44 Squadron commanding officer, W/C Nettleton VC of Augsburg fame. Orders were received on the 13th for an operation against Aachen that night, and a force of 374 aircraft was assembled accordingly. 115 Squadron detailed seventeen Lancasters, which took off between 23.55 and 00.35 with S/Ls Baird and Bazalgette the senior pilots on duty. F/Sgt Peate and crew returned within two hours after DS680 developed a violent shudder, and Sgt Jolly and crew landed fifteen minutes later because of a starboard-outer engine issue. DS690 was outbound over Belgium and approaching the Luxembourg frontier when it crossed paths with the night-fighter of Hptm August Geiger of III/JG.1, and was shot down to crash at 02.10 at les Hayons. Only the flight engineer from the crew of S/L The Hon R A G Baird escaped with his life to become a PoW. The others reached the target to find excellent visibility but some cloud, and arrived ahead of schedule because of a stronger-than-forecast tail wind. The first Pathfinder markers unleashed an unusual amount of activity as a greater number of bomb loads went down in the first minute than was normal. The entire city below seemed to erupt in flames immediately, although the 115 Squadron participants, which carried out their attacks from between 16,000 and 21,000 feet, were unable to track the fall of their bombs. A large explosion was observed along with the glow of fires, and post-raid reconnaissance would confirm a devastating raid, which destroyed almost three thousand buildings, most of which were apartment blocks. Among the twenty aircraft lost was DS660, which was shot down by a night-fighter over the Pas-de-Calais and crashed near Bapaume, killing all but the pilot, F/O Larson RCAF, who was taken into captivity. It is not known whether this event took place during the outbound or homeward journey, but the survival of the pilot alone of the occupants suggests an explosion of the bomb load, which threw him out with his seat-parachute attached, a not unusual occurrence. This points to the Lancaster being outbound, but this is purely speculation on the part of the author.

This was the final operation to involve 3 Group before the start of Operation Gomorrah, and there was barely any activity at all from then until the 24th. S/L Watson was posted in from 1651 Conversion Unit on the 14th as successor to S/L Baird as a flight commander, and P/O Plum was posted to 1678 Conversion Unit two days later at the end of his tour. Sgt Jolly, Sgt Crowther and Sgt Hall were recognised for their valour during the Cologne operation at the end of June, the first two-mentioned receiving the DFM and Sgt Hall the much-coveted CGM (Conspicuous Gallantry Medal). A force of 791 aircraft was assembled on the 24th for the first round of Operation Gomorrah, and, while the crews attended briefing, a new device, which had been available for a year, but had been withheld from operational use in case the enemy copied it for their own use, was being installed into their aircraft. "Window" consisted of tinfoil-backed strips of paper, cut to a precise length, which, when dispensed into the airflow at a pre-determined point on the outward flight, would slowly drift to earth in great clouds, swamping the enemy night-fighter, searchlight and gun-laying radar with false returns, making it impossible to identify genuine aircraft. The Germans had already developed a similar system under the code name Düppel, which had also been withheld for the same reason. 115 Squadron winched either 8,000 or 4,000 pounders into the bomb bays of sixteen Lancasters and added the appropriate number of SBCs of incendiaries, before dispatching them between 22.25 and 22.50 with W/C Rainsford the senior pilot on duty supported by S/L Bazalgette. Having climbed for height over their stations, the squadrons set out for the North Sea to gain operational altitude and form into a bomber stream with the Pathfinders'

H2S marker aircraft in the van and the backers-up spread throughout. Few combats took place during the outward flight, and those aircraft shot down at this stage of the operation were off course, and outside of the protection of the bomber stream, and may have been early returns. Sgt Tinn and crew had to abandon their sortie because of illness among three members of the crew and engine issues, and they were safely back home within two hours of taking-off.

The others pressed on, and, at the appointed time, the assigned crew member in each aircraft began to release bundles of Window through the flare-chute, and would continue to do so until a predetermined point was reached on the return leg. The efficacy of Window was immediately apparent as the head of the stream reached the Hamburg defence zone, and found an absence of the usually efficient co-ordination between the searchlight and gun batteries. Defence from the ground was random and generally ineffective, and, in clear conditions, the Pathfinders were able to produce scattered but acceptably accurate marking of an area close to the city centre. The main force bombing began well, but an extensive creep-back developed, which cut a swathe of destruction along the line of approach, across the north-western districts, and out into open country, where a proportion of the bombing was wasted. The 115 Squadron crews were led to the aiming-point by route markers and carried out their attacks on red and green TIs from between 17,000 and 21,500 feet, from where they could make out the Binnen and Aussen (Inner and Outer) Alster Lakes close to the city centre. On return they reported well-concentrated and huge fires with columns of thick, black smoke ascending towards them. It was an encouraging start to Operation Gomorrah, and a foretaste to the unfortunate population, fifteen hundred of whom already lay dead, of what was to come over the ensuing week. A bonus was the modest loss of just twelve aircraft, and this spoke volumes for the success of Window, which had clearly gained a temporary march on the enemy defences.

On the following night, Harris switched his force to Essen, to take advantage of the body-blow dealt to the enemy defensive system by Window. A force of 705 aircraft was assembled which included fourteen 115 Squadron Lancasters, and they took to the air between 22.37 and 22.50 led by F/L Anderson. There were no early returns to East Wretham, and bombing was carried out on red and green TIs from between 17,000 and 23,000 feet. Very large explosions were observed at 00.38 and 00.43, by which time concentrated fires had begun to take hold along with others scattered right across the city, sending smoke rising into the air. Post-raid reconnaissance confirmed the effectiveness of the raid, which had hit the industrial eastern half of the city particularly hard, and the Krupp works experienced its worst night of the war. Fifty industrial buildings and over 2,800 houses were reduced to rubble, while many others sustained serious damage.

A night's rest preceded round two of Operation Gomorrah, for which 787 aircraft were made ready on the 27th. 115 Squadron dispatched seventeen Lancasters between 22.30 and 22.45 with S/L Watson the senior pilot on duty for the first time since his arrival from 1651 Conversion Unit on the 14th as successor to S/L Baird. W/O Noxon and F/Sgt Blackwell were forced to return early with engine issues, leaving the others to press on in good weather conditions to north-western Germany. What followed their arrival over the city was both unprecedented and unforeseeable, and resulted from a conspiracy of circumstances. The weather during July had been unusually hot and dry, leaving tinderbox conditions in parts of the city. The first spark of ignition came with the Pathfinder markers, which fell about two miles east of the planned city centre aiming-point, but with unaccustomed concentration into the densely populated working-class residential districts of Hamm, Hammerbrook and Borgfeld. The main force crews followed up with uncharacteristic accuracy and scarcely any creep-back, with the 115 Squadron crews attacking from between 14,500 and 23,000 feet and contributing the contents of their bomb bays to the 2,300 tons of bombs falling into this relatively compact area. The individual fires joined together to form one gigantic conflagration, which sucked in oxygen from surrounding areas to feed its voracious appetite. This created winds of hurricane force, and, such was the power of the meteorological phenomenon, that trees were uprooted and flung bodily into the fire, along with debris and people. Temperatures at the heart of the inferno exceeded a thousand degrees Celcius, and the flames only began to subside once all of the combustible material had been consumed. This first recorded example of a bombing-generated firestorm took the lives of over forty thousand people, and the following day brought the first phase of an exodus from the battered city, which would ultimately involve 1.2 million inhabitants. At debriefing the 115 Squadron crews reported well-concentrated fires with smoke rising to 20,000 feet, but, in truth, they had no idea of the extent of the death and destruction taking place beneath them. In return for the scale of success, the Command posted missing a relatively modest seventeen aircraft.

The Pathfinder and main force squadrons drew breath on the 28th, while their aircraft were prepared and serviced, and a force of 777 stood ready by the evening of the 29th to continue the tormenting of Hamburg. 115 Squadron launched fifteen Lancasters from East Wretham with F/Ls Anderson and Starky the senior pilots on duty, and only Sgt Mosen and crew turned back early because of an indisposed rear gunner, probably as the result of oxygen starvation. F/O Barnes was passing over Hemmingstedt on the Schleswig-Holstein peninsular heading for the target, when the immersion pump was switched off in error, cutting all four engines. The bombs were jettisoned live immediately from 15,000 feet, and the aircraft was recovered and flown home safely. The others were guided to the aiming-point by yellow and green TIs, and delivered their loads from between 16,500 and 22,700 feet, observing many large fires around the markers and others scattered around. The Pathfinder markers had again strayed two miles to the east of the city centre, but a little south of the firestorm area, and, following an approach from the north, an extensive creep-back stretched back across the devastation of two nights earlier, before falling onto other residential districts of Wandsbek and Barmbek and parts of Uhlenhorst and Winterhude beyond. Further massive destruction was inflicted through a large area of fire, but there was no repeat of the firestorm. As the defenders began to recover from the effects of Window, so the bomber losses began to escalate, and twenty-eight aircraft failed to return home on this night.

Before Operation Gomorrah was concluded, a force of under three hundred aircraft, consisting of roughly equal numbers of Halifaxes, Stirlings and Lancasters, attacked Remscheid, a town on the edge of the Ruhr south of Wuppertal, and hit it with stunning accuracy, destroying over three thousand houses, and this operation brought down the final curtain on the Ruhr offensive. During the course of the month the squadron operated on just seven occasions, and dispatched 108 sorties for the loss of three Lancasters and crews.

August 1943

Hamburg's current ordeal at the hands of the Command was scheduled to end on the night of the 2/3rd, for which a force of 740 aircraft was assembled. 115 Squadron made ready fourteen Lancasters, which took off between 23.21 and 23.55 with F/Ls Anderson and Eggleston the senior pilots on duty. The weather conditions were good initially, but a towering bank of ice-bearing cloud built over the North Sea, which could not be circumnavigated, and, upon entering it, aircraft were thrown around by violent electrical storms. F/O Alexander of 75(NZ) Squadron later described it as "the most terrifying experience I had ever had, on the ground or in the air", with huge flashes of lightning, thunder, electrical discharges and the instruments going haywire. Not one of the 115 Squadron aircraft reached the target, F/L Eggleston and F/O Barnes both returning early with similar issues affecting their intercom and oxygen systems. The others pressed on to battle with the conditions, but all were persuaded to bomb alternative targets, some of which were creditably close to Hamburg.

Squadron group photo at RAF East Wretham 1943

Had the Pathfinders been able to mark an aiming-point, it might have drawn the main force closer still, but no marking took place and the subsequent bombing was scattered over a wide area of north-western Germany. When dropping their bombs from 18,000 feet W/O Noxon and crew believed that they were over Wilhemsburg, a district of Hamburg located on a number of islands in the Elbe to the south of the city centre. F/L Anderson and crew were over Wesermünde in the Bremerhaven area when the starboard-outer engine began to overheat and a flak barrage compounded their problems. The bombs were jettisoned live from 11,500 feet to help them gain manoeuvrability, and they made it home to report their woes. W/O Hicks and crew reported bombing docks to the west of Hamburg from 8,000 feet, while F/Sgt Peate dumped his cookie live over Cuxhaven from 20,000 feet and brought his incendiaries home. F/Sgt Blackwell and crew failed to reach the target because of severe icing, but claimed to have reached 28,000 feet (possibly incorrectly recorded by the squadron scribe) and bombed Bremervörde, some thirty miles west of Hamburg. F/O Christiansen penetrated to within ten miles of Hamburg's western suburbs before bombing from 13,500 feet and reporting on return the glow of fires visible from the enemy coast. F/Sgt Bradford and crew were heading north towards an area of fire, which they took to be Hamburg, but decided to drop their bombs from 20,000 feet on a built-up area below that they believed to be Buchholz. Sgt Howell and crew were contending with an engine issue when opting to bomb Wenzendorf, a town situated some fifteen miles to the south-west of Hamburg, from 16,000 feet, and they observed explosions.

All of the Lancasters that were going to return to East Wretham were on the ground by 05.40, and this left three unaccounted for among a total loss for the night of thirty aircraft. It would take time for news to filter though concerning their fate, and surviving crews were used to the process of faces disappearing from their midst and the Committee of Adjustment representatives moving quickly to remove all personal items from accommodation areas. By the end of the day new faces would appear, the beds would be occupied by different airmen and life would go on as before, the old faces soon fading from the memory. No trace of DS685 and the crew of F/Sgt Button was ever found, while DS715 was sent crashing to the ground near Harburg, the town facing Hamburg from the South Bank of the Elbe, after being struck by lightning, and took with it the crew of P/O Mosen RNZAF. DS673 fell victim to a night-fighter off the north-western coast of Germany, and crashed into the sea with no survivors from the crew of Sgt Bennett, all of whom were recovered eventually for burial. The squadron's contribution to Operation Gomorrah was sixty-two sorties, of which fifty-one were completed as briefed. (The Battle of Hamburg. Martin Middlebrook.)

Before the next phase in Bomber Command operations occupied its attention, 115 Squadron changed address with a move to the newly-built Little Snoring, a station situated within ten miles of the Norfolk coast, directly south of the resort of Wells next the Sea. The construction had been completed in July, with the intention of it becoming a satellite for nearby Foulsham, but 3 Group decided to bestow full status upon it, and 115 Squadron was its first resident unit. The advance party departed East Wretham on the 5th to prepare the way, and the move was completed by the 7th. Italy was at this time on the brink of capitulation, and Bomber Command was invited to help nudge it over the edge with a week-long series of attacks on its major cities. 1, 5 and 8 Groups began the campaign on the night of the 7/8th, with simultaneous raids on Genoa, Milan and Turin, before a return to Germany involved a major operation against Mannheim on the night of the 9/10th. The raid by more than four hundred aircraft was moderately effective, despite difficulties with the marking plan, and over thirteen hundred buildings suffered serious damage or complete destruction, while much of the city's war industry lost vital production.

115 Squadron was ready to return to the fray twenty-four hours later, and made ready fourteen Lancasters as part of an overall force of 653 aircraft bound for the southern city of Nuremberg. They took off for the first time from their new home either side of 22.00 with S/L Watson the senior pilot on duty, but, sadly, an issue with the rear turret oxygen system forced him to return before reaching the south coast. The others pressed on to find the city largely covered by cloud with tops at 14,000 feet, but the green Pathfinder ground markers were sufficiently visible to guide the main force to the aiming-point. The 115 Squadron crews bombed from between 15,000 and 22,000 feet, and large explosions were witnessed at around 01.07 and 01.30, while scattered fires were reported to be visible from a hundred miles into the return journey. DS665 failed to arrive home with the rest of the squadron, and, inexplicably, it was not

Ground crew of DS682 KO-Y, Aubrey Howell's aircraft.

until 18.00 on the 11th that a telephone message was received from RAF Detling to confirm that the Lancaster had crashed at 04.30 at East Hall Farm, Boughton Monchelsea, some five miles south of Maidstone in Kent, killing P/O Erwin and his crew. The raid produced some useful damage in central and southern districts, and was perhaps the most successful attack yet on this one-time bastion of Nazism.

3 Group's involvement in the Italian campaign began on the 12th with the preparation of the Stirling force for a 3 and 8 Group raid on Turin, while 115 Squadron made ready thirteen Lancasters to join 308 other Lancasters and 183 Halifaxes to attack Milan. They departed Little Snoring between 21.05 and 21.20 with W/C Rainsford the senior pilot on duty, supported by S/L Bazalgette, and all reached the target area after flying out in good weather conditions, which persisted over northern Italy to give clear skies. The target could be identified visually, but the crews bombed on green TIs from between 18,000 and 21,500 feet, observing fires beginning to take hold as they turned away and smoke visible from the Alps. Reports coming out of the city combined the effects of all of the August raids, but the majority of the casualties and the damage to four major factories, including the Fiat motor works, and the railway station probably occurred on this night. The very last attack on an Italian city, in a campaign which had begun in 1940, was mounted on the night of the 16/17th and involved 154 aircraft of 3 and 8 Groups raiding Turin. 115 Squadron provided all fourteen of the Lancasters, and they took off between 20.15 and 20.30 with S/L Watson the senior pilot on duty. F/Sgt Bradford was well on his way across France when the rear turret became unserviceable and he was forced to turn back. The others reached the target area and identified the aiming-point either visually or by green TIs, before bombing from between 8,000 and 18,000 feet. DS661 was attacked by a night-fighter during the bombing run, and F/L Anderson ordered the bombs to be jettisoned live while he and the gunners concentrated on violently corkscrewing to attempt to escape. The enemy broke off the engagement, leaving the Lancaster with non-fatal damage to the starboard fin, aileron and fuselage. The squadron awaited in vain the return of DS684 with the crew of S/L Watson, and it was established later that it had crashed near Alencon in northern France, almost certainly on the way home, without survivors. Many 3 Group Stirling crews found themselves being diverted on their return, and by the time that they got back to their respective stations on the 17th, it would be too late for them to participate in one of the war's most important operations, to be carried out that night. F/L Starky was granted acting squadron leader rank on this day, the 17th, to enable him to assume the duties of a flight commander, and F/O Barnes was elevated to acting flight lieutenant rank.

Since the start of hostilities, intelligence had been filtering through concerning German research into rocket weaponry, and, over a period of time, it became clear that this activity was centred upon the island of Usedom on Germany's Baltic coast. A secret weapons establishment had been built at Peenemünde at the northern end, and it was here that the V-1 flying bomb was discovered by the photographic interpreters at Medmenham, and dubbed the Peenemünde 20, because of the twenty-foot span of its wings. Through the interception and decoding of German Enigma signals traffic through Ultra, it was possible for the brilliant scientist, Dr RV Jones, to monitor V-1 trials over the Baltic, and ultimately to feed disinformation back to the enemy concerning its accuracy against London. Churchill's chief scientific adviser, Professor Lindemann, or Lord Cherwell as he became, steadfastly refused to believe in the feasibility of rocket weapons, and remained unmoved even when confronted with a photograph of a V-2 on a trailer at Peenemünde, taken by a PRU Mosquito as recently as June. It required the combined urgings of Dr Jones and Churchill's son-in-law and Financial Secretary to the War Office, Duncan Sandys, to persuade the Prime Minister of the urgency to act, and it was at last decided to mount an operation at the first available opportunity. This came on the night of the 17/18th, and followed on the heels of the ill-fated American 8th Air Force's twin-pronged raids on Regensburg and Schweinfurt earlier in the day, which cost a staggering sixty bombers.

173

T/O Little Snoring 2025 - target Peenemunde, Germany. Crew on 3rd operation. Crashed at 0214 hours at Ostersoen 1 mile SE of Gedser, Denmark.

F/O F R C Pusey
He was one of a small number of RAF personnel entitled to wear both RAF and USAF wings as he trained in the US and then stayed to train both RAF and USAF pilots hence he had to have his American qualification and earn their wings as well. (Courtesy of Graham Sturrock, and his mother, sister of Frederick)

F/O C G Bruton RCAF (Nav)

The RAF operation was meticulously planned to account for the three vital components of Peenemünde, the housing estate, where the scientific and technical staff lived, the factory buildings and the experimental site. Each was assigned to a specific wave of aircraft, with the Pathfinders charged with the responsibility of shifting the point of aim accordingly. After last minute alterations, 3 and 4 Groups were given the first mentioned, 1 Group the second, and 5 and 6 Groups the third. Thus, 115 Squadron's twelve Mk II Lancasters would be the odd men out in a wave of Stirlings and Halifaxes. The whole operation was to be overseen by a Master of Ceremonies (referred to hereafter as Master Bomber) in the manner of Gibson at the dams, and the officer selected for this hazardous and demanding role was G/C Searby of 83 Squadron, who had stepped into Gibson's shoes at 106 Squadron after Gibson was posted out to form 617 Squadron. Searby's role was to direct the marking and bombing by VHF, and to encourage the crews to press on to the aiming-point, a task requiring him to remain in the target area throughout the attack, a role he had practiced during a not-entirely successful operation on Turin on the night of the 7/8th. In an attempt to protect the bombers from the attentions of enemy night-fighters for as long as possible, eight Mosquitos of 139 Squadron were to carry out a spoof raid on Berlin, led by the highly experienced, and former 49 Squadron commander, G/C Len Slee. It was 21.38 when F/O Pusey and crew took to the air in DS630, to be followed over the ensuing twelve minutes by the others as follows; DS653, F/L Christianson, DS626, F/L Eggleston, DS720, F/L Starky, DS659, F/O Barnes, DS630, F/O Pusey, DS691, F/O Seddon, DS722, P/O Cade, DS683, W/O Boutilier, DS678, W/O Hicks,

DS667, F/Sgt Tinn, DS631, F/Sgt Townsend and DS664, F/Sgt Wolfson. All got away safely, and headed for the narrow neck of southern Denmark, before turning south for the target.

The initial marking of the housing estate went awry, the target indicators falling more than a mile beyond the intended aiming-point, and around the forced workers' camp at Trassenheide. Sadly, grievous casualties were inflicted upon the friendly foreign nationals trapped inside their wooden barracks, some of whom had been instrumental in getting intelligence to London. Once rectified, however, the first phase of the operation proceeded according to plan, the 115 Squadron element bombing from between 7,800 and 12,000 feet and the crews reporting on return bomb bursts, concentrated fires and smoke rising to 8,000 feet. It would be learned later that a number of leading members of the scientific team had been killed. 1 Group's attack on the assembly buildings was hampered by a strong crosswind, which carried the markers towards the sea, but, as bombing was conducted from medium level, they still managed to inflict extensive damage on the site. It was while predominantly 5 and 6 Group Lancasters were in the target area, that the night-fighters belatedly arrived from Berlin, having spotted the commotion over the coastal region a hundred miles away, and taking it upon themselves to head in that direction. Once on the scene, they proceeded to take a heavy toll of bombers, both in the skies above Peenemünde, and on the route westwards towards Denmark. Forty aircraft failed to return home, twenty-nine of them from the final wave, while 3 Group posted missing just three crews, after a relatively quiet time at the head of the raid. All twelve 115 crews bombed the target as briefed, but only eleven made it home, and it was the dispersal of DS630 that stood empty in dawn's early light. P/O Pusey and his crew were on only the third operation of their tour, and they were shot down homebound by a night-fighter to crash near Gedser, Denmark's most southerly point, without survivors. The Pathfinders were generally the first to get back after an operation, but the honour on this night fell to the 115 Squadron crew of F/L Eggleston. It was the final operation of their tour, and they had opened the taps on the powerful Hercules engines for the return flight, landing well ahead of the first 8 Group Lancaster. The operation as a whole was sufficiently effective to push back the development of the V-2 by at least a number of weeks, and the testing of the weapon was moved to Poland, beyond the reach of Harris, while construction was relocated to an underground location at Nordhausen in the Harz Mountains to the south of Hannover.

Harris had long believed that Berlin held the key to ultimate victory. As the seat and symbol of Nazi power, its destruction might so effect morale, that it could weaken the Party's grip on the civilian population, and lead to an uprising. He would state in November, that with the assistance of the American 8th Air Force, he could "wreck Berlin from end to end", and, that though costing between them four to five hundred aircraft, it would cost Germany the war. Having personally witnessed the carnage of protracted land campaigns during the Great War, Harris hoped to achieve victory without the need for a bloody and expensive invasion this time around. It should be remembered, that Harris was the first in history to have at his disposal the theoretical means to win a war by bombing alone, and it is only in the light of more recent conflicts, that we know of the absolute need, in a conventional war at least, to physically occupy the enemy's territory. The Americans, however, were committed to victory on land, and there was never the slightest chance of enlisting their support. Undaunted as always, Harris would go to Berlin alone, and prepared his force for the opening phase of what would become the most bitter and morale-sapping offensive undertaken by the crews of Bomber Command. In the meantime, 3 Group was absent from an unsuccessful attempt by more than four hundred aircraft to hit the Ruhr city of Leverkusen and its important I G Farben chemicals plant on the night of the 22/23rd.

There is some debate as to whether or not the three raids on Berlin conducted during late August and early September constituted the start of the Berlin offensive. Some commentators maintain that it did not begin until mid-November, but there was no doubt in the minds of the authors of the squadron and group ORBs, some of which announced the 23rd of August 1943 as the start of the "Battle of Berlin".

F/Sgt Bert Bradford and Crew

115 Squadron loaded thirteen Lancasters with a cookie each and incendiaries, and launched them towards Germany's capital city between 21.00 and 21.15 with the recently-promoted F/L Christiansen

the senior pilot on duty. They were part of an overall force of 727 aircraft that headed for the rendezvous point over the North Sea, before crossing the Dutch coast near Haarlem and setting course to pass between Bremen and Hannover to bypass the southern rim of Berlin. The plan was then to turn back to approach the city from the south-east and, after bombing, pass out over the Baltic coast and make for the Schleswig-Holstein peninsular. Sadly for 115 Squadron, serviceability proved to be its weakness on this night, and four crews, those of W/O Boutilier, F/O Barnes, F/Sgt Jolly and W/O Hicks, returned early for a variety of reasons and were back home within two hours. The remainder pressed on over heavy cloud, which broke up and cleared altogether as more than six hundred aircraft funnelled towards the bombing run, drawn on by the sight of green TIs on the ground. Unfortunately, the Pathfinders had failed to mark the city centre, and, because crews had decided to cut the corner south of Berlin and approach from the south-west rather than south-east, many bomb loads were wasted in open country and on twenty-five outlying communities. The 115 Squadron crews bombed from between 16,000 and 23,500 feet, and, on return, reported concentrated fires, the glow from which was still visible from a hundred miles away. They also reported fierce defensive activity in the form of flak and night-fighters, which resulted in the Command's heaviest single loss of the war to date, amounting to fifty-six aircraft.

Alarmingly, the Stirlings of 3 Group registered a casualty rate of almost 13%. 115 Squadron's single missing aircraft was DS722, which had to be ditched off the Frisians four hours after take-off. Whether or not the entire crew survived the impact is unclear, but only the pilot, Sgt Townsend RAAF, his flight engineer and bomb-aimer were found by the enemy in the dinghy after a six-day ordeal afloat, and they were taken into captivity. The Master Bomber, W/C Johnny Fauquier, the commanding officer of 8 Group's 405 (Vancouver) Squadron, and later 617 Squadron commanding officer, had been unable to rescue the original plan, despite which, more than 2,600 buildings suffered destruction or serious damage in southern districts, making this operation the most effective yet on Berlin.

A night of mining operations in northern waters followed for sixty-six crews twenty-four hours later, to which 115 Squadron contributed two Lancasters. They took off at 21.25 with the crews of F/L Mott and Sgt Pirie bound for the Frisians, and both, it seems, reached the target area, where the former delivered their mines into the briefed location from 600 feet. F/L Mott had arrived from 1678 Conversion Unit on the 24th, and his time with the squadron would be busy but short-lived. The latter experienced an engine issue which caused them to abandon the sortie, and their return to base, just nine minutes ahead of that of F/L Mott, suggests that they had been very close to completion when the problem occurred. Two nights later F/L Mott and crew were detailed for a further mining operation along with Sgts Pirie and Halley, and they departed Little Snoring at 20.00 bound for the Biscay coast. All three found pinpoints on landmarks surrounding the waters off La Rochelle, and delivered their mines in accordance with instructions from between 700 and 900 feet.

The three-night break for the majority of crews of the heavy squadrons after Berlin ended on the 27th, when Nuremberg was posted as the target for that night. A force of 674 aircraft included a contribution from 115 Squadron of ten Lancasters, which took off in a ten-minute slot from 21.35 with F/L Mott the senior pilot on duty and undertaking his third operation in the space of four nights. They flew out across France over patches of cloud, which had cleared to leave clear skies as the Pathfinders approached the target. F/Sgt Jolly and crew were over the Channel when the compass failed, and Sgt Pirie and crew were an hour-and-a-half into the outward flight when their oxygen system let then down, and both crews were forced to turn back. The others pressed on in the wake of the Pathfinders, whose initial efforts were accurate, until problems with their H2S equipment caused them to drop short in conditions of extreme darkness. The Master Bomber was heard by only 25% of the force, and neither he nor the backers-up among the Pathfinders were unable to rectify the situation. The 115 Squadron crews bombed to the east of the green TIs on instructions from the Master Bomber, and did so from between 19,500 and 22,000 feet, observing concentrated fires and smoke. Unfortunately, a pronounced creep-back led to most of the bombing being wasted in open country to the south-south-west of the city, although some did hit the south-eastern and eastern suburbs. Thirty-three aircraft failed to return, eleven of each type, which meant that the Stirling loss rate was again in excess of 10%. 115 Squadron's DS659 failed to survive an encounter with a ME109 fighter operating under the Wilde Sau system in the target area, and F/L Mott and his wireless operator died in the ensuing crash, while their five colleagues were taken prisoner.

The first major attack on the twin frontier towns of Mönchengladbach and Rheydt was signalled on the 30th, and a force of 660 aircraft assembled accordingly. 115 Squadron loaded eleven Lancasters with either an 8,000 or 4,000 pounder each and filled the available space in the bomb bays with 30lb and 4lb incendiaries, before launching them skyward either side of 00.30 with no senior pilots on duty. The Lancasters were in the first wave of the raid, and all from the squadron arrived to encounter nine-tenths cloud over Mönchengladbach, despite which, the red and green TIs stood out clearly and bombing was carried out from between 18,000 and 22,500 feet. Fires were taking hold as they withdrew, and, by the time the second wave turned up the skies had cleared to leave Rheydt exposed. The raid destroyed a combined total of 2,300 buildings, many of them of an industrial nature, and cost twenty-five Bomber Command aircraft, although none from Little Snoring.

F/L Guy Mott (left) was killed his along with his wireless operator Sgt J Kemm when their Lancaster DS659, KO-T, was shot down attacking Nürnberg on 27/28th August 1943. Navigator P/O CC Boggild RAF (believed in the photo, right) and the other four members of the crew survived as POWs.

Orders were received on the 31st to make ready aircraft for a return to Berlin that night, and it would be a force of 622 aircraft that eventually took off. It would have been more had all eleven 115 Squadron Lancasters managed to get away, but DS691 suffered a last-minute fractured oxygen pipe to the mid-upper turret, while DS620 taxied off the peri-track and collapsed its tail wheel and blocked the path of DS682, forcing the crews of F/Sgt Tinn, P/O Cade and F/O Barnes to stay at home. The remaining eight took off between 20.55 and 21.10 with F/L Anderson the senior pilot on duty, but he and F/Sgt Blackwell were forced to return early with technical issues, further depleting the squadron's effort at the Capital. The route on this night took the bomber stream on an east-south-easterly heading across Texel to a position between Hannover and Leipzig, before turning to pass to the south-east of Berlin and approach the city centre aiming-point on a north-westerly track. The return leg involved a south-westerly course to a position south of Cologne for an exit over the French coast, and the enemy night-fighter controller was able to predict to some extent where to concentrate his fighters. This would be the first occasion on which the Command registered the German use of "fighter flares" to mark out the path of the bombers to and from the target. The Pathfinders encountered five to six-tenths cloud in the target area, and this combined with H2S equipment failure and a spirited night-fighter response to cause the markers to be dropped well to the south of the planned aiming-point. The main force crews became involved in an extensive creep-back, which would stretch some thirty miles into open country and outlying communities. The 115 Squadron element bombed on red and green TIs from between 18,000 and 22,000 feet, before returning to report scattered fires and an impression that the raid had not been successful. This would be confirmed by local reports of just eighty-five houses destroyed, and the disappointment for the Command was compounded by the loss of forty-seven aircraft, more than a third of them Stirlings, and this amounted to a catastrophic 16% casualty figure for the type. During the course of the month the squadron undertook ten operations and dispatched 111 sorties for the loss of eight Lancasters and crews.

September 1943

After completing his tour of twenty-eight operations in August, acting S/L Ian Bazalgette DFC, whose substantive rank was still flying officer, was posted to 20 O.T.U at Lossiemouth on the 1st as a flight commander. 514 Squadron became the latest recruit to 3 Group when it was formed at Foulsham also on the 1st. It was to be the second unit in the group to be fully-equipped with Mk II Lancasters, many of which would be transferred over from 115 Squadron. This would signal a period of reduced operational activity at Little Snoring, while the new G-H blind-bombing device was installed in the squadron's Lancasters and the crews were trained in its use. G-H was similar to mott Oboe in that it relied on a radio pulse from a ground station in England intersecting with a second signal over the target. The aircraft were to fly in gaggles or loose formations of between three and six, and formate on an assigned G-H leader, whose tail fins would be painted in a distinctive way to provide a clear visual reference. When the leaders' bombs were seen to fall away, the other aircraft would release theirs, in a manner similar to the American system. G-H could be employed by day or night, and, in time, almost a year hence, would become a highly successful tool in the hands exclusively of 3 Group, and be used effectively against oil and railway-related precision targets.

The new month's operations began with mining and minor forays on the night of the 2/3rd. Eighty-nine aircraft were sent mining, and among them was the freshman 115 Squadron crew of F/O Newcomb, who took off at 20.55 bound for the Frisians. They found their Gee being jammed in the target area for a radius of fifty-six miles, and brought their stores home for future use. An all-Lancaster heavy force of 316 aircraft was made ready on the 3rd for what would be the final attack on Berlin in the current phase. The numbers would have been greater had not four of the 115 Squadron offering of eleven been cancelled early in the day, and three more become unserviceable at the last minute, leaving just four to take off at 20.40 with F/O Barnes the senior pilot on duty. The course for this night took the bomber stream across the Dutch coast a little south of Den Helder, and continued on a track a few degrees south of due east for a straight leg of 350 miles. At Brandenburg they were then to turn towards the north-east to cross the centre of Berlin, and, having exited the city via its eastern suburbs, head north to Sweden, intentionally violating its neutral airspace, before turning for home over the northern tip of Denmark. The 115 Squadron quartet reached the target, where small amounts of cloud proved to be no hindrance, and dropped their cookie each and incendiaries onto green TIs from between 17,000 and 20,500 feet. The attack appeared to be concentrated and large explosions were witnessed at 23.27 and 23.35, but Sgt Pirie and crew reported a large fire which they considered to be some five miles south of the intended aiming-point. Much of the bombing had, indeed, fallen short along the line of approach from the west, and had hit the residential districts of Moabit and Charlottenburg and the industrial district of Siemensstadt, where a number of important factories suffered a serious loss of production. In the absence of Halifaxes and Stirlings, the Lancasters sustained heavy casualties, with twenty-two failing to return, 7% of those dispatched, but 115 Squadron's only casualty was DS658, which was damaged beyond repair after running off the end of the runway, happily without injury to P/O Barnes and his crew.

Mention has been made of the creep-back phenomenon, which was a common feature of major operations against heavily-defended targets. It resulted from the failure of crews to press on to the aiming-point, and bombing instead the first fires they came upon, progressively shifting the attack back along the line of approach. There were occasions, however, when it could work in the Command's favour, and where twin cities were involved, as in the case of Mannheim and Ludwigshafen, Düsseldorf and Neuss and Mönchengladbach and Rheydt, a creep-back could be incorporated in the plan of attack. The aiming-point on the night of the 5/6th was in the eastern half of Mannheim, with an approach from the west, which would allow the bombing to spread back across the central and western districts before spilling over the Rhine into the eastern districts of Ludwigshafen.

A force of 605 aircraft was made ready, of which just six Lancasters represented 115 Squadron, and they took off at 20.10 with S/L Starky the senior pilot on duty. They flew out across France in better weather conditions than expected, and these would hold good to provide clear skies in the target area. Sgt Halley and crew were forced to turn back with an oxygen supply issue, and S/L Starky and crew were within twenty miles of their objective when attacked from head-on by a JU88 and then from astern. DS682 was riddled with bullets, and the starboard aileron destroyed, which prompted F/L Starky to issue the order to abandon aircraft. The navigator and wireless operator complied, before Starky regained a semblance of control and rescinded the order, before coaxing the Lancaster back to a crash-landing at 01.45 at RAF Ford on the Sussex coast. It is not clear whether the injuries sustained by the second pilot and flight engineer resulted from the engagement or the landing, but the gunners were certain that they had shot down their assailant. The others reached the target to bomb on green TIs from between 19,500 and 21,000 feet, and observed large explosions but few fires. Post-raid reconnaissance revealed that, as anticipated, the bombing had spread back along the line of approach, and spilled across onto the West Bank of the Rhine into Ludwigshafen, wherein lay an I G Farben chemicals plant engaged in the production of synthetic oils. Both cities sustained very heavy damage to housing and industry, the Mannheim authorities describing a catastrophe, while half of almost two thousand fires in Ludwigshafen were classed as large and more than a thousand houses were among the buildings destroyed. The defenders fought back in spirited fashion, leaving the bomber force badly mauled, and thirty-four aircraft failed to return home.

The departure of S/L Bazalgette had created a vacancy for a flight commander, and S/L Annan was posted in from 20 O.T.U on the 6th as his successor. A force of 404 Lancasters and Halifaxes was prepared for a return that night to southern Germany to attack the city of Munich. This meant that 115 Squadron was the only 3 Group unit operating, and loaded a cookie each and incendiaries into five Lancasters before sending them off at 20.10 with F/O Newcomb the senior pilot on duty. He, P/O Harris

Lancaster MkII being serviced at RAF Little Snoring, 1943

180

and Sgts Halley and Pirie and their crews had also taken part in the previous night's six-hour round-trip, and one wonders why they were not rested. They all reached the target area to encounter seven to eight-tenths broken cloud, and bombed on green TIs from between 16,000 and 20,400 feet, observing what appeared to be a concentrated raid with fires beginning to take hold as they turned away. In fact, the Pathfinder sky and ground marking proved to be ineffective and most crews made a timed run from the Ammersee before releasing their bombs on estimated positions. In contrast to the previous night, Munich escaped serious damage, and the cost of the failure to Bomber Command was sixteen aircraft, thirteen of them Halifaxes.

Stations were notified of operations to Berlin on the 8th and 9th, but they were cancelled late on, and the main force crews were given a rest from Germany for the next two weeks. The major activity during the period was undertaken by the Stirlings of 3 Group in company with elements of 4 and 8 Groups against targets in France. F/L Eggleston was officially posted to 84 O.T.U on the 11th, at the end of his tour. On the 14th, F/Sgt Bradford and crew took a brand-new aircraft, DS780, for an air-test and bomb-sight levelling exercise after the ground acceptance checks had been carried out satisfactorily. They took off at 10.53, and all went well until the bomb-aimer called for a height of 2,000 feet to be maintained in order to level the bomb-sight without it jamming. The pilot reported being unable to maintain height and ordered the crew to their crash positions, before the Lancaster slammed into a railway embankment east of Wiggenhall St Mary Magdalan, some four miles north of Downham Market airfield. F/Sgt Bradford and five others were killed, while the wireless operator and bomb-aimer sustained serious injuries. The freshman crews of F/Sgts Hammond and Milgate took off shortly after 19.30 on the 18th to mine the waters in the mouth of the Gironde Estuary on the approaches to the port of Bordeaux in south-western France. They delivered their mines from 800 and 1,000 feet respectively, before returning safely within six hours, F/Sgt Hammond's DS734 displaying slight damage to its starboard tail-plane courtesy of light flak.

The final week of the month brought a return to Germany, and the first of a four-raid series against Hannover which would be spread over a four-week period. According to Martin Middlebrook and Chris Everitt in Bomber Command War Diaries, the first three operations were concentrated but outside of the target, while only the third one succeeded in causing extensive damage, which, if the figures are to be believed, seem to be massively out of proportion. The author contends that the reports of the crews after the first two operations suggest strongly that the damage to Hannover was accumulative over the first three raids and did not result from just one, as will be explained in the following narrative. The telling feature is, perhaps, that no reports came out of Hannover to corroborate the testimony of the crews on the first two raids, although post-raid reconnaissance by the RAF after the second one did show that some of the bombing had fallen into open country. 711 aircraft were made ready for the first operation on the 22nd, of which seven Lancasters were provided by 115 Squadron, and they departed Little Snoring between 19.18 and 19.30 with F/L Anderson the senior pilot on duty. F/Sgt Milgate was an hour out when an intercom issue forced him to turn back, leaving the others to press on across Holland and northern Germany to the target. They encountered good visibility in the target area, but stronger-than-forecast winds caused the marking and bombing to be focussed between two and five miles south-south-east of the city-centre aiming-point. The 115 Squadron crews bombed from between 10,500 and 20,000 feet after identifying it by means of ground detail and green TIs, and five of them returned to report fires and black smoke visible from the Dutch coast 150 miles into the return journey. They were among hundreds of crews to provide similar reports, and, although the Pathfinders admitted to a poor performance on their part, dummy and decoy fires are not capable of lighting up the sky sufficiently to be visible from such a huge distance. Among the twenty-six missing aircraft was 115 Squadron's DS675, which contained the eight-man crew of F/O O'Farrell RAAF, three of whom were members of the RNZAF. They fell victim to a night-fighter in the general target area, and only the navigator and bomb-aimer survived to be taken into captivity.

Lancaster MkII DS608 (above) at dispersal and (below) after crashing on landing after engine failure on 2nd September 1943.

Mannheim was posted to host its second major operation of the month on the following night, and a force of 628 aircraft was made ready. 115 Squadron was still dispatching small numbers of aircraft, and, on this night, six Lancasters took off in a five-minute slot from 19.35 with F/L Anderson the senior pilot on duty. They all reached the target in good weather conditions, and identified the aiming-point in the hitherto less-severely afflicted northern districts by ground detail and yellow, red and green TIs, before bombing from between 13,000 and 20,000 feet. On return they reported observing well-concentrated fires, and the effectiveness of the raid was confirmed by local reports of more than nine hundred houses destroyed along with twenty industrial premises. The bombing again crept back across the Rhine onto the northern rim of Ludwigshafen, where the I G Farben chemicals plant sustained severe damage, and the nearby towns of Oppau and Frankenthal were also afflicted. This proved to be the final operation of the month for the squadron, and it remained at home while a force of 678 aircraft took off on the 27th for round two at Hannover. Stronger-than-forecast winds pushed the focus of the marking and bombing five miles north of the city centre, and, once again, the Bomber Command War Diaries suggests that most of the bombing was wasted on farm land and outlying communities. However, returning crews again claimed to have participated in a highly successful attack, surpassing even the earlier one at this target, and reported numerous large fires and columns of smoke rising to 12,000 feet, with the glow still visible from the Dutch coast. The ground defences were described as ineffective, but night-fighters were very much in evidence, and were probably responsible for the heavy loss of thirty-eight aircraft.

The month ended with a highly successful attack on Bochum in the Ruhr by an initial force of 352 aircraft, which exploited the benefits of Oboe to pound the Altstadt and reduce 527 houses to rubble and seriously damage more than seven hundred others. During the course of the month the squadron operated on seven nights and dispatched thirty-one sorties for the loss of two Lancasters at home and one on enemy territory.

October 1943

There was a hectic start to October for the Lancaster crews, who would be called into action no fewer than six times in the first eight nights. 1, 5 and 8 Groups were the busiest, they alone undertaking raids on Hagen and Munich on the nights of the 1/2nd and 2/3rd respectively, the former with outstanding success. S/L Annan and crew took off at 19.15 on the 2nd to mine the waters off the Frisians, and returned in a little under two hours thirty minutes to report completing their brief from 700 feet. Halifaxes and Stirlings joined in at Kassel on the night of the 3/4th, for which a force of 547 aircraft had been made ready. 3 Group contributed 113 Stirlings, of which ten returned early and six failed to return at all, while 115 Squadron was left at home. Ground haze caused the H2S markers to overshoot the aiming-point, and the main weight of bombs fell onto the western suburbs, where the Henschel and Fieseler aircraft factories were hit, but a stray bomb load also detonated an ammunition dump at Ihringshausen, situated close to the north-eastern suburb of Wolfsanger, which was left devastated by the blast. At 06.52 F/O Newcomb RNZAF and his predominantly Kiwi crew took off in DS721 to carry out a search over the North Sea for crews reported to have ditched on return from Kassel, and no trace of them or the Lancaster was ever seen again.

Frankfurt had always proved a difficult target to hit, but a force of under four hundred aircraft inflicted severe damage on its eastern districts and inland docks area on the night of the 4/5th, for the modest loss of ten aircraft. 115 Squadron remained on the ground for this one, but put crews on standby for operations against Gelsenkirchen on the 5th and Schweinfurt or Frankfurt on the 6th, before both were cancelled. A two-night rest was followed by the notification of an all-Lancaster operation to Stuttgart on the 7th, a particular feature of which would be the first employment in numbers of night-fighter communications-jamming Lancasters operated by 1 Group's 101 Squadron. The device, known as "Jostle", required a specialist operator in addition to the standard crew of seven, who, though not necessarily a German speaker, could recognise the language, and, on hearing it, jam the signals on up to three frequencies by broadcasting engine noise over them. At 101 Squadron the device was referred to as ABC or Airborne Cigar, and, once proved to be effective, ABC Lancasters would be spread through the bomber stream for all major operations, whether or not 1 Group was involved. The Lancaster would also carry a full bomb load reduced by 1,000lbs to compensate for the weight of the equipment and its operator.

A force of 343 Lancasters of 1, 3, 5, 6 and 8 Groups was made ready for Stuttgart, of which thirteen represented 115 Squadron, and they were each loaded with a cookie and mixture of 30lb and 4lb incendiaries. They took off between 21.00 and 21.20 with F/Ls Anderson and Christiansen the senior pilots on duty, but F/L Christiansen turned back early on with an electrical problem, and he was followed home by F/O Cade who reported an indisposed rear gunner. The others pressed on over a cloud-covered France, while Mosquitos carried out a diversionary raid on Munich, which succeeded in delaying the arrival of night-fighters at the primary target. The Pathfinders employed H2S in conditions of ten-tenths cloud, and established two areas of marking, predominantly in residential districts. The 115 Squadron crews bombed from between 18,000 and 21,500 feet, reporting on return the glow of concentrated fires and large explosions at 00.39 and 00.51. Whether the loss of just four aircraft could be entirely credited to ABC is impossible to say, but it was declared to be an effective tool, and paved the way for the creation of 100 Group in November. The new Group, which would be stationed on airfields in Norfolk, would be dedicated to a radio-counter-measures (RCM) role, initially employing Wellingtons, before adding Halifaxes and Stirlings to its strength. Eventually, in 1944, it would be given "Serrate" Mosquito squadrons, which would become the scourge of enemy night-fighters. Stuttgart suffered the destruction of almost 350 houses and apartment blocks, with many thousands of other buildings sustaining damage to some extent.

The third raid of the series on Hannover was posted on the 8th, and a force of 504 aircraft assembled accordingly, among them the last twenty-six Wellingtons, from 300 (Polish) and 432 (Canadian) Squadrons, to carry out a bombing raid in Bomber Command service. 115 Squadron made ready a dozen Lancasters, loading seven of them with an 8,000 pounder and the others with a cookie, and filling the available space with incendiaries. They took off between 23.30 and 23.50 with S/L Annan the senior pilot on duty for the first time, supported by F/L Christiansen. P/O Hicks and crew were out over the North Sea when the rear gunner complained of petrol in his oxygen system, compelling them to turn back, and P/O Harris and crew were over Germany when the W/T equipment broke down to curtail their sortie. The others reached Hannover to find it under clear skies, and the Pathfinders were able to mark the city centre accurately for the first time with red and green TIs. Nine 115 Squadron crews bombed from between 17,000 and 21,800 feet, and returned home to report what appeared to be a successful operation, which had caused extensive fires and a large explosion at 01.40 followed by another at 01.42 that appeared to be oil-related. It is believed that DS691 was on the way home when it was shot down from 20,000 feet by a combination of flak and a night-fighter, and crashed at 01.32 a few miles north-north-east of the target. P/O Cade and four of his crew survived to be taken into captivity, but both gunners lost their lives. The operation cost twenty-seven aircraft in all, in return for the destruction, according to local reports, of the city centre by fire, and a total of 3,932 unspecified buildings, with a further thirty thousand damaged to some extent. This degree of destruction is disproportionate, and, as no reports have emerged to cover the first two attacks on Hannover, it seems clear that this one refers to the cumulative effects of the three raids to date, confirming the conviction among the crews and the author, that the first two had been highly successful.

A long stand-down until the 18th provided the crews with a welcome break, and, during this period, F/L Baigent arrived on posting from the AFDU on the 15th. The offensive inactivity ended on the 18th, when orders came through to mount the fourth and final raid of the series on Hannover. An all-Lancaster force of 360 aircraft was made ready, of which fourteen represented 115 Squadron, and they took off between 18.05 and 18.20 with S/L Annan the senior pilot on duty. DS661 lost its port-inner engine over Nienburg, some twenty-five miles north-west of Hannover, and P/O Harris was forced to turn back after jettisoning his bombs live. W/O Boutilier and crew were about to commence their bombing run when an enemy night-fighter approached from behind, and poured fire into DS683, killing the rear gunner and wounding the wireless operator and flight engineer. The Lancaster had its elevators and trimming controls shot away, and, by the time it reached Little Snoring to crash-land at 22.35, had lost the use of two engines. Only the outstanding airmanship of the crew enabled them to return home, and the pilot and wireless operator received immediate awards of the DFC and DFM respectively. The others bombed on red, green and yellow TIs from between 16,500 and 22,500 feet, but were prevented by cloud from observing the results. Eighteen Lancasters failed to return home, and among them was DS769, in which Sgt Whitehead and his crew lost their lives.

Lancasters MkII LL678 and DS837 in 1943, probably at the manufacturer's airfield or an RAF storage unit prior to delivery. Neither aircraft carries a squadron code at this time. DSD837 was allocated to 426 Sqn and was lost on the fateful night of 16th December 1943, flying into high ground in cloud returning from Berlin. LL678 later moved to 514 Sqn at Waterbeach. She was shot down on 13th June 1944 attacking Gelsenkirchen.

Two nights later, an all-Lancaster force of 358 was assembled to carry out the first major raid of the war on the eastern city of Leipzig. 115 Squadron briefed thirteen crews, and dispatched them between 18.10 and 18.25 with S/L Annan the senior pilot on duty. He turned back almost immediately with an unserviceable Gee-box, and P/O Peate followed him in a little later after compass and engine problems curtailed his sortie. The route for this operation was over northern Holland to pass to the north of Bremen, followed by a south-easterly course to the east of Braunschweig (Brunswick) and then on to the target. The weather conditions over the Continent on this night were appalling, and would defeat a number of crews, including those of F/Sgt Blackwell and P/O Hicks, who reported jettisoning their bombs live over Uelzen, situated some seventy miles east-south-east of Bremen, after encountering severe icing and violent electrical storms. There was no marking at the target, and the other 115 Squadron crews bombed on e.t.a from between 20,500 and 23,000 feet without observing any results. It was an expensive failure, which cost the Command sixteen aircraft, and one of these was 115 Squadron's DS769, which contained the eight-man crew of F/L Anderson, all of whom died when it crashed outbound near Engersen, fifty miles further south-east from Uelzen. This was an experienced crew approaching the end of their tour, and their presence would be missed.

Having already felt the weight of a moderately effective raid at the start of the month, the residents of Kassel must have braced themselves for more of the same as the drone of a large force was heard approaching during the mid-evening of the 22nd. The operation had begun badly for 115 Squadron, which bombed up a dozen Lancasters as part of an overall force of 569, but had one sortie scrubbed at the last minute after the bomb-aimer was taken ill, and another to a burst tyre during the taxy along the perimeter track, which resulted in the Lancaster becoming bogged down. The aircraft behind also became bogged down while trying to edge past, and the three behind that one had their paths to the threshold blocked. This left just six to take off between 18.40 and 18.55, plus F/Sgt Harwick and crew, who had taken off also at 18.40 bound for a mining sortie off the Frisians. In the event, Gee failure would scupper their maiden operation and they would return home early after jettisoning their mines safe. The others pressed on over a cloud-covered Belgium, some encountering electrical storms and icing conditions. P/O Peate and crew suffered a DR-compass malfunction as a result, and let their bombs go live over St-Truiden from 21,000 feet before turning back. As at Hamburg in July, no one could have foreseen the outcome at Kassel, the attack upon which began with the H2S blind markers overshooting, and the possible deployment by the enemy of some decoy target indicators. The latter attracted a proportion of the bomb loads, but, after the Pathfinder visual markers had corrected the initial inaccuracy, the majority of the main force crews produced concentrated bombing of the city centre. The result was a firestorm, which, although less intense than that experienced at Hamburg, never-the-less ripped through residential districts, destroying in its path over 4,300 apartment blocks. A further 6,700 were damaged to some extent, while many industrial premises were badly affected, as were public and administrative buildings and railway installations. The death toll was also high, almost certainly exceeding six thousand people, but, at least, many of the hundred thousand homeless would have been cheered to know, that forty-three of their tormentors would not be returning home. 115 Squadron escaped the carnage, and, along with the rest of the Command, spent the remainder of the month at home engaged in training. During the course of the month the squadron operated on six nights, dispatching sixty sorties for the loss of five Lancasters and four crews.

November 1943

There would be little activity during the first half of November, and just one significant operation would be mounted. Orders were received on the 3rd to prepare a force of 589 aircraft to attack Düsseldorf that night. Incorporated in the plan was an attempt to hit the Mannesmann Rohrenwerke (tubular steel works) on the northern outskirts of the city, employing the new G-H blind bombing device carried by thirty-eight Mk II Lancasters. This would be the first large-scale live trial of G-H, for which 115 Squadron detailed eleven aircraft, and 3 Group's newest addition, 514 Squadron, would be making its operational debut with two aircraft, while the remaining twenty-five Mk II Lancasters were to be provided by 6 Group's 408 and 426 Squadrons. The first departure from Little Snoring was that of F/Sgt James and crew at 18.00 bound for a mining trip to the Frisians. They would deliver their mines according to brief by Gee-fix from 1,000 feet and return safely from an uneventful sortie. The bombing brigade took off between 18.00 and 18.10 with F/L Christiansen the senior pilot on duty, each Lancaster carrying either an 8,000 pounder or a cookie with incendiaries making up the balance of the loads. P/O Harris and crew were an hour out when the loss of oil pressure in two engines forced them to turn back. The others pressed on, unaware that the G-H force was experiencing a high level of early returns, five in all, and that G-H-equipment failure would reduce further the numbers bombing the factory to fifteen. The 115 Squadron ORB scribe would not have been aware of the use of the top-secret G-H on this night, and reported the raid in standard format, recording the bombing as being delivered on red and green TIs from between 20,600 and 21,500 feet. This was, in truth, largely accurate, as only four, according to the 3 Group ORB, bombed by G-H, and the squadron ORB mentions only P/O Newton and crew identifying the target by means of navigational aids. The reporting system in the much-bombed German cities was beginning to break down, and the level of detail coming out of Düsseldorf after this raid was more general than exact. It is known that the main weight of the attack fell on central and southern districts, and caused heavy damage, while several assembly halls in the Mannesmann factory were burned-out.

3 Group was not involved in either of the two medium-scale operations to southern France on the 10th and 11th, but continued to send individual aircraft on mining sorties. Bound for French coastal waters off La Pallice at 00.08 on the 8th, DS825 came to grief when the starboard-outer engine failed halfway down the runway, almost at the point of lifting off. The take-off was abandoned and the Lancaster careered off the runway with the engine on fire, but the crew clambered out of the wreckage without any injuries to report, and before a fire consumed the evidence of the cause of the engine failure. The identity of the pilot was not recorded, but F/L Mackie was recorded as the captain, despite being a bomb-aimer who had been posted in from 1678 Conversion Unit on the 23rd and was undertaking his first operation with the squadron. It was standard practice in Bomber Command for the pilot to be captain, irrespective of his rank, but the 115 Squadron ORB consistently refers to F/L Mackie as captain in the crew of F/Sgt Atkin. The rest of the squadron had been briefed to operate against Augsburg that night, but a cancellation came through after 21.00, and too late for the crews to get to the local watering holes. The same target was posted for the following night, and the cancellation of that one came through even later, after 22.00.

The decks were now cleared for the resumption of the Berlin offensive, with Harris fully aware, after his minute to Churchill on the 3rd concerning American participation, that he would be going alone. F/L Baigent was given the acting rank of squadron leader on the 15th to enable him to perform the role of flight commander. For the re-joining of the rocky road to Germany's Capital an all-Lancaster heavy force of 440 aircraft was made ready on the 18th. A diversion was laid on involving a force of 395 Halifaxes, Stirlings and Lancasters at Mannheim and Ludwigshafen, and 115 Squadron would support both operations. F/O Woolhouse and Sgt Smith and their crews were assigned to southern Germany, while the remaining eleven crews were to be part of the main event. The two elements took off together between 17.48 and 18.05 with S/L Annan the senior pilot on duty and F/L Mackie flying with P/O Hicks. The two forces would cross the enemy coast simultaneously some 250 miles apart to confuse the enemy night-fighter controllers, and the route chosen for the Berlin brigade was via the Frisian island of Texel to a point north of Hannover, and thence to the target to pass over the centre on an east-north-easterly heading. After bombing they would return south of Berlin and Cologne, before crossing central Belgium to gain the English Channel via the French coast. An innovation for this operation was a shortening of the bomber stream to reduce the time over the target to sixteen minutes. When the first Thousand Bomber raid had taken place in May 1942, with an unprecedented twelve aircraft per minute crossing the aiming-point, there was considered to be a high risk of collisions. The number had since been increased to sixteen per minute, with large raids lasting up to forty-five minutes, but, on this night, twenty-seven aircraft per minute were to pass over the aiming-point.

Complete cloud cover was encountered over northern Germany, and an unserviceable DR compass meant that F/Sgt James and crew were unable to locate the primary target. They actually passed to the north of Berlin, and bombed the small town of Bad Freienwalde from 21,000 feet, which was situated to the north-east of the target, and within sight of the Polish frontier. The others found the general area of Berlin, where the marking and bombing was carried out blindly, the 115 Squadron participants delivering their loads from between 20,000 and 22,000 feet on red and green sky-markers. It was impossible to assess the accuracy of the raid until photographic reconnaissance could take place, when it was established, that bombs had fallen into most parts of the city with no point of concentration, and that destruction was on a fairly modest scale. The diversion at Mannheim seemed to succeed in its purpose, and the 115 Squadron duo bombed on red and green TIs from 18,000 feet before returning safely. The losses from Berlin were encouragingly low at just nine aircraft, but among them was the squadron's DS680, which fell victim to the night-fighter of Oblt Eckart-Wilhelm von Bonin of II/NJG.1 on the way home over Belgium, and crashed at Herstal, north-east of Liege, with no survivors from the eight-man crew of P/O Peate RAAF. Twenty-three aircraft failed to return from southern Germany in exchange for some useful industrial damage and the destruction of over three hundred buildings.

On the following night, while the Lancaster crews were rested, 3, 4, 6 and 8 Groups sent their Halifaxes and Stirlings to the Ruhr city of Leverkusen in poor weather conditions. Bombs fell all over the Ruhr, and only one was recorded by local authorities as having hit the intended target. Meanwhile, F/Sgt Lee and crew had departed Little Snoring at 17.40 bound for the Nectarines garden off the Frisians, and they returned at 19.50 to report an uneventful sortie, during which they fulfilled their brief from 900 feet after obtaining a Gee-fix. A call for a maximum effort on the 22nd resulted in 764 aircraft being made ready for the second round of the renewed Berlin offensive. Fourteen 115 Squadron Lancasters took off between 17.24 and 17.55 with F/Ls Baigent and Christiansen the senior pilots on duty, but F/Sgt Atkin, with F/L Mackie on board as navigator, was back within two hours after the rear turret guns jammed while being tested. P/O Halley's sortie lasted a little longer, but an electrical fault in the rear turret ended his participation, leaving the others to press on via a direct route identical to the previous one, with an almost reciprocal return. This was based on a forecast of low cloud and fog over Germany, which would inhibit the night-fighter effort, but broken, medium level cloud over Berlin to facilitate ground marking. An additional bonus was the availability to the Pathfinders of five new H2S Mk III sets, while a new record of thirty-four aircraft per minute passing over the aiming-point would be achieved by abandoning the long-standing practice of allocating aircraft types to specific waves. On this night aircraft of all types would be spread through the bomber stream, which was bad news for the Stirlings, which, by the very nature of their design, would be below the Lancaster and Halifax elements, and in danger of being hit by friendly bombs.

On arrival at the target, it became clear that the forecast had been inaccurate, and that the city was hidden under a blanket of ten-tenths cloud with tops at around 12,000 feet. This meant that ground marking would be largely ineffective, and that the least reliable method of sky-marking would have to be employed. The 115 Squadron crews bombed on red and green parachute flares from between 18,000 and 22,000 feet, and observed the orange glow of many concentrated fires beneath the cloud. Five crews reported a huge explosion at 20.21, and others could still see the reflections in the sky from Hannover, some 150 miles into the homeward leg. No genuine assessment could be provided at debriefing, but all of the indications were of a successful raid, and this was expressed in the 3 Group ORB. In fact, it was the most destructive raid of the war on the Capital, with the central and western districts suffering the heaviest damage. A large area of fire, parts of which almost certainly developed firestorm characteristics, contributed to the destruction of over three thousand buildings, most of them of a residential nature, although industry was also hard-hit, and around two thousand people lost their lives, while 175,000 others were rendered homeless. Twenty-six aircraft failed to return home, and two of them were 115 Squadron Lancasters, DS782, which disappeared without trace with the crew of Sgt Harris, and DS764, which crashed somewhere in western Germany. The body of the pilot, Sgt Smith, was found in the wreckage, but the rest of the crew parachuted into the arms of the enemy to spend the rest of the war as PoWs. The wireless operator, Sgt Deakin, fractured both legs in a heavy landing, and spent time in hospital before joining his crew mates.

Five Stirlings were among the missing, a loss rate of 10% for a type that had long been giving cause for concern through disproportionately high loss-rates. Unlike the Lancaster and Halifax, the Stirling had no development potential, and was restricted by its wingspan to operating at medium level, and by its split bomb bay to a limited bomb load. Harris had never liked the aircraft, and now took the decision to withdraw it from further operations over Germany and to relegate it to other important, but secondary duties. This effectively removed 3 Group from the main battle, leaving only 115 and 514 Squadrons to carry the flag with their Mk II Lancasters, until the other units were gradually converted onto the type over the next ten months. The Stirling would find a new lease of life in 1944 when operating on behalf of the highly secret Special Operations Executive (SOE), helping to supply agents and vital equipment to the resistance organisations in the Occupied Countries, and it would ultimately become the aircraft of choice for both 138 and 161 Squadrons operating out of Tempsford.

W/O Boutilier was rewarded for his service to date by the award on the 23rd of the DFC, and, that night, a heavy force of 365 Lancasters and ten Halifaxes was made ready with some difficulty for a return to Berlin. Back-to-back long-range operations put a strain on those charged with the responsibility of getting the aircraft off the ground, and the Ludford Magna armourers were unable to load all nineteen 101 Squadron Lancasters with the intended weight of bombs, sending them off 2,000lb short. 514 Squadron was about to change address, and would take off from Foulsham and land at its new home of Witchford. 115 Squadron detailed a dozen Lancasters, but only ten presented themselves for take-off between 17.40 and 17.55 led by F/Ls Baigent and Barnes. F/O Woolhouse and crew were forced back early by an unserviceable Gee-box, and this was just one of forty-six crews to return early for a variety of reasons. Another was that of F/O Harris, whose a.s.i failed, and the bombs were dropped live onto Texel from 20,000 feet. There was also evidence over the North Sea of the dumping of bombs by others intending to push on to the target, but wanting to gain more height. It involved largely those from 1 Group, who were shedding their cookies in protest at the A-O-C's policy of loading each Lancaster to its maximum all-up weight at the expense of altitude. The slogan H-E-I-G-H-T spells safety could be found on the walls of most bomber station briefing rooms at the time. The remaining 115 Squadron crews reached the target via the same route adopted on the previous night, and found it covered by ten-tenths cloud. Guided by the glow of fires still burning beneath the clouds from the night before, and the red and green TIs, the 115 Squadron crews bombed from between 20,000 and 22,500 feet to contribute to another stunning blow. Returning crews described the glow of fires visible again from the Hannover area some 150 miles from the target. It was on this night that fake broadcasts from England caused annoyance to the night-fighter force by ordering them to land because of fog over their bases, but they still had a major hand in the bringing-down of twenty Lancasters. Post-raid reconnaissance and local reports confirmed that this operation had destroyed a further two thousand buildings, and killed around fifteen hundred people. This would be one of the few Berlin operations negotiated by the squadron without loss.

The crews were probably still in bed when the advance party left Little Snoring for the squadron's new home at Witchford, situated some ten miles north of Cambridge, where 514 Squadron was preparing to move out and take up residence at Waterbeach. The move was completed on the 26th, in time for the squadron to make ready a dozen Lancasters for round four of the Berlin campaign. They were part of an all-Lancaster heavy force of 443 aircraft, and took off between 17.40 and 17.46 with F/Ls Christiansen and Barnes the senior pilots on duty. A diversionary raid on Suttgart by a predominantly Halifax force followed the same route as those bound for Berlin, which involved an outward leg across the French coast and Belgium to a point north of Frankfurt, where they separated. By this time W/O Boutilier and crew had already turned back for an unspecified reason, having reached the English Channel, and P/O Blackwell and crew had travelled as far as Limburg an der Lahn, to the east of Koblenz, when both starboard engines began to play up. They jettisoned the bomb load live from 18,000 feet onto the small town as they turned back, and observed what turned out to be a 7 Squadron Lancaster exploding and releasing red and green TIs. F/L Barnes and crew found themselves heavily engaged by flak over Brandenburg on the south-western approaches to Berlin, and jettisoned their bombs live from 20,000 feet before heading home. DS793 crashed at Stockheim, twenty miles beyond Frankfurt, and there were no survivors from the crew of F/O Woolhouse. Despite finding Berlin under clear skies, the Pathfinders overshot the city centre aiming-point by six or seven miles, and marked an area well to the north-west, which happened to contain many war-industry factories. The 115 Squadron crews bombed from between 19,500 and 22,000 feet, and returning crews spoke of a mass of fires and thick smoke rising to 15,000 feet. It was learned later that thirty-eight war-industry factories had been destroyed and many others damaged, in return for the loss of twenty-eight Lancasters, many of which had fallen victim to night-fighters on the return flight.

This was the final operation of the month for 115 Squadron, which formed a C Flight on the 28th. During the course of the month the squadron operated on seven nights and dispatched sixty-three sorties for the loss of five Lancasters and four crews.

December 1943

As November had ended, so December began, with the preparation of a heavy force of 440 aircraft, all but fifteen of them Lancasters, after the main Halifax element was withdrawn because of fog over their Yorkshire stations. 115 Squadron made ready eleven aircraft, which took off either side of 17.30 with S.L Annan the senior pilot on duty, and headed for the Norfolk coast between Sheringham and Caistor. The route was again straight-in-straight-out, but, first, the crews had to negotiate a towering front of ice-bearing cloud over the North Sea, which would contribute to a 10% rate of early returns. 115 Squadron suffered a 45% early-return rate as a result of a variety of technical issues afflicting the Lancasters of S/L Annan, F/L Barnes and F/Sgts Clark, Lee and Milgate, who all landed between 19.40 and 20.10. The others pushed on in the continuing adverse weather conditions, which included varying winds that caused navigation problems and dispersed the bomber stream. Enemy night-fighters were up in numbers and would harass the bombers all the way to the target, which was correctly predicted by the controller. The 115 Squadron crews bombed on red and green TIs and ground detail, like burning streets, from between 19,500 and 22,000 feet. By the time that F/Sgt Anderson and crew arrived at the target, the TIs had burned out, so they bombed the north-western edge of the fires based on the glow reflecting through the clouds. They had been hit by flak over Bremen, and whether or not this was the cause of their late arrival on target, or they stumbled into the Bremen defence zone while homebound, is uncertain. What is certain is that they had no business being so far north at any time during the operation, and they were the last to land at 00.30, some fifty minutes behind the penultimate one. Returning crews reported many fires and the glow visible from 120 miles into the homeward leg, and bombing photographs suggested that the raid was only partially successful, causing useful damage in industrial districts in the west and east, but scattering the main weight of bombs over the southern districts and outlying communities to the south. It was a bad night for the bomber force, which lost forty aircraft, mostly in the target area and on the way home, but 115 Squadron bucked the trend, and came through unscathed from Berlin for the second and last time.

Exploiting the enemy expectation that Berlin would be the target again, a force of 527 aircraft was prepared to attack Leipzig on the night of the 3/4th. 115 Squadron loaded eight Lancasters with a cookie and a mixture of 30 and 4lb incendiaries, and launched them from Witchford between 00.30 and 00.40 with S/L Annan the senior pilot on duty. The route aimed directly for Berlin, passing north of Hannover and Braunschweig, before turning towards the south-east, while a Mosquito feint at Berlin confirmed in the mind of the controller that the Capital was the intended target. The night-fighters had managed to

RAF Witchford

infiltrate the bomber stream before the turning-point, but the controller ordered them to head for Berlin, which left the bomber stream to carry out the attack at Leipzig unmolested. The Pathfinders performed well despite a thin layer of ten-tenths cloud at around 6,000 feet, and the 115 Squadron crews carried out their attacks on skymarkers from between 20,500 and 23,000 feet. Seven of them returned to report many fires and smoke rising up through the cloud to 6,000 feet as they turned away, and it was confirmed eventually that a highly effective attack had been delivered. The loss of twenty-four aircraft would have been fewer had many aircraft not inadvertently strayed into the Frankfurt defence zone during the long southern withdrawal, and the flak batteries claimed half of them. DS765 was missing from its Witchford dispersal, and it was learned later that the Lancaster had crashed in Germany, killing F/Sgt Clark DFM and his crew, who had recently been posted in from 620 Squadron.

S/L Grant was posted to the squadron from 1678 Conversion Unit on the 5th, and would fulfil the role of C Flight commander. There was little activity over the succeeding twelve nights, and when elements of the main force were next called to briefing on the 16th, it was to learn that Berlin was the objective for that night. Only the Lancaster crews were involved of the heavy squadrons, and 115 Squadron made ready fourteen of theirs before dispatching them either side of 17.00 with F/Ls Christiansen, Barnes and Seddon the senior pilots on duty. They were to cross the Dutch coast in the region of Castricum-aan-Zee, and then head due east all the way to the target with no deviations. A three-quarter moon would rise during the long return leg over the Baltic and Denmark, but it was hoped that the very early take-off and the expectation of fog to keep the enemy night-fighters on the ground would reduce the risk of interception. F/Sgt Anderson and crew returned early because of an unserviceable rear turret, and a similar problem forced F/O Ryder and crew to turn back and jettison their bombs over Wognum on the Den Helder peninsular. At about the same time DS835 crashed at Heemskerk, close to the coast just south of Castricum, possibly the victim of one of the night-fighters sent to meet the bomber stream at the Dutch coast, and there were no survivors from the crew of P/O Newton and crew.

When F/O Ryder and crew arrived back in the Witchford circuit in DS795, they collided with a Stirling and sustained considerable damage to the tail, but managed to land safely, as, apparently, did the Stirling. The remainder pressed on to find Berlin obscured by ten-tenths cloud, but identifiable by means of red and green sky-markers, which were bombed from between 20,000 and 23,000 feet. The return over Denmark passed largely without major incident, but the greatest difficulties awaited the 1, 6 and 8 Group crews as they arrived home to find their airfields covered by a blanket of dense fog. With little reserves of fuel, the tired crews began a frantic search to find somewhere to land, stumbling blindly through the murk to catch a glimpse of the ground. For many, this proved fatal, while others gave up any hope of landing, and abandoned their aircraft. Twenty-nine Lancasters and a mine-laying Stirling were thus lost, and more than 150 airmen killed in these most tragic of circumstances. To this number was added the twenty-five Lancasters failing to return from the raid, many of which were accounted for by night-fighters over Holland and Germany while outbound. At debriefing some crews reported the glow of fires, while others saw nothing through the cloud, and it was a local report that confirmed a moderately effective raid, which had fallen principally onto central and eastern districts, where housing suffered most.

A three-night break preceded the next major operation, which this time included the Halifax brigade. The target for the night of the 20/21st was Frankfurt, where the Command had enjoyed little success in repeated attempts to date. A force of 650 aircraft was assembled, which included a contribution from 115 Squadron of eleven Lancasters, and they departed Witchford between 17.35 and 17.50 with F/Ls Christiansen and Barnes the senior pilots on duty. F/Sgt Lee and crew were over the Scheldt Estuary when the oxygen system failed, and they were forced to return after jettisoning their bombs over Overflakee. F/O Ryder and crew were beset with icing problems in the same area a few minutes later, and also turned back, to be followed fifteen minutes later by F/L Barnes and crew, who touched down at 20.30 having been compelled by the failure of the oxygen supply to the mid-upper turret to abandon their sortie. The others continued on over Belgium and into Germany, where clear skies had been forecast and a ground-marking plan prepared. In the event, up to eight-tenths cloud concealed most of the ground detail, and a decoy fire site five miles south-east of the city combined with dummy target indicators to lure away the bombing. The 115 Squadron crews identified the target by means of green TIs and delivered their loads from between 19,000 and 22,000 feet, a number of crews observing a huge explosion with sheets of red flame at 19.47. The raid was saved from failure by the creep-back, which, on this occasion, worked in the Command's favour by spreading back from the decoy fire site to hit a residential district, where more than 450 houses were destroyed. A diversionary raid on Mannheim by elements of 1 and 8 Groups failed to fool the night-fighter controller, and forty-one aircraft did not make it home from Frankfurt.

W/C Rainsford was posted to HQ 33 Base on the 21st at the conclusion of his tour as commanding officer, and S/L Annan was elevated to wing commander rank as his successor. It should be remembered, that W/C Annan's substantive rank was still flight lieutenant. Orders came through on the 23rd for the continuation of the relentless campaign against Berlin, and a predominantly all-Lancaster force of 371 aircraft was made ready. 115 Squadron loaded thirteen Lancasters with a cookie each and incendiaries, and launched them into the cold night air between 00.35 and 00.50 with S/L Baigent the senior pilot on duty. The route to the target was somewhat circuitous, and took the bomber stream in a south-easterly direction to the Scheldt Estuary, before hugging the Belgian/Dutch frontier to cross into Germany south of Aachen, as if threatening Frankfurt. When a point was reached south of Leipzig, the route turned sharply towards the north and Berlin, while a Mosquito feint suggested Leipzig as the target. Between 03.20 and 03.45 the crews of F/Sgt Whyte, F/Sgt Lee and F/Sgt Anderson returned home after suffering a variety of technical problems over Belgium, leaving the others to press on to find the target enveloped in cloud. This might not have been critical had the Pathfinders not suffered an unusually high failure rate of their H2S equipment, which resulted in scattered and sparse sky-marking. The 115 Squadron crews found red and green marker flares at which to aim their bombs from between 18,000 and 22,000 feet, and observed well-concentrated fires and two large explosions at 04.04 and 04.24, the latter emitting red flame. Two south-eastern suburbs sustained the most damage, with 287 houses and other buildings suffering destruction. In return, a relatively modest sixteen Lancasters failed to return, among them the squadron's DS773, which crashed somewhere in northern Germany killing P/O Pirie and his crew.

The Christmas period passed in peace and traditional style before the final major raid of the year was posted on the 29th. The target was Berlin, for which a force of 712 aircraft was assembled, and, for the Lancaster squadrons, this was to be the first of three trips to Berlin in an unprecedented five-night period spanning the turn of the year. It was at this juncture that the intolerable strain on the crews of successive long-range flights in difficult weather conditions would begin to show. 115 Squadron made ready a record nineteen Lancasters, which took off either side of 17.30 with S/L Baigent the senior pilot on duty. The bomber stream was routed out over the Dutch Frisian islands pointing directly for Leipzig, and, having reached a point just to the north of that city, was to turn to the north towards Berlin, while Mosquitos carried out spoof raids on Leipzig and Magdeburg. All of the 115 Squadron participants reached the target to find complete cloud cover, and aimed their bombs at red and green marker flares from between 18,500 and 22,000 feet, observing a number of explosions along with the glow of concentrated fires. F/Sgt Lee and crew were on their way home in DS834 when they were intercepted by a night-fighter and shot down to crash near Weert in south-eastern Holland. Four members of the crew lost their lives, but F/Sgt Lee and his navigator fell into enemy hands, while the flight engineer managed to evade a similar fate through the assistance of the magnificent Dutch resistance organisation. Local reports confirmed that the attack had been restricted to southern and south-eastern districts, where more than three hundred buildings had been destroyed. During the course of the month the squadron operated on six nights, and dispatched seventy-six sorties for the loss of four Lancasters and crews.

January 1944

Not only was this the "winter of discontent" for the crews of Bomber Command, the beleaguered citizens of Berlin were also feeling the strain of the constant round of attacks on their city. They were, however, a hardy breed, and proud of their status as Berliners first and Germans second. Just like their counterparts in London during the Blitz of 1940, they bore their trials with fortitude and humour, and developed a spirit of community to help them through the worst moments. They paraded banners through the shattered streets proclaiming, "you may break our walls, but not our hearts", and took comfort from the most popular song of the day, Nach jedem Dezember kommt immer ein Mai, After every December comes always a May. The sentiment of the lyrics hinted at a change of fortune with the onset of spring, although, as the year turned, both they and the bomber crews must have been hoping that Harris would turn his attention elsewhere much sooner. It was not to be, and, before New Year's Day was over, the first of a 421-strong all-Lancaster force had taken to the air to adopt an almost direct route to the Capital. Of a record twenty-one Lancasters detailed by 115 Squadron, only sixteen made it to take-off between 00.30 and 00.50, each aircraft carrying a cookie and incendiaries, and with S/Ls Baigent and Grant the senior pilots on duty. Between 02.30 and 02.45 the crews of F/Sgt Hayes, F/Sgt Milgate and S/L Grant returned with a variety of technical issues, leaving the others to press on across a cloud-covered northern Germany to find the target completely concealed and sky-marking in progress. The squadron's crews bombed from between 16,000 and 21,500 feet, observing the glow of fires, but no detail, and all but one made it home to a safe landing. DS796 was force-landed four miles south-south-west of Ely at 07.39, and, although the Lancaster was written off, the crew of F/Sgt Chantler walked away to return to duty. They would survive the Berlin offensive, but sadly, not their tour. The operation was a failure, which scattered bombs across the southern fringes of the city, causing only minor damage, while the main weight of the attack fell beyond the city boundaries into wooded and open country. The disappointment was compounded by the loss of twenty-eight Lancasters.

A heavy force of 362 Lancasters and nine of the new Mk III Hercules-powered Halifaxes was made ready on the 2nd for a return to Berlin that night. There was snow on the ground, and many of the crews called to briefing were still tired from the almost-eight-hour round trip the night before, and in a mutinous frame of mind at being on the Order of Battle again. 115 Squadron detailed twenty Lancasters, but only thirteen presented themselves for take-off either side of 00.30 with F/Ls Christiansen and Howell the senior pilots on duty. The outward route crossed the Dutch coast near Castricum and took the bomber stream to a point south-east of Bremen, followed by a dogleg to the north-west and, finally, a ninety degree change of course to the south-east in the Parchim area to leave a ninety-mile run to the target. F/Sgt Gibson's oxygen supply somehow became disconnected as he and his crew approached the Dutch coast, causing him to black out temporarily, and, when he had recovered, he ordered the cookie and some incendiaries to be jettisoned over the North Sea. W/O Jolly was close by, when severe icing froze his instruments, and he dumped his bombs live on Den Helder from 15,000 feet before turning back and landing a few minutes after F/Sgt Gibson. P/O Canning and crew were well into Germany when the compass became unserviceable, also through severe icing, and they dumped the contents of their bomb bay on Bremen after turning back. The route changes worked well in throwing off the night-fighters, but they would congregate in the target area after the controller correctly identified the Capital as the target forty minutes before zero-hour. The 115 Squadron crews bombed from between 19,000 and 21,500 feet either on sky-markers or on the glow of fires beneath the cloud cover, and W/O Robbins and crew reported smoke rising to 20,000 feet as they turned away. It was not possible to make an accurate assessment of the outcome, and the impression was of an effective attack. In fact, it had been another failure, which had scattered bombs across the city and destroyed just eighty-two houses for the loss of twenty-seven Lancasters, mostly to night-fighters in the target area. The squadron's DS667 was one of those to go down in the Berlin defence zone, and although all of the crew survived to be taken prisoner, the pilot, F/Sgt Hayes, succumbed to his severe injuries three weeks later.

Berlin would now be left to the Mosquitos of 8 Group until the final third of the month, and, in the meantime, over three hundred aircraft raided the Baltic port of Stettin on the night of the 5/6th. The attack, which did not involve 115 and 514 Squadrons, began well, before deteriorating slightly as it progressed, but the central districts suffered heavy damage, and eight ships were sunk in the harbour. This was the last major operation for more than a week, and had again been conducted by an all-Lancaster heavy force. The main force Halifax crews had sat out the New Year thus far, and it was a force of 496 Lancasters and two Halifaxes that was made ready on the 14th for that night's operation. There must have been a degree of relief, when the red tape on the wall maps was seen to terminate short of Berlin, and point the way instead to Braunschweig (Brunswick), an historic and culturally significant city situated a little to the east of Hannover, for which this would be the first major raid of the war. There would be those among the assembled masses who remembered the difficult and costly series of raids against the latter during the autumn, and Brunswick was to prove to be an equally testing target. Not at briefing was the recently-commissioned and tour-expired P/O Boutilier DFC, who was posted on this day to 1678 Conversion Unit.

E J Thompson (M/UG) AH Howell (Capt.) RS Stewart (Nav) RF Millett (W.Op)H T Macwilliams (B/A) RS Brown (Flt. Eng.) J Masson (Rear Gunner)

115 Squadron prepared a record twenty-two of its Lancasters, loading seven with an 8,000 pounder and incendiaries and fifteen with a 4,000lb cookie and incendiaries. They took off between 16.55 and 17.15 with S/L Baigent the senior pilot on duty, and headed out towards Germany's north-western coast, where they were met by part of the enemy night-fighter response. F/Sgt Bishop and crew returned early after excessive vibration and an inability to maintain height forced them to turn back from a position over the North Sea. Complete cloud cover dictated the use of red and green sky-markers, which the 115 Squadron crews bombed from between 19,000 and 22,000 feet and assessed the operation as a success. F/Sgt Fogaty and crew observed a white glow in the clouds, which indicated to them that fires were burning below, and a large explosion at 19.26 was followed by a sheet of flame. They were attacked by a night-fighter on the way home, which blew away the starboard-inner engine, sending pieces of it through the wing and fuselage, and it was only through the very best crew co-operation that they managed to bring DS629 to a safe landing on the emergency strip at Woodbridge. The enemy fighters would score consistently all the way in and out, and would account for the majority of the thirty-eight missing Lancasters. 115 Squadron's DS720 was probably shot down while outbound, and crashed near Hannover with no survivors from the eight-man crew of P/O Blackwell RNZAF. LL673 was on the way home when the end came at Gittelde, midway between Salzgitter and Göttingen, and F/L Christiansen RNZAF died with his eight-man crew, which included second pilot, F/L Vinson, who had been posted in from 1678 Conversion Unit on the 5th. The attack almost entirely missed the city, and fell mostly onto outlying communities to the south. The Pathfinders, in particular, had been taking a beating since the turn of the year, with 156 Squadron alone losing fourteen Lancasters and crews, four and five on Berlin, and five again on Brunswick. There was something of a crisis in Pathfinder manpower, and a number of sideways postings took place to ensure a leavening of experience in each squadron. One of the solutions was to take the cream from among the crews emerging from the training units, rather than wait for them to gain experience at a main force squadron.

The first maximum effort of the year was called for on the 20th, for a raid that evening on Berlin. A force of 769 aircraft was made ready, of which twenty-one represented 115 Squadron. They took off between 16.30 and 17.10 with F/Ls Harris and Seddon the senior pilots on duty, and headed for the west coast of the Schleswig-Holstein peninsular at a point opposite Kiel. W/O Robbins returned early with a starboard-inner engine issue, and he was followed home ten minutes later by W/O McCann, whose compass had become unserviceable, and ten minutes later still by F/Sgt Rodger with a rear turret problem. The night-fighters were again able to infiltrate the bomber stream early on and inflict heavy casualties throughout the approach to the target and much of the withdrawal stages. F/Sgt Anderson and crew were deep into Germany when they discovered a navigation error, which left them with insufficient time to reach the target, and they touched down at 21.00. Forty-five minutes later F/O Rodger and crew arrived back to report bombing Hamburg from 18,000 feet after their rear-turret gave up the ghost. Meanwhile, complete cloud over Berlin again necessitated the use of sky-marking, leaving the 115 Squadron crews to bomb on red and green sky-markers from between 19,500 and 22,000 feet. It was not possible to assess the results, but the glow of widespread fires convinced them that an accurate attack had taken place. The Command paid the heavy price of thirty-five aircraft, one of which was 115 Squadron's LL650, which was shot down by a night-fighter after leaving the target, and crashed ten miles to the south-south west of Berlin city-centre. P/O Canning and all but one of his crew lost their lives, the rear gunner alone surviving to fall into enemy hands. It was some time later, before it was established that the hitherto less-severely damaged eastern districts had been hardest hit in a moderately successful raid.

Lancaster Mk II - LL673 KO-G.

F/L J H Christiansen (Pilot)   *Sgt R A Rodhouse (FE)*

F/O C H Wright RNZAF (BA)   *P/O J L Boswell-Kitching RNZAF (RG) F/O F A Braithwaite RNZAF (W.Op)*

All the crew were lost on 14th January 1944 on a raid on Brunswick

196

Twenty-four hours later, the city of Magdeburg was selected to host its first major operation of the war. A force of 648 aircraft was made ready, of which fourteen Lancasters represented 115 Squadron. They took off between 20.05 and 20.32 with S/L Baigent the senior pilot on duty, and there were no early returns to deplete the number reaching the target area. Situated some fifty miles east-south-east of Braunschweig, Magdeburg was on a route that threatened first Hannover, then Braunschweig and, finally, Berlin, which meant that the enemy night-fighter controller had a relatively simple task to direct his response. Enemy radar was able to detect H2S transmissions during night flying tests and equipment checks, and the night-fighter controller was, thereby, always aware of an imminent heavy raid. On this night, the night-fighters were able to infiltrate the bomber stream even before the German coast was crossed, and the recently-introduced "Tame Boar" night-fighter system provided a running commentary on the bomber stream's progress, enabling the fighters to latch onto the bombers and remain in contact. Some main force aircraft were now equipped with H2S, and, having been driven to the target early by stronger-than-forecast winds, a proportion of them opted to bomb ahead of the Pathfinders. The resultant fires and some decoy markers attracted other crews, and the Pathfinders were unable to centralize the attack. The 115 Squadron crews identified the target by means of red and green sky-markers and fires already burning, and bombed from between 19,000 and 22,000 feet. On return, a number reported a flash some twelve minutes after bombing, that lit up the clouds for seven seconds, and two large explosions were noted at 23.15. Fires that initially seemed to be scattered, appeared to become more concentrated as the crews headed for home, and the impression was of a successful operation. A record total of fifty-seven aircraft failed to return, the majority having fallen victim to night-fighters, and the Halifax contingent suffered particularly heavy casualties amounting to 15.6%. Among the twenty-two missing Lancasters was 115 Squadron's DS777, a C Flight aircraft, which had been shot down by a night-fighter in the target area, killing F/Sgt Moncrieff RAAF and three of his crew. No post-raid reconnaissance was attempted, and there was nothing emerging from Magdeburg to provide an assessment of the outcome, although the consensus was that most of the bombing had missed the city.

Five nights of rest preceded the next series of operations, which was to involve the crews in an unprecedented three trips to Berlin in the space of four nights. An all-Lancaster heavy force of 515 aircraft was made ready on the 27th, sixty-two of them belonging to 3 Group, whose conversion programme from the Stirling was gathering pace. 115 Squadron bombed up twenty MK IIs, and they departed Witchford without mishap either side of 18.00 with S/L Grant the senior pilot on duty. A complex route would take the bomber stream towards the north German coast, before swinging to the south-east to enter enemy territory over the Frisians and northern Holland. Having feinted towards central Germany, suggesting Leipzig as the target, the force was then to turn north-east to a point west of Berlin, from where the final run-in would commence. The long return route passed to the west of Leipzig before turning due east to pass north of Frankfurt and cross Belgium. F/Sgt Campbell and crew returned early after the wireless became unserviceable, leaving the others to press on towards the target. A mining diversion off Heligoland, combined with dummy fighter flares and route-markers, was partially successful in reducing the numbers of enemy night-fighters making contact, and it was a relatively intact bomber force that approached the target over ten-tenths cloud with tops at 15,000 feet. This necessitated the Pathfinders' use of sky-marking, and it was the red and green flares that led the 115 Squadron crews to the aiming-point, where they bombed from between 19,000 and 22,000 feet. On return they would report the glow of fires and the appearance of a successful raid, the 3 Group ORB describing it as probably one of the best yet. Of course, not all would make it back to debriefing, and thirty-three Lancaster dispersals stood empty in dawn's early light. Among the casualties were two from Witchford, one of which sent out a weak SOS signal, picked up at Binbrook at 00.55. Sadly, despite an extensive search by the air-sea rescue service, no trace of LL682 and the crew of F/Sgt Morris was ever found. LL668 was on the way home when it crashed at Steinberg on the western fringe of the Frankenwald in south-eastern Germany, and there were no survivors from the crew of F/O Ryder. Reports from Berlin described bombs falling over a wide area, more so in the south than the north, and

L-R: F/L. Hicks (Pilot), F/Sgt A W Todd RNZAF (B/A) P/O C F Farquharson (W Op) Lancaster LL648 KO-B 115 Sqn All crew KIA on Berlin raid, 31 January 1944.

damage to fifty industrial premises, a number of them engaged in important war work, while twenty thousand people were bombed out of their homes. A feature of the campaign was the number of outlying communities being afflicted, and, on this night, sixty-one recorded bombs falling.

Halifaxes were included in the force of 677 aircraft made ready for a return to the Capital on the following night. 115 Squadron detailed fifteen Lancasters, but only nine presented themselves for take-off between 00.14 and 00.29. S/L Grant was the senior pilot on duty as they crossed the east coast on a heading for the Schleswig-Holstein peninsular, but the Witchford numbers became depleted with the early return of F/L Hicks and F/Sgt Atkin (F/L Mackie) and their crews within minutes of each other at around 04.15, the former with an engine issue and the latter through severe icing that prevented them from climbing. The others continued on to approach the target area this time from the north-west, having overflown southern Denmark. They found Berlin covered by ten-tenths thin cloud, and the Pathfinders employed both ground and sky-marking to good effect. The TIs could be seen burning on the ground, but it was mostly the red and green sky-markers that led the 115 Squadron crews to the aiming-point, where they bombed from between 20,000 and 21,000 feet. The five crews returning between 07.55 and 08.50 were confident that a successful operation had taken place, but, it was clear also that it had been an expensive night for the Command. Night-fighters had been very active over the target, and many of the missing forty-six aircraft had fallen victim here. 115 Squadron's LL649 was almost certainly one of these, and only the bomb-aimer survived from the crew of P/O Tinn. The fate of DS833 has never been established, and F/L Harris and his crew have no known graves. They were an experienced crew, two-thirds of the way through their tour, and would be particularly missed at Witchford. News coming out of Berlin suggested that western and southern districts of the city had sustained the greatest damage to industry and housing, but many administrative buildings in the centre were also afflicted, and local reports told of 180,000 people being bombed out of their homes. Many bombs fell outside of the city again, and, on this night, seventy-seven outlying communities found themselves under attack.

After a night's rest a force of 534 aircraft was made ready on the 30th for the final operation of this concerted effort against Berlin. 115 Squadron bombed up eleven Lancasters and dispatched them between 17.15 and 17.30 with S/Ls Baigent and Grant the senior pilots on duty. S/L Grant and crew were back home within two hours after an engine issue curtailed their sortie, leaving the others to press on and follow a route similar to that adopted two nights earlier. The bomber stream remained relatively free of harassment until approaching the target, where it was greeted by ten-tenths cloud and Pathfinder sky-marking in progress. The 115 Squadron crews bombed on these from between 16,000 and 21,500 feet, and all commented on the smoke and the glow of fires beneath the cloud, which, according to some, was still visible from a hundred miles into the return flight. They also described intense night-fighter activity in the target area, and S/L Baigent's LL626 sustained damage as a result. F/Sgt Whyte and W/O Jolly and their crews witnessed a sudden explosion at 20.28 and were among nine crews to make it home to land between 23.25 and 00.56. They were the lucky ones, as thirty-three others failed to return, among them the squadron's LL648, which crashed in the target area with no survivors from the experienced and largely Kiwi crew of F/L Hicks RNZAF. Central and south-western districts suffered heavy damage and serious areas of fire, and at least a thousand people were killed, but other parts of the city were also hit, and many bomb loads were again scattered liberally onto outlying communities. This would prove to be the last concerted effort to destroy Berlin, although two further heavy raids would take place, one in February and another in March, before the campaign finally ended. Germany's Capital had been sorely afflicted by the three latest operations, but was still a functioning city, showing no signs of imminent collapse. During the course of the month the Squadron operated on eight nights, dispatching 127 sorties for the loss of eleven Lancasters and ten crews.

February 1944

Bad weather during the first two weeks of February allowed the crews to draw breath and the squadrons to replenish. Harris had intended to maintain the pressure on Berlin, and would have launched a further attack, had he not been thwarted by the conditions. On the evening of the 5th, F/Sgt Bishop and crew took DS827 for a night Bullseye (cross-country) exercise with an American, 1st Lt Weber USAAF, on board as a passenger. The Lancaster crashed at Great Dunmow in Essex at 20.20, with sufficient force to bury the engines, and killing all on board. The squadron carried out training on each day thereafter, and it was not until the 13th that an operation was posted, only to be cancelled in mid-afternoon. When the Pathfinder and main force crews next took to the air in numbers, it would be to participate in a record-breaking operation, which would also be the penultimate raid of the war by RAF heavy bombers on Berlin. A force of 891 aircraft was assembled on the 15th, and this was the largest non-1,000 force to date, and, therefore, the greatest ever sent against the Capital. It was the first time that more than five hundred Lancasters and three hundred Halifaxes had operated together, and they would carry in their bomb bays the greatest-ever tonnage of bombs. 115 Squadron dispatched nineteen Lancasters either side of 17.30, with S/L Baigent the senior pilot on duty and the newly-promoted S/L Mackie DSO flying as usual as bomb-aimer to F/Sgt Atkin.

The route out headed for the western coast of Denmark, crossing the Schleswig-Holstein peninsular and entering Germany via the Baltic coast between Rostock and Stralsund, before heading straight for the target, and exiting south of Hannover and Bremen and across Holland to the Castricum area. Extensive diversionary measures included a mining operation in Kiel Bay ahead of the arrival of the bombers, a raid on Frankfurt-an-Oder to the east of Berlin by a small force of 8 Group Lancasters, and Oboe Mosquitos attacking five night-fighter airfields in Holland. W/O Robbins and crew were less than an hour out when the starboard-inner engine expired, forcing them to turn back. The others pushed on over ten-tenths cloud, which persisted throughout the operation, and were guided to the target by red and green sky-markers, which they bombed from between 19,000 and 22,000 feet. Returning crews reported many fires beneath the clouds, but some felt the attack to be less concentrated than the one on the 30th of January. Heavy flak was reported to be reaching 22,000 feet, and the last crews to leave the target

Harry Rossiter and crew

area watched smoke rising beyond 20,000 feet. Forty-three aircraft failed to return home, and among them were two from Witchford as Berlin continued to claim 115 Squadron lives. LL651 crashed near Neuruppin some forty miles before reaching the target, and only the navigator in the crew of F/Sgt Whyte survived to fall into enemy hands. LL689 had almost run the gauntlet of the defences on the way home, and was over the Ijsselmeer, when it was intercepted by Oblt Schnaufer, one of the Luftwaffe's foremost night-fighter pilots. The Lancaster went down into the water, breaking up on the way, and throwing the navigator and bomb-aimer into space, where they were able to deploy their parachutes. F/Sgt Ralph and the remainder of the crew perished, but the two survivors were rescued from the water and soon joined their colleagues as PoWs. Those reaching the Capital had delivered 2,640 tons of bombs causing extensive fire and blast damage within the city's central and south-western districts. Over a thousand houses were destroyed, along with hundreds of temporary wooden barracks, which had been erected to provide emergency living accommodation for those rendered homeless over the past months. Industry also suffered during the attack, and the, now, familiar scattering of bombs onto outlying communities did not detract from its effectiveness.

After another three nights on the ground, Leipzig was posted as the target for 823 aircraft, of which twenty Lancasters were provided by 115 Squadron. They took off either side of midnight and headed for the Dutch coast, where a proportion of the Luftwaffe Nachtjagd was waiting for them, while others had been drawn away by a mining diversion off Kiel. F/Sgts Wood, Moon and Rodger returned early with technical problems between 02.25 and 03.12, leaving the others embroiled in a running battle all the way into eastern Germany. Inaccurately forecast winds caused some aircraft to arrive at the target early, and they were forced to orbit, while they waited for the target indicators to go down. The local flak batteries accounted for around twenty of these, while four other aircraft were lost through collisions. The 115 Squadron crews arrived to find ten-tenths cloud and sky-marking in progress, at which they aimed their bombs from between 19,000 and 23,000 feet. The operation appeared to them to be fairly concentrated, with smoke seen to be rising through the clouds as they turned away and the glow of fires visible for some fifty miles. The actual outcome was inconclusive in the face of the complete cloud-cover, but what was not in question was the enormity of the Command's losses. When all of the returning aircraft had been accounted for, there was a massive shortfall of seventy-eight, representing 9.5% of those dispatched, and this was the heaviest loss of the war to date by a clear twenty-one aircraft. A disproportionately high loss rate among the Merlin-powered Mk II and V variants of the Halifax of 13.3% saw them join the Stirlings in exile from German skies. This would mean that some of 4 Group's premier squadrons would be off the order of Battle for a few weeks, while they took delivery of the much-improved Mk III.

Despite this depletion of available numbers, a force of 598 aircraft was made ready on the 20th for an operation that night against Stuttgart, which would be the first of three against the city over a three-week period. 115 Squadron loaded eighteen Lancasters, eight with an 8,000 pounder, five with a cookie and five with a mixture of 2,000 and 1,000 pounders, all with incendiaries to make up the weight. They took off in a half-hour slot from midnight with S/L Grant the senior pilot on duty, but W/O Robbins and crew turned back over the Channel after two engines began to malfunction. A North Sea sweep and a diversionary raid on Munich two hours ahead of the main activity caused the Luftwaffe to deploy its forces early, and this allowed the bomber stream to push on unmolested into French airspace, where the cloud remained at ten-tenths with tops at 8,000 feet all the way into southern Germany. The cloud thinned in the target area to five to eight tenths, and the visibility was excellent as the crews drew a bead on the Pathfinder red and green sky-markers and TIs on the ground. The 115 Squadron crews bombed from between 19,000 and 23,000 feet, observing many large fires, and, on return, they reported the glow still visible from 250 miles into the return flight. Despite some scattering of bombs, local reports described central districts, and those in a quadrant from north-west to north-east suffering extensive damage, and a Bosch factory was one of the important war industry concerns to be hard-hit. In contrast to twenty-four hours earlier, a modest nine aircraft failed to return, and, having escaped the carnage at Leipzig, 115 squadron almost came through unscathed again. Sadly, LL729 crashed at 06.45 at Shillington, eleven miles south-south-east of Bedford, and there was total loss of life among the crew of F/Sgt Wood RAAF.

In an attempt to reduce the prohibitive losses of recent weeks, a new tactic was introduced for the next two operations. A force of 734 aircraft was assembled on the 24th for an operation to the centre of Germany's ball-bearing production, Schweinfurt, situated some sixty miles to the east of Frankfurt in southern Germany. The plan called for 392 aircraft to depart their stations between 18.00 and 19.00, and to be followed into the air two hours later by 342 others in the hope of catching the night-fighters on the ground refuelling and rearming as the second wave passed through. 115 Squadron made ready nineteen Lancasters, six of them assigned to the first phase, and they took off between 18.49 and 18.55 with S/L Grant the senior pilot on duty. The remaining thirteen departed Witchford between 20.44 and 21.11 led by F/L Halley, and only F/Sgt Birnie and crew returned early, having reached Selsey Bill on the south coast. They apparently picked up a hole in the tail-plane, and jettisoned their bombs before landing safely at Lyneham in Wiltshire shortly after midnight. Visibility in the target area was good, and the Pathfinders were able to employ ground-marking, which appeared to be accurate and sufficiently concentrated to provide a good reference for the main force crews. The second phase crews described the glow from the resultant fires visible from two hundred miles away as they approached, and the 115 Squadron crews from both waves recorded bombing from between 18,000 and 22,000 feet. Smoke was seen to emanate from the many fires, and all indications suggested an effective raid. Unfortunately, both phases of the operation had suffered from undershooting after some Pathfinder backers-up failed to press on to the aiming-point. In that regard it was a disappointing night, but an interesting feature was the loss of 50% fewer aircraft from the second wave in comparison with the first, in an overall casualty figure of thirty-three. The squadron's LL701 failed to return from the early shift, and was lost without trace with the crew of F/L Hornby, while LL644 crashed in southern Germany during the second phase, and there were no survivors from the crew of F/O Nice, which contained three members of the RCAF.

Lancaster KO-Y on a daylight raid to Cologne 1944

On the following day, almost six hundred aircraft were prepared for a similar two-phase assault that night on the beautiful and historic city of Augsburg, situated around thirty miles north-west of Munich. 115 Squadron contributed thirteen Lancasters to the second phase of the operation, and they took off between 21.29 and 21.46 with no senior pilots on duty. They flew out over ten-tenths cloud that had dissipated by the time the target drew near, and, on arrival, it was possible to gain a visual reference. They bombed from between 19,500 and 21,500 feet, aiming at TIs and fires, and were able to see the glow in the sky from a hundred miles away. A relatively modest twenty-one aircraft failed to return, but all from 115 Squadron arrived home safely to make their reports of a successful operation. It was one of those rare occasions, when all facets of the operational plan came together in near perfect harmony, and it spelled disaster for this lightly-defended treasure trove of culture. The heart of the city was torn out by blast and fire, while almost three thousand houses were destroyed, along with buildings of outstanding historical significance. There was also some industrial damage, and around ninety-thousand people were bombed out of their homes. This was the final operation of the month, which had seen the squadron operate on just five nights, and dispatch eighty-nine sorties for the loss of six Lancasters and crews.

March 1944

March would bring an end to the winter campaign, but a long and bitter month would have to be endured first before any respite came from long-range forays into Germany. The crews had enjoyed a few nights off when the second raid of the series on Stuttgart was posted on the 1st, for which a force of 557 aircraft was made ready, including eighteen Lancasters representing 115 Squadron. Take-off from Witchford was accomplished without incident between 23.28 and 23.52 with S/L Grant the senior pilot on duty, and there were no early returns. They flew out over ten-tenths cloud with tops at between 12,000 and 17,000 feet, and encountered similar conditions in the target area. The Pathfinders employed a combination of sky and ground-marking, which returning crews would describe as scattered, and the markers were bombed from between 19,000 and 22,000 feet. It was not possible to assess the accuracy of the attack, although large fires were evident from the glow in the sky visible from 150 miles away. The presence of thick cloud all the way there and back made conditions difficult for enemy night-fighters, and a remarkably modest four aircraft failed to return. It was eventually established that the raid had been an outstanding success, which had caused extensive damage in central, western and northern

P/O Dick Treasure RNZAF stands with his air and ground crew at RAF Witchford on completion of his operational tour in May 1944. He was awarded a DFC.

districts, where a number of important war-industry factories, including those belonging to Bosch and Daimler-Benz, sustained damage.

There would not be another maximum-effort operation for two weeks, and it was during this period, that the first salvoes were fired in the pre-invasion campaign under the Transportation Plan. This required the systematic destruction by bombing of the French and Belgian railway networks, and it fell to the Halifaxes of 4 and 6 Groups to open proceedings at Trappes, to the west of Paris, on the night of the 6/7th, which gave an opportunity for the Merlin-powered examples of the type to extend their operational career, until they finally disappeared from the bombing scene altogether during May. Twenty-four hours later it was the turn of Le-Mans, this operation bolstered by the addition of thirty-two Mk II Lancasters from 115 and 514 Squadrons to make a total force of 304 aircraft. The fourteen 115 Squadron aircraft took off between 19.39 and 19.52 with S/L Baigent the senior pilot on duty, he now the bearer of a Bar to his DFC. They encountered ten-tenths cloud in the target area, but most could pick out the glow of red TIs on the ground, and bombed them from between 11,000 and 12,000 feet. P/O Vipond and W/O Treasure failed to identify the target, and jettisoned part of their load before returning safely with the others.

The main force returned to the fray in numbers on the night of the 15/16th, when a massive force of 863 aircraft was made ready for the third raid on Stuttgart. 115 Squadron loaded six Lancasters with an 8,000 pounder each and sixteen with a cookie, along with incendiaries all round, and they became airborne in a twenty-minute slot by 19.39 with S/L Baigent the senior pilot on duty. They crossed the French coast at 20,000 feet over broken cloud with clear conditions above, and it was soon afterwards that P/O Hookway and crew turned back with engine failure. The others pressed on to the target, and, it was as they approached it that the night-fighters made contact and began to score heavily. F/Sgt Williams and crew found themselves under attack by a JU88 when twenty miles south-south-east of Karlsruhe, and sustained damage to the starboard wing and fin, before going on to bomb. Their Monica tail-warning radar would pack up on the way home. The Pathfinders were up to six minutes late in opening the attack, and employed both sky and ground-markers, the former drifting in the wind and scattering. The 115 Squadron crews bombed on whatever markers presented themselves, mostly green and red TIs, and did so from between 19,000 and 21,700 feet, observing a spread of fires, including two large ones ten miles apart. It would be established later that some of the early bombing had been accurate, but that most of the loads had undershot and fallen into open country. In return for this disappointing outcome, thirty-seven aircraft failed to return, and, after two loss-free operations, 115 Squadron was forced to post missing the crew of P/O Rodger. He was killed with four of his crew, when LL693 was shot down over southern Germany, and only the wireless operator and rear gunner survived as PoWs.

Many operations had been mounted against Frankfurt, only one of which had, thus far, been really effective. This state of affairs was about to be rectified, however, and the first of two raids against this southern powerhouse of industry was posted on the 18th, for which a force of 846 aircraft was made ready. 115 Squadron loaded six Lancasters with an 8,000 pounder each, five with a cookie and eleven with 1,000 pounders, all with incendiaries for good measure, and sent them off between 19.35 and 19.55 with S/Ls Baigent and Grant the senior pilots on duty. W/O Hemming's sortie was abandoned when his 8,000 pounder came loose and fell out at 20.28 within a mile of the north-western edge of Cambridge. The Lancaster was flown out to sea to open the bomb bay in case other bombs had become detached, but none had, and they were all returned to store. The other squadron representatives pressed on to southern Germany in good weather conditions, to find haze and three-tenths cloud in the target area. DS629 was attacked by three night-fighters as it closed in on the bombing run, and the port-outer engine was hit and the turrets sprayed. The engine caught fire over the target, and, although the flames were extinguished, it remained unserviceable, and the starboard-outer would also lose power on the way home to a landing at Coltishall at 02.24, where the wounded rear gunner was taken to hospital and the Lancaster was declared to be beyond economical repair. F/Sgt Birnie and crew overshot Frankfurt after missing route markers, and bombed a searchlight concentration on the edge of Ludwigshafen from 20,000 feet as a last-resort target. The remaining squadron crews carried out their attacks from between 19,000 and

Lancaster MkII DS689 KO-S

204

21,500 feet, and contributed to an outstandingly successful raid, which left six thousand buildings destroyed or seriously damaged in predominantly eastern, central and western districts. Twenty-two aircraft failed to return, and among them was LL640, which crashed in Germany, possibly south of the Ruhr on the way home, and P/O Frampton RNZAF died with all but his flight engineer, who was captured.

On the 20th, DS661 swung off the runway during take-off for a training flight, tore off its undercarriage and was written off, although F/Sgt Oldham and his crew emerged unscathed. The residents of Frankfurt were given just four days to try to recover their lives before the approach of another large force of bombers was announced over the radio and the scramble for the air-raid bunkers began. 816 aircraft had been made ready on bomber stations the length of eastern England following the posting of Frankfurt as the target earlier in the day. At briefings crews were told of diversions and an indirect route across Holland, followed by a southerly course to the target, which represented a complete departure from the standard course across France and or Belgium for attacks on southern Germany. 115 Squadron had responded with twenty Lancasters, which assembled for take-off in the early evening, with F/Sgt Atkin's LL622 at the head of the queue and flight commander S/L Mackie occupying his usual position as his bomb-aimer. They rolled down the runway at 18.38 and the others had all followed them into the air by 19.04, before F/Sgt Cameron and crew were forced to turn back with an oil-pressure problem and landed after seventy minutes aloft. The remainder pressed on over a thin layer of broken cloud, and reached the target to find Pathfinder ground-marking in progress. The night-fighter controller had been confused by the route, and had predicted Hannover as the likely target, as a result of which, the bomber stream remained largely free from attack. The 115 Squadron crews identified the aiming-point either visually or by red and green TIs, and bombed from between 19,500 and 21,500 feet, observing large fires as they turned away, which were still visible from a hundred miles. F/Sgt Pope and crew had other matters on their mind as they struggled to get home after flak had severely damaged DS766. They decided to land at the emergency strip at Woodbridge near the Suffolk coast, but came down short of the runway at Bredfield just after midnight, killing the pilot and three others and severely wounding three survivors, one of whom succumbed to his injuries on the 26th. Thirty-three aircraft failed to make it back in return for another highly successful assault on Frankfurt, which resulted in half of the city being deprived of gas, electricity and water for a prolonged period. The Frankfurt that had existed for centuries was now gone, its cultural history lost forever, its industry ravaged and a further 120,000 of its people left homeless. Thirty-six hours later 162 Fortresses of the USAAF 8th Air Force used it as an alternative target after failing to reach Schweinfurt.

The stage was now set for the nineteenth and final operation of the campaign against Berlin, which had begun back in August. It was more than five weeks since the main force had last visited the Capital, and 811 aircraft were made ready on the 24th for what would be the final raid of the war by RAF heavy bombers on Germany's Capital. 115 Squadron contributed eighteen Lancasters, and sent them skyward between 18.34 and 18.50 with F/L Seddon RAAF the senior pilot on duty in LL726. The other aircraft and crews for this momentous occasion were LL622 P/O Atkin (S/L Mackie), LL704 P/O Anderson, LL652 P/O Gibson, DS620 P/O Hammond, DS678 P/O McCann, LL695 P/O McKechnie, LL641 P/O Milgate, LL667 P/O Moon, LL694 P/O Vipond, DS682 W/O Hammond, DS781 W/O Treasure, LL624 F/Sgt Cameron, LL666, F/Sgt Campbell, LL646 F/Sgt Chantler, DS664 F/Sgt Newman, DS728 F/Sgt Taylor and LL730 F/Sgt Williams. They had a long flight ahead of them, which would take them across the North Sea to the Danish coast near Ringkøbing and then to a point on the German Baltic coast near Rostock. When north-east of Berlin they were to adopt a south-westerly course for the bombing run, and, once clear of the defence zone, dogleg to the west and then north-west to pass around Hannover on its southern and western sides, before heading for Holland and an exit via the Castricum coast. The extended outward leg provided a time-on-target of around 22.30, but an unexpected difficulty would be encountered, which would render void all of the meticulous planning. The existence of what we know as "Jetstream" winds was unknown at the time, and the one blowing from the north with unprecedented strength on this night pushed the bomber stream south of its intended track. Navigators, who were expecting to see the northern tip of Sylt on their H2S screens, were horrified to find the southern end, which meant that they were thirty miles south of track, and about to fly over Germany rather than Denmark. A "windfinder system had been set up to help with navigation, and this used designated crews to establish wind strength and direction and send their findings to the raid controllers, who would collate the figures, adjust them as necessary and rebroadcast them to the whole force. The problem on this night was that the windfinders refused to believe what their instruments were telling them. Winds in excess of one hundred m.p.h had never been encountered before, and, fearing that they would be disbelieved, many modified the figures downward. The same thing happened at raid control, and the figures were modified again, so that the information rebroadcast to the bomber stream bore no resemblance to the reality of the situation.

W/O Treasure and crew had crossed the Schleswig-Holstein peninsular on the German side, and had reached an island to the east of Kiel when the port-inner engine failed. They turned back and bombed a flak concentration in the Kiel area, before eventually arriving home almost six hours after taking off. W/O Hemming and crew were so far south of where they were supposed to be, that they stumbled into the Hamburg defence zone and were hit in the port-inner and starboard-outer engines. The former caught fire and the latter stopped, leaving the crew with no option but to drop their bombs live from their current altitude of 12,000 feet, and try to make it home. In this endeavour they were successful, and touched down some seven hours after taking off. F/Sgt Williams and crew crossed paths with a night-fighter over the Baltic, which set off a fire in the bomb bay. Whether or not the bombs were immediately jettisoned is not known, but a decision was taken to try to reach Sweden, which failed because of the Lancaster's inability to maintain height. Having crossed the German coast, the bomb-aimer, Sgt Meikle, decided the time had come to open the hatch in the floor of his compartment and leave LL730, which subsequently crashed at Kröpelin to the west of Rostock, killing all still on board.

Above and overleaf: Lancaster LL704 KO-H, which crashed near Nurtingen on 31st March 1944 after being shot down on the Nuremberg raid. All the crew became POWs.

207

The remaining 115 Squadron crews pressed on to the target with the bomber stream now in total disarray and all timings inconsequential. The Pathfinders employed both sky and ground-markers, but the former drifted with great speed towards the south-west, where many bomb loads would follow. The 115 Squadron crews reported bombing on red and green TIs and marker flares from between 20,000 and 21,200 feet, describing the marking as scattered generally, but concentrated on the eastern side of the city, and claimed to see the glow in the sky for half an hour into the return flight. They were the lucky ones, for not all of the crews arrived home to tell their stories at debriefing. As a consequence of the wind, many aircraft found themselves over the heavily-defended Ruhr as they tried to plot a course to the Dutch coast, and the flak batteries had a field day. A massive seventy-two aircraft were missing, and an estimated two-thirds of them are believed to have fallen victim to flak, while night-fighters claimed the others, including all three of the 115 Squadron casualties heading for home. DS678 was skirting Leipzig at 20,000 feet when the end came, and P/O McCann RCAF died with four others of his crew, while the two survivors were taken into captivity. LL694 had reached Holland before it was pounced upon by one of Germany's foremost aces, Hptm Martin Drewes of III/NJG.1, who shot it down to crash near Deventer at 00.20, killing P/O Vipond and his crew. Finally, DS664 was caught by a JU88 while approaching the south-eastern end of the Ruhr at 19,000 feet, and a fierce fire began to consume the inside of the fuselage. F/Sgt Newman gave the order to abandon ship at 18,000 feet, but the rear gunner, Sgt Alkemade, found his parachute destroyed, and the flames beginning to infiltrate his turret. Faced with the prospect of death by fire or descent from a great height, he opted for the latter, and departed the aircraft resigned to his fate. He lost consciousness on the way down, and awoke later in a snowdrift, suffering from burns and shrapnel wounds, but otherwise undamaged by the three-mile fall to earth. His captors initially refused to believe his remarkable story, but ultimately found the necessary evidence to confirm his incredible escape, which was attributed to falling through fir trees and into deep soft snow, while in a state of complete limpness. Shortly after he began his descent, the Lancaster exploded, flinging the navigator and wireless operator into space, and they also survived to be taken into captivity. The bodies of F/Sgt Newman and three others were found in the wreckage at Schmallenberg, a small town situated between the Edersee and Wuppertal. An assessment of the raid revealed that more than a hundred outlying communities had been afflicted by bombs, while most of the damage within Berlin itself had involved housing in the south-western corner. In his outstanding book, The Berlin Raids, Martin Middlebrook provides an analysis of the performance of squadrons during the nineteen operations to Berlin between the 23rd of August 1943 and the 24th of March 1944. It reveals that 115 Squadron was the only 3 Group unit to take part in every one, and dispatched a total 259 Lancaster sorties, a figure representing more than half of all 3 Group Lancaster sorties. The twenty-one missing aircraft was the most in 3 Group and represented a loss rate of 8.1%, which was also the highest loss rate among Lancaster squadrons in the Command as a whole.

On the 25th C Flight began the process of converting to the Merlin-powered Mk I and Mk III Lancasters which would soon replace the trusty Mk IIs that had given such good service for the past twelve months. In the meantime, and even though the Berlin offensive was now over, the winter campaign still had a week to run, and two further major operations for the crews to negotiate. The first of these was posted on the 26th, and would bring a return to the old enemy of Essen that night, for which a force of 705 aircraft was made ready. 115 Squadron bombed up eleven Lancasters drawn from A and B Flights, and dispatched them between 20.05 and 20.14 with F/Ls Halley, Seddon, Hammond and Milgate the senior pilots on duty. F/Sgt Caigenard and crew returned after seventy-five minutes with a port-inner engine problem, and were followed home a few minutes later by F/Sgt Bertram with an identical issue. The cause of P/O Anderson's early return shortly after 22.00 was an hydraulics leak that rendered the rear turret inoperable. The others pushed on to find the target under eight-tenths cloud with tops at 14,000 feet, but Oboe performed well and enabled the Pathfinders to mark the city with red and green TIs, which

A crew believed to be that of P/O L J Halliday. The members of that crew were) P/O L J Halley (Capt.) P/O J Atkinson (Nav.) Sgt. W Pettit (W.Op) Sgt. F Pick (B/A) Sgt Wyatt (M/UG) Sgt Cook (RG).

which were visible despite the cloud. Bombing took place from between 19,000 and 21,500 feet, and all eight 115 Squadron crews returned safely, having been unable to assess the results of their efforts. Post-raid reconnaissance soon confirmed another outstandingly destructive operation against this once elusive target, thus continuing the remarkable run of successes here since the introduction of Oboe to main force operations a year earlier. Over seventeen hundred houses were destroyed in the attack, and dozens of war industry factories sustained serious damage for a modest loss of nine aircraft.

The winter campaign was to draw to a close with a deep-penetration operation into southern Germany to attack Nuremberg on the night of the 30/31st. The plan of operation departed from normal practice in only one important respect, and this was to prove critical. It had become standard routine over the winter to employ diversions and feints to confuse the enemy night-fighter controllers. Sometimes they were successful and sometimes not, but with the night-fighter force having clearly gained the upper hand with its "Tame Boar" running commentary system, all possible means had to be adopted to protect the bomber stream. During a conference held early on the 30th, the Lancaster Group A-O-Cs expressed a preference for a 5 Group-inspired route, which would require the aircraft to fly a long straight leg across Belgium and Germany, to a point about fifty miles north of Nuremberg, from where the final run-in would commence. The Halifax A-O-Cs were less convinced of the benefits, and AVM Bennett, the Pathfinder chief, was positively overcome by the potential dangers and predicted a disaster, but he was overruled.

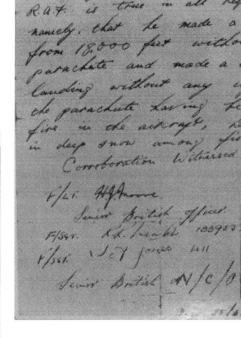

Sgt Nicholas Alkemade who survived an 18,000 ft. fall from his burning Lancaster without his parachute, much to the disbelief of his German captors.

A force of 795 aircraft was made ready, of which ten Lancasters were provided by 115 Squadron, and the crews attended briefings to be told of the route, wind conditions and the belief that a layer of cloud would conceal them from enemy night-fighters. A Meteorological Flight Mosquito crew radioed in to cast doubts upon the weather conditions, which they could see differed markedly from those forecast. This also went unheeded, and, from around 21.45 for the next hour or so, the crews took off for the rendezvous area, and headed into a conspiracy of circumstances, which would inflict upon Bomber Command its blackest night of the war.

The 115 Squadron crews were airborne between 22.29 and 22.43 with S/L Grant the senior pilot on duty, and it was not long into the flight before they and the other crews began to notice some unusual features in the conditions, which included uncommonly bright moonlight, and a crystal clarity of visibility, which allowed them the rare sight of other aircraft in the stream. Once at cruising altitude, the forecast cloud was conspicuous by its absence, and, instead, lay beneath them as a white tablecloth, against which they were silhouetted like flies. Condensation trails began to form in the cold, clear air to further advertise their presence to the enemy, and the jetstream winds, which had so adversely affected the Berlin raid a week earlier were also present, only this time from the south. As the final insult, the route into Germany passed close to two night-fighter beacons, which the enemy aircraft were orbiting while they awaited their instructions. S/L Grant had turned back by this time after the heating system to the turrets failed, and he jettisoned the 8,000 pounder a few miles north-west of the Scheldt Estuary. He and his crew, therefore, avoided the carnage, which began over Charleroi in Belgium, and from there to the target, the route was sign-posted by the burning wreckage on the ground of eighty Bomber Command aircraft. The windfinder system broke down again, and those crews who either failed to detect the strength of the wind, or simply refused to believe the evidence, were driven up to fifty miles north of their intended track, and, consequently, turned towards Nuremberg from a false position. This led to more than a hundred aircraft bombing at Schweinfurt in error, and together with the massive losses sustained before the target was reached, this reduced considerably the numbers arriving at the briefed destination. The 115 Squadron crews bombed on red and green TIs and sky-markers from between 20,000 and 21,500 feet and observed many fires. In fact, Nuremberg escaped serious damage as many of the Pathfinder markers were carried beyond the city and into open country. Bucking the trend, both 115 Squadron casualties occurred while they were on their way home, LL704 crashing south of Stuttgart through the combined efforts of flak and a night-fighter, but F/Sgt Fogaty and his crew escaped by parachute to be taken into captivity. They were halfway through their tour, but F/Sgt Thomas and his crew all died on their first operation together, when LL622 became the last but one of the night's victims at the hands of a night-fighter over Belgium, and crashed on the edge of the historic battlefield of Waterloo. LL646 was lucky to survive an attack from astern by a JU88 over the target, which caused damage to the starboard-inner engine and propeller, and set fire to some hung-up incendiaries. The wireless operator put out the flames with an extinguisher, and F/Sgt Lemoine and crew brought the wounded Lancaster back to land at Graveley with diminishing fuel reserves. Ninety-five aircraft failed to return home, and many others were written off in crashes, or with battle damage too severe to repair. During the course of the month the squadron operated on eight occasions and dispatched 135 sorties for the loss of eleven Lancasters and eight complete crews.

April 1944

That which now faced the crews was in marked contrast to what had been endured over the winter months. The Transportation Plan, already being prosecuted by the Stirlings and Halifaxes of 3, 4 and 6 Groups, would now become the overriding priority for the whole of the Command. In place of the exhausting slog to distant targets in Germany on dark, often dirty nights, shorter range hops to France and Belgium would become the order of the day in improving weather conditions. Such operations, however, would prove to be equally demanding in their way, and would require of the crews a greater commitment to accuracy, to avoid, as far as possible, civilian casualties. As events were to prove, this was an impossible quest, and French civilians would suffer a torrid time under RAF bombs. The main fly in the ointment as far as the crews were concerned, was a dictate from on high, which decreed that most such operations to the occupied countries were worthy of counting as just one-third of a sortie towards the completion of a tour. It was not a popular move, and until this flawed policy was rescinded, an air of discontent pervaded the bomber stations. Despite the prohibitive losses during the winter campaign, the Command was in remarkably fine fettle to face its new challenge. Such were the numbers of aircraft and crews available to Harris, that he could assign targets to individual groups, to groups in tandem or the Command as a whole according to operational requirement, and safe in the knowledge that any size of force had the hitting power to complete the job. This meant that he could achieve that which had eluded his predecessor, namely, to strike simultaneously at multiple targets in sufficient strength to make an impact. Although pre-invasion considerations would now take priority, Harris would never entirely abandon his favoured policy of city-busting, and whenever an opportunity arose, he would strike.

It was not until the second week of April that the new offensive began in earnest, and this provided 115 Squadron's A Flight with the opportunity to continue its conversion to Merlin-powered Lancasters, while Mk IIs would remain on charge with S/L Baigent's B Flight for the time-being. On the 9th, a force of 239 aircraft of 3, 4, 6 and 8 Groups was made ready to attack the Lille-Delivrance goods station, while others, including ten Lancasters of 115 Squadron, were assigned to the important marshalling yards at Villeneuve-St-George on the southern outskirts of Paris. The Witchford element took off between 21.30 and 21.39 with W/C Annan the senior pilot on duty, each carrying ten 1,000 pounders and four 500 pounders. The weather conditions were excellent, and clear skies greeted them as they crossed the French coast at 14,000 feet. The target could be identified visually, but the 115 Squadron crews aimed for the red and green TIs that had been accurately placed by the Pathfinders, delivering their hardware from between 13,000 and 14,500 feet in the face of little opposition. Many bomb bursts were observed along with orange explosions, and, to those high above, the raid appeared to be highly successful. In fact, many bomb loads had fallen into adjacent residential districts, where four hundred houses had been destroyed or seriously damaged. Ninety-three people were killed, but this was far fewer than had died in the simultaneous operation at Lille, many miles to the north, where over two thousand items of rolling stock had been destroyed, and buildings and installations seriously damaged, but at a collateral cost of 456 French civilians' lives.

On the following day plans were drawn up for the destruction of five railway yards in France and Belgium, each, with the exception of one, assigned to a single group. Laon, in north-eastern France, was to be attacked by a heavy force of 148 Lancasters from 3 and 6 Groups, of which eighty-four were provided by 3 Group. 115 Squadron made ready twenty-three Lancasters, and dispatched them between 01.10 and 01.38 with S/Ls Baigent and Grant the senior pilots on duty and S/L Mackie in his usual position as bomb-aimer in the crew of P/O Atkin. They crossed the French coast in clear skies at 14,000 feet, and identified the aiming-point by means of red and green TIs. The bombing was carried out from between 9,000 and 11,500 feet, and appeared to be accurate, returning crews declaring a successful operation, a sentiment echoed in the 3 Group ORB. Post-raid reconnaissance revealed, however, that this was the night's only failure, and that the yards had escaped serious damage after only one corner had been hit.

P/O R P Cagienard (Pilot)

Sgt C P Kelly (Flt.Eng)

F/Sgt F A Foster (Nav)

Sgt W Shorten William (W/Op)

P/O J M MacLeod (BA)

Sgt F D King (M/UG)

P/O A C Letcher (RG)

Lancaster DS734 was shot down by a night fighter on the Karlsruhe operation of 24/25 April 1944. All the crew were killed. P/O Letcher had added three years to his age to join the RCAF. He was actually 18 years old.

213

Aachen was a major railway centre with marshalling yards at both the western and eastern ends, but the attack planned for the night of the 11/12th was clearly designed as a city-busting exercise for which a force of 341 heavy aircraft was drawn from 1, 3, 5 and 8 Groups. 115 Squadron detailed six Lancasters, which took off either side of 21.00 with the Australian F/Ls Hammond and Milgate the senior pilots on duty. The bomber stream climbed to 18,000 to 20,000 feet by the time it reached 03.00E, and maintained that altitude to the target, where six to seven-tenths cloud was encountered. Red and green TIs identified the aiming-point, and the attack appeared to be fairly accurate, with many bomb bursts and fires observed. The crews maintained height on the way home until fifty miles from the coast, at which position they began a gentle descent to exit enemy territory at 15,000 feet or above. Reports coming out of Aachen revealed this to be the city's worst experience of the war to date, with extensive damage in central and southern districts, disruption of its transport infrastructure and a death toll of 1,525 people.

Stand-downs and minor operations occupied the next week, during which time, on the 14th, Bomber Command became officially subject to the dictates of the Supreme Headquarters Allied Expeditionary Force (SHAEF) for the pre and post-invasion period, and would remain thus shackled and under the orders of General Dwight Eisenhower until the Allied armies were sweeping towards the German frontier at the end of the summer. Preparations were put in hand on the 18th to resume attacks on railway targets, and elements of 1, 3 and 8 Groups were combined to make up a force of 273 Lancasters assigned to the marshalling yards at Rouen in northern France. 115 Squadron set a record of dispatching twenty-six Lancasters between 22.27 and 22.55 with S/Ls Baigent and Grant the senior pilots on duty. They arrived in the target area to find clear skies but some ground haze, despite which, the crews were able to identify the target visually by a bend in the River Seine and by lights in a street in a built-up area. The Pathfinders established two distinct areas of marking, which the Master Bomber had to interpret, before ordering crews to bomb to the south-east of the red and green TIs. Many of the 115 Squadron crews picked up the instructions and complied, dropping their loads of 1,000 and 500 pounders from between 12,500 and 14,500 feet in the face of negligible opposition. Bomb bursts and fires were observed, which confirmed in the minds of the participants that a successful attack had taken place. The operation was concluded without loss until home airspace was regained, at which point, enemy intruders, that had infiltrated the bomber stream unnoticed, made their presence known. As LL667 was on final approach to Witchford shortly after 02.00, it was set upon by an enemy intruder and shot down, killing P/O Birnie and his crew. A little over an hour and a half later, an identical fate befell the crew of F/L Eddy RNZAF in LL867. ED631 suffered an undercarriage collapse when three-quarters of the way down the runway, but Sgt Lemoine and his crew walked away, and the Lancaster would be repaired and returned to service.

Orders were received on the 20th to prepare for an operation that night against Cologne, which would be the main operation on a busy night for the Command. Railway yards at La Chapelle, Ottignes and Lens would occupy other elements of the Command, and, together with minor operations, would result in a record number of 1,155 sorties. A heavy force of 357 Lancasters from 1, 3, 6 and 8 Groups would be supported by twenty-two Pathfinder Mosquitos to attack the Rhineland Capital, and the twenty-two 115 Squadron participants departed Witchford either side of midnight with S/Ls Baigent and Grant the senior pilots on duty. They had been told at briefing to cross the enemy coast at 20,000 feet, and then climb, cloud and no Pathfinders. Some crews bombed on e.t.a before the first red sky-markers with yellow stars appeared, which were between six and twelve minutes late and scattered. The 115 Squadron crews bombed from between 18,000 and 21,500 feet, and observed the red glow of fires in the cloud, but most returned with low expectations concerning the outcome of the attack, and the consensus was of a poor performance. ND805 landed at Woodbridge with a damaged starboard wing after being hit by eleven incendiaries from above, which also caused a fire in the fuselage that was dealt with by the crew. Theybefore nosing down to increase speed through the defended area, where they arrived to find ten-tenths reported actually hearing a huge explosion emanating from the target, which, as post-raid reconnaissance and local reports later revealed, had suffered extensive damage, particularly in northern

214

and western districts. More than eighteen hundred housing units had been destroyed, and 192 industrial premises damaged to some extent, along with 725 dwelling units with commercial buildings attached. 1,290 individual fires were recorded, and the death toll was put at 664, most of whom perished while sheltering in basements. Only four aircraft failed to return, but among them was the squadron's DS728, which fell victim to flak in the target area, killing both gunners and delivering F/Sgt Bertram and four of his crew into enemy hands.

Two nights later, a force of 596 aircraft was made ready to deliver a standard city-busting raid on Düsseldorf. Only 5 Group would be unrepresented, having now effectively become an autonomous entity with its own target marking force. As a result of the Group's highly successful trials with Mosquitos in a low-level visual marking role, pioneered by W/C Cheshire and Co at 617 Squadron, 83 and 97 Squadrons had been returned to it from 8 Group with their Lancasters, along with 627 Squadron's Mosquitos. This was a blow to Pathfinder pride, and, from then on, 5 Group would be referred to in Pathfinder circles somewhat disparagingly as the "Independent Air Force" or the "Lincolnshire Poachers". On this night at least, 5 Group did not come out on top, after failing to strike effectively at Brunswick when employing the low-level marking method for the first time at a heavily defended German urban target. 115 Squadron's twenty-one Lancasters took off between 23.01 and 23.29 with S/Ls Baigent and Grant the senior pilots on duty, and joined the rest of the force in adopting the tactics of height-gaining and shedding before bombing. They arrived over the target in very clear conditions, identifying the aiming-point by the river and the concentrated red and green Pathfinder TIs. They bombed from between 17,500 and 23,000 feet, and, in contrast to the attack on Cologne, were confident in the effectiveness of their work. Huge explosions and large fires, the latter visible from a hundred miles into the return flight, convinced them that Düsseldorf was undergoing a torrid time. It was not a one-sided affair, however, and losses among the bombers reached twenty-nine. Night-fighters accounted for

115 Squadron air gunners, RAF Witchford 1944

215

The Merlin-powered Lancaster Mk I / III replaced the Bristol Hercules-powered MkII from March 1944. The MkII had been produced as a precaution against an anticipated shortage of Merlins; by early 1944 it was clear that production of the iconic Rolls-Royce engine was not in any danger of failing. The MkIII was powered by Merlins built by the American company Packard. This magnificent study is of a Merlin-powered Lanc; however, the part serial just visible between the roundel and tailplane shows that this was not an aircraft allocated to 155 Squadron.

many, but the 115 Squadron casualty was caused by flak in the target area, and involved the crew of the recently-commissioned P/O Chantler. They, it will be remembered, had force-landed on return from Berlin on New Year's Night early on in their tour, but now all perished in the wreckage of ND753 on the northern outskirts of the city, and this was the first 115 Squadron Merlin-powered Lancaster to be lost. Post-raid reconnaissance and local reports confirmed that Düsseldorf had been pounded to the extent that over two thousand houses had been either destroyed or seriously damaged, dozens of industrial premises had been hit, and around twelve hundred people had lost their lives.

Orders came through on the 24th to prepare for an operation that night against Karlsruhe, a city situated a few miles from the French frontier some thirty miles south of Mannheim. A force of 637 aircraft included twenty-one Lancasters representing 115 Squadron, which took off in a half-hour slot either side of 22.00 with S/L Baigent the senior pilot on duty. P/O Cameron and crew were just approaching Dieppe on the French coast when a generator problem ended their sortie, and they jettisoned their cookie before turning back. It was a night of unfavourable weather conditions and ten-tenths cloud over the target, according to the 3 Group ORB. However, some crews were able to identify ground detail, like the River Rhine to the west, and the red and green TIs on the ground were visible to others, and, again, opinion was divided between scattered and concentrated. Bombing took place from between 15,000 and 22,000 feet, and the many fires seen to be burning seemed to indicate a successful operation. F/L Shadforth's ND800 was hit by flak and damaged further by a night-fighter, leaving electrical wiring shorting out and leaving both gunners and the wireless operator wounded. They landed at Manston at 03.40 to allow the casualties to be taken to hospital. Nineteen aircraft failed to return, and among them were two belonging to 115 Squadron. HK542 crashed shortly after crossing the frontier into Belgium on the way home, and there were no survivors from the crew of F/Sgt Bennett. F/Sgt Cagienard and his crew were a little nearer home and closing in on Antwerp when the end came for DS734 near Mechelen, again with fatal consequences for all on board. This proved to be the last Mk II Lancaster to be lost in service with 115 Squadron. An analysis of the raid revealed it to have been disappointing, and had hit only the northern rim of the city in the face of a strong wind, but, even so, one report gives a figure of nine hundred houses being either destroyed or seriously damaged. Mannheim, Ludwigshafen, Darmstadt and Heidelberg also reported being under attack as bombs were sprayed liberally around south-western Germany.

Another busy night of multiple operations on the 26/27th caused feverish activity on bomber stations in all group areas. 493 aircraft were made ready for Essen, of which twenty Lancasters were provided by 115 Squadron, while the "Independent Air Force prepared a force of more than two hundred aircraft for Schweinfurt with a sprinkling of 101 Squadron ABC Lancasters to offer some RCM protection. A predominantly Halifax force, also of more than two hundred aircraft, was to return to the railway yards at Villeneuve-St-Georges, while other support and minor operations would bring the number of sorties to more than a thousand. The 115 Squadron element departed Witchford between 22.55 and 23.17 with S/L Baigent the senior pilot on duty and S/L Mackie flying with P/O Atkin. The weather outbound was good, with little cloud and excellent visibility in the target area, where the Pathfinders performed well to mark the aiming-point for the main force crews. The 115 Squadron element bombed on red and green TIs from between 19,000 and 24,000 feet, and observed large, red explosions, many fires and copious amounts of black smoke. All were unanimous in their assessment that this was a highly successful raid, and it cost a very modest seven aircraft.

The highly industrialized town of Friedrichshafen was posted as the target for a force of 322 Lancasters of 1, 3, 6 and 8 Groups on the 27th. Situated on the shores of the Bodensee, close to the Swiss frontier, the town was associated particularly with the production of tank engines and gearboxes, and these factories were to be the principal objectives on a night of full moon light to aid identification and accuracy. Diversionary measures were put in place to try to avoid the carnage that had occurred in similar conditions during the Nuremberg raid just a month earlier. 115 Squadron contributed eighteen aircraft, which took off either side of 22.00 with S/L Baigent the senior pilot on duty and S/L Mackie also on the Order of Battle. F/Sgt Burdett and crew were soon back on the ground after a variety of technical issues ended their sortie, but the others reached the target area to be greeted by clear skies, which enabled them to identify ground detail. The initial Pathfinder TIs were thought to be a little scattered, but this was soon rectified, and the Witchford crews bombed either visually or on red and green TIs from between 16,500 and 21,500. Many fires and explosions were observed, but few crews hung around to admire the view as night-fighters made contact while the bombing was in progress, and accounted for the majority of the eighteen Lancasters shot down. 115 Squadron's ND803 was actually a victim of the local flak, and crashed into the Bodensee with no survivors from the crew of F/Sgt Stewart. Post-raid reconnaissance confirmed the raid to have been highly successful in hitting the factories, and in destroying over 60% of the town's built-up area. German authorities would confirm later that this was the most damaging raid of the war on tank production. During the course of the month the squadron took part in nine operations, and dispatched 167 sorties for the loss of seven Lancasters and crews.

May 1944

The first night of May brought operations against railway installations, while elements of 1 and 5 Groups attacked aircraft plants and a motor works. A 3 Group force of ninety-six Lancasters and sixteen Stirlings was assigned to the railway stores and repair depot for the Northern French system at Chambly, situated north of Paris. The 115 Squadron element of seventeen Lancasters took off between 22.38 and 22.57 with F/L Rash DFC the senior pilot on duty. F/O Clarey arrived back shortly after midnight with the DR

Crew of Lancaster HK542 KO-J, killed when the aircraft was shot down on the Karlsruhe raid of 24/25th April, 1944. Above: F/Sgt P A Bennett, pilot (left) and Sgt. J F Plummer, flight engineer (right). Below: F/O A D L Hoffman, navigator (left) and P/O J E Zegarchuk RCAF, bomb aimer (right).

unserviceable, but the others all reached the target to find clear skies, which enabled them to identify ground detail. They were under instructions not to bomb until told to do so by the Master Bomber, and if nothing was heard from him by H+2, to bomb on any TIs visible. In the event, the Master Bomber's instructions were clearly heard, and the Stirlings were sent in at 14,000 feet while the Lancasters remained between 7,000 and 10,000 feet. The 115 Squadron element bombed on yellow TIs from between 6,800 and 10,000 feet, and contributed to a highly successful operation that left the target severely damaged and out of action for more than a week. This was the last operation by the squadron to involve Mk II Lancasters, which were passed on to 514 Squadron, 6 Group and training units.

The perils of operating over the occupied countries was brought home forcibly to 1 and 5 Groups on the night of the 3/4th, when forty-two Lancasters were lost attacking the panzer training camp and motorized transport depot at Mailly-le-Camp in north-eastern France. 3 Group was not called into action again until the night of the 7/8th, when a relatively small force was made ready to join elements of 8 Group to target the Chateau Bougon airfield at Nantes in north-western France. 115 Squadron put up ten of fifty 3 Group Lancasters detailed to take part, and they took off between 00.15 and 00.47 with no senior officers to take the lead. After the initial marking was somewhat scattered, the Master Bomber brought the raid on track, and bombing took place from between 7,000 and 10,000 feet. Fires were observed with thick, black smoke, and post-raid reconnaissance confirmed that the runways had been left cratered and the hangars damaged. On the following night, thirty Lancasters from the group failed to score any hits on a gun battery at Cap Griz Nez, necessitating a return on the night of the 9/10th, when it would be one of seven coastal batteries in the Pas-de-Calais area to be targeted by more than four hundred aircraft. With D-Day now less than a month away, coastal batteries were to feature prominently, and, in order to maintain the conviction in the enemy's mind that the landings would take place in the Calais area, the main focus, for the time being, would be in this region. 115 Squadron prepared sixteen Lancasters for Cap-Gris-Nez, and sent them off between 02.55 and 03.15 with S/L Grant the senior pilot on duty. All arrived in the target area to find fair but hazy conditions and a Master Bomber to control the attack. Bombing took place from between 5,000 and 7,000 feet on a choice of red, green and yellow TIs, and most appeared to fall within the confines of the target.

A return to the railway campaign was posted on the 10th, when five marshalling yards were earmarked for attention, those at Courtrai in Belgium assigned to eighty 3 Group Lancasters. 115 Squadron loaded nineteen of them with fourteen 1,000 pounders each and unleashed them between 22.03 and 22.22 with F/L Shadforth the senior pilot on duty. They all arrived in the target area to find good conditions and a Master Bomber on hand to direct the attack. Bombs went down from between 9,000 and 11,000 feet, and many fires in the target area confirmed an accurate attack. Four similar targets, a military camp and a gun battery would provide employment for around seven hundred aircraft on the night of 11/12th. 115 Squadron made ready five Lancasters for the marshalling yards at Louvain (Leuven), situated some twenty-five miles south of Antwerp, and loaded each with ten 1,000 pounders and five 500 pounders. They took off either side of 23.00 with S/L Grant the senior pilot on duty, for what was to be a two-phase operation. F/Sgt Thornton's sortie lasted an hour and forty minutes after his forward escape hatch blew away. The others pushed on into an unanticipated strong headwind, which delayed their arrival in the target area, and, although the Witchford crews were able to identify the target by the white TIs, which they bombed from between 8,000 and 9,000 feet according to the instructions of the Master Bomber, the later arrivals found the TIs to be no longer visible. ND923 fell victim to a night-fighter in the target area, and there were no survivors from the eight-man crew of S/L Grant, who had been such an important part of the squadron for a long time. The bombing caused damage mostly to workshops and other buildings, but a follow-up raid by 6 Group twenty-four hours later completed the job.

On the night of 11/12th May 1944, 115 Sqn joined an attack on railway marshalling yards at Leuven, Belgium. Lancaster ND923 came to grief when shot down at 0027hrs at Wilsele. There were no survivors from the eight crew. Left to right: S/L JR Grant MID, P/O J Rodgerson, bomb aimer (Photo: D. Tyers); P/O Stanley Waller, navigator (Photo: Elisabeth Brown); Sgt W G Parry, wireless operator (Photo: Gillian Appleton). Below: Route map for the raid.

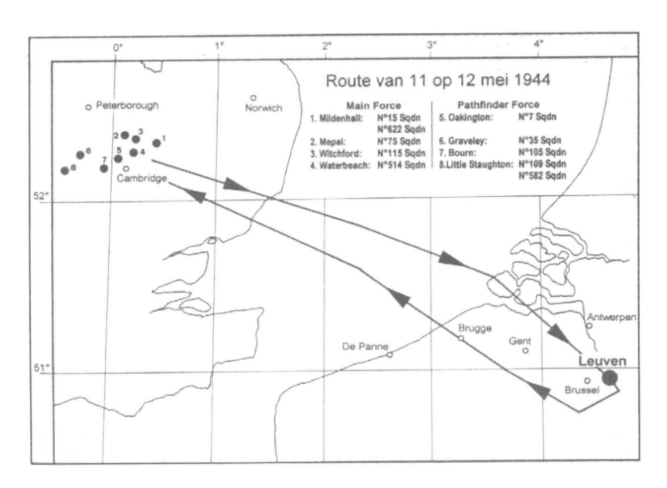

Contemporary photos of damage caused during the Leuven raid.

221

After a period of reduced activity in mid-month, five railway yards were posted as the targets on the 19th, those at Le Mans assigned to 3 Group, which detailed a hundred Lancasters as the main force. 8 Group would provide twelve additional Lancasters and four Mosquitos to take care of the marking and Master Bomber duties, while 115 Squadron bombed up twenty-four Lancasters with ten 1,000 and four 500 pounders each. They took off between 22.08 and 22.30 with F/L Andersen the senior pilot on duty, and all reached the target to find ten-tenths cloud. They identified the target by means of green and yellow or red and yellow sky-marker flares, and bombed them from between 5,000 and 10,500 feet. The first phase appeared to progress well, but the second phase crews were unable to hear the Master Bomber because of a transmitter in another Lancaster jamming his broadcasts, after which the bombing became scattered. 7 Squadron provided the Master Bomber and deputy on this night, the former, W/C Barron DSO & Bar, DFC, DFM, a young, but highly experienced Pathfinder from New Zealand, who typified the 8 Group spirit. Both he and his deputy, S/L Dennis DSO, DFC, were shot down by flak in the target area and killed along with thirteen others, many of whom were senior and decorated. The only other failure to return from this operation was the 115 Squadron Lancaster, HK547, which also went down over the target after being hit by flak. There were no survivors from the eight-man crew of P/O Atkin, with whom, it will be recalled, the now tour-expired S/L Mackie DSO had flown on many occasions.

Orders were received on 1, 3, 5 and 8 Group stations on the 21st for 510 Lancasters to be made ready for the first heavy raid on Duisburg for a year. 115 Squadron responded by bombing up twenty-six Lancasters, six with an 8,000 pounder and the remainder with a 2,000 pounder each and incendiaries all round, but one would be forced to drop out at the last moment with an engine issue. Crews had been told at briefing to adhere to the plan for the outward route, which, for 3 Group, involved a few aircraft gaining height as they adopted a north-westerly course as far as Sleaford, so as not to cross into enemy radar cover earlier than necessary. The 3 Group element would rendezvous with 1 Group at 18,000 feet at 03.00E, before crossing the enemy coast at 20,000 feet and climbing to 22,000 or 23,000 feet, and then increasing speed for the run across the target. Twenty-five Lancasters departed Witchford between 22.29 and 23.07 with F/Ls Andersen, Shadforth, McKechnie and Martin the senior pilots on duty, and all reached the Ruhr, which they found to be concealed beneath ten-tenths cloud with tops at 20,000 feet, into which the markers fell almost before they could be seen. F/Sgt Francis and crew overshot Duisburg, and bombed the island of Schouwen in the Scheldt Estuary from 19,000 feet by H2S on the way home. F/Sgt Oldham and crew also overshot the target, and dropped their bombs on what they believed to be Düsseldorf from 20,000 feet, observing a large, red glow. The others bombed from between 18,000 and 22,000 feet, some on red sky-markers and others on either H2S or the glow of fires, and all but one returned home with little useful information to report. The loss of twenty-nine aircraft was a reminder that the Ruhr had lost none of its venom, and ND754 was the 115 Squadron representative among them. It was sent crashing to earth in the target area by the local flak, and only the wireless operator from the eight-man crew of F/L Andersen escaped with his life to become a PoW. Post-raid reconnaissance revealed that 350 buildings had been destroyed in the southern half of the city, and 665 others had been seriously damaged.

On the following day Dortmund was posted as the target, and a heavy force of 361 Lancasters was duly made ready on 1, 3, 6 and 8 Group stations. As in the case of Düsseldorf, this would be Dortmund's first visit since the two devastating attacks exactly a year earlier. 115 Squadron detailed twenty Lancasters, all but one of which made it to take-off between 22.40 and 23.03 with F/L McKechnie the senior pilot on duty. The 3 Group element climbed away into heavy cloud and severe icing conditions, which persuaded twenty-five of eighty-four crews to abandon their sorties and turn back before reaching enemy territory. F/Os Miller and Wesley, P/O Cameron and F/Sgts McLachlan and Robertson were the 115 Squadron early-returnees for a variety of technical reasons, leaving the others to push on in improving conditions to find no more than two-tenths cloud in the target area. The Pathfinders laid red and green TIs, which the 115 Squadron crews bombed from between 15,000 and 21,000 feet, observing many fires, some with oily smoke, and the consensus was of an accurate and effective raid. Eighteen Lancaster failed to return, and among them was ND745, which crashed in the Antwerp region of Belgium, killing F/O Ward and three of his crew, and delivered the three survivors into enemy hands. It soon emerged, that the main weight of the attack had fallen onto mainly residential districts in the south-east of the city, where six industrial premises and more than eight hundred houses had been destroyed, and almost as many seriously damaged.

The important railway hub-city of Aachen was the next to be targeted, in the knowledge that it was a vital component in the enemy's communications system, and would be employed to transport men and equipment to the Normandy coast to counter the invasion. At briefings on the 24th, the 442 crews from all but 5 Group were assigned to attack either the Aachen-West yards or those to the east of the town at Rothe-Erde, but the size of the force suggested that this was to be an area attack also, which was intended to cause disruption to the built-up area between the yards. 3 Group supported the operation with forty-three Lancasters, but the twenty 115 Squadron aircraft on operations that night were not among them, having been assigned instead to bomb a coastal battery at Boulogne, almost certainly one of two such sites situated at either end of the little seaside resort town of Le Portel. Code-named Religion and Andante, these two long-range batteries had been attacked in early September of the previous year under Operation Starky, which had been devised to simulate the assembly of an invasion force to test the enemy's response. They had apparently escaped damage, but the town had sustained heavy damage and civilian casualties in the process of trying to hit them. The Witchford crews began taking off at 00.01 with F/L Shadforth the senior pilot on duty, and all reached the target to find clear conditions and green TIs on the ground to aim at. They delivered their loads of 1,000 and 500 pounders from between 6,500 and 9,000 feet in the face of negligible opposition, and returned to report what appeared to be a successful raid. Meanwhile, serious damage had been inflicted on Aachen and the surrounding villages, leaving almost fifteen thousand people bombed out of their homes.

It was considered necessary to target Aachen's Rothe Erde yards again, and plans were put in place on the 27th to send a force of 162 Lancasters and eight Oboe Mosquitos of 1, 3 and 8 Groups back there on what was to be a night of intense Bomber Command activity involving more than eleven hundred sorties. 115 Squadron's twenty-one Lancasters departed Witchford between 00.25 and 00.50 with F/Ls Shadforth, Rash and McKechnie the senior pilots on duty, and only P/O McBride and crew came home early after finding that HK544 was unwilling to maintain height above 15,500 feet. The remainder pressed on to the target, which was identified by red and green TIs, and bombed from between 11,000 and 14,000 feet before returning safely home to report many fires and thick, black smoke eventually obscuring the ground. The raid, which, according to local people, lasted only twelve minutes, halted all through-traffic and razed to the ground the adjacent suburb of Forst.

On the 28th, and at very short notice, 3 Group was ordered to provide the main force for an attack on the railway yards at Angers in north-western France. Ninety-eight Lancasters were detailed, but insufficient time to bomb them up before take-off at 18.00 led to fourteen being cancelled, leaving eighty-four to join thirty-four Lancasters and eight Mosquitos of 8 Group. The plan was to fly out in daylight via Land's end at 2,000 feet, to a point over the Atlantic some ninety miles west of Brest, and then follow the coastline until south-west of the target, before heading inland while gaining height to between 8,000 and 10,000 feet for the bombing run. 115 Squadron dispatched thirteen Lancasters after cancelling eight, and they took to the air between 18.25 and 19.05 with F/L Martin the senior pilot on duty. All reached the target, which was identified visually by the River Maine and by white and yellow TIs, and bombed from between 7,500 and 10,000 feet. Crews reported observing bursts in the marshalling yards and a deep, red explosion at 23.54. Sadly, despite the success of the raid, a large proportion of the bombing strayed onto residential districts, destroying eight hundred buildings, and killing 254 French civilians.

3 Group put together a force of fifty Lancasters on the 30th for a return to the coastal battery south of Boulogne, with 8 Group Mosquitos on hand to provide the marking. 115 Squadron provided ten of the heavy brigade, which took off between 22.59 and 23.10 with no senior pilots on duty. They all arrived in the target area to find good, if hazy conditions, and bombed on the red TIs from between 6,000 and 8,000 feet. The consensus on return was that, if the marking had been accurate, then so had the attack. A two-wave assault on the railway yards at Trappes was planned for the last night of the month, for which 115 Squadron made ready nineteen Lancasters to contribute to an overall force of 219 aircraft drawn from all but 5 Group. They took off either side of midnight bound for the Trappes-West yards with F/Ls Rash and Martin the senior pilots on duty, but the numbers were reduced by four early returns landing between 01.26 and 02.45. F/Sgts Garside and Thornton and P/O Holder were put off by the electrical storms and icing conditions in a bank of ten-tenths cloud across their route, while F/L Martin suffered a port-inner engine failure. The others reached the target to find clear skies and good visibility, which enabled them to identify the aiming-point visually from their bombing height of between 8,000 and 10,000 feet. Despite the good visibility, they had a choice of white, green and yellow TIs to aim at, and complied with the instructions of the Master Bomber to conclude a successful operation. Just four Lancasters failed to return, and among them was LL936, which crashed near Chandelle, some twenty miles south-west of the target, and there were no survivors from the predominantly Kiwi crew of F/Sgt McLachlan RNZAF. During the course of the month the squadron took part in thirteen operations, and dispatched 218 sorties for the loss of five Lancasters and crews.

Don Cameron's Crew with Lancaster ME836 KO-Charlie, RAF Witchford 1944

The Burgess crew at RAF Witchford in 1944. Back row l to r: Taffy Ginsburg (Navigator); Harry O'Cavanagh (Bomb Aimer); Rex Reeves (W.Op/AG). Front row l to r: Frank Howe (Flt. Eng.); Buzz Burgess (Pilot); Dana Duthie (R/G) RCAF. (Photo: Rex Reeves)

June 1944

The first week of June was dominated by unsettled weather, and the impending launching of the invasion force. 3 Group remained on the ground on the 1st, but was called into action on the 2nd to support the invasion-deception attacks on coastal batteries in the Pas-de-Calais area. A total of 271 aircraft included fifteen Lancasters belonging to 115 Squadron, which took off between 01.05 and 01.26 with no senior pilots on duty, and headed for Wissant, situated between Calais and Boulogne. They reached the target area to find ten-tenths cloud, which prevented seven crews from identifying the aiming-point, and they jettisoned part of their loads before returning home. The remaining eight crews bombed on red and green markers from between 5,000 and 8,000 feet, but could only guess at the results of their efforts. Although they would not have been told, the outcome of the attack was strategically unimportant. On the following day elements of 1, 3 and 8 Groups were made ready for attacks on two similar sites, 115 Squadron loading ten Lancasters with a cookie and sixteen 500 pounders each to drop onto a target near Calais, almost certainly at Sangatte. They took off between 00.25 and 00.39, again with no senior pilots in action, and, this time found the target area to be free of cloud. The aiming-point was identified visually and by red and green TIs, which were bombed from between 7,500 and 12,000 feet, and a large, orange-coloured explosion at around 01.30 confirmed the accuracy of the raid.

3 Group remained at home on the night of the 4/5th, while elements from the other groups attacked three coastal batteries in the Pas-de-Calais, and another at Maisy, situated between the Normandy beaches code-named Omaha and Utah, which were soon to be the scene of American landings. The weather over the Channel had been giving cause for concern, with cloud-filled skies, gusty winds and choppy seas, and, when the decision was finally taken to launch Operation Overlord in the early hours of the 6th, there

was a distinct sense of uncertainty at HQ. Briefings took place on all bomber stations, but there was no direct reference to the invasion itself. Instead, crews were warned to adhere strictly to specified flight levels, and were prohibited from jettisoning bombs over the sea. 1,012 aircraft were to be involved in the bombing of ten coastal batteries covering the landing areas, and twenty-four of the 107 Lancasters of 3 Group were provided by 115 Squadron. The crews had been briefed to attack the site at Ouistreham, to the north-east of Caen, and they departed Witchford between 03.25 and 03.51 with the newly-promoted S/L Rash the senior pilot on duty. They each carried ten 1,000 and four 500 pounders, and all reached the target area, where red and green markers identified the aiming-point. Bombing was carried out chiefly on the red marker flares from between 9,000 and 11,500 feet, but heavy cloud obscured the ground for most crews, and they could only guess at the outcome. Some of those returning in dawn's early light were rewarded with the sight through occasional breaks in the cloud of the greatest armada in history, ploughing its way sedately across the Channel below. 3 Group was also involved in spoof and diversionary operations, which were highly successful in misleading the enemy.

Another thousand aircraft were made ready to take part in operations on D-Day night, when road and railway communications were to be bombarded in and around nine towns leading to the beachhead. A hundred 3 Group Lancasters were assigned to an important railway junction at Lisieux some twenty miles to the east of Caen, for which 115 Squadron loaded twenty-three Lancasters with eighteen 500 pounders each and dispatched them between 00.01 and 00.28 with F/Ls McKechnie and Norbury the senior pilots on duty. They all reached the target area to find a thin layer of cloud at 3,000 feet, but the Oboe markers were clearly visible, and some crews even made out ground detail. Not all crews heard the Master Bomber, and bombed predominantly on the red markers from between 1,500 and 5,500 feet, although W/O Shapley and P/O Francis did pick up his broadcasts and bombed on yellow TIs in accordance with his instructions. Returning crews reported bomb bursts within the marked area, and a large orange explosion was noted at 01.29, but F/O Wesley and crew were not at debriefing having failed to return in LM533, the fate of which has never been determined.

450 aircraft were detailed for attacks on four railway targets on the following night, for which 115 Squadron made ready eighteen Lancasters. The target was to be a junction at Massy-Palaiseau on the south-western approaches to Paris, for which the 115 Squadron element departed Witchford either side of 00.30 with W/C Annan the senior pilot on duty. The weather conditions were as forecast, with ten-tenths cloud between 5,000 and 7,000 feet, above which night-fighters were operating in numbers and taking a heavy toll of bombers as they made their way to the target. HK548 was closing in on the aiming-point when it was shot down by a night-fighter, and, although the bomb-aimer and one of the gunners perished in the crash, P/O Law RAAF and the remainder of his crew escaped by parachute to ultimately evade capture. HK552 came down at Montchauvet to the west of Paris and a few miles to the south of Mantes-la-Jolie, and only the navigator escaped with his life from the crew of F/Sgt Todd RAAF. LL864 crashed to the north-west of Mantes-la-Jolie close to Giverny, and P/O Maude and his crew all lost their lives. ND760 had reached the north-western suburbs of Paris when a night-fighter detonated the bomb load over Puteaux and spread the Lancaster and crew of P/O Quinton over quaysides and stretches of the Seine. ND761 was probably heading away from the target when it was intercepted and shot down to crash four miles north-north-west of Rambouillet without survivors from the crew of F/L Norbury. It is likely that ND790 had also delivered its bombs and was heading home when the end came for it and the crew of P/O Francis at Houdan to the west of Paris and a short distance to the north-west of Rambouillet. There must have been shock at Witchford when only twelve crews attended debriefing to give their reports of bombing the target from between 4,000 and 6,500 feet on red and green TIs. To lose six Lancasters on a single operation meant accepting the fact that forty-two of the men who had attended briefing would not be coming home. It would be some time afterwards that news came through from the Red Cross that only six had survived, by which time the squadron would be populated largely by new crews as other losses and postings ensured a constant influx of new faces through the door. This would

prove to be the squadron's blackest experience of the war, and, during the course of the summer, a number of other squadrons would suffer similar or worse tragedies, but they would not be allowed to interfere with the business in hand, and 115 Squadron would soon be back in harness.

Following two nights off the Order of Battle the squadron prepared twenty-two Lancasters on the 10th for an attack on the marshalling yards at Dreux, situated some twenty-five miles to the west of Paris. They were part of a ninety-strong 3 Group force assigned to this target, and took off between 23.00 and 23.35 with S/Ls Shadforth and Rash the senior pilots on duty. Each Lancaster had been loaded with eighteen 500 pounders, and all made it to the target where good weather conditions greeted them. Bombing took place from between 7,000 and 9,000 feet either visually or on green and yellow markers under the guidance of the Master Bomber, and, although there was some scattering in the early stages, all of the indications, including large explosions either side of 01.00, suggested a successful operation. Night-fighters proved to be a little troublesome on the way home as far as the Channel Islands, and F/O Clarey and crew reported three combats but no damage to either party. It was similar fare on the following night for elements of 1, 3, 4 and 8 Groups among which four railway targets were divided. 3 Group prepared fifty Lancasters for a railway junction at Nantes in north-western France, and 115 Squadron contributed seventeen of them, sending them off either side of midnight with S/L Rash the senior pilot on duty. F/Sgt Garside returned early with a starboard-outer engine failure, and he was followed home by F/O Miller, whose rear gunner became ill. The others pressed on to the target, where layers of cloud between 2,000 and 7,000 feet impeded the marking and bombing. The Master Bomber called the crews down to below the cloud base, but not all heard his instructions, and those that did found it difficult to fix on the well-placed markers from such low level. The others bombed on the glow of the markers from up to 8,000 feet, and returned with little to report because of the cloud. F/Os Chatterton and Clarey and F/L McKechnie returned with holes from light flak as evidence of their low-level attacks, but there were no crew casualties and the holes were soon patched up.

Lancaster KO-Z with Flt Lt Rowe-Evans and air and ground crews

W/C Devas was posted in from 514 Squadron at Waterbeach on the 12th, where he had been a flight commander, and succeeded W/C Annan as commanding officer. He presided over his first operation on the day of his appointment, which was the opening round in a new campaign against Germany's synthetic oil industry. 303 Lancasters of 1, 3 and 8 Groups were to attack the Nordstern Synthetic oil plant at Gelsenkirchen, while other elements of the Command continued the assault on communications in support of the ground forces. 115 Squadron loaded eight Lancasters with a cookie and sixteen 500 pounders each, and launched them off the end of the runway either side of 23.30 with S/L Shadforth the senior pilot on duty. After climbing out they made for the rendezvous point with 1 Group at 03.00E, before climbing to cross the Dutch coast at between 20,000 and 22,000 feet, and then descending gently to fly over the aiming-point at 18,000 feet at 180 i.a.s. The first TIs were estimated by H2S-equipped crews to be eight miles south of the intended aiming-point, and they attracted a number of bomb loads before the situation was rectified by the second batch of TIs falling in exactly the right place. The 115 Squadron crews dropped their loads on red and green TIs from between 17,500 and 20,000, and many explosions were observed, accompanied by copious amounts of black smoke. Such installations were always hotly defended, and seventeen Lancasters failed to return, among them HK545, which was claimed by flak in the target area, killing S/L Shadforth DFC and his crew, two of whom were holders of the DFM. He had only recently been promoted to the role of flight commander, and became the squadron's second senior officer to be lost in the space of four weeks. Post-raid reconnaissance revealed that the plant had been left inoperative for several weeks, at a cost to the enemy war effort of a thousand tons of vital aviation fuel per day.

The first daylight operations since the departure of 2 Group from Bomber Command a year previously, were mounted against E-Boats and other light marine craft posing a threat to Allied shipping supplying the beachhead. They were based at Le Havre, and were to be attacked in two phases on the evening of the 14th, first by a predominantly 1 Group force, and then by 3 Group in the fading light. At the head of the force, hot on the heels of the Oboe Mosquitos came twenty-two Lancasters of 617 Squadron carrying the Barnes Wallis-designed 12,000lb Tallboy earthquake bombs, and these did enormous damage to the pens, even penetrating the reinforced concrete roofs in places. The twenty-two 115 Squadron aircraft were safely airborne by three minutes after midnight, each carrying eleven 1,000 and four 500 pounders with F/L McKechnie the senior pilot on duty. Each squadron was a polyglot of nationalities, and the importance of the Commonwealth to RAF Bomber Command was demonstrated on this night by the fact that half of the 115 Squadron pilots were non-RAF, four representing the RAAF, five Canada and two New Zealand, with many crewmen also coming from these magnificent countries. They all reached the target to find favourable weather conditions, accurate marking in progress and a Master Bomber on hand to direct the bombing, The 115 Squadron participants delivered their loads from between 13,000 and 15,000 feet onto red and green TIs, and all returned safely to report a highly successful operation, that had left the target area a mass of flames, and few, if any, enemy craft still serviceable.

A similar operation against Boulogne twenty-four hours later would prove to be equally effective, but would be carried out in the absence of a 3 Group contribution. 3 Group found itself assigned to the marshalling yards at Valenciennes, a French town on the River Scheldt close to the Franco/Belgian frontier, and made ready ninety-nine Lancasters of which twenty represented 115 Squadron. The Witchford aircraft were each loaded with eighteen 500 pounders, and took to the air between 23.05 and 23.27 with no pilots above flying officer rank. They arrived in the target area to find cloud with a base at 7,000 feet, and not everything proceeded according to plan. The Master Bomber called the crews down to bomb from beneath the cloud base, but the TIs were scattered, and he held up the bombing while the aiming-point was remarked. This time the TIs undershot, and the Master Bomber issued instructions to the crews to overshoot by two seconds, which caused confusion and a partial scattering of bombs as they approached from a variety of headings. The 115 Squadron crews bombed from between 6,500 and 10,000 feet, and, to them, at least, the attack appeared to be accurate, creating many fires. The delay allowed night-fighters the time to get amongst the bombers, and five failed to return, among them 115 Squadron's HK550. The pilot, F/O Amaka RCAF, and his bomb-aimer were able to save themselves before the crash in the Pas-de-Calais region near Marquion, and they ultimately evaded capture, but their crew colleagues all perished.

The month's second new campaign, this one against flying bomb launching and storage sites, was opened on the night of the 16/17th by elements of 1, 4, 5, 6 and 8 Groups, while other elements of the Command carried out the second raid in the oil offensive at Sterkrade/Holten in the Ruhr. 3 Group stayed at home, but made ready seventy-seven Lancasters and twenty Stirlings on the 17th to pitch against the marshalling yards at Montdidier in north-eastern France. This was one of three targets to be attacked that night, and the fourteen 115 Squadron representatives took off between 01.01 and 01.21 with F/L McKechnie the senior pilot on duty. They reached the target area to find impossible conditions of thick cloud, and it soon became clear to the Master Bomber that there was no point in continuing. He sent the force home, but twelve crews failed to hear his instructions and bombed on the red glow of target markers in the cloud. P/O Cameron and F/Sgt Muir were among these, and let their bombs go from 10,000 feet without observing any results. It was a similar story at the Aulnoye marshalling yards, and the only operation to be completed was that by 4 Group Halifaxes at St-Martin-l'Hortier. Only one aircraft failed to return from these raids, and that was 115 Squadron's HK559, which dived into the ground at Gannes, just south of the target, and exploded with great force, presumably with the bombs still on board, killing P/O Traill RAAF and his crew.

3 Group detailed a hundred Lancasters on the 21st, for what would be its first genuine daylight operation since 1941. There had been recent dawn and dusk raids with take-off or landing in daylight, but the attack on the Domleger flying bomb site would take place entirely in daylight, and would provide useful experience for future operations. The plan called for aircraft to form up in loose pairs within their squadron, and to fall in behind a leader at 9,000 feet over Braintree in Essex, who would fire a succession of six red Verey Lights to identify himself. The formation was then to climb to 14,000 feet for the flight to the target, situated some twenty miles inland from Cayeux-sur-Mer, and bomb from between 12,000 and 14,000 on whatever markers were visible. 115 Squadron made ready eighteen Lancasters, loading each with eighteen 500 pounders, and dispatched them between 17.55 and 18.16 with W/C Devas leading for the first time. The first attempt at building a formation proceeded remarkably well, despite a tendency by some crews to go their own way. They were greeted by ten-tenths cloud in the target area, which completely swallowed up the markers so that not even a faint glow remained to aim at. The Master Bomber had no choice but to send the force home with its bombs, but valuable lessons had been learned that would serve the group well in the months ahead. That night, 5 Group entered the oil campaign for the first time, when sending forces to Wesseling, near Cologne, and Scholven-Buer in the Ruhr, with a few 1 and 8 Group aircraft in support. Night-fighters turned the occasion into a disaster, and four 5 Group squadrons each lost six aircraft at Wesseling in return for modest success.

V-Weapon storage sites were referred to in ORBs as "constructional works", largely because they were still in the process of being completed, and the target for one hundred 3 Group Lancasters on the 23rd was such a site at L'Hey, situated south-east of Calais. 115 Squadron loaded twenty Lancasters with eleven 1,000 and four 500 pounders each, and launched them off the end of the runway between 23.00 and 23.20 with F/Ls McKechnie, McFetridge and McBride the senior pilots on duty. They all reached the target to find ten-tenths cloud, through which the glow of red markers was clearly visible, and bombing took place from between 7,000 and 9,000 feet. It was not possible to assess the outcome, but the 3 Group ORB expressed a reason to suppose that the effort had been successful. After a few nights off the Order of Battle, 3 Group detailed a hundred Lancasters on the 27th to attack a flying-bomb supply dump at Biennais located a few miles inland from the Normandy coast. 115 Squadron loaded twenty-

P/O C McBride and his crew at Witchford in 1944

The McKechnie crew with Lancaster ND758, A4-A. They served with the squadron between March and July 1944. From l to r: Joe Harper, Bernard Payne, Ernie Wilkins, Don McKechnie, Frank Leatherdale, Ken Derby, Arthur Franc.

230

four Lancasters with eighteen 500 pounders each, and dispatched them either side of 23.30 with the same senior pilots on duty as for the previous operation. Again, all reached the target area to encounter ten-tenths cloud, through which they bombed on the glow of red TIs from between 13,000 and 14,000 feet, without being able to make an assessment. A number of white or yellowish explosions were observed by many crews between 01.12 and 01.15, but the 3 Group ORB expressed doubts about the success of the operation. There were no losses, but HK556 was hit by an unidentified object, probably a bomb, and sustained a damaged port-inner propeller, while ME834 landed at Woodbridge with flak damage.

Another genuine daylight operation was planned for the evening of the 30th, in support of ground forces, for which 3 Group detailed 127 Lancasters. 115 Squadron was able to offer a magnificent twenty-seven aircraft, each of which was loaded with eleven 1,000 and four 500 pounders to deliver onto a road junction at Villers-Bocage, situated a few miles north of Amiens, through which the Germans were planning to send an armoured division to inhibit the Allied break-out from Caen. W/C Devas was the senior pilot on duty as the Witchford element took off either side of 18.00 to form up into loose pairs in squadron formation, and, on the way south, the force picked up a Spitfire escort provided by 11 Group. The cloud that had characterised the month was broken on this occasion, and, although it had been planned to bomb from between 12,000 and 14,000 feet, some crews came down to 4,000 feet to ensure accuracy. P/Os Garside and Oldham were the 115 Squadron representatives among these, bombing from 4,000 and 5,000 feet respectively, while the rest of the squadron remained at between 11,500 and 12,500 feet, aiming either for red TIs or the edge of the smoke as directed by the Master Bomber. The entire target area was soon obscured by smoke and dust from the many explosions, and it was seen to be rising through 2,000 feet as the force turned away. The operation was entirely successful in preventing the German advance, and the Army commanders sent a message of congratulations to Bomber Command HQ. It had been a challenging month for the whole Command as the workload increased, and 115 Squadron played a full part, operating on fifteen occasions, dispatching 256 night and 49 daylight sorties for the loss of ten Lancasters and crews.

July 1944

The first few days of the new month were dominated by daylight raids on flying bomb sites, 3 Group's involvement coming on the 2nd, when 119 Lancasters were detailed and made ready for an attack on the supply depot at Beauvais in Normandy. 115 Squadron loaded twenty-five Lancasters with eleven 1,000 and four 500 pounders each, and dispatched them between 12..38 and 13.00 with F/L McBride the senior pilot on duty. 11 Group was on hand again to provide a fighter escort, and the force reached the target area to find three to four-tenths cloud and the Pathfinder markers clearly visible on the ground. The 115 Squadron crews bombed from between 4,000 and 13,000 feet with absolutely no opposition to distract them, and the attack appeared to be concentrated and successful. On the 5th, King George VI and Queen Elizabeth visited the squadron, accompanied by the Princess Elizabeth, to present nineteen medals. Out on the dispersals work went on as normal to prepare twenty-four Lancasters for the night's operation against a constructional works at Watten, according to the squadron ORB as compiled by F/L Heness, or Wizernes according to the 3 Group scribe. Both were located in the Pas-de-Calais, and, whichever was correct, was one of four V-Weapon launching or storage targets to be attacked that night by 540 aircraft of 3, 4, 6 and 8 Groups. The 115 Squadron element took off either side of 23.00 with F/Ls McBride, Martin and Rowe-Evans the senior pilots on duty, and each carrying the usual bomb load of eleven 1,000 and four 500 pounders. They all reached the target area to find good, but hazy weather conditions, and carried out the bombing on red and green TIs from between 7,800 and 10,000 feet. Returning crews reported fires in the target area and the operation was deemed to have been successful.

The Royal Family visiting RAF Witchford 5th July 1944

Aircrew honoured in the Investiture at RAF Witchford on 5th July 1944. Left to right: F/Sgt ?; DFM; W/O Boutilier (Canada); F/O Len Halley DFC (Newfoundland); F/O Webb DFC; F/L Ron Stewart DFC; F/O Philips DFC; F/L Aubrey Howell DFC; F/O Ron Birchall DFC (Bill Jolley's crew); S/L Geo. Mackie DSO (A Flt Commander); F/O Ron Hulse DFC (Ray Milgate's Crew); W/C Rainsford DFC (C.O.115); F/L Ray Milgate DFC (RAAF); F/L Seddon DFC (RAAF); F/L Geoff Hammond DFC (RAAF); S/L Baigent DFC & Bar (B Flight Commander) (NZAF); W/C Bobby Annan DSO (C.O. 115). S/L Clufas DFC (Canada).

A major operation was planned against fortified villages around Caen on the evening of the 7th to provide support for the Canadian and British ground forces in their push to spread out from the town. It would be carried out by 460 aircraft from 1, 4, 6 and 8 Groups, while 3 Group focussed its attention elsewhere, detailing a hundred Lancasters to attack the marshalling yards at Vaires to the east of Paris. 115 Squadron made ready twenty-two Lancasters, which took off between 22.35 and 22.56 with F/Ls McKechnie and Rowe-Evans the senior pilots on duty. They all reached the target to find excellent visibility, which enabled them to pick out ground detail and bomb from between 12,000 and 15,000 feet either visually or on the red, yellow and green TIs. A large, red explosion was observed at 01.33, followed by a steady fire, which was thought to be a fuel dump, and not a single aircraft was lost in completing this successful raid. A return to flying-bomb launching sites by daylight on the 9th involved fifty 3 Group Lancasters, of which twenty-six belonged to 115 Squadron. The details in the squadron and group ORBs are not in harmony, the former recording Nucourt, to the north-west of Paris, as the target and the latter Lisieux, situated some fifteen miles from the Normandy coast. The author believes Lisieux to be correct as Nucourt is cited as the objective for twenty-four hours later. Whichever, the target was one of six similar sites earmarked for destruction by 347 aircraft drawn from 3, 4, 6 and 8 Groups. According to the squadron ORB the Witchford element took off between 04.00 and 04.35 with W/C Devas the senior pilot on duty, and each carrying eleven 1,000 and four 500 pounders. The all arrived in the target area to find thick cloud that hid the TIs from view and made it impossible to achieve any degree of concentration. Bombing took place from between 13,000 and 17,000 feet, almost exclusively on the basis of Gee or DR, and it is unlikely that the target sustained meaningful damage. Just one Lancaster failed to return from this operation, and, according to Bill Chorley's Bomber Command Losses for 1944, it was a 622 Squadron aircraft shown as taking off for Lisieux at noon, which adds further weight to the suspicion that the author of the squadron ORB, F/L Heness, may have recorded matters incorrectly.

It was a similar story of weather conditions on the 10th, when 1, 3 and 8 Groups joined forces to try to eliminate the flying-bomb storage dump at Nucourt, but could produce only scattered bombing in the face of ten-tenths thick cloud. 115 Squadron sat this one out, and it was the 12th before it was next called into action to prepare twenty-two Lancasters for another attack on the marshalling yards at Vaires, this one to be carried out in daylight. 3 Group contributed 110 Lancasters to the operation that was to be conducted in concert with elements of 1 and 8 Groups, and the Witchford gang took off either side of 18.00 with the newly-promoted S/L McFetridge the senior pilot on duty. When they arrived at the target to encounter thick cloud and no hope of an effective attack, the Master Bomber sent them home, and twenty of the squadron participants responded accordingly. Somehow, W/O Andrewartha managed to identify the canal and also saw a red marker, which he bombed from 15,500 feet, while F/L Belyea aimed his eighteen 500 pounders on a yellow marker from 14,600, both before picking up the Master Bomber's instruction to abandon the operation.

3 Group was, in fact, the least employed group during the second third of the month, and it was the 15th before orders were received at Witchford to prepare for an operation that night. Twenty-three Lancasters were loaded with eighteen 500 pounders each and dispatched between 21.40 and 22.01 with S/L McFetridge the senior pilot on duty. Their destination, in company with seventy-seven others from the group, was the marshalling yards at Châlons-sur-Marne, situated south-east of Reims in north-eastern France. P/O Pellew and crew were well on their way to the target when problems with Gee and the oxygen system forced them to turn back, and they arrived home shortly after F/Sgt Franks and crew had landed with engine problems. The others reached the target area to find the ground obscured by cloud, upon which the Master Bomber called the force down to below the cloud base at 8,000 feet. Not all complied, most finding yellow and green TIs to aim at from higher altitudes, with the 115 Squadron element spread between 7,500 and 12,000 feet. An exceptionally large explosion was observed at 01.34, and many fires were reported by returning crews. LL944 had reached England when the starboard-inner

engine burst into flames, and F/O Gadd RCAF ordered all but his flight engineer to take to their parachutes. They drifted safely to earth, and the Lancaster landed at Witchford without further incident.

Despite accurate attacks on the marshalling yards at Vaires, the Germans were able to effect repairs quickly by drafting in French civilian forced workers. Orders were received on the 17th for another operation against the yards, for which 115 Squadron made ready twenty-four Lancasters. This operation is not mentioned in the 3 Group ORB or in Bomber Command War Diaries, but, according to the 115 Squadron ORB, the Witchford crews took off in two waves between 11.00 and 12.45 with F/Ls Belyea, Folkes and McBride the senior pilots on duty, only to be recalled, and all had brought their bombs back by 14.25. Crews were early out of bed on the 18th to help prepare the way for the British Second Army's armoured attack under Operation Goodwood. 942 aircraft were made ready to attack five fortified villages to the east of Caen at first light, and twenty-five Lancasters at Witchford were loaded with eleven 1,000 and four 500 pounders each before being launched into the air between 04.03 and 04.40 with F/Ls Belyea, McBride and Martin the senior pilots on duty. They all reached their target at Emieville to find it clearly identifiable, either visually or by yellow TIs, and bombing took place under the guidance of a Master Bomber from between 8,000 and 10,000 feet. The attacks at each aiming-point were concentrated and many fires were observed in the woods, where German infantry and its equipment were concealed. Returning crews reported paratroops dropping south of Ouistreham and much transport to the north of the target. On return, 115 Squadron's LM616 crashed onto West End Farm at Great Offley near Hitchen in Hertfordshire at 07.15, killing P/O Letts and his crew, and also the three occupants of the farmhouse, which was demolished.

Preparations were put in hand during the day for an operation that night against a railway junction at Aulnoye in north-eastern France, while 5 Group went to a similar target at Revigny, which had thwarted two earlier attempts by 1 Group. 115 Squadron contributed twenty-four Lancasters to the 3 Group force of 127, and they took off either side of 22.30 with F/Ls Belyea, Folkes and McBride the senior pilots on duty. F/Sgt Braun and crew returned early with engine issues, and F/Sgt Morgan and crew were unable to identify the target on e.t.a, and jettisoned their bombs safe. The others managed to locate the target either visually or by red and green TIs, which they bombed from between 8,000 and 11,000 feet, some observing an explosion at 00.57. Meanwhile, the 5 Group force had been badly mauled by night-fighters, losing twenty-four aircraft, and this, together with extensive Bomber Command activity over the oil refineries at Wesseling and Scholven-Buer, may have contributed to the loss of just two 3 Group Lancasters. One of these, however, was the squadron's LL943, which crashed on the Belgian side of the frontier with France with no survivors from the crew of F/O Pellew RAAF.

Two nights later, 3 Group was ordered to return to the oil campaign with a raid on the refinery at Homberg, to the north-west of Duisburg in the Ruhr. A 3 Group force of 128 Lancasters included twenty-two provided by 115 Squadron, in addition to which a number of ABC Lancasters from 1 Group would provide RCM support, while others from 8 Group took care of illuminating and marking in concert with Oboe Mosquitos. The Witchford element took off between 22.47 and 23.30 with the newly-promoted S/L Martin the senior pilot on duty, and each bearing aloft a cookie and sixteen 500 pounders. All reached the target, which was identified by red and green TIs, and bombing took place from between 17,500 and 20,000 feet. A large orange-red explosion at 01.21 was followed by sparks and a large amount of black smoke, which increased in volume as it rose into the air. Enemy night-fighters latched onto the bombers as they approached the target, and followed them out as far as the Dutch coast scoring heavily. C Flight's ND913 crashed at Papendrecht in the Scheldt region of southern Holland, killing F/O Clarey RAAF and his crew, and this was just one of twenty Lancasters to be lost. It was a disastrous night for 75(NZ) Squadron from Mepal, where seven empty dispersals were silent testimony to the fortunes of life in Bomber Command. 115 Squadron's LM510 almost became another missing statistic after being attacked over the target by a night-fighter from starboard quarter down, which shot away both turrets during its first pass. A second attack a minute later shattered the pilot's instrument panel, caused a fire in his oxygen system in the cockpit and destroyed the compass. F/Sgt Gaston corkscrewed all the way home, navigating by Gee and, eventually, the North Star, before landing at Woodbridge, where the starboard undercarriage collapsed, damaging the Lancaster beyond repair. During the engagement all crew members picked up wounds or injuries of some sort, to which the wireless operator and rear gunner would succumb. F/Sgt Gaston RCAF was awarded the DFM for his exploits, and would ultimately be commissioned. The operation was successful, and production of aviation fuel, which had stood at 6,000 tons a day back in April, now fluctuated between 120 and 970 tons per day and was a major setback to Germany's war effort.

Orders were received on the 23rd to prepare for the first heavy raid on a German urban target for two months, for which a force of 629 aircraft was made ready. 3 Group detailed a hundred Lancasters, of which twenty-one represented 115 Squadron. They took off for Kiel between 22.30 and 23.00 with F/Ls Belyea and Folkes the senior pilots on duty, carrying a total of ten cookies, 124 x 500 pounders and sixty "J" Type cluster projectiles. 100 Group was on hand to provide a strong "Mandrel" RCM screen, and, when the force appeared suddenly and with complete surprise from behind it, it was already too late for the naval port. A thin layer of ten-tenths cloud lay over the target, but the red and green TIs stood out

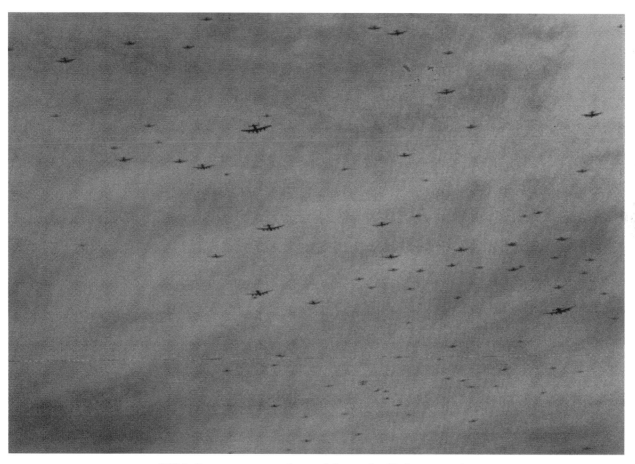

100+ Lancasters outbound for a daylight operation

235

Above: Lancaster A4-E 'Emily' of C Flight is waved off on an op. The extended bomb bay can be seen clearly. The aircraft was flown by P/O Alf Sweeney in 1944. Below: The Sweeney crew with 'Emily'. L to R: Sgt. E Richards RCAF; Sgt. Fred Goff; F/O John Isaacs; F/O Alf Sweeney; Sgt. Bill Watts; Sgt. John Ingram; Sgt Cecil Unstead.

clearly enough for the crews to identify the aiming-point and bomb under the instructions of a Master Bomber from between 17,500 and 21,000 feet. Around half a dozen explosions were observed at 01.24, and it was with confidence in the effectiveness of their work that crews reported to debriefing on return. Post-raid reconnaissance confirmed extensive damage in all parts of the town, but, in particular, in the port area, wherein lay the U-Boot yards and naval facilities. Many delayed action and dud bombs added to the difficulties for the rescue services, and this would be Kiel's worst experience of the war.

On the following day preparations were put in hand for the first of what would be a series of three raids on Stuttgart over five nights. A force of 461 aircraft included twenty Lancasters from 115 Squadron, which departed Witchford between 21.34 and 21.55 with S/L McFetridge the senior pilot on duty. All reached the target to encounter eight to ten-tenths cloud with tops at 6,000 feet, but the Pathfinders had prepared both sky and ground-marking, and those crews unable to see the red and green TIs on the ground, aimed at the parachute flares to deliver their loads from between 19,000 and 21,000 feet. An orange explosion was observed at 01.46, and the glow of fires was penetrating the clouds as the force turned away. Night-fighters were troublesome south-east of Paris, and were probably responsible for the failure to return of twenty-one aircraft. 115 Squadron came through unscathed, and responded to the call for a return to Stuttgart on the 25th by making ready seventeen Lancasters as part of an overall force of 550 aircraft. They took off between 21.35 and 21.53 with F/Ls Belyea and McBride the senior pilots on duty, but six abandoned their sorties, mostly because of severe icing that prevented them from climbing to operational height through a bank of cloud barring their passage over the Channel between 7,000 and 16,000 feet. F/Os Hockey, Garside, Osborne, Sweeney and Ward and F/Sgt Frank all returned home between 00.14 and 02.37, leaving the others to press on to the target, ironically through the same layer-cloud that now afforded protection from night-fighters. They were greeted over southern Germany by clear skies and slight ground haze, which proved to be no impediment, and the aiming-point was identified by flares and red and green TIs. The bombing was carried out with accuracy and concentration from between 9,500 and 20,000 feet to leave many fires marking out the pattern of the streets. Returning crews reported two large explosions at 02.15, and the consensus was of a successful raid, for the loss, on this occasion, of just twelve aircraft.

The final raid on Stuttgart was posted on the 28th, and a force of 494 Lancasters of 1, 3, 5 and 8 Groups was made ready, while preparations were put in hand on some 1, 6 and 8 Group stations for a simultaneous operation against Hamburg by three hundred aircraft, which should divide the enemy night-fighter response. While the Witchford crews were attending briefing, the armourers were loading fourteen of nineteen Lancasters with six 1,000 and three 500 pounders, and the others with seven 1,000 and two 500 pounders. They took off between 21.40 and 22.10 with F/Ls Belyea and McBride the senior pilots on duty, but F/Sgt Morgan returned shortly after midnight with an unserviceable artificial horizon. The others pressed on across France, where bright moonlight above the cloud tops favoured the enemy night-fighters, which pounced upon the bomber stream, causing havoc and claiming thirty-nine Lancasters, 7.9% of the force. Some 3 Group crews used the cloud as cover, and crossed France at between 5,000 and 7,000 feet, but then came under fire from light flak, particularly around Orleans. The 115 Squadron participants avoided the unwelcome attention from the air and the ground, and reached the target to find a layer of thin, ten-tenths cloud between 8,000 and 15,000 feet, despite which, the aiming-point was well marked by red and green Pathfinder TIs and flares. They bombed on these from between 17,000 and 21,500 feet, and reported many large explosions, one of particular interest at 01.56, and the glow of many fires reflected in the cloud. They also commented on the number of combats in the target area, and F/O Bickford and crew claimed the destruction of a JU88, which had attacked their Lancaster at 01.34. The three-raid series caused heavy damage in Stuttgart's central districts, and, by the end, much of the city lay in ruins, with over eleven hundred of its inhabitants having lost their lives. The heavy losses were repeated among the Hamburg force as they returned home, only to a lesser extent, and the twenty-two failures to return brought the night's missing tally to sixty-one four-engine bombers.

F/L P W Bickford and crew with Lancaster MkIII LM693, KO-T. All were killed on 16/17th September 1944 on a mission to support Operation Market Garden, possibly due to a collision with 90 Sqn Lancaster LM169, WP-R2.

The 30th brought further operations in support of mostly American ground forces at six locations in the Villers-Bocage – Caumont area south-west of Caen, for which 692 aircraft were made ready. The target for twenty Lancasters of 115 Squadron was at Amaye-sur-Seulles, and they took off between 05.57 and 06.16 with F/Ls Folkes and Miller the senior pilots on duty. Weather conditions in the target area were challenging in the extreme with low cloud, and the Master Bomber at Amaye called the crews down to below the cloud base, where the yellow, red and green Oboe TIs could be seen. Bombing was carried out from between 1,000 and 3,000 feet under the instructions of the Master Bomber, and some aircraft closest to the ground were hit by bomb splinters. Many explosions were observed before the area became concealed by large amounts of smoke, and the consensus was of a concentrated and accurate attack. Fifteen of the 115 Squadron crews landed at Woodbridge because of the low cloud over Witchford, but four others managed to get down there. Missing from either station was PB130, which crashed on French soil, killing Sgt Thompson RCAF and his crew, which included three other members of the RCAF. The cause of the loss is not known, but it is possible that the Lancaster fell victim to friendly bombs when flying at very low level. Only two of the six aiming-points were attacked in the unfavourable weather conditions, leaving more than three hundred aircraft to bring their bombs home. During the course of the month the squadron operated on fifteen occasions, dispatching 192 night and 142 daylight sorties for the loss of five Lancaster and four complete crews.

August 1944

The first week of August was devoted to daylight operations against flying-bomb sites, and 777 aircraft were made ready on the 1st to attack multiple sites. 115 Squadron loaded fifteen Lancasters with a mixture of 1,000lb and 500lb bombs, and launched them from Witchford between 16.04 and 16.17 with

S/L McFetridge the senior pilot on duty. They were bound for Coulonvillers in the Pas-de-Calais, as part of a 3 Group force of fifty aircraft and reached the target area to find impossible conditions of thick cloud, which left the Master Bomber with no option other than to call off the attack and send the crews home. The following day brought clear conditions for operations against four flying-bomb-related sites, but 3 Group committed only its diminishing Stirling brigade and left the Lancasters on the ground. They were called to arms on the 3rd, however, as 1,114 aircraft were made ready to attack three flying-bomb stores at Bois de Cassan, Foret de Nieppe and Trossy-St-Maximin. 3 Group provided 113 Lancasters for the first-mentioned situated in the L'Isle-Adam area to the north of Paris, of which twenty-two represented 115 Squadron. They took off between 11.50 and 12.20 with S/L Martin the senior pilot on duty, each loaded with eleven 1,000 and four 500 pounders, and headed south to pick up the Spitfire escort provided by 11 Group. They all reached the target to find clear conditions, which enabled them to identify the aiming-point visually or by Pathfinder flares and deliver their bombs in accordance with the Master Bomber's instructions, mostly into the burgeoning smoke, from between 15,800 and 18,000 feet. The entire site soon became obscured, and returning crews described an accurate and concentrated attack with opposition only from flak, which caused damage to F/O Culver's starboard wing.

It was left to almost three hundred aircraft of 6 and 8 Groups to continue the flying-bomb campaign on the 4th, with a return to the Bois-de-Cassan and Trossy sites. The Master Bomber for the latter, by 8 Group, was the former 115 Squadron flight commander, S/L Ian Bazalgette, who, it will be recalled, had been posted to 20 O.T.U at Lossiemouth in September. There he had remained, frustrated and desperate to return to operational duty at the first opportunity. Feeling threatened by the prospect of remaining an instructor, he wrote to the former 7 Squadron and 3 Group stalwart, W/C "Hamish" Mahaddie, who was in charge of recruiting for the Pathfinders under the unofficial appellation of the "Pathfinder Horse Thief". He begged Mahaddie to rescue him from this posting, pointing out, that he would be far more useful to the war effort in an operational capacity with 8 Group. He got his wish with a posting to 635 Squadron in April 1944, and, on this day, and while undertaking his fifty-eighth sortie, his aircraft was severely damaged, lost both starboard engines and was on fire. Despite this, he pressed on to mark the target, knowing that the success of the attack depended upon him, then, having baled out most of his crew, he attempted a forced-landing in France. On touch-down, the Lancaster exploded, killing Bazalgette and the other two occupants, one of whom had already been mortally wounded. For his outstanding gallantry and devotion to duty, he was posthumously awarded the Victoria Cross.

Meanwhile, elements of 1, 3 and 8 Groups were sent to attack oil storage depots at Bec-d'Ambes and Pauillac, situated on the banks of the Gironde on the approaches to the port of Bordeaux. 3 Group had detailed 101 Lancasters for the former, of which twenty were provided by 115 Squadron, and they had departed Witchford between 13.27 and 13.55 with S/Ls McFetridge and Smith the senior pilots on duty. They were escorted to the target for the first time by "Serrate" Mosquitos belonging to 100 Group, flying out over Land's End to a point at 06.00W, and then in to 02.00W at 1,000 feet, before climbing to a planned bombing height of between 7,000 and 9,000 feet. The attack was carried out in excellent conditions with no opposition in the air or on the ground, the 115 Squadron crews delivering their loads from between 6,000 and 9,000 feet. At least eight explosions were observed in and around the oil-storage tanks, and a destroyer-type vessel moored at the northern end of the jetty was hit in the stern. Smoke was rising high into the air as they turned away, and the target was seen to be burning fiercely. Spitfires of 11 Group covered the withdrawal over the Brest peninsular, and no aircraft were lost. Pauillac was posted as a target again on the following day, along with another at Blaye, situated on the eastern bank closer to Bordeaux, and Bassens, which was on the outskirts of Bordeaux itself. 115 Squadron contributed twenty-one Lancasters to the 3 Group force of 106 aircraft, and they took off between 14.15 and 14.35 led by F/Ls Miller, Belyea and Sutherland. The 100 Group Mosquito escort was picked up as they crossed out over Land's End to follow a similar course to that adopted on the day before. This time, however, they were to climb to between 15,000 and 17,000 feet for the bombing run because of the

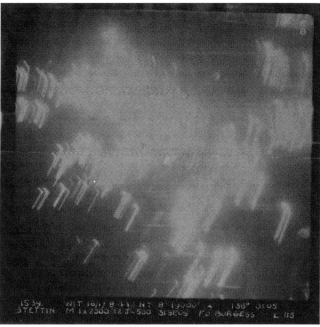

Two target photos from August 1944. Left: A daytime raid on the Bec d'Ambes Oil Storage Depot. Right: Stettin on the night of 16/17th August, taken by the bomb aimer of F/O Burgess' crew in KO. The ORB summary read: "16 aircraft attacked Stettin while two more were mining. This operation was carried out to help the Russians as most of the supplies for East Prussia passed through Stettin. The attack was fairly good, and many fires were started. The Germans appear to have been taken by surprise."

expected response from the flak batteries surrounding the port. A port-wing-low attitude persuaded W/O Andrewartha and crew to turn back when over the sea, leaving the others to press on to find five-tenths cloud over the target, through which the aiming-point was clearly visible. They bombed either on yellow TIs or fires according to the Master Bomber's instructions, but not necessarily from the briefed altitudes, in fact, the bombing heights for the 115 Squadron crews ranged from between 3,500 and 15,000 feet. Many oil explosions were observed either side of 19.00, with flames leaping to 750 feet and black smoke rising many thousands of feet into the air. As they flew north over the site of the previous day's operation, the enemy destroyer was seen to be badly charred and down by the stern. Mustangs patrolled the target area to keep enemy fighters away, and Spitfires were once more on hand to see the bombers safely across the Brest peninsular. All 115 Squadron aircraft were safely back home by 22.23 after an eight-hour round-trip, and the crews were able to report another highly successful attack.

Over a thousand aircraft were made ready on the 7th to employ against five enemy positions facing Allied ground forces. 3 Group detailed a hundred Lancasters to attack enemy troop concentrations and communications in the Mare de Magne region of Normandy, and 115 Squadron contributed eighteen of them. They took off between 21.40 and 21.59 with S/L Martin the senior pilot on duty, and all reached the target area to encounter favourable conditions. It had been pre-arranged that the aiming-point be marked for the Pathfinder element by the coning of friendly searchlights, Bofors tracer and star-shells, and the Witchford crews aimed at the marker flares and red TIs from between 7,000 and 9,400 feet. The bombing was well-concentrated and a huge artillery barrage from behind Allied lines added to the discomfiture of the enemy positions to leave the area obscured by smoke. There was little flak, but enemy night-fighters made their presence felt, and a bomber was seen to fall from the skies over the target

The following night brought a return to the oil offensive by elements of 1, 3 and 8 Groups, which were handed two storage dumps as targets. 3 Group detailed 104 Lancasters for the Forêt de Lucheux site, situated west-south-west of Arras, of which twenty-five were provided by 115 Squadron, and they took off in a thirty-minute slot either side of 22.00 with S/Ls McFetridge, Martin and Smith the senior pilots on duty. They crossed the French coast at 17,000 feet before losing height to cross the aiming-point at 210 i.a.s at around 12,000 feet. The weather was favourable as the 115 Squadron crews arrived and identified the target in the light of Pathfinder flares, before delivering their eighteen 500 pounders each onto green TIs and fires from between 8,000 and 13,000 feet as directed by the Master Bomber. The dump was hidden in a wood, which erupted as many oil-explosions tore it to pieces, and large columns of black smoke were reaching 8,000 feet as the bombers turned away. They had run into many searchlight cones on the way in, and it was the same on the way out, although flak was negligible. HK549 was ensnared in a cone, which was evaded after F/O Hill dived from 9,000 to 5,000 feet, but, unfortunately, the intercom broke down for a few moments, during which time the rear gunner, presumably believing the end to be nigh, baled out. The single loss from the operation was 115 Squadron's LM166, which crashed in the general target area on the edge of the Pas-de-Calais, killing W/O Leggett and two of his crew, while the four survivors landed in Allied held territory to return home.

A flying-bomb storage depot at Fort d'Englos near Lille was posted as the target for ninety-nine 3 Group Lancasters on the 9th, although the 3 Group ORB identifies it as a petrol storage site. Twenty aircraft were provided by 115 Squadron, and they departed Witchford between 21.50 and 22.23 with S/L Smith the senior pilot on duty. F/L Belyea was soon on his way home again, however, after the starboard-inner engine failed, leaving the remainder to press on to the target, where good conditions prevailed. Despite this, the Pathfinder markers were somewhat scattered, a situation exacerbated by a confused Master Bomber, and this led to inaccurate bombing in the early stages at what was, anyway, a small target. The majority of the 115 Squadron participants aimed at red and green TIs from between 12,000 and 14,000 feet, some undershooting by two seconds in accordance with the instructions of the Master Bomber. All returned safely to report an orange explosion at 23.18 and clusters of fires, but a generally scattered pattern of bombing. An accurate assessment was made impossible by the volume of smoke drifting across the target area, but, it is believed that the operation was successful.

Railway targets had taken something of a back seat thus far during the month, but this was rectified on the 11th, when elements of 1, 3, 4 and 8 Groups were made ready to attend to marshalling yards at Douai, Somain and Lens and a bridge at Etaples. 115 Squadron bombed up twenty-seven Lancasters as part of a 3 Group force of 120 assigned to the Lens yards, situated to the south-west of Lille in the Pas-de-Calais. S/Ls McFetridge and Smith were the senior pilots on duty as they took off between 14.05 and 14.30, and headed for the south coast to pick up the fighter escort. They all arrived in the target area to find favourable conditions, which enabled them to identify ground detail, and bomb on yellow, red and green TIs or on smoke from between 13,600 and 16,000 feet. A dull, red explosion was observed at 16.32, and many other bomb bursts were seen on the track and a bridge over the canal before smoke obscured the area. One Lancaster from 514 Squadron was hit by a bomb from above, which sliced off the nose and took with it the bomb-aimer, who was seen to fall without a parachute to his inevitable death.

The first operations of the month to industrial Germany were posted on the 12th, one to Braunschweig (Brunswick) in northern Germany and the other to Rüsselsheim in the south, where the Opel motor works was the objective. Both operations were to be supported by 115 Squadron, and fourteen of its Lancasters were included in the overall force of 379 Lancasters and Halifaxes assigned to the former, in what was essentially an experiment to ascertain the ability of crews to locate and bomb a target on the strength of their own H2S equipment without the assistance of Pathfinders. This may have been an attempt to ease the enormous work-load being heaped upon 8 Group by the concurrent campaigns against railways, oil, flying bombs and city-busting, whilst also providing tactical support for the ground forces. S/L Martin was the senior pilot on duty among the Witchford brigade as they took off either side of 22.00, but the numbers became depleted as F/Ls Garside and McBride turned back with engine problems, S/L Martin with complete intercom failure and F/O Frankland through the failure of the electrical heating to the rear turret, all landing between 23.40 and 00.01. The others reached the target, locating it by H2S or e.t.a and the glow of fires beneath the ten-tenths cloud, and bombed from between 18,000 and 21,000 feet. A very large explosion was observed at 00.07, and some crews caught sight of the built-up area on fire through occasional breaks in the cloud. The general belief, however, was that the attack was scattered and mediocre, the disappointment of which was compounded by the loss of twenty-seven aircraft, or 7.1% of those dispatched. There was little opposition over the target, but night-fighters made their presence felt on the way home, and they were probably responsible for the loss of the two 115 Squadron failures to return. Both ND927 and PB127 crashed in Germany with one survivor each, and, in an unusual coincidence, it was the pilot in both cases. F/O Hockey and F/L Belyea respectively escaped with their lives to become PoWs, which suggests the possibility that the Lancasters broke up in mid-air before the other crew members had time to attach their parachutes. Local reports described a heavy raid, with bombs falling also on outlying communities up to twenty miles away.

Meanwhile, nine 115 Squadron Lancasters had taken off for Rüsselsheim at the same time as the Braunschweig element, with F/L Miller the senior pilot on duty, but F/Sgt Morgan was forced to return early with oxygen-system failure. The others flew out over ten-tenths cloud across France, but this had become well-broken by the time the target area hove into sight. The 115 Squadron crews identified the aiming-point by means of red and green TIs, and bombed from between 15,000 and 18,000 feet, although too early in the attack to make an assessment of the results. The impression was of a scattered raid, although the 3 Group ORB was more positive and recorded a successful operation. In fact, some damage had been inflicted on the Opel works, which had been turned to manufacturing aircraft components and tanks, but it would be necessary for the Command to return later in the month to try to finish the job. This operation was probably still in progress when F/L Johnson and F/O Bickford and their crews departed Witchford for Falaise to take part in an attack on an enemy troop concentration and a road junction to the north of the town. They identified the target by means of Pathfinder flares before bombing on red and green TIs from between 8,000 and 8,400 feet in accordance with the Master Bomber's instructions. The attack was believed to have been effective, and all surviving participants in the night's activities had returned to base by 03.30.

The afternoon of the 14th brought eight hundred aircraft into action against seven enemy positions ahead of Canadian forces pushing towards Falaise. 3 Group detailed a hundred Lancasters, of which twenty were provided by 115 Squadron, and they were loaded with eleven 1,000 and four 500 pounders each before taking off either side of 14.00 with S/Ls Martin and Smith the senior pilots on duty. They arrived in the target area to find clear conditions and the aiming-point well marked by red and green TIs, and bombed from between 8,700 and 10,000 feet. The attack appeared to be scattered at first, but the Master Bomber, who was praised in the 3 Group ORB as being particularly good in directing the bombing clearly and skilfully, brought it back on track despite the aiming-point becoming covered by smoke and dust from other nearby aiming-points. Most of the bombing at the other sites was carried out accurately, but, confusion over identification flares from the ground and target indicators may have led to the accidental "friendly fire" incident, in which thirteen Canadian soldiers were killed, fifty-three others wounded, and some equipment destroyed.

In preparation for his new night offensive against industrial Germany, Harris ordered a large-scale assault on nine night-fighter airfields in Holland and Belgium on the 15th. 1,004 aircraft were made ready, including nineteen 115 Squadron Lancasters, which took off between 10.08 and 10.31 with S/L Smith the senior pilot on duty. Their destination was St-Trond (Sint Truiden) as part of a hundred-strong 3 Group force, and all from Witchford arrived in the target area to find ideal conditions in which to let go their loads of eleven 1,000 and four 500 pounders each. The target was identified visually, and the runway intersection bombed from between 9,500 and 15,800 feet under the instructions of the Master

Bomber. Returning crews described the attack as well concentrated, commenting that little remained of the airfield and its buildings, and reported also observing elements of the fighter escort strafing the ground. As they flew back some of the other targets came into view, and these were described also as well-bombed.

On the 16th, 1,188 aircraft were detailed for two major operations that night and a variety of support and minor operations. The Baltic ports of Kiel and Stettin were to occupy the bulk of the numbers, with 461 Lancasters assigned to the latter, while a mixed force of 348 Lancasters and Halifaxes attended to the former. 115 Squadron contributed eighteen Lancasters to the 3 Group force of ninety-seven for Stettin, and had ten of them loaded with a 2,000 pounder each plus twelve "J" Type cluster projectiles, while the remainder would carry a load of one 2,000 pounder each with thirteen or fourteen No 14 cluster projectiles. They took off between

St Trond Airfield. 15th August 1944

21.05 and 21.25 with F/Ls Chatterton, Folkes, Johnston, Miller and McBride the senior pilots on duty, and headed out across the North Sea at under 1,000 feet as far as 05.00E to try to remain under the enemy radar. Meanwhile, 145 aircraft from training units were carrying out a North Sea sweep and others were engaging in mining duties off Germany's Baltic coast, all of which helped to keep enemy defensive measures to a minimum. All from Witchford reached the general target area, where seven-tenths cloud occupied the space between 15,000 and 20,000 feet, and P/O Wadham and crew saw a red TI, which they bombed from 19,500 feet. Soon afterwards they observed fires beneath the clouds to the south, and realised that they had bombed the naval port of Swinemünde. They were not alone, as F/O Brown and crew also bombed there from 20,500 feet after spotting incendiary fires. The performance of the Master Bomber was described in the 3 Group ORB as poor, recording that few crews heard his instructions to bomb from below the cloud base at 14,000 feet. The 115 Squadon element aimed their bombs at red and green TIs from between 13,500 and 20,000 feet, some believing the raid to be scattered, while others saw a good concentration of bombs around the markers and a large oil explosion. Despite the doubts and the performance of the Master Bomber, the operation was outstandingly successful, and destroyed fifteen hundred houses and twenty-nine industrial premises. Five ships were sunk in the harbour, while a further eight sustained serious damage, and 1,150 people lost their lives, and this was achieved for the loss of just five Lancasters, none of which belonged to 3 Group. The Kiel operation enjoyed moderate success, inflicting heavy damage on the town's docks area, but a proportion of the effort fell away from the target. Bremen was posted as the target on the 18th, and a heavy force of 281 Lancasters and Halifaxes was made ready. 115 Squadron briefed twenty-one crews as part of the 120-strong 3 Group effort, and they departed Witchford between 21.30 and 21.55 with S/L Smith the senior pilt on duty. F/O Davidson and crew were out over the North Sea when the mid-upper turret became unserviceable, and they were forced to turn back, leaving the others to press on to the target under clear skies. They were guided to the aiming-point by Pathfinder flares, and delivered their 8,000 or 4,000 pounders and incendiaries from between 16,000 and 20,000 feet, afterwards observing many large, red explosions and fires. Smoke was rising through 13,000 feet as they turned away, and it was clear that this major city and port had suffered catastrophic destruction. Post-raid reconnaissance and local reports confirmed the enormity of the devastation, which included over 8,500 houses and apartment blocks and an indeterminate number of industrial premises destroyed, some in firestorm conditions. Eighteen ships were also sunk in the

Lancaster KO-W (top) and with the W. Johnson crew and ground crew members.

Publicity photo taken at RAF Witchford 1944

harbour, while more than a thousand people lost their livesand this was by far the city's worst night of the war.

After a hectic first three weeks of the month, the greater part of the Command enjoyed six nights away from the operational scene, until orders came through on the 25th to prepare for a return that night to Rüsselsheim for another shot at the Opel works. Its destruction was to be entrusted to 412 Lancasters of 1, 3, 6 and 8 Groups, and 3 Group put together a force of 130 aircraft, of which twenty-four were provided by 115 Squadron. Each carried a 4,000 pounder and incendiaries as they took off between 20.23 and 20.50 with S/L McFetridge the senior pilot on duty. Clear skies greeted their arrival in the target area, and they delivered their loads onto red and green TIs from between 8,000 and 19,000 feet, observing a large, orange explosion at 01.00, which lit up the sky. Oily smoke was rising through 14,000 feet as the force retreated towards the Belgian frontier, and it was south of Koblenz where PD274 collided with another Lancaster and lost both port engines. F/L Aldridge RCAF and his crew were forced to abandon their chariot to its fate as it fell through 6,500 feet, and all were taken prisoner on the ground. The Canadian navigator sustained a broken leg, which would keep him in hospital for most of his period of captivity. The others from the squadron returned safely, two with fairly minor damage, and all were diverted to other stations because of adverse weather conditions at home. The operation was only partially successful, local reports admitting that the forge and gear-box assembly departments were out of action for several weeks, but large stocks of ready-made parts allowed production to continue almost unaffected.

This final week of the month would prove to be expensive for 115 Squadron, which was called upon on the 26th to provide twenty-two aircraft as part of an overall force of 372 Lancasters for a raid on Kiel. They took off between 20.09 and 20.45, twelve carrying a cookie and ten an 8,000 pounder each, all with incendiaries to complete their loads. F/Ls Folkes, Hill, Johnston and McBride were the senior pilots

Bremen 18/19 August 1944   *Kiel 26/27 August 1944*

on duty as they headed out to the North Sea at below 2,000 feet as far as 05.00E. F/O Osborne and crew turned back after an hour because of an unserviceable rear turret, while P/O Ellison and crew were two hours into the outward flight when their sortie was curtailed by the failure of the port-outer engine. The others pressed on in favourable if hazy conditions, and had to run the gauntlet of flak from the coast and over Kiel itself. Those reaching the target found a smoke screen in operation, but, also well-concentrated red and green TIs at which to aim their bombs from between 16,000 and 19,000 feet. Many fires were observed, and the impression, as the force turned away, was of a highly destructive assault. Night-fighters were out in numbers on the way home, and were probably responsible for the majority of the seventeen missing Lancasters. C Flight's HK556 and HK560 failed to return to Witchford, and were lost without trace with the crews of F/O Holder and F/Sgt Braun respectively, while LM127 is known to have crashed in the North Sea off the Danish coast, killing F/O Morgan and his crew. Local reports confirmed the extensive damage caused in the town centre and surrounding districts, where the fires had been fanned by a strong wind.

On the 28th, small scale operations were mounted against twelve flying bomb sites in the Pas-de-Calais, as Allied forces prepared to take the region, and this concluded the campaign which had begun in earnest in mid June. 115 Squadron was not involved, but made ready twenty-one Lancasters on the 29th to contribute to a force of 402 detailed to attack Stettin for the second time in two weeks. The Witchford gang took off between 21.08 and 21.30 with S/L McFetridge the senior pilot on duty, and carrying between them nine 8,000 pounders, seven cookies, five 1,000 pounders and seventeen hundred 30lb and 4lb incendiaries. F/O Ward and crew turned back within the hour with a failed starboard-inner engine, leaving the others to push on over cloud towards the eastern Baltic, where the skies cleared and the target could be identified visually. The 115 Squadron element bombed on red and green TIs from between 15,000 and 19,000 feet, and returning crews reported observing a concentration of explosions in the docks area, followed by large volumes of smoke. Night-fighters had been active over Denmark, and flak in the target area had been fierce, and, sadly, two crews were not present at debriefing at Witchford. News eventually filtered through concerning their fate, when it was leaned that ME718 had crashed near Ove on the eastern side of Denmark's North Jutland, killing F/L Chatterton RCAF and his crew, while

246

PB131 had gone down beyond the target in Poland. The consequences for the crew of F/O Berkeley were the same, however, and the wireless operator was only seventeen years old when he met his death. (Bomber Command Losses 1944. W R Chorley.) HK555 sustained flak damage to its front end and cockpit, and the pilot, F/Sgt Potter RAAF, was wounded in the leg. He received permission to land in Sweden, but opted to head back home, where he landed safely at 07.10. The operation was another huge success, which destroyed 1,569 houses and thirty-two industrial premises, seriously damaged many more, and sank or damaged 31,000 tons of shipping. The death toll was also high, at 1,033, with a similar number sustaining injury, and it was a fact, that, unlike many urban targets, Stettin never escaped lightly.

Le Havre 5th September 1944

Although the V-1 threat had been largely nullified, the V-2 remained operational, and its mobile launchers woud be almost impossible to take out. This left the storage sites as essential targets, and nine such sites in northern France were earmarked for attention by daylight on the 31st. 115 Squadron prepared sixteen Lancasters as part of the 3 Group effort, and they took off between 16.09 and 16.40 with W/C Devas taking the lead. Their destination was Pont-Remy, situated just to the south-east of Abbeville in northern France, but they found the area covered by cloud, and had to orbit a number of times before identifying the target. Located in a wood, it was a very small objective, and the crews, having bombed visually from between 12,700 and 16,000 feet, were disappointed by their efforts. A number of hits were observed on the aiming-point, and an explosion at 18.15 was followed by black smoke, but, generally, the bombing was scattered. During the course of the month the squadron took part in eight daylight operations and eleven by night, dispatching a record 353 sorties for the loss of nine Lancasters and eight complete crews.

September 1944

September would be dominated by a campaign to liberate the major French ports still in enemy hands, beginning with Le Havre, and, in preparation, six airfields in southern Holland were earmarked for attention by 675 aircraft in daylight on the 3rd. 3 Group was assigned to Eindhoven, and detailed fifty Lancasters, ten of which belonged to 115 Squadron. They were loaded with eleven 1,000 and four 500 pounders each, and dispatched between 15.41 and 15.50 with F/Ls Folkes and Hill the senior pilots on duty. They all arrived over the target to find five-tenths cloud, through which they were able to make a visual identification of the aiming-point, and bombed on well-placed TIs from between 13,000 and 16,000 feet. All had returned safely home by 19.01 to report an accurate and successful raid.

3 Group put up 136 Lancasters for the first of a series of attacks on enemy strong-points around the port of Le Havre on the 5th, and they were to join up with elements of 1 and 8 Groups to make up an overall force of 348 aircraft. Not mentioned in the 3 Group ORB are five Stirlings from 149 Squadron, which was the last operator of the type as a bomber, and was in the final stages of converting to Lancasters. The Witchford brigade of twenty took off between 17.15 and 17.50 with W/C Devas the senior pilot on

duty, and all reached the target in excellent conditions to deliver their loads onto the easily-identifiable aiming-point from between 12,000 and 13,500 feet. It was estimated that 90% of the bombs fell within the defined target area, and the operation was deemed to be a success. The process was repeated on the following day by a heavy force of 311 Lancasters and three Stirlings with thirty Mosquitos in attendance. 115 Squadron launched twenty-two Lancasters from Witchford between 15.41 and 16.40 with S/L Smith the senior pilot on duty, and each carrying the usual eleven 1,000 and four 500 pounders. A band of cloud between 7,000 and 8,000 feet was pouring rain onto the enemy positions below, but this was small beer compared with the ironware raining down onto them from the cloud base as the attack began. The bombing was well concentrated around the Pathfinder flares, and fires were seen to develop in the docks area.

The weather remained unfavourable while a force of 304 Lancasters of 1 and 3 Groups was made ready for round three against Le Havre on the 8th. In addition to twenty-five Mosquitos, four Stirlings from 149 Squadron would carry out the final bombing sorties by the type, although it would continue to operate with distinction with the secret SOE squadrons based at Tempsford. 115 Squadron contributed twenty-one Lancasters for the morning attack, and they took off between 06.05 and 06.35 with S/L Smith the senior pilot on duty. The operation was to be conducted against two aiming-points, and those, including the 115 Squadron element, arriving at the first, encountered cloud with a base at 3,000 feet. They experienced great difficulty in identifying it and also in hearing the Master Bomber's transmissions. Five of the Witchford crews were among 109 to bomb, doing so from between 2,000 and 5,000 feet, before the Master Bomber called off the attack in view of the close proximity of Allied ground forces. He sent the remaining aircraft home, where, at debriefing, a number of crews reported seeing a Lancaster on fire in the target area. As HK579 was one of three failures to return, the conclusion was that it had fallen victim to light flak, and this was soon confirmed when news came through of the survival of five crew members. They had parachuted into Allied-held territory, but, sadly, F/Sgt Kilsby and his rear gunner had lost their lives.

Elements of 4, 6 and 8 Groups set off to continue the assault on the 9th, but the operation was abandoned in the face of poor visibility before any bombing took place. The campaign against the enemy positions continued on the 10th, when 992 aircraft were made ready to target eight separate strong-points, each to be individually marked by Pathfinders. 115 Squadron loaded seventeen Lancasters with eleven 1,000 and four 500 pounders each, and sent them skyward between 15.33 and 15.57 with S/L McFetridge the senior pilot on duty. The weather had improved to leave clear skies in the target area, and all from Witchford located the aiming-point, Alvis IV, visually, before, in accordance with the Master Bomber's instructions, bombing a hundred yards short of the red TIs from between 10,500 and 11,000 feet. Many medium red explosions were observed, and all of the day's attacks were concluded successfully. The final blow would be delivered on the afternoon of the 11th by 171 aircraft of 4, 5, 6 and 8 Groups, a few hours after which the German garrison surrendered to British forces.

While the above operation was in progress, three other forces were in action over the Ruhr targeting synthetic oil refineries at Castrop-Rauxel, Kamen and Gelsenkirchen. 3 Group had detailed a hundred Lancasters for Kamen, a town situated on the north-eastern edge of the Ruhr, and twenty-two of these were provided by 115 Squadron. They had been loaded with a cookie and sixteen 500 pounders each, and had taken off between 16.07 and 16.35 with the station commander, G/C Sims, the senior pilot on duty, and S/L Smith in support. The squadrons flew out in formation all the way to the target area, where they separated into pairs in a line-astern arrangement, safe in the knowledge that they were operating under the umbrella of twenty squadrons of Spitfires, and three each of Mustangs and Tempests. The weather conditions at Kamen were good, and the crews were able to identify the refinery visually and by the red TIs, which they bombed from between 16,500 and 19,000 feet under the watchful eye of the Master Bomber. Many fires were observed, and the black smoke that was rising through 15,000 feet as the aircraft withdrew, was still visible from forty-five miles into the return flight. That night, 5 Group devastated the university city of Darmstadt in a firestorm that left 70,000 people homeless out of a population of 120,000, and killed 12,300 others.

Two city-busting operations were posted on the 12th, both of them in southern Germany, at Frankfurt and Stuttgart, the former to be carried out by 378 Lancasters and nine Mosquitos of 1, 3 and 8 Groups. 115 Squadron contributed twenty-one Lancasters to the 3 Group force of 119, and they departed Witchford between 18.40 and 18.56 with S/L McFetridge the senior pilot on duty. F/Os Davidson and Frankland returned early with technical issues, leaving the others to push on across France in fine weather conditions that allowed the crews to identify the city visually and by Pathfinder flares. They bombed on red and green TIs from between 16,500 and 17,500 feet, observing many fires to take hold and a dull, red explosion at 23.05. What they couldn't know was that the Frankfurt emergency services were still helping out at nearby Darmstadt, and were unable to douse the fires that devastated the western districts in what would prove to be the last major raid of the war on this city. It was a similar story of destruction at Stuttgart, where the northern and western districts were devastated by a predominantly 5 Group force, and a minor firestorm erupted.

An oil store at Wassenaar, to the north of the Hague, was posted on the 14th as the target for a small 3 Group force of thirty Lancasters, with five Lancasters and ten Mosquitos of 8 Group to carry out the marking. The likelihood was that it was, in reality, a suspected V-2 store, and represented an extremely small and challenging objective. Ten 115 Squadron Lancasters took off between 13.00 and 13.11 with S/L McFetridge the senior pilot on duty, and reached the target area in good conditions to bomb from between 11,500 and 12,000 feet on the red TIs as directed by the Master Bomber. Four aircraft returned with flak damage, but there were no losses, and crews were confident that, if the markers had been accurate, they had done their job.

The ill-fated airborne landings in Holland under Operation Market Garden were to be launched in the early hours of the 17th, and 3 Group was called upon to support the endeavour by attacking the railway bridge at Moerdijk in the south of the country. Forty-eight Lancasters were made ready on the 16th, 115 Squadron contributing a dozen of them, and they took off between 21.20 and 21.34 with S/L McFetridge the senior pilot on duty. They reached the small target to find clear conditions, which allowed a visual identification, and concentrated bombing was carried out onto red TIs from between 9,000 and 10,000 feet. Hits were observed, as was an orange-red explosion at 22.58, and all but one crew returned to Witchford to report a successful operation. Sadly, LM693 had collided with LM169 of 90 Squadron, and both Lancasters plunged into the Dutch countryside without survivors. The experienced F/O Bickford RCAF and his predominantly RCAF crew could not have been far from completing their tour and would be missed. Post-raid reconnaissance confirmed that the bridge had been hit and severed.

Later on the morning of the 17th, 762 aircraft took off to deliver three thousand tons of bombs onto enemy positions around Boulogne. 3 Group detailed a hundred Lancasters for two aiming-points, and the thirteen 115 Squadron participants got away between 09.59 and 10.15 with S/L Smith the senior pilot on duty. They all reached the target to bomb from between 2,200 (F/L Muir) and 8,800 feet, overshooting the red TIs by 250 yards as directed by the Master Bomber. This part of the operation was successful, but the bombing of the second 3 Group aiming-point became scattered and the Master Bomber decided to call a halt. This was not critical, and, within about a week, this port too was returned to Allied control. That evening 3 Group ordered forty Lancasters to be made ready for a target at Zaltbommel in support of Operation Market. It may have involved the bridge over the River Waal some thirty miles south-west of Arnhem, but the squadron ORB describes this as a "secret duty", and notes that each aircraft was loaded with seven containers. The ten 115 Squadron participants took off between 19.20 and 19.35 led by S/L McFetridge, and reached the target to make a visual identification by a bend in the river, and deliver their stores from between 2,500 and 3,000 feet. Parachutes were seen to open, suggesting that the containers were carrying equipment, and, perhaps, arms for the ground forces. Red flares and white flashes like fireworks were observed, and returning crews were confident of a successful outcome. F/O Dugdale reported that one of his containers struck the bomb-bay doors and caused a small explosion, which led to a hydraulics leak and the failure of the rear turret.

Only Calais of the northern French ports now remained in enemy hands, and the first operation to redress that situation was mounted on the 20th. A force of 646 aircraft was assembled with a contribution from 3 Group of 150 Lancasters. 115 Squadron loaded their twenty-five with eleven 1,000 and four 500 pounders each, and launched them between 14.36 and 14.54 with F/Ls Brown, Cunningham, Muir and Stechman the senior pilots on duty. The squadrons flew out in formation, and two 622 Squadron Lancasters collided in cloud over Essex and crashed without survivors. (Bomber Command Losses 1944 records this as a training accident). The 115 Squadron crews delivered their attacks from between 2,000 and 3,000 feet, F/O Josling and crew doing so on three engines having lost their port-outer while outbound. The operation was decared to be successful at all aiming-points, and was concluded for the loss of a single 514 Squadron Lancaster.

Before the next raid took place on the port, a force of 549 aircraft was assembled from 1, 3, 4 and 8 Groups to attack the Ruhr city of Neuss, situated across the Rhine from Düsseldorf. 3 Group put up 159 Lancasters, of which twenty-two were provided by 115 Squadron. They took off between 19.20 and 19.55 with F/Ls Castle, Cunningham, Muir and Stechman the senior pilots on duty. F/O Russell lost an engine soon after take-off, but continued on, while F/Sgt Adams and crew returned early after the bomb-aimers hatch blew in and then fell out. The others encountered ten-tenths cloud over the target with tops as high as 12,000 feet, and the bombing had to be carried out on the glow of marker flares or the fires already burning. The 115 Squadron crews delivered their eleven 1,000 and four 500 pounders each from between 10,000 and 20,300 feet, but were unable to assess what was happening on the ground. In fact, the docks and industrial districts had sustained heavy damage, and residential property was also severely afflicted.

Left: Boulogne, 17th September 1944. Right: Calais 27th September 1944. The ORB read: 'Gun positions attacked in this area by 18 aircraft of 115 Sqn, the bombs were concentrated, and the area plastered.'

It was later on the 24th, that the second operation took place to dislodge enemy ground forces from Calais and its environs. 188 Lancasters and Halifaxes were made ready, 3 Group providing just thirty of the former, although none from Witchford, but very low cloud in the target area allowed only 126 aircraft to bomb on Oboe skymarkers before the Master Bomber called a halt to proceedings. Eight aircraft that came down to deliver their attacks from below the cloud base were shot down by light flak. It was the same story on the 25th, when 115 Squadron dispatched a record twenty-nine Lancasters between 08.10 and 08.35, as part of an overall force of 872 aircraft. W/C Devas the senior pilot on duty, and he reached the target area with the rest of the squadron to be greeted by ten-tenths low cloud, and to be sent home with his bombs. The effort was divided on the 26th, when over five hundred aircraft attacked four gun emplacements at Cap Gris Nez, while 191 others sought out enemy positions at Calais. 115 Squadron dispatched eighteen Lancasters to Cap Gris Nez between 11.25 and 11.45 with F/L Clark the senior pilot on duty, and all identified the aiming-point by means of Pathfinder flares and red TIs, and bombed from between 3,000 and 4,000 feet. Returning crews spoke of yellow smoke to the south of the target, and the target itself being pitted with craters.

Low cloud over Calais would continue to be a problem for 341 aircraft from 1, 3, 4 and 8 Groups on the 27th, among which were thirteen 115 Squadron Lancasters. They had taken off between 07.25 and 07.50

Lancaster NN706 'B' with the crew of F/L Cunningham. L-R F/Sgt Turner (M/UG), Sgt Hart, (Flt. Eng.), F/Sgt Saville (RG), F/L Cunningham (Pilot), Sgt. Snidall (W.Op), F/Sgt Nield (Nav), F/O Smardon (BA) (Photo: Fred Nield)

as part of a 3 Group contribution of 120 Lancasters, divided between two aiming-points on a 40/80 split, and led by F/Ls Culver, Cunningham, Osborne and Talbot. The cloud base was at around 5,000 feet, and it was from between this level and 6,500 feet that the 115 Squadron crews delivered their bombs onto red TIs in accordance with the Master Bomber's instructions, in what became an accurate attack. Just one aircraft failed to return, 115 Squadron's LM738, which crashed with great force in the target area, killing F/O Wibberley and all but his bomb-aimer, who managed to take to his parachute and land in Allied-held territory with a broken arm. On the following day the squadron made ready thirteen Lancasters to support another assault by elements of 1, 3, 6 and 8 Groups on six coastal batteries at Cap Gris Nez. They took off between 08.01 and 08.10 led by S/L Smith, but they were among three-quarters of the 494 aircraft involved to be sent home with their bombs in the face of ten-tenths cloud. It mattered little, as the aim had already been achieved, and, within days, Canadian forces would take control of the port. During the course of the month the squadron took part in seventeen operations, and dispatched 296 sorties, eighty-five by night and 211 by day, for the loss of three Lancasters and the equivalent of two complete crews.

October 1944

On the 1st of October a new squadron was formed at Witchford, to which 115 Squadron would eventually donate its C Flight as the nucleus. That would happen later in the month, and, in the meantime, the first crews to join 195 Squadron would be posted in from 3 LFS on the 7th. It would be some weeks before the liberated French ports could be cleared of mines, and the installations destroyed by the retreating enemy forces repaired. The advancing Allied forces' insatiable appetite for materials and supplies demanded that other ports be made available also, and, to this end, operations during September had included strikes against enemy gun emplacements on the island of Walcheren in the Scheldt Estuary. These were barring the approaches to Antwerp, but were difficult targets to hit. It was decided, therefore, to breach the sea walls, in order to inundate the low-lying land, waterlog the batteries, and create a terrain which would be hard to defend when the ground forces went in. On the 3rd of October, a heavy force of 252 Lancasters was made ready to attack the sea wall at Westkapelle, at the island's most westerly point, in eight waves of thirty aircraft each, after the marking had been carried out by Oboe Mosquitos. 3 Group put up 120 Lancaster, twenty of which represented 115 Squadron, and they departed Witchford between 12.05 and 12.45 with F/Ls Clarke, Cunningham, Easterman, Fuller and Osborne the senior pilots on duty. Each lifted a cookie and six 1,000 pounders into the air, and all made it to the target, which was identified visually and by Pathfinder flares. Bombing took place on red TIs from between 4,000 and 6,500 feet, and the first breach was created by the fifth wave. Subsequent bombing widened the gap to around a hundred yards, and the flood waters had penetrated seven hundred yards inland by the time the last aircraft turned away. These attacks against sea walls and coastal batteries would continue throughout the month, mostly in the hands of 5 Group, but 3 Group would have an opportunity to play its part again.

A new and important role was beckoning for 3 Group but, for the time being, it would take its place on the Order of Battle as the Command returned to industrial Germany in increasing numbers and with an unprecedented weight of bombs. Saarbrücken was posted as the target on the 5th, for which 3 Group contributed 184 Lancasters to the force of 531 drawn also from 1 and 8 Groups. 115 Squadron set a new record of thirty Lancasters, which took off between 17.00 and 17.30, with W/C Devas the senior pilot on duty and each carrying eleven 1,000 and four 500 pounders. The purpose of the operation was to cut enemy rail communications to the advancing American Third Army, but this first attack on the city for two years was intended to achieve much more. The 3 Group effort was divided between the marshalling yards and the town on a 121/63 split, but the Master Bomber and Deputy disagreed as to which markers on the railway yards were accurate, and only 50% of the crews had bombed by the time he called a halt and sent the rest home with their bombs. Fifteen of the 115 Squadron crews had identified the target visually and by Pathfinder flares, and delivered their loads onto red and green TIs from between 11,000 and 15,000 feet. The remainder, however, arrived on the scene to be told to turn round and go home. The attack on the town was delivered through three-tenths cloud and proceeded according to plan, causing massive damage for the loss of three Lancasters. 115 Squadron's PD344 was involved in a mid-air collision with 75(NZ) Squadron's ND904 south-south-west of Bitburg, and both Lancasters plummeted to earth before any crew members could save themselves. It is not known whether the incident occurred on the way to the target or homebound, but the lack of reports of a flash suggest that both aircraft may have been empty and, therefore, on their way home. F/Sgt Henderson and his crew were buried initially at Wolsfeld, close to the crash site, but were ultimately reinterred in the Rheinberg War Cemetery along with the 75(NZ) Squadron crew. Local reports revealed that 5,882 houses had been destroyed, largely in the Altstadt and Malstatt districts, but the relatively modest death toll of 344 people suggests that, what was now a front-line city, had been partially evacuated.

Dortmund was posted as the target on the 6th for what would be the opening round of a new and devastating Ruhr campaign. 3, 6 and 8 Groups were called upon to provide a force of 523 aircraft, for which 115 Squadron made ready twenty-five Lancasters in a 3 Group contribution of 171. They departed Witchford between 16.25 and 17.14 with S/L Smith the senior pilot on duty, and he had the new station commander, G/C Reynolds, performing the role of second pilot. F/Os Gaston and Potter returned early at 18.30 and 19.51 respectively with technical issues, leaving the others to press on to the Ruhr under clear skies, guided by Pathfinder flares and red and green TIs on the aiming-point. They bombed from between 17,300 and 20,000 feet, and observed many large explosions, a sea of flames and black smoke rising to meet them. Only two 3 Group aircraft failed to return, and, once again, the unlucky squadrons were 115 and 75(NZ). This time it was not a collision, and, as the flak had been reported to burst well

Lancaster ME692 KO-G was lost without trace on the Wilhelmshaven raid of 15th October 1944

Emmerich 7th October 1944. The ORB noted: '23 aircraft took part in an extremely successful attack on this town which had not been attacked before. Bombing was visual and very concentrated and smoke was seen up to 14,000 ft. A very good prang.'

below the bombers, it was most likely that a night-fighter, waiting on the periphery of the target, had claimed LL880, and brought about the deaths of W/O Erickson and his crew.

Orders were received on the 7th for operations that afternoon against the German frontier towns of Cleves and Emmerich, which lay about four miles apart on opposite sides of the Rhine, through which enemy forces might attempt to advance on the exposed Allied right flank following the "bridge too far" failure at Arnhem. Eighty 3 Group crews were briefed for Cleves (Kleve) and seventy-five for Emmerich in overall forces of 351 and 340 aircraft respectively, and it was for the latter that twenty-three 115 Squadron Lancasters took off either side of noon with F/Ls Brown, Castle, Clarke, Cunningham, Easterman, Osbourne and Talbot the senior pilots on duty. They flew out in good weather conditions, and all reached the target, perched on the northern bank of the Rhine, and identified it visually and by Pathfinder flares. F/O Hynes and crew suffered a hang-up over the aiming-point, and went round again for another try, this time employing the jettison toggle, but, again, without success. As a last resort F/O Hynes dived

115 Sqn Crew of Lancaster HK598 L-R Sgt Savage (M/UG), F/Sgt Radcliffe (W.Op). F/Sgt Hogben (Gunner), Sgt Hughes (Nav), F/L Ward (Pilot), F/Sgt Smith (B/A), Sgt Tarr (RG), Sgt Frank Rutter (Flt.Eng.) (Photo F Rutter)

the Lancaster and pulled up sharply to try to dislodge the hardware, but the bombs remained stubbornly on board, and he was forced to proceed to the jettison area, where they were released by hand. The others bombed from between 12,000 and 13,000 feet, and watched the town disappear beneath smoke and flames, one crew noting that the only part of the town not to be on fire was the south-western corner. A local report described the destruction of 2,424 buildings with many hundreds severely damaged, and a death toll in excess of seven hundred people.

There were no other major outings for 3 Group thereafter until the commencement of Operation Hurricane, a campaign designed as a demonstration to the enemy of the overwhelming superiority of the Allied air forces ranged against it. A force of 1,013 aircraft was assembled to hit Duisburg, of which 196 represented 3 Group, and twenty-five of these 115 Squadron. They departed Witchford between 06.50 and 07.25 with F/Ls Clark, Cunningham, Fuller (with S/L Frankland as second pilot), Stechman and Talbot the senior pilots on duty, and headed out to fulfil their briefs to aim for a specific railway junction and factory or the built-up area in general. They arrived over the already-battered city shortly after breakfast time to be greeted by five-tenths cloud, and followed the Master Bomber's instructions to bomb as best as they could. The 115 Squadron participants complied from between 17,800 and 20,000 feet in the face of fairly heavy flak, and observed many explosions, particularly in the docks area. Almost four and a half thousand tons of bombs rained down, the vast majority of them high explosives, as it was assumed, that there was little material left of a combustible nature. Fourteen aircraft failed to return, mostly having fallen victim to the local flak batteries, and 115 Squadron had the misfortune to be represented by two of them. Only the pilot, F/O Lister, survived the destruction by flak of HK599, and he was taken prisoner, while F/O Price RCAF and four of his predominantly Canadian crew perished in ND805, leaving only the flight engineer and navigator to survive as PoWs.

Once the crews had returned, C Flight was posted across the tarmac, on paper at least, under the command of S/L Farquharson, who, it will be recalled, had completed a tour with 115 Squadron earlier in the war, and had now returned to the operational scene. These crews would become the nucleus of 195 Squadron to provide the experience, and would operate that night under the orders of 115 Squadron, but in the name of 195 Squadron, as the new unit went to war for the first time as part of the force of 1,005 aircraft setting off once more for Duisburg. Other 195 Squadron pilots would accompany five of the twenty-two 115 Squadron crews as second pilots, and they took off between 22.25 and 23.20 with S/L Smith the senior pilot on duty. It was a remarkable fact, that the Command had been able to launch 2,018 heavy bombers in less than twenty-four hours, and did so without any participation by 5 Group, which would take advantage of this night's activity over the Ruhr, to finally nail Brunswick, after so many marginally effective operations against it during the year. F/O Gaston turned back with engine issues before the first hour was done, and F/O Hynes was also in the early stages of his sortie when the bomb load fell out during a circuit check. Finally, F/O Ward was ninety minutes out when defective instruments forced him to turn round, and this left nineteen from the squadron to press on to the target, where they were greeted by good visibility. They were able to make a visual identification of the release-point guided by the fires still burning from the morning raid and by Pathfinder flares, and aimed their 1,000 and 500 pounders at red and green TIs from between 10,000 and 21,000 feet. The attack took place in the face of quite heavy flak, despite which, the bombing appeared to be more concentrated than the morning effort, and six large explosions were observed at around 01.25. A modest seven aircraft failed to return, but nine thousand tons of bombs during the course of the 14th had left Duisburg devastated and paralyzed.

On the following day, the 15th, seven 115 Squadron crews were called to briefing to learn that they were to be part of seventy-strong 3 Group force, which would join up with 436 other aircraft from all but the "Independent Air Force". Their target for the final time during the war was to be the naval port of Wilhelmshaven. They took off between 17.40 and 18.00 with F/L Clarke the senior pilot on duty, but

Lancaster MkII KO-H with George Henry and crew.

F/O Potter and crew dropped out some ninety minutes after take-off because of a defective oxygen supply to the flight engineer. The others reached the target to find cloud and haze, through which the red and green TIs could be made out, and bombing took place from between 11,500 and 20,000 feet. A large, orange explosion was observed at 19.49, but the attack appeared to be scattered, and there was little to inspire confidence among the crews that their efforts had been worthwhile. Bomber Command claimed severe damage to business and residential areas, but little information came out of the town to confirm one way or the other. One of the squadron's veteran Lancasters, ME692, a veteran of sixty-nine operations, went missing without trace on this night, and it took with it the eight-man crew of F/O Perry. The eighth crew member was S/L Franklin, who had joined 195 Squadron as a flight commander from 3 LFS on the 7th, and was flying as second pilot.

On the 16th, the former 115 Squadron commander, W/C Rainsford, returned to Witchford temporarily from 33 Base to oversee 195 Squadron's administration, and W/C Burnside arrived on the following day to take command, to be joined by S/L Brentnall as the replacement flight commander after the loss of S/L Franklin. 3 Group had been training for some time for its new role, which would give it some measure of independence from the main force. The G-H device, which could be described as Oboe in reverse, had been undergoing trials for a considerable time, and had, as already mentioned, been employed in a limited way against targets in Germany. Now it was to become a 3 Group preserve, and would be used with great effect until the end of the war against urban areas, and such precision targets as railway and oil installations. G-H equipped aircraft, with highly distinctive fin markings, would lead a gaggle of aircraft into the attack, and the release of the leader's bombs would be the signal for those following to do likewise. G-H raids would be predominantly by daylight, but the system could, and indeed, would be employed with equal effectiveness by night.

3 Group would venture forth for the first time in its new role on the morning of the 18th, to attack Bonn, a small city situated some twenty miles to the south-east of Cologne, which had little previous damage that might cloud the assessment of the G-H performance. A force of 128 Lancasters was made ready, of

which sixteen belonged to 115 Squadron and took off between 08.25 and 08.40 with F/Ls Castle, Clark, Osborne and Stechman the senior pilots on duty. The intention was for the force to divide into vics of three, each with a G-H leader, but matters did not proceed precisely according to plan, and some G-H leaders found themselves alone, while others had four or five Lancasters for company. Contrary to expectations of ten-tenths cloud over the target, they were met with only three to five-tenths and an unexpectedly heavy flak barrage, which broke up the formations. Another problem was the fading of the G-H pulse, which led to some crews bombing visually, and this was the experience of most of the 115 Squadron crews, who released their loads from between 16,000 and 19,000 feet. Initial undershooting was rectified, but bombing became scattered towards the end of the raid, although most of the hardware fell within the confines of the city, and one bomb was seen to explode on a bridge at 11.05. Only one Lancaster was lost, and this was 115 Squadron's HK544, which went missing without trace with the crew of F/O Smith RAAF. Despite the element of uncertainty, post-raid reconnaissance revealed that the raid had destroyed seven hundred buildings, including many of a cultural nature, and had torn out the heart of the old city, leaving many public buildings and residential areas burned-out.

Stuttgart was posted as the target for the night of the 19/20th, for which 565 Lancasters of 1, 3, 6 and 8 Groups were made ready. 3 Group detailed 176 aircraft, 115 Squadron loading seven of its own with a cookie, six 1,000 and two 500 pounders, and ten with a cookie and ten SBCs of incendiaries. In addition, as 195 Squadron was still not yet officially operational, a further six Lancasters from C Flight were also bombed up for the use of 195 Squadron crews. This was to be a standard city-busting raid to be conducted in two waves, separated by four-and-a-half hours, and the first Witchford element of twelve Lancasters took off between 17.30 and 17.44 with F/L Clarke the senior pilot on duty. They flew out over cloud, which persisted all the way to the target, where the Pathfinders were dispensing Wanganui (skymarker) flares with red with yellow stars, and also red and green TIs. F/O Dowling described the target area as glowing as bright as day, and reported a white explosion at 20.44. The 115/195 Squadron crews bombed from between 16,000 and 19,000 feet, some observing the faint glow of the TIs on the ground, while most aimed for the skymarkers. Capt Martin of the RSAAF witnessed three huge, red explosions at 20.35, and confirmed that the entire target area was lit-up. His was one of a number of aircraft to sustain minor flak damage. As the first wave crews headed home, the eleven second-wave participants took off between 22.00 and 22.20 with F/Ls Castle, Mills, Stechman and Talbot the senior pilots on duty. They reached the target to find the same conditions of ten-tenths cloud and the glow of fires beneath, and bombed on the skymarkers from between 15,800 and 18,500 feet, many observing large orange explosions at 01.05. Although not as concentrated as intended, the raid inflicted heavy damage on central and eastern districts, whilst also spilling over onto nearby towns, and the important Bosch factory was among the buildings to sustain damage.

On the 21st, 3 Group was invited to attack three coastal batteries at Flushing on the island of Walcheren, and detailed twenty-five Lancasters for each. The 115/195 Squadron element of twenty-five departed Witchford between 11.11 and midday, each carrying fourteen 1,000 pounders. 115 Squadron was led by six pilots of flight lieutenant rank, and there were no early returns to deplete the weight of bombs reaching the target. There were no Pathfinders on hand to provide marking, and, according to the 115 Squadron report, most of the bombs delivered from between 7,500 and 10,000 feet, fell into the water. The 3 Group report, however, described all three aiming-points to be "respectively straddled by bombs", and one was reported to have blown up.

The Group prepared to carry out its second G-H raid on the 22nd, when the Ruhr city of Neuss was to be the target. A force of one hundred Lancasters was made ready, of which 115 and 195 Squadrons provided four and two respectively, and they took off at 13.15 with F/Ls Mills and Talbot the senior pilots on duty. The forming-up process again proved to be challenging, but, once accomplished, the operation proceeded according to plan with a strong G-H pulse throughout the attack, which was delivered from between 17,000 and 17,500 feet through ten-tenths cloud. The raid lacked the concentration achieved at Bonn, local reports putting a figure of around 630 houses seriously damaged or destroyed along with twenty-one industrial buildings, but no aircraft were lost and it was another step towards perfecting the system.

The Hurricane force was briefed for a huge assault on Essen on the evening of the 23rd, for which a force of 1,055 aircraft was assembled and loaded with 4,500 tons of bombs, 90% of which were high-explosive. This was, in fact, the largest force ever to be dispatched by the Command to a single target, and, once more, it would be achieved without the presence of 5 Group. Twenty-three Lancasters were bombed-up at Witchford, seventeen belonging to 115 Squadron's A and B Flights, and six to C Flight, the last-mentioned to be occupied by 195 Squadron crews. They took off between 16.20 and 16.45 with F/Ls Clarke, Hynes, Stechman and Talbot the senior pilots on duty, each Lancaster carrying in its bomb-bay a cookie and mixture of 1,000 and 500 pounders and No 14 Cluster Projectiles. They all reached the target to find ten-tenths cloud with tops at between 10,000 and 14,000 feet, over which the Pathfinders delivered concentrated red and green Wanganui flares. The 115/195 Squadron element bombed from between 16,000 and 21,000 feet, and observed the glow of explosions and fires from what appeared to be an accurate and effective raid. Local reports listed more than six hundred buildings destroyed and a further eight hundred seriously damaged, with 662 fatalities.

A force of 771 aircraft was detailed to return to the tortured city on the afternoon of the 25th, the day on which C Flight became physically part of 195 Squadron, and took with it its A4 code letters, but not before operating for the final time as part of its parent unit. 115 Squadron made ready twenty Lancasters from A and B Flights, and five from C Flight to be operated by 195 Squadron crews, as part of the 3 Group contribution of 170, and they took off between 13.05 and 13.30 with W/C Devas the senior pilot on duty. They all reached the target to find seven to ten-tenths cloud cover, but with sufficient gaps to enable some crews to identify the aiming-point. The 115/195 Squadron crews bombed either on red flares or green TIs from between 18,500 and 22,000 feet under the guidance of an effective Master Bomber, and all but one returned safely to report observing a number of huge explosions. PD276 was one of just four failures to return, and it was learned that F/O Stuart RAAF and his crew, which included two other members of the RAAF and one of the RCAF, had been killed in the crash to an unknown cause in Germany. The attack was, actually, more damaging than that by the larger force two days earlier, and had destroyed 1,163 buildings and killed more than eight hundred people, but, by this time anyway, the once mighty Essen had lost its status as a major centre of war production.

The Ruhr city of Leverkusen was selected to host the next G-H raid on the 26th, and this would provide 195 Squadron with the opportunity to undertake its maiden operation as an independent unit. In the absence of a 115 Squadron contribution, the operation proceeded according to plan with G-H working well, and returning crews claimed a successful attack, which was confirmed by photographic reconnaissance. However, whether or not the I.G. Farben chemicals plant, the intended aiming-point, was hit, is not known. The main operation on the 28th would involve the Hurricane force against Cologne, but, before that, 3 Group detailed seventy-six Lancasters for a morning attack on three coastal batteries at Flushing on Walcheren, for which the eight 115 Squadron participants took off between 09.05 and 09.59 with the newly-promoted S/L Castle the senior pilot on duty. They all identified the target visually and by Pathfinder flares, and bombed on red and green TIs from between 8,000 and 9,000 feet, before returning home to report an accurate and concentrated attack, which produced a large explosion at 10.33.

Cologne's first visit by the Hurricane force was to be a two-phase affair delivered by a force of 773 aircraft, of which a dozen Lancasters were to be provided by 115 Squadron. They departed Witchford between 13.01 and 13.10 with F/Ls Clark, Hynes, Milne and Russell the senior pilots on duty, and

Lancaster PB584 with the crew of . L-R: Sgt D Cook (W.Op), Sgt L Parsons (RG), Sgt R Base (Flt. Eng.) Capt. R Martin RSAAF (Pilot), Sgt P Purdy (Nav) not on raid, Sgt A Andrews (M/UG) F/O J Bowles (BA) (Photo R Base)

reached the target to find clear conditions. They bombed on red TIs from between 17,500 and 21,000 feet, and observed a very accurate and concentrated raid, during which they saw a bridge demolished

Crew of Lancaster PD577 'P', 115 Sqn. L-R: F/Sgt 'Red' Eva (BA), F/Sgt/ 'Fitz' Fitzgerald (W.Op), F/O 'Jock' Milne (Pilot), Sgt 'Paddy' Power (M/UG), Sgt Allan Wilson (Nav), Sgt Turberville (Flt/Eng) and Sgt.Evans (RG). (Photo: A Wilson)

Various photographs of the crew of F/Sgt John Boden and their Lancaster PD276, KO-X. Above left: 'All set to go.' Above right: Back row: L-R: Sgt John Ottewell (Nav), Sgt. Chas Sheppard (M/UG), F/Sgt John Boden (Pilot), Sgt. Ken Acklund (Flt.Eng.), Sgt. Tom Lapin (W.Op) Front row, L-R:F/Sgt Alan Guilfoyle (BA), Sgt Chas Sargeant (RG) (Photo: K Ackland)

and a large explosion was witnessed at 15.48. Local reports confirmed the enormity of the destruction, which left more than 2,200 apartment blocks and many industrial premises in ruins. There was also massive damage to power stations, along with railway and inland harbour installations, and 630 German people lost their lives. 115 Squadron's NF960 was one of seven missing aircraft, and only the bomb-aimer and flight engineer from the crew of F/L Hynes RNZAF survived to fall into enemy hands.

The campaign to dislodge enemy forces from Walcheren was drawing to a close on the 29th as seventy-five Lancasters from 3 Group were being made ready to return to three coastal batteries. According to the 3 Group ORB, the targets were at Flushing on the southern edge of the island, while the 115 Squadron scribe records Westkapelle at the most westerly point as the location. They were among 358 aircraft drawn from 1, 3, 4 and 8 Groups to be committed to the attack on eleven aiming-points, for which the 115 Squadron element of eight Lancasters took off either side of 10.00 with F/Ls Cunningham, Mills and Ward the senior pilots on duty. All three 3 Group targets were clearly visible through large gaps in the cloud, and, although two were accurately bombed, the markers at the third were wrongly placed, and crews who had not identified the aiming-point visually and ignored them, wasted their bombs there. The final attack on the Walcheren defences would be delivered by 5 Group on the following day, but there would be a week of heavy ground action before the island was finally taken, and the port of Antwerp would remain out of commission until the end of November.

Cologne's ordeal was not yet over, and 905 aircraft were made ready to continue its agony on the 30th. 3 Group detailed ninety-nine Lancasters, of which seventeen would represent 115 Squadron, and they took to the air between 17.55 and 18.15 with F/Ls Cunningham, Milne, Russell and Ward the senior pilots on duty. F/O Grant and crew were forced to return early after the pilot's escape hatch blew off and left a largish hole in the mid-upper turret, but the remainder all reached the target, guided by Pathfinder flares, and found ten-tenths cloud, through which they bombed on red and white skymarkers from between 18,000 and 24,000 feet. It was impossible to make an assessment, but it was clear from the large explosions and glow of fires reflecting in the cloud that the operation was massively destructive. This would be confirmed later by local reports, which described a number of districts as being 'thoroughly ploughed-up". On the following evening a force of 493 aircraft representing 1, 3, 4 and 8 Groups returned to Cologne to continue the torment. 115 Squadron dispatched eleven Lancasters between 18.00 and 18.30 with S/L Castle the senior pilot on duty, and they again encountered ten-tenths cloud, through which they bombed on red and white skymarkers from between 18,700 and 21,000 feet. Explosions and the orange glow of fires confirmed the intensity of the bombing, which fell mostly into southern districts and left the city effectively paralyzed. During the course of the month the squadron dispatched 158 night and 163 day sorties on eighteen operations for the loss of eight Lancasters and crews.

November 1944

3 Group opened its November account with a G-H raid on the oil plant at Homberg, north-west of Duisburg on the 2nd. 184 Lancasters were detailed, of which sixteen represented 115 Squadron, and they departed Witchford either side of 11.30 led by six pilots of flight lieutenant rank. All arrived in the target area to find five-tenths cumulus cloud, and identified it either visually or by green skymarkers. The standard G-H system was extended on this occasion to allow a large number of leaderless aircraft to deliver their bombs onto skymarkers dropped by the G-H leaders, and the 115 Squadron crews carried out their runs across the aiming-point from between 18,800 and 21,800. As the aircraft wheeled away, fires were seen to be burning and black, oily smoke from the refinery was drifting through 12,000 feet. That evening, almost a thousand aircraft took the Operation Hurricane message to Düsseldorf, and, in the absence of a 115 Squadron presence, destroyed or seriously damaged five thousand houses and apartment blocks, in what was the final heavy raid of the war on this Ruhr city.

177 Lancasters were detailed on the 4th for a G-H raid that afternoon on the town of Solingen, perched on the southern fringe of the Ruhr near Remscheid. 115 Squadron loaded fifteen cookies and a single 8,000 pounder into the bomb bays of its Lancasters, and filled them up with 1,000 and 500 pounders and cluster bombs, before launching them skyward between 11.15 and 11.34 with F/Ls Cunningham, Davidson and Milne the senior pilots on duty. The formation process went smoothly, and all from Witchford arrived in the target area to find seven to ten-tenths cumulus cloud, through which some ground detail could be identified. There were also red skymarkers from the G-H leaders, and the 115 Squadron element mostly bombed these from between 18,000 and 22,500 feet, assessing the attack as scattered, partly as a result of a strong wind driving the skymarkers across the target. Fires were seen in the town, and some crews reported observing two Lancasters explode in the air and a third crash with both port engines ablaze. Flak was light and ineffective, which meant that the four missing aircraft were most likely brought down by friendly bombs. There was much sadness at Witchford when three crews from 195 Squadron failed to return home, and, while the two Lancasters destroyed by mid-air explosions are known to have come from Witchford, the one seen to crash was either the third 195 Squadron victim or a 75(NZ) Squadron aircraft.

The group was ordered to return to Solingen on the following day, this time with a force of 173 Lancasters, of which sixteen were provided by 115 Squadron. They took off between 10.20 and 11.05 with F/Ls Cunningham, Davidson and Milne the senior pilots on duty, and all reached the target to bomb from between 13,500 and 18,800 feet through ten-tenths cloud on either a G-H leader or G-H red flares. The crews were unable to assess the outcome, but local reports showed it to have been outstandingly successful in terms of damage to housing and industry, listing 1,300 houses and eighteen industrial building as destroyed and a further sixteen hundred seriously damaged. Sadly, there was also the inevitable human toll, which amounted to well over a thousand lives. The 3 Group ORB claimed this to be the most successful G-H raid to date. Gelsenkirchen wilted under a heavy bombardment by seven hundred aircraft on the 6th, which 3 Group sat out in order to prepare for its first night G-H raid against the almost virgin target of Koblenz. 115 Squadron provided fourteen of the 128 Lancasters to be employed against this medium-sized town situated some fifty miles south-east of Cologne. The number would have been greater but for a delay in bombing up at Methwold, which caused the cancellation of twenty-one aircraft. The Witchford element took off either side of 17.00 with S/L Castle the senior pilot on duty, and all reached the target, which was identified visually by a river junction or by red and green markers dropped by the G-H leaders. The weather was clear, and the pattern of streets stood out clearly in the light of the flares as the bombs were delivered from between 17,500 and 18,000 feet. The built-up area soon became a sea of flames, which would remain visible for seventy miles into the return trip, and a large explosion was witnessed at 19.32. It would become clear after the war, that around 58% of the town had been destroyed, and a two-mile stretch across the centre, which had contained many ancient and cultural buildings, had been erased.

There was an early start to proceedings for 136 crews of 3 Group on the 8th, who had been detailed for an operation against the Meerbeck synthetic oil refinery at Homberg. 115 Squadron briefed twelve crews, and they took off between 08.10 and 08.35 with F/Ls Cunningham and Mills the senior pilots on duty. Cloud over the stations caused some difficulties in forming up, and an hour into their outward flight, P/O Ingham and crew had to turn back when the second pilot became indisposed. The others all pressed on to the target, where a large gap in the clouds enabled them to identify it visually and by G-H flares. Bombing took place from between 17,000 and 18,500 feet in the face of an accurate and sprited flak response, despite which, the crews observed their hardware to fall onto the aiming-point. Two large fires broke out, sending a column of black smoke spiralling upwards to conceal the ground, after which the attack became somewhat scattered.

The oil plant at Castrop-Rauxel was posted as the target on the 11th, and this required another early start for ten 115 Squadron crews. They took off between 08.25 and 08.45 as part of an overall force of 122 aircraft, with F/Ls Davidson and Gorrie the senior pilots on duty, but F/O Gadd and crew turned back within the hour because of engine issues. The target was found to be hidden beneath ten-tenths cloud, and bombing took place either on G-H leaders or their marker flares from between 18,000 and 22,300 feet. No assessment was possible, but the attack was believed to be accurate and no losses were incurred. 195 Squadron moved out of Witchford on the 13th, and took up residence at Wratting Common, where it would remain until after the war. The oil offensive continued at Dortmund on the 15th, for which 3 Group detailed 177 Lancasters, nineteen of them provided by 115 Squadron. The Witchford element took off between 12.32 and 12.47 with S/L Castle the senior pilot on duty, and all reached the target to encounter ten-tenths thick cloud that completely obscured the ground. Bombing was carried out on G-H leaders and flares from between 16,500 and 19,500 feet, and the attack appeared to be concentrated. Two Lancasters were seen to explode in the air after being hit by the intense flak barrage, and the failure to return of two Witchford crews provided their identity. HK595 contained the nine-man crew of flight commander, S/L Castle, which included a second pilot and an additional gunner, while F/L Davidson RCAF and his crew were in NN706, and not a single man survived. In all, five members of the RCAF

262

and three of the RAAF perished, and only four sets of remains from S/L Castle's crew were recovered for burial.

As American forces advanced towards the Rhine, Bomber Command was called upon to cut communications behind enemy lines by bombing the towns of Düren, Jülich and Heinsberg, situated in an arc from north to east of Aachen. A force of 1,188 was assembled from all groups and divided amongst the targets, with elements of 1, 5 and 8 Groups assigned to Düren, 4, 6 and 8 Groups to Jülich and 3 Group to Heinsberg. 182 Lancasters were bombed up on 3 Group stations, and fourteen 115 Squadron Lancasters departed Witchford either side of 13.30 with F/Ls Mills and Milne the senior pilots on duty. The target was found to be visible through three to five-tenths cloud, and a Master Bomber was on hand to direct proceedings. Sadly, W/C Watkins, the commanding officer of XV Squadron, was shot down, leaving his Deputy to step in and control the bombing, which he did expertly. He directed crews to ignore the G-H markers, which were inaccurate because of an error in calculating the release co-ordinates, and ensured that the bombing, which was carried out by the 115 Squadron crews from between 7,500 and 10,000 feet, hit the town and all but erased it from the map. While more than three thousand people lost their lives in Düren, Heinsberg had been almost completely evacuated, and fifty-two civilians paid the ultimate price for remaining. In the event, the American push faltered in difficult ground conditions, which prevented the use of tanks. W/C Watkins, who was the only survivor, is shown in Bomber Command Losses as the pilot, but he was, in fact, one of a few navigators to attain squadron command, and the crewman listed as the navigator was the pilot.

The Gadd crew. L to R: Bill Smith, George Brown, George Hawkins, Ken Gadd (Captain), Don Miller, Ken Bradfield, Doug Marsh.

Orders were received on the 20th for 3 Group to return to the Meerbeck oil plant at Homberg, and a force of 185 Lancasters was made ready accordingly. 115 Squadron briefed fifteen crews, who took off between 12.35 and 12.55 with F/Ls Gibson, Gorrie and Milne the senior pilots on duty. F/O Jenkins and crew were almost two hours out when their port-inner engine failed, and they jettisoned their cookie before bringing the remaining bombs home. The others battled the conditions of towering, ice-bearing clouds, which made forming up on a leader almost impossible. Some crews climbed to 25,000 feet to avoid the cloud, while others found a clear lane at around 20,000 feet and managed to latch onto a G-H leader. All from Witchford reached the target and bombed from between 18,000 and 23,000 feet in what degenerated into a scattered and largely ineffective attack. The importance to the German war effort of this target demanded a return, which was put in hand on the following day with the preparation of a G-H force of 159 Lancasters. 115 Squadron's contribution was again fifteen aircraft, which took off either side of 12.30 with the newly-promoted S/L Clarke the senior pilot on duty. Weather conditions were a vast improvement on the previous day as all of the 115 Squadron crews reached the target to find it clearly visible and the G-H leader orbiting without bombing. There was a high level of G-H-set unserviceability, and the flak was sufficiently accurate to upset the runs of those with a G-H leader. Most of the 115 Squadron crews bombed visually from between 19,000 and 21,500 feet, and judged the attack to be accurate based on fires and smoke seen emanating from the plant. The Bomber Command report was more expansive, describing a vast sheet of yellow flame followed by black smoke rising to a great height.

G-H was proving to be very effective in the hands of 3 Group against oil refineries, and the Group was ordered to send a force to dismantle the Nordstern plant at Gelsenkirchen on the 23rd. 168 Lancasters were made ready, of which twenty belonged to 115 Squadron. They departed Witchford between 12.34 and 13.10 led by six pilots of flight lieutenant rank, a number of them newly-promoted. F/O Pickering and crew were soon on their way home after their port-outer engine failed, but the remainder carried on in conditions ideal for a G-H raid, with a layer of ten-tenths cloud at 12,000 feet and clear skies above. Flak was only moderate, and the formations held firm as they traversed the aiming-point. The 115 Squadron crews were in the second wave and delivered their bombs by G-H leader or on red flares with stars from 18,800 to 20,400 feet between 15.19 and 15.25. No assessment could be made because of the cloud, but the consensus was of a successful operation.

Seventy-five 3 Group Lancasters conducted a trial operation on the 26th, to establish the range at which G-H could remain effective. Railway yards at Fulda were selected as the objective, in a region south of the now famous Eder Dam. The attack was not successful, but all aircraft returned safely home. 115 Squadron was not involved in the operation, but lost the crew of F/Sgt Crebbin, who disappeared without trace over the North Sea during the afternoon while engaged in an H2S training exercise in PD293. The Kalk-Nord marshalling yards in the eastern side of Cologne was posted as the target for a G-H raid on the 27th, for which 3 Group detailed 169 Lancasters, twenty of them provided by 115 Squadron. They departed Witchford between 12.14 and 12.34, led again by pilots of flight lieutenant rank, and all reached the target area to find moderate to heavy accurate flak. It seemed that the lead navigator in the spearhead had taken the formations through most of the Ruhr defences before arriving at the yards. The squadron's HK624 was shot down to crash in the Mülheim district on the East Bank of the Rhine within sight of the aiming-point, and there were no survivors from the nine-man crew of F/O Ingham, which included a second pilot and an additional gunner. The remaining 115 Squadron crews, who were part of the first wave, bombed with a G-H leader from 19,000 to 22,000 feet between 15.02 and 15.06, and returned, some with flak damage, to report observing explosions around the aiming-point. It was on this day that W/C Devas relinquished command of the squadron on posting to 31 Base for Air Staff duties, and W/C Shaw came in the opposite direction as his successor to see the squadron through to the end of the bombing war, and almost to the total cessation of hostilities.

Orders were received on the 28th for a 3 Group night attack on the Ruhr city of Neuss to follow up on one delivered by elements of 1, 6 and 8 Groups on the previous night. Unusually for a G-H raid, there was no specific target other than the built-up area, for which a force of 145 Lancasters was made ready. 115 Squadron put up sixteen Lancasters, whose crews had to wait until 02.54 before take-off began. S/L Clarke was the senior pilot on duty as they all became safely airborne by 03.21, fifteen of them carrying a cookie and 1,000 and 500 pounder plus incendiaries, while F/L Jenkins had a 12,000 pounder on board along with 500 pounders. F/L Holloway lost power in both port engines which prevented him from climbing to operational height, and he turned back after around ninety minutes. The others continued on to find the target concealed beneath ten-tenths cloud, and bombed on red Wanganui flares with green stars from 19,000 to 20,000 feet between 05.30 and 05.42. Returning crews commented on the markers going down late and that they were scattered, which led to scattered bombing, and this was partly confirmed by local reports of modest property damage to mostly residential districts.

3 Group divided its forces on the morning of the 30th, preparing sixty Lancasters each for synthetic oil plants at Osterfeld and Bottrop, both situated to the north-east of Oberhausen in the heart of the Ruhr. 115 Squadron bombed up fifteen Lancasters, and dispatched them to the former between 10.31 and 10.49 with F/L Milne one of the senior pilots on duty and sharing his cockpit with W/C Shaw. The conditions of ten-tenths cloud with tops at 12,000 feet were favourable for a G-H raid, allowing the G-H leaders to be clearly seen by those maintaining contact with them, but they also released flares for those remaining unattached. Two Lancasters were seen to be shot down by flak over the target, one belonging to 75(NZ) Squadron and the other to 115 Squadron. PD367 crashed with great force, and there were no survivors from the crew of the highly-experienced F/L Holloway DFM, who was on his second tour, having undertaken his first with 99 Squadron. The rest of the squadron bombed in formation from 19,000 and 20,000 feet between 13.09 and 13.11, and observed thick, black smoke rising through the clouds. The aircraft from one unspecified base arrived seven minutes late, affecting the intervals between waves and this led to a degree of congestion on the way out. During the course of the month the squadron carried

Lancaster NN754 of 'C' Flight, with armourers prior to being 'bombed up'.

out fourteen operations and dispatched 172 daylight and forty-one night sorties for the loss of five Lancasters and crews.

December 1944

December began for 3 Group with the preparation on the 2nd of ninety-three Lancasters for a daylight G-H raid on the Hansa benzol plant at Dortmund. 115 Squadron loaded thirteen aircraft with ten 1,000 pounders each, and launched them skyward between 13.03 and 13.30 with F/Ls Gadd and Jenkins the senior pilots on duty. Conditions were ideal for a G-H attack with thick, ten-tenths cloud up to 13,000 feet and clear skies above to aid forming up. F/L Gadd was forced to turn back with a failed starboard-outer engine, leaving the others to press on to the target, which was identified by G-H flares. The squadron element bombed from between 18,300 and 21,000 feet in the face of a heavy flak barrage, which, according to most was inaccurate, although F/O Olorenshaw and crew would beg to differ after picking up damage to the main-plane, fin and rudder. A greater danger was falling bombs, which caused F/O Snyder and crew to experience a squeaky-bum moment. This was the first time that all G-H aircraft detailed to bomb on G-H were successful, for which the 3 Group ORB praised the crews and the radar tradesmen. The attack appeared to be concentrated, and was completed without loss.

The Ruhr was the destination once more on the 4th, this time for a G-H force of 160 Lancasters, of which seventeen were made ready by 115 Squadron. Fourteen of them were loaded with a cookie, two with an 8,000 pounder and one with a 12,000lb blockbuster, all with a selection of 500 pounders and or incendiaries. They took off between 11.40 and 11.55 bound for Oberhausen with W/C Shaw the senior pilot on duty for the first time, but F/O Roberts turned back early on with a port-outer engine issue. The winds at cruising altitude were lighter than forecast, and this resulted in the leaders flying too fast and the stream becoming strung out. Fortunately, no enemy fighters appeared, other than a very small jet-propelled aircraft near the target, where all arrived to find nine to ten-tenths cloud. Bombing took place mostly in G-H formation and partly on a concentrated bunch of flares, the 115 Squadron crews attacking from between 19,000 and 21,000 feet. Returning crews were unable to offer an assessment of the results, but a local report revealed heavy damage in the town centre around the railway station. 472 houses were destroyed and a similar number seriously damaged along with a number of industrial and public buildings.

The important railway centre of Hamm was posted as the target for ninety-four 3 Group Lancasters on the 5th, while fifty-six others went for the Urft Dam in the Eifel region south-east of Aachen, towards which American ground forces were advancing. Eighteen 115 Squadron crews were briefed for the Hamm raid, and departed Witchford either side of 09.00 with S/L Clarke and the newly-promoted S/L Gorrie the senior pilots on duty. They flew to the target in good formation, but P/O Kerrins was unable to find it, presumably after failing to attach himself to a G-H leader, and he abandoned the sortie. The others found nine-tenths strato-cumulus, through which the bombing was carried out by the 115 squadron element on G-H from between 19,000 and 22,000 feet. For the first time since daylight operations had resumed in June, a force of enemy fighters made a determined attack, which was dealt with by the 11 Group fighter escort, and just one straggling 195 Squadron Lancaster was damaged by a BF109G, which was claimed as shot down. The Lancaster eventually force-landed in a ploughed field near Ghent in Belgium. It was established later, that almost 40% of Hamm's built-up area had been destroyed in this attack of modest size.

Lancaster PB756. Her first operation was 16 December 1944 and she flew 31 operations. Flak damage was sustained on five of them. Note the yellow bars on the rudder denoting status as a G-H Leader.

Crew of Lancaster NN706 'B', No. 115 Sqn. Back row, L-R Sgt. Bill Phillips (Flt.Eng.), F/Sgt Les Algar (M/Under/G), not on raid. F/O David Jenkins (pilot), F/O Bill Patton (BA), F/Sgt Harry Rossiter (W.Op). Front row, L-R Sgt George Goulborn (RG) and Sgt Reg Begon (M/G). The same crew took part on the operation of 29th October 1944. Taken on December 16th 1944 before take-off on their last mission. (Photo: Rossiter & Goulborn)

The busy first week of the new month continued on the 6th with orders to prepare for what, that night, would be the group's deepest penetration into Germany for six months. The target was the synthetic oil refinery at Leuna, near Merseburg, one of numerous such sites located to the west of Leipzig in eastern Germany, some 250 miles from the Dutch frontier and five hundred miles from the bomber bases of eastern England. 123 aircraft were made ready by 3 Group to join forces with 352 others from 1 and 8 Groups, and the 115 Squadron element of fourteen took off either side of 17.00 with the newly-promoted S/L Mills the senior pilot on duty. A serious fuel leak into the fuselage could not be stemmed by chewing gum, and F/O Dowling and crew decided, sensibly, to turn back. Petrol fumes from the starboard-inner engine caused F/L Gaston's mid-upper gunner to pass out, and he was removed from the turret for treatment as this sortie was also abandoned. These were just two of fifteen abortive sorties to afflict the group, for which the severe icing weather conditions were believed to be largely responsible. The Pathfinders had prepared for "Newhaven" marking (ground), with emergency Wanganui (skymarking) if required, and this proved to be the case as ten-tenths cloud was unexpectedly encountered over the target. The skymarkers were plentiful, continuous and concentrated, and the squadron element bombed from between 20,000 and 23,000 feet in the face of a strong flak defence, which, fortunately, exploded below their flight level. Large explosions and fires were reflected in the clouds, and, although no immediate assessment could be made, photographic reconnaissance showed the effort to have been worthwhile.

On the 8th, 3 Group prepared 163 Lancasters for a G-H attack on marshalling yards in Duisburg, for which the 115 Squadron element of twenty took off between 08.16 and 08.41 with W/C Shaw and S/L Mills the senior pilots on duty. As they flew out the crews encountered thick layers of cloud up to 25,000 feet, which prevented them from forming up. However, so accurate was the navigation, that, as they emerged into clear air, they were able to create a compact stream and line up behind a G-H leader. Bombing was carried out from between 19,000 and 21,000 feet through nine-tenths cloud, and the challenging conditions persisted all the way home, where the crews were unable to offer an assessment. The group was ordered to return to Osterfeld on the 11th, where two aiming-points, the benzol plant and the marshalling yards, were to be attacked. Fifty-two and ninety-eight Lancasters respectively were made ready, of which eighteen were provided by 115 Squadron. It is not known to which aiming-point they had been assigned as they took off between 08.31 and 08.50 with S/Ls Clarke and Mills the senior pilots on duty. Forming up and climbing to operational height was made difficult by cloud up to 15,000 feet over the stations and for the outward flight. By the time the target was reached, the cloud tops were at 18,000 to 19,000 feet, which pushed the bombing height above what had been intended, and the G-H flares quickly disappeared from sight. The 115 Squadron crews bombed from between 19,000 and 21,000 feet as part of what they described as a well-concentrated stream, and returned with little to report. The 3 Group assessment was of a scattered attack at both aiming-points.

The Ruhrstahl steelworks at Witten, a large mining town tucked in a pocket of the Ruhr south-west of Dortmund and south-east of Bochum, was posted as the target for 140 Lancasters of 3 Group on the 12th, for which 115 Squadron made ready eighteen aircraft. They took off between 10.57 and 11.45 with S/L Mills the senior pilot on duty, and there were no early returns to deplete the Witchford effort. The bomber stream became divided on the run in to the target, with the Methwold element and some from 31 Base (Stradishall, Chedburgh and Wratting Common) about seven miles ahead of the main stream. The bulk of the fighter escort remained with the rear section, but the fighter leader had the foresight to send one squadron ahead to cover the lead group, which was fortuitous, as the Luftwaffe was waiting for them over the Ruhr, having chosen this day to mount its largest effort since daylight bombing operations began in June. A strong force of BF109s managed to break up the forward section of bombers, shooting down, among others, four 195 Squadron Lancasters, and this led to a scattered start to the attack. However, on observing the events ahead, the main section tightened its formation, which helped to create very concentrated bombing, and forty of the forty-six G-H leaders were able to use their equipment effectively. The 115 Squadron element attacked from between 20,000 and 21,500 feet on G-H over ten-tenths cloud, but an orange explosion was seen by a number of crews through a gap in the cloud, and this was followed by brown smoke. F/O Durham and crew returned without the trailing edge of the port main-plane after it was torn off in a collision with a 75(NZ) Squadron Lancaster over the target. Eight Lancasters failed to return from this raid, which missed the steelworks, but destroyed 126 houses and five industrial premises and killed around four hundred people.

A fighter escort was to accompany the 3 Group force of 138 Lancasters to the railway yards at Siegen on the 15th, for which twenty-one 115 Squadron participants took off between 11.08 and 11.37, but bad weather prevented the fighters from taking off, and the bombers were recalled. Of many bombs wasted by being jettisoned into the sea were twenty-one cookies. The operation was rescheduled for the following day, when a force of 108 Lancasters of 3 Group included twenty-one from Witchford, the latter taking off between 11.12 and 11.27 with F/Ls Dagnon, Jenkins, Keddilty and Russell the senior pilots on duty. They climbed into ice-bearing cloud that stretched from base to 06.00E at 20,000 feet, and this persuaded sixteen crews to turn back, three of them from 115 Squadron. Capt Martin RSAAF lost sight of the formation and circled at 6,500 feet, where he spotted two other Lancasters, and climbed to 8,000 feet while setting course for Beachy Head. After climbing again to 20,000 feet and seeing no other aircraft, he descended to 8,000 feet into rain and ice, at which point his a.s.i froze and he abandoned the sortie. F/O Hill also lost sight of his colleagues, and headed for Waterbeach to latch on to aircraft from there. He found three, but lost them again in cloud, so climbed to 18,000 feet and set course for the Channel, only to find himself ten minutes behind schedule when halfway across and turned back. F/Sgt Noble managed to get a Gee-fix on his G-H leader, but lost him when he turned sharply in cloud, and decided to turn back from the French coast when alone and still in cloud at 11,000 feet. The others pressed on to the fighter escort rendezvous point, where the cloud began to break up, and it was discovered that the leaders were fifteen minutes ahead of schedule. While they orbited to lose time, the others were able to form up into an orderly stream, which reached the target over nine-tenths cloud to carry out their attack. The 115 Squadron element bombed from between 17,800 and 19,000 feet, but the cloud prevented an assessment, although a number of crews observed an orange explosion followed by brown smoke. Post-raid reconnaissance revealed that only a few bombs had hit the railway yards, and the main weight of the attack had fallen on the town and nearby Weidenau. Many public buildings and houses were destroyed in a town never before singled out for attack, and 348 people lost their lives on the ground. Just one Lancaster was lost from the operation, and that was LL944 of 115 Squadron, which was shot down by a fighter, and crashed a dozen miles east of Bonn, killing F/O Robertson and three of his crew, while three others survived to be captured. As events were to prove, this was the squadron's final casualty of the year, and from now until the end of the war, losses would average just one per month.

The German break-out in the Ardennes, which became known as the Battle of the Bulge, began on this day, and, on the 19th, 3 Group was given the task of bombing the railway yards at Trier, the city on the banks of the Moselle River, lying within sight of the Luxembourg frontier and the closest urban centre to the enemy front. On this occasion, the town itself was the main victim, so a second assault was mounted in two waves on the 21st. Having sat out the earlier raid, 115 Squadron made ready twenty Lancasters as part of the overall 3 Group force of 113 aircraft. The numbers would have been greater had not the thirty-two Lancasters from the 31 Base airfields been prevented from taking-off by fog and low cloud. The 115 Squadron element departed Witchford either side of 12.30 with S/L Gorrie the senior pilot on duty, and managed to form up with the others into a concentrated stream. However, as they approached the target over ten-tenths cloud, vapour trails became so thick that the aircraft ahead were obscured. It had been planned to carry out a visual attack with a Master Bomber and Deputy, but the low cloud completely hid the ground and a code word was transmitted by the Master Bomber to switch to G-H. The majority of Witchford crews complied from between 17,000 and 19,000 feet, but four failed

Lancaster HK687 A4-D 115 Sqn, C Flt, with crew

to find a G-H leader and held on to their bombs. F/O Mason lost his port-inner engine to an oil leak while outbound, but continued on to complete his sortie and return safely. A column of smoke was observed to be rising from the town, but no assessment could be made, and by the time that a local report spoke of heavy casualties from this operation, another had taken place.

The third and final raid on this city was to be mounted on the 23rd, for which a 3 Group force of 153 Lancasters was made ready. 115 Squadron contributed twenty-one aircraft, which took off between 11.30 and 11.49 with S/L Clarke the senior pilot on duty. The intention was again to bomb visually on TIs dropped by G-H under the control of a Master Bomber, S/L Scott of 90 Squadron, and, this time, the conditions proved to be ideal with clear skies and good visibility. One TI was off target, a situation which the Master Bomber dealt with skilfully, and the attack fell squarely into the target area, which was soon covered by smoke and dust. The flak over the front line was considerable, predicted and accurate, but was less troublesome over the target as the 115 Squadron crews delivered their loads from between 16,000 and 20,000 feet. It was impossible to make an assessment of the results, but a local report was clear that it was the city's worst experience of the war. On the afternoon of Christmas Eve, the Group sent a hundred Lancasters to attack Hangelar airfield near Bonn, all but one of the crews returning home to spend the final wartime Christmas in relative peace. 115 Squadron had been told to prepare twenty-one Lancasters, but the requirement was cancelled and Witchford's Christmas started a little earlier than some.

On Boxing Day, crews from all of the Groups were roused into action to provide tactical support for the ground forces resisting the enemy push near St Vith. 115 Squadron was not called into action until the following day, when elements of 1, 3, 5 and 8 Groups made up a force of two hundred Lancasters and eleven Mosquitos to attack the railway yards at Rheydt. 115 Squadron had been ordered to provide twenty-three Lancasters, but, when take-off time arrived at 12.47, only seven were fit for action because of severe icing. They were all airborne by 13.05 with S/L Clarke the senior pilot on duty, and all made

270

it to the target where they bombed in clear conditions either visually or on TIs from between 18,000 and 20,500 feet. The main weight of bombs was observed to fall in the southern end of the marshalling yards, although some overshot and landed in the town to the east. The target area was covered by a mass of fires emitting brown and grey smoke, and returning crews were confident that they had fulfilled their brief. The single missing aircraft was from 75(NZ) Squadron, and was seen to spin down after being hit by friendly bombs.

The Group ended the year with operations against railway yards, beginning with those at Gremberg on the eastern side of Cologne on the 28th. 167 Lancasters were made ready for the G-H attack, including twenty-one at Witchford, and they took off between 12.07 and 12.44 with S/Ls Clarke and Mills the senior pilots on duty. All reached the target to encounter ten-tenths cloud, and delivered their bombs by G-H from between 19,000 and 21,500 feet before returning safely home. It was not possible to provide an assessment, but smoke was seen to be rising through the cloud-tops as the bombers turned away, and some crews reported seeing the glow of TIs in the yards and explosions. On the following day orders came through for attacks on two railway yards at Koblenz, one of the main centres serving the Ardennes battle front. The Mosel yards south of the river were handed to a 4 Group main force of Halifaxes with Pathfinder support, while the Lützel yards in the north were to be the target for a 3 Group G-H force of eighty-five Lancasters, of which twenty were to be provided by 115 Squadron. They took off between 11.46 and 12.32 with W/C Shaw and S/L Mills the senior pilots on duty, and all reached the target to find clear conditions and moderate to intense heavy flak. The 3 Group force had been timed to carry out its attack from between H+8 and H+12, hard on the heels of the 4 Group raid to the south, which was planned to finish at H+8. In the event, the tail end of the 4 Group bomber stream became entangled with the spearhead of 3 Group, and this, together with the accurate flak, caused some difficulties, which were compounded by a weak G-H tracking pulse and a less-concentrated stream than of late. Fires were already burning fiercely further south as the 3 Group attack began, but only fifteen of an intended thirty-two crews bombed on G-H, while the others did so either visually or on G-H Flares. The Witchford gang delivered their bombs from between 18,500 and 20,000 feet, and a 12,000 pounder was observed to fall into the marshalling yards, while other bombs hit the town. Nine Lancasters returned to Witchford displaying battle damage courtesy of the flak, and one bomb-aimer sustained a leg wound.

A similar target at Vohwinkel, situated south-west of Wuppertal and north of Solingen, was posted on the 31st, and a G-H force of 155 aircraft made ready. 115 Squadron contributed twenty Lancasters, and they took off between 11.33 and 11.57 with S/Ls Clarke and Mills the senior pilots on duty. P/O Burbridge and crew were about ninety minutes out when the port-outer engine lost power and had to be shut down, and they returned to land at 15.08. The others pushed on to the target, where flak was again plentiful and accurate on the run-in over Düsseldorf and Leverkusen, but dwindled to almost nothing over the target. The formation was good until a stronger-than-forecast wind caused a scattering of the stream towards the south, but some of the bombing, which took place through broken cloud from between 19,000 and 21,000 feet, found the mark, and bursts were observed in the marshalling yards, where fires were started. However, perhaps the main weight of the raid fell to the south-west of the target and in Solingen, where eighty-three people lost their lives. Three 115 Squadron Lancasters sustained flak damage, and two others belonging to 218 Squadron failed to return after falling victim to friendly bombs. During the course of the month the squadron carried out fourteen operations, thirteen by day and one by night, and dispatched 248 sorties for the loss of a single Lancaster and crew.

The rebirth of 3 Group was now complete after its virtual removal from the front line a year earlier, and, particularly from the start of the Transportation Plan onwards, it had regained its rightful place at the forefront of Bomber Command operations. With G-H in its hands, it had become a vital component in the destruction of Germany's communications system and oil industry, and with the rest of the Command, faced the coming year with a spirit of confidence and an expectation of victory.

Above: Lancaster NG205 KO-K and L – R: Jackie Kingham (M.U.G.), Bill Whitling (W/Op), Reg Whiting (F.Eng.), F/L Gordon Gibson RAAF (Pilot), Ray Wilkins (Nav.), Bob Measom (Rear Gunner) F/L. Morgan RAAF (B/A) (Courtesy of Bob Measom). Below: Flak and cannon damage sustained by NG205, flown by F/L Gordon Gibson during final approach of daylight attack on Duisburg 8th December 1944. Mid upper turret out of action and gunner wounded. The fighter was beaten off by fire from the manually operated rear turret.

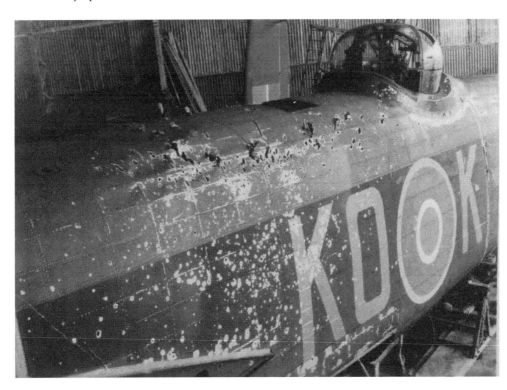

January 1945

Much remained to be done, before the proud and tenacious enemy finally laid down his arms, and many Bomber Command squadrons would continue to sustain heavy casualties right up to the end. 115 Squadron, in contrast, would negotiate the last four months of the bombing war relatively easily, although the year began with a tragic loss to remove any trend towards complacency. The incident arose out of the Luftwaffe's ill-conceived, and ultimately ill-fated Operation Bodenplatte (Baseplate), which was intended to destroy large numbers of Allied aircraft on the ground at the recently liberated airfields in France, Holland and Belgium. Almost the whole day fighter strength was committed at first light on New Year's Day to low-level strafing and bombing attacks, and those that survived the airfield flak defences, were forced to run the gauntlet of Allied fighters to get home. Around 250 aircraft were sacrificed in this way, in return for some degree of success, which the Allies could make good, literally, within hours from their enormous stockpiles. Not so the Luftwaffe, which lost somewhere in the region of 150 pilots killed, wounded or captured, and it was a setback from which it would never fully recover. Inevitably, the attacks created itchy fingers among the Allied flak crews, and any aircraft coming within range over the ensuing twenty-four hours were likely to receive a hot reception, irrespective of their nationality.

Bomber Command operations had been going on throughout New Year's Day by the time that a force of 146 Lancasters of 3 Group took off in the late afternoon to return to the railway yards at Vohwinkel. The Witchford element of fifteen was airborne between 16.03 and 16.29 with S/L Mills the senior pilot on duty, and headed out via the southerly route to the Ruhr across Belgium. They were subjected to Allied flak over the front, while the German batteries opened up with a heavy, predicted barrage between Cologne and Bonn, west of Siegen and on the run-in to the target, where fifteen searchlights were operating. The weather conditions were clear and ground detail could be easily identified in the light of the G-H flares as the TIs went down punctually

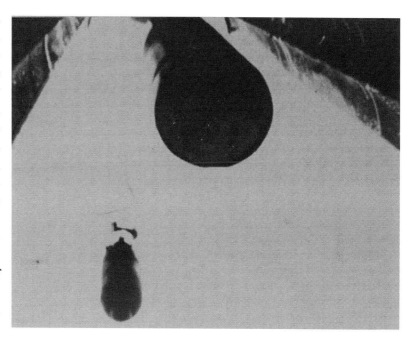

'Bombs Away'

and accurately, and a stronger-than-forecast wind was the only challenge. All 115 Squadron participants were present in the reasonably concentrated G-H formation as bombing took place from between 19,400 and 21,000 feet, and smoke, fire, bomb bursts and a large, yellow explosion were evidence of the accuracy of the assault. Single-engine enemy fighters were much in evidence, and a ME262 jet was also seen, but it was American flak over Namur in Belgium that accounted for the 115 Squadron casualty. NG332 plunged to earth to crash at 20.10 onto farmland, before S/L Mills and the other seven occupants could take to their parachutes. This truly Commonwealth crew, which was made up of members of the RAF, RNZAF, RAAF and RCAF, would be sorely missed back at Witchford.

Staff of the Technical Wing heralf the New Year: L – R: W/C Shaw, Avro Rep, Mrs. Wright, S/L Wright CTO, Mrs Humphries, F/O Penney, F/O Judson, F/L. W Jones, G/C Reynolds, Sgt. Shepherd, Unknown.

Some of the heaviest raids of the war on Germany's cities would take place over the next three months, and the first of these was directed at Nuremberg on the night of the 2/3rd. 3 Group contributed ninety-five Lancasters to the overall force of 514 of the type drawn from 1, 3, 6 and 8 Groups, and the dozen 115 Squadron participants took off either side of 15.30 with no pilots on duty above flying officer rank. Weather conditions were again favourable as the force made its way across France to the target, and it was as F/O Hallam and crew were closing on the German frontier south-east of Nancy that they discovered a complete failure of the bomb-release circuitry, and were forced to abandon their sortie. The Pathfinder element exploited the clear visibility to produced accurate and concentrated marking of the city centre, and the Witchford crews bombed on red and green TIs from between 16,000 and 18,000 feet at around 19.30. On return they reported observing many explosions, and fires that could be seen from almost two hundred miles into the return flight, and also noted passing close to a burning Ludwigshafen, whose two I.G Farben chemicals factories had been attacked by elements of 4, 6 and 8 Group. Post-raid analysis confirmed that the centre of Nuremberg, particularly the eastern half, had been destroyed, and that the castle, council house and most of the churches had been raized to the ground along with two thousand preserved medieval houses. More than four and a half thousand apartment blocks were also destroyed in north-eastern and southern districts, and important industrial areas had sustained severe damage.

3 Group would be the only one to be called into action on the 3rd, and their targets were benzol plants at Castrop-Rauxel and Dortmund in the Ruhr, for which forty-nine and fifty Lancasters respectively were made ready. The former was carried out first and was successful, before the 115 Squadron element of twelve departed Witchford between 12.38 and 13.00 with S/L Clarke the senior pilot on duty. They were bound for the Huckarde district in the northwest of Dortmund to hit the Hansa Plant, which was situated just a few miles to the south-east of the Castrop-Rauxel target. They were flying into the sun, which

made it difficult to create a compact formation, and the stream was somewhat elongated as they approached the target to find ten-tenths cloud with tops at 10,000 to 12,000 feet and clear skies above. These were ideal conditions for a G-H attack, which was carried out from 20,000 feet in the face, initially, of slight flak, which became more intense as the attack developed. A 622 Squadron Lancaster was seen to explode over the target, and this would be the only casualty of the operation. The cloud prevented an assessment of the raid, but smoke was seen to be rising through the cloud-tops as the force withdrew.

Alternating between oil and railway objectives when operating alone, 3 Group was ordered on the 5th to send 160 Lancasters to bomb the area of Ludwigshafen containing its marshalling yards. 115 Squadron made ready twenty-one Lancasters, which took off between 11.13 and 11.45 with W/C Shaw the senior pilot on duty, supported by S/L Gorrie with his all-officer crew. They all reached the target area to find clear skies, which provided the flak batteries with an unobstructed view of their quarry, and prompted them to fill the sky with hot, bursting metal. The G-H tracking pulse proved to be weak, and this combined with the flak to produce a scattered formation and attack. The Witchford element bombed from between 14,100 and 20,300 feet, and all returned to report observing explosions, fires and smoke. The ground crews were left with the task of patching up the thirteen Lancasters bringing home flak damage. Post-raid reconnaissance revealed that a proportion of the bombing had fallen into Ludwigshafen's northern suburbs and outlying communities, where more than five hundred houses had been destroyed or seriously damaged, along with eighty-seven industrial buildings.

Evidence that the enemy defences were by no means spent came with the loss of thirty-one Halifaxes and Lancasters while raiding Hannover on the evening of the 5th. The main operation on the 6th was to be conducted by elements of 1, 4, 6 and 8 Groups against Hanau in southern Germany, while 1 and 3 Groups joined forces to attack the area within the Ruhr city of Neuss containing the marshalling yards. 115 Squadron contributed seventeen Lancasters to the 117 provided by 3 Group in the overall force of 147 aircraft, and they departed Witchford either side of 16.00 with S/L Clarke the senior pilot on duty. F/O Evans and crew turned back with a number of issues, leaving the others to arrive in the target area to find thin ten-tenths cloud obscurring the ground. However, the G-H-delivered TIs could be seen through it, allowing crews the choice of bombing either on these or on the skymarkers. The 115 Squadron crews dropped their loads of a cookie, ten 500 and six 250 pounders each from between 19,500 and 20,100 feet, before returning safely to report facing moderate heavy flak, a few searchlights, and a red glow of fires reflecting on the clouds. Post-raid reconnaissance confirmed that some of the bombing had fallen into the railway yards, but also into the city, where more than seventeen hundred houses, nineteen industrial and twenty public buildings had been destroyed or seriously damaged. It was a further demonstration of the enormous destructive power of what, by current standards, was only a modest force. The last major raid of the war on Munich was scheduled to take place twenty-four hours later, and would involve a force of 645 Lancasters drawn from 1, 3, 5, 6 and 8 Groups. 3 Group's contribution was to be ninety-six aircraft, of which eighteen would represent 115 Squadron, and they took off between 18.32 and 19.15 with W/C Shaw the senior pilot on duty. W/O Hills and crew turned back early on with a starboard-inner engine problem, leaving the others to press on to the target, where the Pathfinders arrived late, before delivering skymarkers over the cloud-covered city. Searchlights could be seen playing on the underside of the cloud, and a moderate amount of heavy, inaccurate flak was encountered, while white, red and yellow glows provided evidence of fires on the ground. The 115 Squadron crews were part of the second phase of the operation, and observed fires already burning as they bombed from between 18,000 and 21,000 feet. They returned to report thin smoke rising through 19,000 feet as they turned away, and the glow of fires remaining visible for 150 miles into the return journey. This final major raid on Munich produced severe damage in central and industrial districts, but no local reports emerged to confirm or deny.

After a rather hectic start to the month, the crews, no doubt, appreciated an opportunity to relax before the next onslaught, which began with a daylight G-H raid on the Uerdingen railway yards at Krefeld on the 11th. Eighteen 115 Squadron Lancasters were made ready as part of the 3 Group force of 152, and they took off between 11.33 and 11.57 with F/Ls Dowling, Keddilty, Olorenshaw, Robson and Stirling the senior pilots on duty. F/O Kerrins and crew returned early with a port-outer engine problem, but the remainder pressed on to the Ruhr to encounter ten-tenths cloud. A strong wind delayed their arrival slightly, but the formation was fairly compact as bombing took place from between 19,200 and 21,000 feet, and the general impression was that the main weight of the attack had fallen into the marshalling yards and town area. This was confirmed by a local report, which described the raid as a "Grossangriff" (large attack), the highest classification, that had decimated the eastern districts where the railway yards were situated.

A similar target at Saarbrücken was posted as the destination for 158 Lancasters of 3 Group on the 13th, for which 115 Squadron made ready twenty aircraft. They took off between 11.37 and 12.13 with S/L Clarke the senior pilot on duty, and all arrived in the target area as part of a solid and compact formation. The G-H blue-puff smoke markers stood out clearly against the snow-covered ground as the bombs went down from between 19,000 and 20,000 feet to be followed by dense black and brown smoke and fires. F/L Keddilty's rear turret became unserviceable after being flooded by oil, but this was the only incident involving a 115 Squadron aircraft, which were all diverted to land at Exeter. A number of crews reported observing a Lancaster with a feathered engine firing a red flare to attract a fighter escort, but it was apparently ignored. The raid was believed to be successful, with, perhaps, some overshooting, but a second raid by elements of 4, 6 and 8 Groups was sent there later that night, and this was followed up on the 14th by another 3 Group G-H raid, which did not involve 115 Squadron.

The only aircraft scheduled to operate by daylight on the 15th were 140 Lancasters of 3 Group, which were to be divided between two benzol-producing sites, one at Erkenschwick, near Recklinghausen, and the Robert Muser plant in the Langendreer district of Bochum. The 115 Squadron element of twenty-one Lancasters was assigned to the latter, and took off between 11.27 and 11.46 with S/L Gorrie the senior pilot on duty. They all arrived in the target area to find ten-tenths cloud with tops at 6,000 feet, and the green and blue smoke-puff markers could be seen from some distance. The consensus, according to the 3 Group ORB, was that the blue ones were more effective than the green, while the 115 Squadron ORB recorded mixed opinions ranging from the greens being very visible to invisible. Bombing took place on both from between 18,600 and 20,000 feet in the face of intense flak, which inflicted damage on five of the Witchford aircraft. The two attacks appeared to be effective, but it seems that there was no post-raid reconnaissance to confirm the outcome one way or the other.

The night of the 16/17th found 137 Lancasters of 3 Group being prepared to attack a synthetic oil refinery at Wanne-Eickel, a western suburb of Herne situated south of Recklinghausen and north of Bochum. 115 Squadron briefed twenty-one crews, all but one of which took off between 23.05 and 23.44 with S/L Clarke the senior pilot on duty. F/O O'Halloran would arrive home at the same time as the others, having not completed the sortie because of icing of the butterfly throttles, which prevented him climbing to bombing height, but cleared on the way home. It was a similar story of icing and an inability to climb that forced F/O Wilson and crew to abandon their sortie, and their return also coincided with that of the rest of the squadron. The bombing took place from between 18,300 and 20,200 feet over ten-tenths cloud on both sky and ground markers, but the TIs were all but obscured by the cloud, leaving the crews to aim for the skymarker flares or the glow of fires beneath the cloud. All but one Lancaster returned from an inconclusive operation, which did not benefit from post-raid reconnaissance.

On the 22nd, and after a few days break from operations, Duisburg was posted as the destination for 286 Lancasters of 1, 3 and 8 Groups, which were to target a benzol plant in the Bruckhausen district to the north of the city centre, and the Thyssen steelworks further to the east in what the 115 Squadron ORB records as being located in the Hamborn district. The 3 Group force of 130 Lancasters was assigned to the latter and included a contribution from 115 Squadron of eighteen, which departed Witchford between 16.55 and 17.13 with a whole host of pilots of flight lieutenant rank leading the way. All reached the target area, where Pathfinder Mosquitos carried out the marking in clear conditions and visibility so good that crews were able to identify ground detail. The 115 Squadron crews bombed from between 19,000 and 20,300 feet, but W/O Hulme suffered a complete failure of the bomb-release system, which forced him to jettison his load safe on the way home. The others reported flak co-operating with searchlights and fighters circling beacons, but the overriding impression was of large explosions, fires and thick, black smoke drifting across the target area. Post-raid reconnaissance revealed that both targets had been severely damaged, while a local report assumed that the steel works had been the intended target.

Following another lengthy break from operations, 3 Group made ready a force of 153 Lancasters on the 28th to target the Gremberg marshalling yards, situated on the East Bank of the Rhine south-east of Cologne city centre. 115 Squadron bombed up twenty-one aircraft, and launched them skywards between 10.16 and 10.45 with pilots of flight lieutenant rank again leading the way, although the newly-promoted Major Martin RSAAF probably outranked them all. The flight out was conducted through condensation trails that provided challenging conditions in which to form up and maintain close contact, but all reached the target to find clear conditions which afforded a visual identification of the aiming-point. F/L Sherwood suffered a complete hang-up over the target, but the others released their loads from between 18,100 and 20,000 feet in the face of quite intense and accurate flak, which seemed to be fitted with proximity fuses. Seven of the squadron's Lancasters were hit, and F/L Grant's bomb-aimer sustained a neck wound. Bombing was described by some as a little scattered, but many bomb bursts and explosions were observed within the railway yards, and the operation was deemed to be successful.

The Uerdingen yards at Krefeld were to provide the final challenge of the month for 115 Squadron, which made ready twenty-one Lancasters on the 29th as part of a 3 Group G-H force of 148. The Witchford element took off between 10.15 and 10.40 with W/C Shaw the senior pilot on duty supported by S/Ls Gorrie and Morgan, and all reached the target area, this time in less demanding conditions. The forming-up process went well at first, and the Master Windfinder System, being employed for the first time, also seemed to be successful. During the run-in the third wave cut across the second wave, and some 115 Squadron crews were forced to descend a little. There was also a complaint on return that the 75(NZ) Squadron aircraft had not observed a line-astern approach, which made it impossible to form up on them. The target was covered by eight to ten-tenths cloud, through which the 115 Squadron crews bombed from between 18,000 and 19,000 feet, and a large mushroom of white smoke was seen to rise through the cloud-tops. No aircraft were lost, but a number of 115 Squadron Lancasters sustained damage from falling shrapnel. During the course of the month the squadron undertook thirteen operations, and dispatched 234 sorties for the loss of a single Lancaster and crew.

February 1945

3 Group was immediately into action on the first day of the new month, preparing a force of 160 Lancasters to attack the marshalling yards at Mönchengladbach, which had become a frontier town. At Witchford twenty-one Lancasters were loaded with a cookie each and a selection of high-explosives and/or incendiaries, and were sent off the end of the runway between 13.03 and 13.34 with S/L Gorrie the senior pilot on duty. All reached the target area, where the approach was made over eight to ten-tenths cloud, but the rear half of the formation unaccountably turned between two and six miles to

L-R: K H Barnard (Nav), T E Masefield (Flt.Eng), A H Gibbons (Pilot), (M/UG) A E Lester (M/UG), C Mayne (W.Op/AG)
J Murphy (RG), R Strelchuk (BA)

starboard, while the front half carried straight on. The 115 Squadron element remained compact and was guided to the target by G-H leaders and a Gee-fix, and a few blue-puff smoke markers could be seen ahead about five minutes before the release-point. Bombing took place from between 18,200 and 20,700 feet, but cloud largely concealed the points of impact, although some crews did observe some incendiaries in fields and others in a built-up area. One large explosion was witnessed along with fires, and another concentration of bomb-bursts reflecting in the cloud could not be placed, but black smoke was rising through the cloud-tops by the end of the raid to suggest that some success had been gained.

Until the night of the 2/3rd, the spa city of Wiesbaden, situated some twenty miles to the west of Frankfurt, had experienced numerous small-scale attacks from the air, but never a major Bomber Command attack. A heavy force of 495 Lancasters of 1, 3, 6 and 8 Groups was made ready to rectify this, 3 Group providing 158 aircraft including twenty-one from Witchford, the latter taking off between 20.43 and 21.04 with S/L Clarke the senior pilot on duty. It would not be a good night for the group, and matters began to go awry early on with some aircraft becoming bogged down while taxiing and preventing others from taking off. Two 90 Squadron Lancasters collided over Suffolk while outbound, and the commanding officer was killed with his crew, and the newly-appointed 149 Squadron commanding officer would fail to return. The 115 Squadron element got away without incident, but F/L Noble and crew turned back after an hour because of a burst hydraulic pipe. The others reached the target area to find ten-tenths cloud with tops at 16,000 feet, expecting to bomb on Pathfinder ground-marking. However, the density of the cloud obscured the TIs, and the 3 Group crews bombed on G-H, H2S or DR, the 115 Squadron element doing so from between 19,000 and 20,500 feet. Returning crews described a red, yellow and white glow under the clouds and bright, red explosions followed by black smoke, but also witnessed what they described as "scarecrows", or flak shells designed to mimic a bomber being blown to pieces. Of course, these did not exist, and it was, in fact, the end of a 428 Squadron Lancaster that F/L Strange and crew had seen at 23.47. Flak was described as slight, but the vapour trails of enemy fighters criss-crossed the night sky, and it is perhaps surprising that just seven aircraft were lost to enemy action. The consensus was of a widely-spread raid that had fallen mostly into the target city, and this was confirmed by a local report, which recorded that around a thousand buildings, mostly houses, had been destroyed or seriously damaged, and that a thousand people had lost their lives.

Orders were received on the 3rd for 3 Group to prepare for an attack on the Hansa benzol plant in the Huckarde district of Dortmund that night, and detailed a force of 149 Lancasters accordingly, including twenty-four provided by 115 Squadron. The Witchford element took off either side of 16.30 with S/Ls Clarke and Gorrie the senior pilots on duty, but technical problems soon intervened to reduce the numbers available to hit the target. F/O Stone's port-outer engine failed just two minutes after take-off, and P/O Knapp had a similar experience involving his starboard-outer at the same time, while S/L Gorrie abandoned his sortie after two hours, when his a.s.i iced up in an already sluggish-performing PA181. The others pressed on to the target area under clear skies, but haze presented identification problems, and, for the first time in months, searchlights were very active and coned a number of aircraft. The 3 Group ORB commented on flak following the bombers on the run-in, but stopping short of the release-point, suggesting that, perhaps, the batteries were short of ammunition and were ordered to use their shells sparingly. The main problem on this night, however, was a simultaneous raid by elements of 1 and 8 Groups on the Prosper benzol plant at Bottrop, some twenty miles to the west of Dortmund. This raid was seen to be going well, and the lack of flak and markers over Dortmund persuaded some crews that the few markers they could see ahead were dummies. Five of the 115 Squadron crews joined in the attack at Bottrop, leaving the others to continue on to Dortmund, where the raid developed slowly, but was thought to be concentrated. The Witchford crews bombed from between 17,500 and 20,000 feet after running the gauntlet of searchlights, flak and night fighters, and two Lancasters returned with damage. Post-raid reconnaissance suggested that the main weight of the attack had fallen to the north and north-west of the Hansa plant.

L-R: K H Barnard (Nav), A H Gibbons (Pilot), A E Lester (M/UG), C Mayne (W.Op/AG), R Strelchuk (BA), T E Masefield (Flt.Eng), J Murphy (RG),

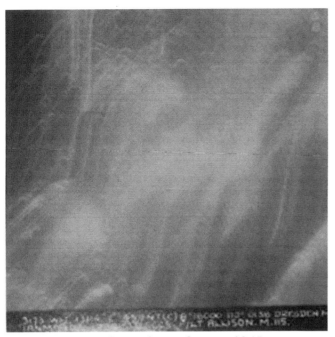

Dresden 13/14 February 1945

This short-lived, generally ineffective phase of operations for 3 Group would culminate in an attack on the Hohenbudberg railway yards at Krefeld carried out in the early morning of the 9th. 151 Lancasters had been made ready, of which twenty-one represented 115 Squadron. They departed Witchford between 03.21 and 04.05 with S/L Gorrie the senior pilot on duty and no fewer than thirteen pilots of flight lieutenant rank. One of these, F/L Snyder, was some twenty miles west of Abbeville, when the starboard-inner engine began to surge and cut and create a vibration that could not be rectified, forcing him to turn back. The others pushed on in unfavourable weather conditions to reach the target, where the ground was visible and red TIs could be seen. A simultaneous attack by Halifaxes on the oil plant at Wanne-Eickel, some twenty-five miles to the north-east of Krefeld, could also be observed, and S/L Gorrie, finding no marking at his briefed target, decided to join in there, delivering his load from 18,500 feet onto red TIs. Perhaps, as he was returning, he observed TIs going down on Hohenbudberg at 06.22, and this was where the rest of the squadron bombed on red TIs and skymarkers from between 18,000 and 20,000 feet, during which F/L Pickering and crew noted a large reddish explosion followed by black smoke at 06.25. F/O Blackwood and crew thought the skymarkers to be about seven miles to the east of the target, but the general impression was of a reasonably concentrated attack. Cloud had built for the homeward flight, with tops at 23,000 feet, but all from Witchford made it safely home, where they would learn that the operation had failed to hit the railway yards.

A few nights of rest preceded the first of the Churchill-inspired series of operations against Germany's eastern cities under Operation Thunderclap. The historic, beautiful and culturally significant city of Dresden was selected to receive the first blow, which was to be delivered on the night of the 13/14th by an all-Lancaster heavy force in a two-phase operation. The plan called for 5 Group to open the proceedings with 244 aircraft, and for 529 aircraft from 1, 3, 6 and 8 Groups to follow up three hours later. 3 Group assembled a force of 160 Lancasters, of which twenty-one were provided by 115 Squadron. They took off between 21.41 and 22.12 with S/L Clarke the senior pilot on duty, and all reached the target area, to which the deep, red fires from the 5 Group attack drew them on from eighty-five miles away. The thin layers of cloud that had caused some difficulties for the first phase had now drifted away, leaving a naked and ill-defended target at the mercy of the second-phase force. F/L Roberts and crew ran into cloud with tops at 20,500 feet on e.t.a., and orbited without seeing the target, upon which the bombs were jettisoned from 20,000 feet. It was then that they saw Dresden on fire some ten to fifteen miles away on the port beam. F/O Stone and crew located what they believed was Leipzig, and flew on without finding Dresden, and ultimately bombed on the estimated position of Chemnitz from 20,000 feet. The remainder delivered their loads from between 18,000 and 20,400 feet, contributing to the 1,800 tons of bombs following on the heels of the eight hundred tons dropped by 5 Group. The entire built-up area appeared to be ablaze, with smoke rising to 15,000 feet, and the glow from the burning city remained visible for two hundred miles into the return journey. What was not understood by the bomber crews was that a firestorm had erupted of similar proportions to that at Hamburg in July 1943, and this would result in massive casualties. 115 Squadron had enjoyed almost six weeks of loss-free operations since the first night of the year, but PB686 did not return home on this night with the others. It was quickly established, however, that F/O Dick and all but one of his crew had survived, after being forced to abandon their aircraft through an engine fire when over France on the way home. They were soon back in the bosum of the squadron, sadly, without their rear gunner, who had failed to survive.

A few hours after the Bomber Command attack, 311 American B17s delivered a further 771 tons of bombs, aiming ostensibly for the railway yards, and sent some of the escort fighters down to strafe traffic on the roads around the city to increase the level of chaos. The population of Dresden had been swolen by a massive influx of refugees from the eastern front, and it was this that initially led to an inflated death toll of up to 250,000 people. A figure of 25,000 fatalities has since been settled upon, which made this the second highest death toll after Hamburg resulting from a Bomber Command operation.

The lack of a coherent defence from the city, its doubtful strategic significance and cultural history, and the scale of destruction all led to an hysterical reaction, and, with his eyes set firmly on the coming peace and the inevitable general election, Churchill, a former champion of area bombing, now chose to distance himself from Bomber Command, and effectively accused Harris of bombing for the sake of creating terror. It should be understood, that Harris had no interest in Dresden, preferring instead to return to Berlin, but he was constantly hounded by Chief-of-the-Air-Staff Sir Charles Portal on Churchill's urgings to attack Dresden to help the Russian advance, and, ultimately, was ordered by him to carry out the raid. It should also be clear, that before deciding to attack the city, the Americans had identified some fifty factories contributing to the war effort. The fact that a firestorm developed was an accident of nature, a meteorological event, which could not be predicted and arose out of a conspiracy of conditions on the ground and the concentration of the bombing. The casualty figure does not come close to the 40,000 deaths in one night at Hamburg, which, curiously, did not generate the same level of outrage, and the American raid is barely mentioned. It was decided in Germany and by the "hindsight" liberal brigade in this country that Harris was responsible, and he would be unjustly vilified for the rest of his life, would be the only commander in the field not to be honoured after the war, his men would be denied a campaign medal until being insulted by the award of a clasp after most of them had passed away, and they would have to wait seventy years before a memorial to them was erected in London.

Operation Thunderclap moved on to Chemnitz on the following night, for another two-phase raid, in which the 5 Group Lancasters would be replaced by 4 Group Halifaxes in an overall force of 717 aircraft. 3 Group made ready 151 Lancasters, which included a contribution from 115 Squadron of twenty-one. They took off between 20.18 and 21.10, led by a whole host of pilots of flight lieutenant rank, and made their way into eastern Germany under clear skies until about fifty miles from the target, where the cloud began to build to eight to ten-tenths between 14,000 and 16,000 feet. The 115 Squadron crews could see the target burning from 120 miles away after the attack by the first wave, and then bombed either on skymarkers or the glow from beneath the clouds from between 17,500 and 21,000 feet. The cloud prevented an assessment of results, but the target was seen to be well-alight, with many explosions and bomb bursts, with, perhaps, a scattering to the south-east, where woods were thought to be on fire. For the second night running, 115 Squadron registered a missing aircraft, but this time there was no good news concerning the crew. LM725 came down in north-eastern France, 5 miles west-south-west of Vanciennes, and F/O Slogrove died with the other occupants.

On the 16th, a hundred Lancasters of 3 Group undertook the first of a series of operations against the town of Wesel, situated on the Rhine close to the advancing Allied ground forces. In two main offensives five weeks apart, the unfortunate town would be all but levelled in an attempt to render it untenable for the enemy troops gathered there. The purpose of this operation was to block the advancement of enemy reinforcements intending to oppose the Canadian First Army attack between the Maas and the Rhine. 115 Squadron made ready twenty-one Lancasters and unleashed them between 12.21 and 13.04 with W/C Shaw the senior pilot on duty. The weather conditions provided good visibility, which allowed for a compact formation, and concentrated skymarking all-but ensured a destructive raid. Bombing took place on G-H or visually from between 17,800 and 20,000 feet, and the town was soon ablaze with many fires, much dust and smoke, and an explosion was observed near the marshalling yards with another close to the river. A span of one of the road bridges was seen to be down before smoke drifted across the target area to obscure it. W/C Shaw returned to report a hang-up over the target, which caused him to orbit three times and released the cookie manually, before dumping the others in the jettison area. This first attack was accurate and loss-free, inflicting heavy damage on the town and railway, and probably causing heavy casualties before a general evacuation took place.

Almost three hundred aircraft of 4, 6, and 8 Groups were thwarted by cloud on the following day, and the Master Bomber abandoned the raid very early on. 3 Group was ordered to return on the 18th, for which 160 Lancasters were made ready, twenty-one of them by 115 Squadron. They departed Witchford between 11.51 and 12.08 led by pilots of flight lieutenant rank, but F/L Snyder lost his starboard-inner engine three-quarters of the way down the runway, and managed to struggle into the air on three, before making it to the jettison area to get rid of the dead weight in his bomb bay. The others reached the target to find it obscured by ten-tenths cloud, but G-H worked satisfactorily, and smoke-puff markers provided a good reference. W/O Gibbins had lost an engine outbound, but carried on and bombed from 13,000 feet. The others carried out their attacks from between 18,000 and 19,500 feet, but were prevented by the cloud from observing the results. The assault on this unfortunate town continued on the 19th, when 168 Lancasters were prepared by 3 Group, twenty of them at Witchford, where take-off took place between 13.06 and 13.46 with Major Martin probably the senior pilot on duty. They all reached the target area to encounter seven-tenths cloud, through which some ground detail could be identified, and bombing was carried out on G-H from between 13,800 and 20,000 feet. A cluster of explosions was observed in the town, smoke was seen to be rising through the cloud-tops, and one aircraft was seen to explode in the air, although that was also reported as a scarecrow. The victim was the 90 Squadron Lancaster of the commanding officer, W/C Dunham, which spread itself far and wide over the target area and Xanten to the west. W/C Dunham had recently succeeded W/C Bannister after his death at the start of the month in a collision with the Lancaster being flown on this operation by W/C Dunham. Another report concerned condensation trails travelling vertically to 25,000 feet to the east of the target, and these were clearly created by ME163 Komet rocket-powered fighters.

The penultimate raid of the war on the much-bombed city of Dortmund was launched late on the 20th, and involved a heavy force of 514 Lancasters drawn from 1, 3, 6 and 8 Groups. 115 Squadron contributed ten Lancasters to the 3 Group force of 111, and they took off between 21.55 and 22.14 with pilots of flight lieutenant rank taking the lead. The weather in the target area was very much as forecast, with a thin layer of ten-tenths stratus at low level, through which the Pathfinder TIs could be seen. The Witchford crews bombed from between 19,700 and 21,000 feet in the face of searchlights and moderate to strong heavy flak, and black smoke was seen to be rising through the clouds as they turned away. Jet fighters and a JU88 were seen along with fighter flares and air-to-air tracer, and the whitish glow of fires could be seen up to a hundred miles into the return flight, with a dull red glow hanging over the city. Post raid reconnaissance revealed that the southern half of the city had sustained the level of destruction intended for it, but its greatest ordeal still lay in the future.

It was back to the Ruhr oil industry for 3 Group on the 22nd, with raids on two refineries, one at Oberhausen-Osterfeld involving eighty-two Lancasters from 33 Base and Methwold, and the other situated further to the east in the Buer district of Gelsenkirchen, which was to be attacked by eighty-five Lancasters from 31 and 32 Bases. 115 Squadron dispatched twenty aircraft between 12.03 and 12.40 with a bunch of flight lieutenant pilots leading the way, and, having circled to gain height, they set course for Osterfeld. F/O Kerrins's port-inner engine cut thirteen minutes after take-off, forcing him to jettison his cookie and twelve 500 pounders safe, although the cookie detonated on impact. The others pressed

Lancaster HK798 C Flight in February 1945. The aircraft features the extended bomb bay for an 8,000lb 'Blockbuster' bomb.

on to find clear skies over the Ruhr with haze, through which they could make out ground detail. The formation was compact until the target was reached, at which point moderate to heavy predicted flak broke it up, and this would lead to some scattered bombing in the early stages. They located the target by blue smoke-puffs and bombed on G-H from between 17,500 and 21,000 feet, scoring many hits as the attack developed, and one very large explosion was witnessed. By the end of the raid the target and surrounding built-up area were seen to be well-alight and emitting large amounts of smoke, while, over to the east, they could see evidence of a successful assault on the other target. They ran into flak again over the front line on the way home, but it was the Ruhr flak that had caused damage to fourteen of the Witchford Lancasters.

A G-H attack on the Alma Pluto benzol plant at Gelsenkirchen was planned for the following day, for which 133 Lancasters were made ready. 115 Squadron loaded one of its own with an 8,000 pounder and five 500 pounders, and eleven others with a cookie each plus either eleven or twelve 500 pounders, and sent them off either side of noon with flight lieutenant pilots again the most senior on duty. W/O Gibbins and crew abandoned their sortie because of engine problems, leaving the others to carry on to the target in challenging conditions of cloud with tops at between 16,000 and 24,000 feet. At times the horizontal visibility was reduced to two hundred yards, and this caused major problems for the forming-up process. Somehow, the crews managed to latch on to a G-H leader, and bombing took place from between 20,000 and 21,500 feet through ten-tenths cloud, which prevented an assessment of results. That night elements of 1. 6 and 8 Groups carried out the only area raid of the war on the city of Pforzheim, situated north-west of Stuttgart in southern Germany, and created a firestorm in which seventeen thousand people lost their lives.

The benzol-producing refinery at Kamen had been raided by elements of 4, 6 and 8 Groups on the 24th, when the main weight of bombs seemed to have fallen onto the town itself rather than the intended target. On the 25th, 3 Group prepared a force of 153 Lancasters to rectify the failure, and the 115 Squadron element of sixteen departed Witchford between 09.22 and 09.44 led by W/C Shaw. They all reached the target area, and were under fire from the ground from the moment they entered enemy territory until they vacated it. Despite this unwanted attention, the bombers were able to form into the ideal long and narrow stream, which was guided to the aiming-point by blue smoke-puff markers. Bombing took place on G-H through ten-tenths cloud from between 19,000 and 21,800 feet, as always in daylight, under the umbrella of a fighter escort. Cookie-bursts and explosions were reflected in the clouds, and, as they passed beyond the target, a break in the cloud allowed some crews to look back at the effects of the raid, but they were able to gain only an impression of fires and thick, greyish smoke. All from Witchford returned safely, but five Lancasters did so bearing the scars of battle courtesy of flak.

The Squadron made ready eighteen Lancasters on the 26th to support an attack by the group on the Hoesch benzol plant at Dortmund. They took off between 10.30 and 10.53 with S/L Gorrie the senior pilot on duty and ME803 KO-L undertaking its one-hundredth sortie in the hands, on this occasion, of F/L Roberts and crew. They all reached the target area to find ten-tenths cloud with tops at around 9,000 feet and a stronger-than-forecast wind, which caused some long gaps between squadrons, although the Witchford formation remained compact. They were guided to the aiming-point by red smoke-puffs, which the wind dispersed very quickly, and bombing took place from between 18,800 and 20,500 feet through the cloud. All returned safely home, five with slight flak damage, but no crews would be able to provide an assessment of the outcome. ME803 circled Witchford triumphantly amidst great enthusiasm on the ground, and it was declared a memorable day in the history of 115 Squadron and a great tribute to the work of the ground staff.

The Alma Pluto coking plant at Gelsenkirchen was posted as the target for 149 Lancasters of 3 Group on the 27th, for which 115 Squadron made ready twenty aircraft. Eighteen of them were loaded with a cookie and eleven or twelve 500 pounders, while the remaining two would carry an 8,000 pounder each and five 500 pounders. They took off between 11.06 and 11.55 with no pilots above flight lieutenant rank, and all reached the target area, where the cloud was ten-tenths with tops at between 7,000 and 10,000 feet. They were guided to the aiming-point by skymarkers, and bombed on G-H leaders from between 19,500 and 21,000 feet, although again without being able to observe the results. Flak was persistent and accurate, and nine Lancasters returned to Witchford with holes to be patched up by the ground crews.

The busy end to the month concluded with a return to the Ruhr on the 28th to attend to the Nordstern synthetic oil plant at Gelsenkirchen. A 3 Group force of 156 Lancasters included eighteen provided by 115 Squadron, which took off between 08.52 and 09.15 with W/C Shaw the senior pilot on duty. F/O Knapp and crew returned early with an unserviceable starboard-inner engine, leaving the others to continue on to the target over ten-tenths cloud. The stream formed up well, but there were long gaps between the squadrons by the time the bombing run began. The G-H tracking pulse from station 114 failed at 12.04, right in the middle of the timing for the attack between 12.00 and 12.09, fortunately though, as no crews reported a problem, it was believed that the bombing had begun early and was over before the problem arose. The green smoke-puff markers were reported to be concentrated, and the attack was carried out from between 17,500 and 19,500 feet through the cloud that obscured the results. However, thick, black smoke was seen to rise up through the clouds before spreading out to form a three-mile-wide mushroom. During the course of the month the squadron operated on sixteen occasions, and dispatched 305 sorties for the loss of two Lancasters, one crew and a rear gunner.

March 1945

The 1st of March brought the final heavy raid of the war on Mannheim, while 151 Lancasters of 3 Group were sent to Kamen in the Ruhr for another swipe at the oil refinery. 115 Squadron supported the operation with seventeen aircraft, which took off between 11.45 and 12.03 with no senior pilots on duty. F/L Hill's sortie was over almost before it began after black smoke was seen to issue from his port-inner engine on take-off. The others pressed on, and formed a compact stream, but, it seems, that the lead squadron failed to pick up the G-H tracking pulse and overshot the final turning point ahead of the target, before orbiting and then converging on the main stream from a variety of angles. F/L Stephens complained that 149 Squadron came over the starboard flank of the Witchford element and remained there, rather than pulling ahead, and squeezed them uncomfortably into what became a congested stream. Ten-tenths cloud obscured the ground, but the blue smoke-puff markers were well concentrated, and bombing took place on the G-H leaders from between 18,000 and 19,700 feet. No results were observed, and the tone of the 3 Group ORB suggested a scattered and disappointing operation.

On the 2nd, the already tormented city of Cologne was the subject of briefings across the Command, as 858 aircraft were prepared to carry out the very last raid upon it of the war. It was to be a two-phase operation involving 703 aircraft for the main attack in the morning, and this would be followed in the afternoon by 155 Lancasters of 3 Group. The first wave inflicted massive damage in clear conditions, and they were well on their way home when the 115 Squadron element of nineteen began taking off at 12.02, and all were safely in the air by 13.07. The operation seemed to be proceeding according to plan as the target drew near, but then the G-H releasing station suffered a technical failure, and the squadrons were forced to orbit many times awaiting instructions. The city was covered by ten-tenths cloud, but clear skies to the east prompted an instruction to bomb the eastern side of the Rhine visually, and, it seems, that only 115 Squadron picked up the message. Three of its crews returned with the rest of the force without bombing, but the remainder found built-up areas beneath them and attacked them from

Air and ground Crew together after this aircraft had just landed from a daylight raid on Dortmund on 12th March 1945.

between 16,000 and 19,500 feet. Bombing photographs showed that the towns receiving the loads were located south-east of Cologne between Bonn and Koblenz, among them Remagen, Linz, Bad Hönningen and Anderbach. Just four days hence, the once proud Rhineland Capital would be captured by American forces.

3 Group continued its assault on the enemy's communications system with an attack on the extensive marshalling yards at Wanne-Eickel/Herne on the 4th, for which 115 Squadron was not called into action. The group detailed a force of 170 Lancasters on the 5th to target the Consolidation benzol plant in the Schalke district of Gelsenkirchen, and, this time, 115 Squadron made ready twenty aircraft, which took off between 10.34 and 10.55 with Major Martin probably the most senior pilot on duty. All reached the target area to find seven to ten-tenths cloud with tops at 8,000 feet, but a thin layer of cirrus at the bombing height of 18,000 to 21,000 feet impaired visibility. The G-H run was good, and a cluster of smoke-puffs indicated that the bombing, in the face of slight but accurate moderate flak, should be concentrated. The Witchford crews bombed with their G-H leaders from between 18,800 to 20,000 feet, but could not determine the fall of their cookie and fifteen 500 pounders each. Having escaped serious damage on the night after Dresden, Chemnitz was targeted again on the night of the 5/6th by a Thunderclap force of 760 aircraft. 3 Group was not involved as this eastern city succumbed to a concentrated raid, in which the central and southern districts were consumed by fire.

The Wintershall oil refinery at Salzbergen was posted as the target on the morning of the 6th, for which 3 Group put together a force of 119 Lancasters, sixteen of them provided by 115 Squadron. They took off between 08.28 and 08.46 with pilots of flight lieutenant rank leading the way, and all reached the target area just across the Dutch frontier and about twenty-five miles west of Osnabrück. The weather in the target area, of ten-tenths cloud with tops at between 9,000 and 12,000 feet, was ideal for a G-H attack, and the blue smoke-puff markers were clearly visible as the Witchford element bombed with their G-H leaders from between 18,000 and 19,200 feet. The results could not be observed, but a black patch on the cloud and a column of grey smoke rising through 10,000 feet was evidence of a successful operation.

That evening the campaign against Wesel was renewed in an attempt to destroy the bridges over the Rhine, which were the only ones intact north of Cologne, and providing an escape route for enemy ground forces retreating to the East Bank to establish resistance. 3 Group made ready eighty-seven Lancasters in two separate forces of thirty-eight and forty-nine, which would take off eight hours apart to follow up an attack by fifty-one Mosquitos of 8 Group. 115 Squadron dispatched five Lancasters between 18.17 and 18.27 with F/Ls Allison, Stephens and Stirling the senior pilots on duty, and all reached the target area to find that a thin layer of ten-tenths cloud with tops at 16,000 feet was obscuring ground detail. Bombing was carried out on G-H leaders from 18,000 feet, and cookie bursts and explosions were observed below the cloud. Moderate flak and fighters, including jets, were encountered over the target and front line, but the Witchford quintet returned safely just before midnight to make their reports. It was 02.40 when F/L Evans lifted off the runway for the second phase, and F/L Durham was the last of the six participants to depart at 02.54. They all reached the target area to bomb with their G-H leaders through ten-tenths cloud from between 18,000 and 18,500 feet, and were rewarded with the sight of bomb flashes and a glow in the cloud.

The one and only raid of the war on the eastern town of Dessau was scheduled to take place on the night of the 7/8th at the hands of a 1, 3, 6 and 8 Group force of 526 Lancasters. 3 Group contributed 124 Lancasters, of which seventeen represented 115 Squadron, and they departed Witchford between 17.15 and 17.37 with no senior pilots on duty. They all reached the target, which, since 1925, had been home to the famous Bauhaus architectural school, to find breaks in the cloud that afforded them a sufficiently good view of the ground to enable them to pick out detail. The Pathfinder skymarkers identified the aiming-point, and bombing was carried out from between 17,500 and 21,000 feet to leave the town devastated. Widespread fires revealed a distinct pattern of streets, and many explosions were observed, including one producing a large bluish flash at 22.08. At 22.18 a section of the town burning with white flames suddenly erupted in a terrific red burst, and continued to burn red. Night fighters infiltrated the bomber stream from the Rhine, and flak intensified over Braunschweig and Magdeburg. There was also a mention of "scarecrows" over the Ruhr on the way home, but these would have been some of the eighteen Lancasters that failed to return home. The operation caused extensive damage in the town centre and residential, industrial and railway districts, all of which would have to be completely rebuilt after the war, sadly, in the Eastern Bloc style of concrete architecture.

The busy month continued on the 9th with the posting of two Emscher-Lippe benzol plants at Datteln as the targets for the group. 160 Lancasters were made ready and they would be divided equally between the north and south aiming-points identified as A and B. 115 Squadron loaded seventeen Lancasters, all but one of them with a cookie and fourteen or fifteen 500 pounders, and one with a 12,000 pounder, and dispatched them between 10.35 and 10.59 with no pilots above flight lieutenant rank. They all reached the target situated on the north-eastern edge of the Ruhr, and encountered ten-tenths cloud with tops at between 8,000 and 10,000 feet. They were guided to the aiming-point by blue smoke-puff markers, but the formation was ragged as the bombs were delivered on G-H from between 18,600 and 21,500 feet. This suggests that the Witchford crews were attacking aiming-point A, as the 3 Group report describes it as scattered, while the bombing of aiming-point B was recorded as excellent and was confirmed by post-raid reconnaissance. The formation of convection cloud confirmed the existence of fires beneath, and dark grey smoke was seen to rise through the cloud-tops to 12,000 feet. A bonus was the breaching in two places of the adjacent Dortmund-Ems Canal, which was rendered completely unnavigable.

The Scholven-Buer synthetic oil refinery at Gelsenkirchen was posted as the next target for the group on the 10th, for which a force of 155 Lancasters was made ready. 115 Squadron supported the operation with fifteen Lancasters, which took off between 12.15 and 12.31 with no pilots above flight lieutenant rank. All reached the target area to be guided to the aiming-point by blue smoke-puff markers, and bombing took place through ten-tenths cloud on G-H from between 19,500 and 20,500 feet. No results could be observed other than smoke rising up through the clouds, but post-raid reconnaissance confirmed that a very accurate and effective blow had been delivered against the enemy's declining oil industry.

A new record was set by the Command on the late morning of the 11th, when 1,079 aircraft took off to hit Essen for the last time. 3 Group put up 143 Lancasters, of which fifteen represented 115 Squadron, and they departed Witchford between 11.44 and 12.08 with no pilots on duty above flight lieutenant rank. F/L Reid turned back with engine issues after two hours, leaving the others to continue on to find the target area covered by ten-tenths cloud with tops at 7,000 feet. The group bombed on G-H from between 19,000 and 19,600 feet, and observed little other than two large, red explosions and black and grey smoke discolouring the clouds. A total of 4,661 tons of bombs left the city in a state of paralysis and 897 people dead, and it would soon fall into the hands of Allied ground forces. The record lasted for a little over twenty-four hours, and was surpassed by a force of 1,108 aircraft departing their stations for the final area raid of the war on Dortmund in the early afternoon of the 12th. 3 Group supported the operation with 159 Lancasters, of which sixteen were provided by 115 Squadron. They took off between 12.55 and 13.21 with Major Martin probably the senior pilot on duty among a bunch of flight lieutenants, and all reached the target area after flying out in a somewhat ragged bomber stream, which they managed to close up before bombing took place on G-H from between 19,000 and 20,000 feet. The Germans were firing up blue smoke-puffs ten miles south-west of the target, but they did not deceive either the Pathfinder or G-H marker crews. A circle of black smoke rose up through the clouds and continued to climb, remaining visible for a hundred miles into the return journey.

Unidentified crew and aircraft after landing at RAF Witchford 12th March 1945

Benzol plants at Datteln and Hattingen were handed to 3 Group as its targets on the 14th, and eighty and eighty-nine Lancasters respectively were detailed. 115 Squadron made ready twenty-one aircraft for the latter, which was situated in Henrichschütte, a north-eastern suburb of the Ruhr town to the north of Wuppertal. They departed Witchford between 13.23 and 13.47 with Major Martin probably the senior pilot on duty among numerous flight lieutenants, and made their way to the target through flak from the Rhine eastwards and then to the south, much of it coming from the Remscheid, Solingen and Bochum areas. Bombing took place through ten-tenths cloud on G-H from between 17,200 and 19,500 feet, and no results were visible. All made it home, but six Lancasters bore the evidence of the flak activity. Clearer skies over Datteln allowed the flak there to break up the bomber stream, and the attack was assumed to be less effective. The group received orders on the 17th to continue the assault on the Ruhr synthetic oil industry, this time targeting the Gneisenau coking plant at Dortmund and the Auguste Viktoria benzol plant at Hüls, situated north of Krefeld. 167 Lancasters were divided between the two, 115 Squadron making ready twenty-one for the latter, which took off between 11.45 and 12.03 with pilots of flight lieutenant rank taking the lead. They flew out over ten-tenths cloud with tops at 8,000 to 10,000 feet, and this persisted all the way to the target, where additional wispy cirrus with tops at 22,000 feet created challenging conditions for station-keeping. The 115 Squadron formation spread out a little as a result, but crews were still able to bomb with their G-H leaders, doing so from between 19,500 and 22,500 feet without observing the results. Similar conditions were present some thirty miles to the west over Dortmund, and it is believed that both operations were effective.

The 18th followed a similar pattern with orders being received for attacks on oil-related plants at Bruchstrasse on the West Bank of the Rhine at Duisburg and also a return to the Henrichschütte plant at

288

Hattingen. 115 Squadron was assigned to the former, and dispatched seventeen Lancasters between 11.45 and 12.08 with S/L Gorrie the senior pilot on duty. The formation remained compact for the outward flight, but became spread-out five minutes before the target was reached, where cloud was ten-tenths with tops at 12,000 feet. It may have been accurate flak which caused the bomber stream to break up, and F/L Evans's Lancaster sustained damage to the nose and starboard mainplane. Some crews orbited to port behind the raid leader, and S/L Gorrie described the attack as a shambles after bombing took place on G-H from between 18,000 and 19,500 feet. Some others thought the stream to be reasonably well-together, but none could make an assessment of the outcome.

The squadron was not involved at Gelsenkirchen on the 19th, but dispatched twenty-four Lancasters from Witchford between 09.30 and 10.22 on the 20th to attack the railway yards at Hamm as part of an overall force of ninety-nine. Major Martin and other pilots of flight lieutenant rank led the way, and all but F/L Algeo and crew made it to the target, they being forced to abandon their sortie because of an engine issue. The formation held together well as it approached the target to find five to seven-tenths cloud with tops up to 8,000 feet, and crews were able to identify the aiming-point visually through gaps. Bombing took place on G-H from between 17,500 and 20,500 feet in the face of a flak defence, which was also met east of Cologne, and eight Lancasters returned home bearing battle damage. Some crews were able to report observing bomb bursts in the marshalling yards along with three explosions and much smoke.

Marshalling yards at Münster and a nearby railway viaduct were the targets for a 3 Group force of 161 Lancasters on the 21st, of which eighteen were provided by 115 Squadron. They took off between 09.34 and 10.08 with W/C Shaw the senior pilot on duty supported by S/L Gorrie, but the latter was one of three to abandon their sorties because of engine issues, W/O Cameron and F/Sgt Kitson being the others. Those reaching the target area found clear skies, but, through no fault of their own, delivered what was only a partially successful attack. The G-H coordinates for the two aiming-points had been reversed, and this led to the main weight of the attack falling on the smaller target, the viaduct. Bombing took place from between 19,000 and 19,500 feet either by visual reference assisted by blue smoke-puff markers or on G-H, and, according to returning 115 Squadron crews, despite an early scattering of bombs, the railway yards were hit squarely, and fires emitted brown and pinkish smoke which was rising through 8,000 feet as they turned away. Flak in the target area was heavy and accurate, and the stream had to run the gauntlet over the front line, but all from Witchford returned home, seven of them with flak damage.

On the 22nd 3 Group prepared a force of one hundred Lancasters to carry out an area raid on the town of Bocholt, situated close to the front line north of Wesel. 115 Squadron was not required to support the operation, which left the town on fire, but was back on the Order of Battle on the 23rd to provide seven Lancasters for a 3 Group attack by eighty aircraft on what remained of Wesel. The purpose of the operation was to soften it up ahead of the Rhine crossing by the British Second Army, and the Witchford element took off between 14.35 and 14.43 with Major Martin probably the senior pilot on duty. F/O O'Halloran was forced to turn back with Gee and G-H failure, leaving the others to press on to the target, which they found under clear skies. They bombed on G-H from 21,000 feet and produced a concentrated pattern of bombing right on the aiming-point, which left the town covered by smoke. Some of the German forces were so traumatized by the experience, that the town was taken on the following morning at a cost to the British of just thirty casualties. It was forty-eight hours before many of the enemy prisoners had recovered sufficiently to be interrogated, and a message of congratulations from Field Marshal Montgomery and General Dempsey was received at 3 Group HQ.

115 Squadron briefed twenty-one crews on the 27th for an attack that morning on a benzol plant at Sachsenring, a northern suburb of Hamm. This was one of two such targets in the Hamm area, the other, according to the 3 Group ORB, located at Konigsborn, which the author has been unable to trace. A total of 150 Lancasters were detailed by 3 Group to divide between the two aiming-points, the Witchford

element taking off either side of 10.30 with S/L Gorrie the senior pilot on duty. F/O Burbridge returned after two hours, and S/L Gorrie abandoned his sortie also, both after the failure of their port-outer engines. The others flew on to encounter ten-tenths cloud in the target area with tops at 13,000 feet. Bombing was carried out on G-H from between 18,500 and 21,000 feet, the G-H leaders responding to a strong release-pulse which all-but guaranteed accuracy. Cloud hid the results, but the presence of black smoke rising through the clouds from both targets confirmed the effectiveness of the operations.

The final operation for the group in this penultimate month of the bombing war was posted on the 29th and was to be against the Hermann Goering benzol plant at Salzgitter, situated to the south-west of Braunschweig (Brunswick). 115 Squadron supported the 130-strong 3 Group operation with twenty-one Lancasters, which took off between 12.20 and 13.38 with Major Martin probably the senior pilot on duty among a host of others of flight lieutenant rank. They flew out in heavy cloud with tops at 21,500 feet and visibility down to about fifteen hundred yards, which may have been responsible for F/O Hannah losing sight of a G-H leader and opting to drop his cookie on a last resort target south-east of Arnsberg at the eastern end of the Ruhr, and his 500 pounders on Dortmund. F/O Burbridge experienced similar difficulties, and, despite a strong release-pulse, saw no other aircraft or smoke within five minutes of starting his bombing run, and believed that he had passed Salzgitter while port of track. He turned back and bombed the first target of opportunity close to the track, which turned out to be Holzminden, located some fifty miles west south-west of the intended target. The others carried out their attacks on G-H from between 17,000 and 22,000 feet, but the cloud tops at 23,000 feet forced the formation to spread out, and it was believed that the bombing was likely to be scattered. This was the first occasion on which the new G-H/H2S Mk III equipment had been employed as a marking device, but the cloud caused the smoke-puff markers to be hidden from the following aircraft. It had been a good month for 115 Squadron, during which not a single aircraft had been lost from 311 sorties launched on nineteen operations.

April 1945

The Group's April account was opened on the night of the 4/5th, when joining forces with elements of 6 and 8 Groups to attack the oil refinery at Leuna near Merseburg, situated to the west of Leipzig in eastern Germany. 188 of the 327 Lancasters were provided by 3 Group, and twenty-one of these departed Witchford either side of 19.00 with W/C Shaw the senior pilot on duty. F/O Graham and crew turned back after an hour or so with an unserviceable rear-turret, leaving the others to press on across Belgium to pass south of Bonn and traverse central Germany. It was when south of the small town of Sinn, some fifteen miles west-north-west of Giessen that HK555 collided with a Lancaster from 186 Squadron, and both aircraft plunged to the ground with just one survivor from the latter. Thus was registered the final operational casualty of the war for 115 Squadron, and the names of F/L O'Halloran and his seven man crew were the last to be entered into the long Roll of Honour. The others reached the target area to find broken cloud with tops at 3,000 to 5,000 feet, and, for most of the raid, the ground would be hidden. The Pathfinders were responsible for the marking and arrived late, but, once released, their skymarkers were concentrated, and even their TIs could be seen through occasional gaps in the cloud. Both were used by the 115 Squadron crews to bomb from between 17,000 and 21,000 feet, after which they observed bomb bursts, large explosions, small fires and a yellowish glow on the clouds. Earlier in the day 5 Group had attacked the underground V-2 factory at Nordhausen in the Harz mountains, which had been hastily set up after Peenemünde and employed brutal slave labour. The fires from the burning barracks accommodation and other site buildings were still visible as the Leuna force flew back towards the west.

In late February one of the squadron's Lancasters had been sent to Netheravon for experiments in loading food stuffs to be air-dropped to PoWs in Germany. Trials had been conducted using standard bomb doors and also the bulged doors as used when a 12,000 pounder was in the bomb bay. On the 6th of April, the A-O-C and other ranks from air commodores to squadron leaders were assembled at Witchford to observe live tests, one of which was conducted while the aircraft was still on the ground. On the 7th, Major Martin and crew flew HK798 to Bomber Command HQ and conducted a demonstration drop over Lacey Green airfield in front of a gathering of staff officers, who were suitably impressed by what they saw. Supplies were contained in six SBCs with a combined weight of 1,254lbs, which represented 20% of a full load.

On the 9th, 1 and 3 Groups provided the main force of 591 Lancasters for a raid on Kiel, where the U-Boot construction yards and a number of moored capital ships were the main attraction. 115 Squadron made ready thirty Lancasters, which took off between 19.32 and 19.56 with S/L Gorrie the senior pilot on duty. F/O Dick and crew were back in the circuit within the hour because of port-inner engine failure, but the remainder all reached the target area, where they were greeted by clear skies and up to fifty searchlights. They bombed either visually or on Pathfinder TIs from between 17,000 and 20,300 feet, under the guidance of a Master Bomber, and observed many bomb bursts and large explosions at 22.35, 22.37 22.41 and 22.43, which resulted in one large fire and numerous smaller ones. The glow of the burning port remained visible for up to 120 miles into the return flight, and it was clear that a devastating attack had taken place. Post-raid reconnaissance revealed that the Deutscher Werke U-Boot yards had sustained severe damage, the pocket battleship Admiral Scheer had capsized and the Emden and Admiral Hipper were left in a state of disrepair. The bombing had spilled inevitably into the town and its residential districts, where much further destruction occurred.

Kiel's port area was posted as the target again on the 13th, with the U-Boot construction yards the main objective, for which a 3, 6 and 8 Group force of 482 Lancasters and Halifaxes was assembled. 3 Group put up 199 of the Lancasters, of which twenty-one were provided by Witchford, and they took off between 20.25 and 20.40 with pilots of flight lieutenant rank taking the lead. They all arrived in the target area to find ten-tenths thin stratus with difficult winds, and Pathfinder marking in progress under the control of a Master Bomber. Bombing took place from between 16,000 and 21,000 feet on skymarkers and the TIs visible through the cloud, while the defenders responded with searchlights and a moderate heavy flak barrage that sent tracer shells up to 17,000 feet. Many bomb bursts were observed, followed by large explosions, numerous large and small fires and smoke rising up through the cloud. The operation appeared to be successful, although a local report described the main weight of the attack falling two miles from the port area and into the suburb of Elmschenhagen.

Briefings took place on the 14th for what would be the final area raid of the war by RAF Bomber Command. The target was to be Potsdam, situated some fifteen miles to the south-west of Berlin, and this would be the first incursion by RAF heavy bombers into the Capital's defence zone since the final raid of the Berlin offensive more than a year earlier. 1, 3 and 8 Groups assembled a force of five hundred Lancasters, 198 of them provided by 3 Group, and the 115 Squadron element of twenty-nine took off between 18.03 and 18.32 with S/L Gorrie the senior pilot on duty. They all arrived in the target area to find clear skies, which enabled them to bomb from between 18,000 and 21,000 feet either visually or on the Pathfinder TIs under the instructions of the Master Bomber. The attack appeared to be very concentrated, and its effectiveness was confirmed by large explosions, volumes of black smoke and fires visible for some seventy miles into the return flight. Little information came out of the city, but some of the bombing apparently spilled over into northern and eastern districts of Berlin, and a figure of five thousand fatalities was suggested but not confirmed.

All of the groups contributed to the force of 969 aircraft made ready on the 18th for a huge assault on the fortress island of Heligoland, which was home to a town, a naval base, an airfield and coastal defences. 3 Group detailed 254 Lancasters of which thirty-two represented 115 Squadron, and they made their way to the runway threshold shortly before 10.00 with W/C Shaw the senior pilot on duty. S/L Gorrie's PA181 burst its port tyre while taxiing, and had to be scrubbed, leaving the remaining thirty-one to take off between 10.08 and 10.42. F/L Burbridge returned early with a port-inner engine oil leak, but the others all reached the target area to find clear skies and barely any flak to interfere with the attack. A Master Bomber was on hand to direct proceedings, and bombing was carried out visually by the 115 Squadron participants from between 15,500 and 17,000 feet. Apart from a degree of undershooting which wasted bombs in the sea, the majority fell squarely onto the island, which soon disappeared beneath black smoke issuing from the many fires, some of which were devouring oil-storage tanks. The smoke had climbed to 20,000 feet by the time the final aircraft retreated to the south-west, and the island was left looking like a cratered moonscape, with three or four motor boats making for the Danish coast in the wakes of four larger vessels. 617 and 9 Squadrons would follow up next day to target the coastal defences with Grand Slams and Tallboys, by which time the island had probably already been abandoned.

RAF Witchford Watch Office

L-R: W Fisher (Flt.Eng.), H E Harrison (Nav.)R Burbridge (Pilot), P Pollock (W.Op) H.R. Sydney (AG) L. Ireland (AG), C Walker (A.B.) (Photos: H R Sydney)

3 Group sent a small G-H force of forty-nine Lancasters to Munich on the 19th, to attend to the Pasing railway yards, and, what appeared to be a concentrated attack was delivered through cloud without loss. 115 Squadron remained on the ground at Witchford, where a number of 3 Group dignitaries welcomed Lord Trenchard in the afternoon. He addressed a gathering of air and ground personnel, before proceeding to the officers' mess for tea, after which, S/L Gorrie and crew carried out a supply-dropping display. The oil campaign in Germany was brought to a conclusion by 3 Group on the 20th, when it was called upon to bomb a fuel storage depot at Regensburg, way down in the south. A force of one hundred Lancasters carried out a G-H attack, which, after initial undershooting, appeared to find the mark, and much smoke seemed to confirm an effective raid. 115 Squadron did not take part, and remained inactive until the 22nd, when orders were received to prepare for an operation in support of the British XXX Corps, which was poised to launch an assault on Bremen. 1, 3, 6 and 8 Groups assembled a force of 767 aircraft to bomb the city's south-eastern suburbs, and the 3 Group element of 193 Lancasters included twenty-one from Witchford, which took off between 15.25 and 15.46 with F/L Keddilty the senior pilot on duty. They all reached the target area to find cloud patially obscuring the ground, and bombed visually or on G-H from between 16,000 and 17,700 feet. 3 Group was the first to attack, causing smoke and dust very quickly to cover the aiming-point and persuade the Master Bomber to call a halt to proceedings and send the 1 and 6 Group aircraft home with their bomb loads intact. Smoke was rising through 5,000 feet as the force turned away, and, although the effectiveness of the raid was unclear, news would be received of further damage to more than three thousand buildings. After three days of fighting, the city would become the first German port to fall into Allied hands after six thousand German troops surrendered.

3 Group detailed 110 Lancasters on the 24th in response to orders to attack the marshalling yards at Bad Oldesloe, a town situated between Hamburg and Lübeck. 115 Squadron dispatched twenty-one aircraft between 07.10 and 07.32 with F/L Keddilty probably the senior pilot on duty. No one knew that this would be the final offensive activity of the war for 3

F/L. Burbridge with Crew and Ground Crew at Netheravon in preparation for test drop for Operation Manna, 22nd April, 1945

Group squadrons, and F/O Graham and crew were to miss out after their port-outer engine failed and forced them to return early. The others pressed on to run the familiar gauntlet of flak from the Dutch coast inland, but it was not particularly troublesome and was not responsible for the lack of a compact formation on the way to the target. Fortunately, the stream had tightened up by the time that the target hove into sight beneath three-tenths cloud with tops at 4,000 feet. Bombing was carried out on G-H from between 17,000 and 19,000 feet, and was very concentrated, crews reporting many bombs hitting track and falling within the marshalling yards, where explosions and fires sent volumes of smoke skyward. A local report would describe the town as unprepared for an attack from the air, and approximately seven hundred people lost their lives in residential districts adjacent to the yards. All returned safely to Witchford, and, at 13.09, F/O Carberry RAAF and crew had the honour of being the last to land from a 115 Squadron offensive operation.

This operation ended 3 Group's war, and it sat out the final acts of the Command's offensives, which took place on the 25th. In the morning, 1, 5 and 8 Groups attacked the SS barracks at Hitler's Eaglesnest retreat at Berchtesgaden, and, later in the day, 4, 6 and 8 Groups bombed gun emplacements on the island of Wangerooge. That night, 5 Group raided an oil refinery at Tonsberg in Norway, and then, for the heavy crews at least, it was all over. On the 27th, W/C Shaw was posted from the squadron, to be replaced by the thirty-six-year-old W/C Harley Stanton, who arrived from 138 Squadron at Tuddenham, where he had been serving as a flight commander, a role he had also performed at 149 Squadron. W/C Stanton had been commissioned in 1932, and had served in Malaya in 1941 in the temporary rank of wing commander. During the course of the month the squadron took part in seven operations, dispatching 174 sorties for the loss of a single Lancaster and crew. Since May 1940, when strategic bombing began, the squadron had delivered 22,839.65 tons of bombs.

A 115 Sqn Lancaster dropping food to Dutch civilians during Operation Manna, May 1945

Operation Manna, the dropping of vital food supplies to the starving Dutch people still under occupation, began for 3 Group on the 29th, when ninety-four sorties were launched to the Hague area. 115 Squadron dispatched eight Lancasters between 12.35 and 12.52 with S/L Gorrie the senior pilot on duty. Each of the Lancaster s carried five packs weighing a total of 5,955lbs, and all reached the drop zone to find rain and seven-tenths cloud at the northern aiming-point with tops up to 1,500 feet, while there was ten-tenths cloud with tops at 800 feet at the southern aiming-point. The Lancasters came down to 500 feet for the drop, and saw the magnificent sight of thousands of deliriously happy Dutch people in the streets and on roof-tops welcoming their saviors with flags and whatever else they could grab to wave. The drop zones were marked by 8 Group Mosquitos and identified by a white cross, and the drops were reasonably successful, despite many of the sacks bursting on impact. The squadron contributed twenty aircraft for drops in the Rotterdam area on the 30th, and Operation Manna would continue until hostilities ceased on the 8th of May. Operation Exodus, the repatriation of Allied PoWs, in which the squadron was also to participate, would continue for some time thereafter.

There is no question, that 115 Squadron possesses an unequalled wartime record of service. The fact that it despatched the second highest number of sorties by the Command's heavy units, speaks volumes for the commitment of those involved, both in the air and on the ground. Few of its members gained fame, and it prosecuted its war almost with anonymity, but it, never the less, became the 3 Group flagship, in deed, if not in name. While the other units of 3 Group struggled to maintain a level of efficiency with Stirlings, 115 Squadron soldiered on with Wellingtons until 1943, before becoming the first to operate the Hercules-powered Mk II Lancaster in squadron strength. When Stirlings were withdrawn from operations over Germany in November 1943, the Lancasters of 115 Squadron and eventually 514 Squadron alone carried the 3 Group banner to Berlin and other cities. The squadron ended the war with an enviable record of service, which, in addition to the above, showed it to have recorded the fourth highest number of bombing raids in Bomber Command, the sixth highest number of overall operations in Bomber Command, the fourth highest number of Lancaster sorties in Bomber Command, the highest number of Wellington operations in Bomber Command, the highest number of Wellington sorties in Bomber Command, the highest number of Wellington overall operations in 3 Group, the highest number of Wellington sorties in 3 Group, the highest number of Lancaster overall operations in 3 Group and the highest number of Lancaster sorties in 3 Group. Inevitably, the squadron's high rate of sorties resulted in the loss of many aircraft and crews, 208 in all, and it was the only squadron to break the barrier of two hundred aircraft lost operationally. This figure included the highest number of Wellington operational losses in Bomber Command and the highest number of Lancaster operational losses in 3 Group. Despite this, its ratio of losses to sorties shows only an average percentage casualty rate.

Above: Fg Off Varney's crew on 27 May 1945. L-R: Sgt W Hill (RG,) F/O J Varney (Capt).F/S R Cole (A/B, F/S R Goode RAAF (W.Op), F/O J Ward (Nav), F/S S Morris (Flt. Eng.), Sgt. J Hillier (M/UG). Below: An unidentified crew.

A selection of photos taken by the crew of F/L Puddick.

115 Sqn wireless operators gather for a celebratory photo at the end of the war.

An unidentified crew of 115 Sqn.

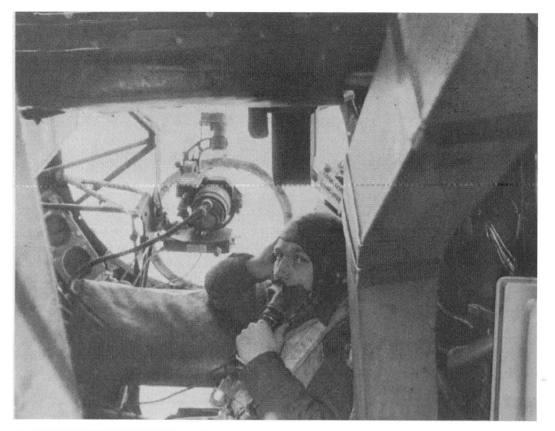

Unidentified bomb aimer (top) and navigator (above), at their posts.

115 Squadron

MOTTO: **DESPITE THE ELEMENTS**   Code **KO IL A4**

Stations

MARHAM	15.06.37. to 24.09.42.
KINLOSS (Detachment)	30.03.40. to 18.04.40.
MILDENHALL	24.09.42. to 08.11.42.
EAST WRETHAM	08.11.42. to 06.08.43.
LITTLE SNORING	06.08.43. to 26.11.43.
WITCHFORD	26.11.43. to 28.09.45.

Commanding Officers

WING COMMANDER H G ROWE DFC	15.03.39. to 27.12.39.
WING COMMANDER G H MILLS DFC	27.12.39. to 30.06.40.
WING COMMANDER H I DABINETT	01.07.40. to 20.01.41.
WING COMMANDER A C EVANS-EVANS	20.01.41. to 19.05.41.
WING COMMANDER R E SHARP	19.05.41. to 14.08.41.
WING COMMANDER T O FREEMAN DSO DFC	14.08.41. to 05.06.42.
WING COMMANDER F W DIXON-WRIGHT DFC	05.06.42. to 26.07.42.
WING COMMANDER A G S COUSENS DFC	30.07.42. to 16.12.42.
WING COMMANDER A F M SISLEY	16.12.42. to 30.03.43.
WING COMMANDER J B SIMS	30.03.43. to 01.06.43.
WING COMMANDER F F RAINSFORD DFC	01.06.43. to 21.12.43.
WING COMMANDER R H ANNAN DSO	21.12.43. to 12.06.44.
WING COMMANDER W G DEVAS DFC AFC	12.06.44. to 27.11.44.
WING COMMANDER R H SHAW	27.11.44. to 27.04.45.
WING COMMANDER H STANTON	27.04.45. to 21.07.45.

Aircraft

WELLINGTON I	04.39. to	11.39.
WELLINGTON IA	09.39. to	08.40.
WELLINGTON IC	04.40. to	03.42.
WELLINGTON III	11.41. to	03.43.
LANCASTER II	03.43. to	05.44.
LANCASTER I/III	03.44. to	09.49.

Operational Record

OPERATIONS	SORTIES	AIRCRAFT LOSSES	% LOSSES
678	7753	208	2.7

CATEGORY OF OPERATIONS

BOMBING	MINING	LEAFLET
593	81	4

<u>WELLINGTONS</u>

OPERATIONS	SORTIES	AIRCRAFT LOSSES	% LOSSES
390	3075	98	3.2

CATEGORY OF OPERATIONS

BOMBING	MINING	LEAFLET
332	54	4

<u>LANCASTERS</u>

OPERATIONS	SORTIES	AIRCRAFT LOSSES	% LOSSES
288	4678	110	2.4

CATEGORY OF OPERATIONS

BOMBING	MINING
261	27

Aircraft Histories

WELLINGTON.   **To March 1943.**

L4221	From A&AEE. To 3GRU.
L4295	From 38Sqn. Became ground instruction machine.
L4299	To 20 OTU.
L4300	To 20 OTU.
L4301	To 18 OTU.
L4305	To 20 OTU.
L4306	To 214Sqn.
L4307	To 38Sqn.
L4317	To 15 OTU.
L4318	To 15 OTU.
L4319	To 148Sqn.
L4321	To 20 OTU.
L4323	To 15 OTU.
L4324	To 11 OTU.
L4325	To CGS.
L4333	To 215Sqn.
L4334	To 15 OTU.
L7774	From 214Sqn. Returned to 214Sqn.
L7796	To 9Sqn.
L7798 KO-S	From 148Sqn. To 218Sqn.
L7801 KO-H	From 148Sqn. To 15 OTU.
L7810 KO-R	From 38Sqn. FTR Boulogne 23/24.2.41.
L7812	To 149Sqn.
L7845 KO-W/U	From 149Sqn. To 40Sqn.
L7854 KO-S	From 38Sqn. To 29 OTU.
L7895 KO-G	From 311Sqn. To 29 OTU.
N2755	To 12 OTU.
N2756 KO-U	To 38Sqn.
N2759	To 38Sqn.
N2760 KO-R	To 38Sqn and back. To 27 OTU.
N2855	To 38Sqn.
N2875	To 305Sqn.
N2876	To 11 OTU.
N2877	To 75Sqn.
N2878	From 214Sqn. To 38Sqn.
N2884	To 38Sqn.
N2885	From 99Sqn. To 311Sqn.
N2899	To 304Sqn.
N2900	To 38Sqn.
N2901	To 75Sqn.
N2902	To 3FPP.
N2947	To 1 AAS.
N2948 KO-A	Crashed on take-off from Marham while training 24.2.40.
N2949 KO-H	FTR from reconnaissance sortie off Denmark 7.4.40.
N2950 KO-J	Crashed during emergency landing at Marham while training 23.3.40.

N2987 KO-O	Crashed in Huntingdonshire while in transit 19.3.40.
N2988 KO-Q	To CGS.
N2989 KO-V	To 304Sqn.
N2990	To 11 OTU.
P2524 KO-F	FTR from reconnaissance sortie off Denmark 7.4.40.
P9207	From 38Sqn. To 218Sqn.
P9224 KO-I	From 149Sqn. To 311Sqn.
P9226 KO-D	From 38Sqn. To 311Sqn.
P9227 KO-A	From 38Sqn. FTR Bremen 18/19.7.40.
P9229 KO-S	FTR Duisburg 15/16.5.40.
P9230 KO-R	To 311Sqn.
P9235 KO-G	From 38Sqn. To 311Sqn.
P9236 KO-B	Destroyed by fire on the ground at Marham 11.7.40.
P9271 KO-O	To 12STT.
P9283 KO-U	From 9Sqn. Force-landed at Oulton 27.10.40.
P9284 KO-J	To 38Sqn and back. FTR Stavanger 11.4.40.
P9285 KO-T	To 38Sqn and back. To 27 OTU.
P9286 KO-K	From 38Sqn. FTR Hamburg 16/17.11.40.
P9290 KO-K	From 38Sqn. To 12 OTU.
P9291	From 38Sqn. To 218Sqn.
P9292	From 38Sqn. To 75Sqn.
P9296	From 38Sqn. To 218Sqn.
P9297 KO-F	From 38Sqn. FTR Dinant 21/22.5.40.
P9298 KO-H	FTR Cambrai 20/21.5.40.
P9299 KO-O/T	To 38Sqn and back. To 218Sqn.
P9300 KO-Q	To 12 OTU.
R1004 KO-U	Abandoned near Cambridge on return from Bremen 11/12.2.41.
R1033 KO-D	To 38Sqn.
R1034 KO-J/W	From 311Sqn. To 38Sqn and back. To 22 OTU.
R1063 KO-D	FTR Münster 6/7.7.41.
R1084 KO-Q	Crash-landed in Norfolk on return from Hanover 11.2.41.
R1094	To Malta.
R1179 KO-W	To 15 OTU.
R1219 KO-D	To 101Sqn.
R1221 KO-F	Crashed on approach to Marham on return from Brest 23.2.41.
R1222 KO-H	From 15Sqn. FTR Duisburg 15/16.7.41.
R1238 KO-A	Crashed on approach to Finningley on return from Bremen 12.2.41.
R1269	To 1429Flt.
R1280 KO-H	From 15Sqn. Crash-landed near Oakington on return from Brest 4.5.41.
R1332 KO-X	From 99Sqn. FTR Emden 26/27.9.41.
R1379 KO-B	FTR Hamburg 10/11.5.41.
R1468 KO-Q	Crashed while trying to land at West Raynham on return from Mannheim 28.8.41.
R1470 KO-H	Shot down by intruder over Norfolk on return from Brest 4.4.41.
R1471 KO-V/T	FTR Mannheim 5/6.8.41.
R1474	To 149Sqn.
R1500 KO-K	FTR Hanover 14/15.8.41.
R1501 KO-X	Crashed on take-off from Marham when bound for Cologne 26/27.6.41.
R1502 KO-W	FTR Bremen 13/14.7.41.
R1505 KO-U	To 101Sqn.

R1508 KO-T	Crash-landed at Manby on return from Hamburg 30.6.41.
R1509 KO-P	FTR Hamburg 29/30.6.41.
R1517 KO-Z	Crashed soon after take-off from Marham for air-test 17.6.41
R1713	To 218Sqn.
R1721 KO-R	From 22 OTU. Crashed on approach to Marham on return from Hamm 13.6.41.
R1772 KO-M	FTR Kiel 7/8.9.41.
R1798 KO-B	FTR Berlin 7/8.9.41.
R1805	Damaged beyond repair on operations 27.6.41.
R3150 KO-E	To 37Sqn.
R3151 KO-D	To 20 OTU.
R3152 KO-J	FTR Dinant 21/22.5.40.
R3153 KO-V	To 218Sqn.
R3154 KO-Q	Crashed in Yorkshire on return from Stavanger 1.5.40.
R3155 KO-P	To A&AEE.
R3156	To 75Sqn.
R3157	To 75Sqn.
R3158	To 75Sqn.
R3159	To 75Sqn.
R3160	To 149Sqn.
R3198 KO-R	From 38Sqn. To 22 OTU.
R3202 KO-J	FTR Hamburg 2/3.8.40.
R3213 KO-S	From 38Sqn. FTR Hamburg 16/17.11.40.
R3232	To 214Sqn.
R3237 KO-D	To 5FP. Converted to MkXVI.
R3238 KO-H	Abandoned over Essex on return from Bremen 11/12.2.41.
R3276 KO-B	Force-landed in Norfolk on return from Mannheim 23.8.40.
R3278 KO-D	To 148Sqn.
R3279 KO-X/D	FTR Brest 2/3.3.41.
R3291	To 38Sqn.
R3292 KO-F	FTR Osnabrück 30.9/1.10.40.
T2465 KO-O	From 38Sqn. FTR Hamm 29/30.12.40.
T2466 KO-C	FTR Mannheim 11/12.12.40.
T2507 KO-Q	To 38Sqn.
T2509 KO-W	Ditched on return from Berlin 15.11.40.
T2511 KO-P/W	To 27 O.T.U.
T2520 KO-A	Crashed in Wales on return from Bordeaux 9.12.40.
T2549 KO-K	From 99Sqn. FTR Osnabrück 30.9/1.10.40.
T2551	To 38Sqn.
T2560 KO-E	Crashed in Wiltshire during operation to Brest 22/23.4.41.
T2563 KO-J/D	Shot down by intruder near Norwich on return from Essen 13.8.41.
T2606 KO-H	To 17 OTU.
T2613 KO-R	From 311Sqn. Crashed in Buckinghamshire during ferry flight 30.10.40.
T2713	From 149Sqn. To 20 OTU.
T2742	To 38Sqn.
T2803	To 99Sqn.
T2805	To 75Sqn.
T2887 KO-B	To 218Sqn.
T2963 KO-A	From 15 OTU. Crashed on approach to Woodbridge on return from Cologne 24.6.41.
W5459 KO-L	FTR Bremen 29/30.6.41.

W5526		To 218Sqn.
W5566		To 305Sqn.
W5684	KO-G	Abandoned over Devon on return from Brest 3/4.9.41.
W5710	KO-J	Abandoned over Norfolk on return from Mannheim 28.8.41.
X3341	KO-W	FTR Lübeck 28/29.3.42.
X3342		From 9Sqn. To 23 OTU.
X3343		To 23 OTU.
X3344		To 419Sqn.
X3345		To 156Sqn.
X3348		To 9Sqn.
X3351	KO-T	From 9Sqn. FTR from mining sortie 31.12.42/1.1.43.
X3354		From 9Sqn. To 27 OTU.
X3364		To 425Sqn.
X3365		To 20 OTU.
X3391		To 101Sqn.
X3392		To 420Sqn.
X3393	KO-H	To 425Sqn and back. To BDU via 1483Flt and back. FTR Turin 9/10.12.42.
X3394		Crashed in Norfolk while training 11.11.41.
X3397		From 75Sqn. To 16 OTU via manufacturers.
X3402		To 57Sqn.
X3408		To 75Sqn.
X3412	KO-L	FTR Hamburg 26/27.7.42.
X3413		To 150Sqn.
X3414		To 103Sqn.
X3416		From 75Sqn. To 419Sqn.
X3417		To 156Sqn.
X3419	KO-T	FTR Essen 8/9.3.42.
X3423		To 9Sqn.
X3424		To 9Sqn.
X3445		To 17 OTU.
X3447		To 101Sqn and back. To 16 OTU.
X3448		From 57Sqn. To 103Sqn.
X3450		From 57Sqn. To 150Sqn.
X3464	KO-B	From 101Sqn. FTR Nuremberg 28/29.8.42.
X3466	KO-N	FTR Stuttgart 6/7.5.42.
X3468		To 75Sqn.
X3471		To 16 OTU.
X3472		To 101Sqn.
X3488		To 75Sqn.
X3539		From 75Sqn. Returned to 75Sqn.
X3540	KO-X	From 75Sqn. To 75Sqn and back. FTR Essen 29.10.42.
X3554	KO-Q	FTR Bremen 25/26.6.42.
X3555	KO-W	FTR Emden 22/23.6.42.
X3560	KO-K	From 9Sqn. FTR Duisburg 13/14.7.42.
X3561	KO-X	FTR Duisburg 21/22.7.42.
X3565		To 30 OTU.
X3584		From 75Sqn. To 57Sqn.
X3589	KO-F	FTR Essen 26/27.3.42.
X3591	KO-K	FTR Stuttgart 6/7.5.42.
X3592		To 419Sqn.

X3593 KO-C	FTR Gennevilliers 29/30.4.42.
X3596 KO-B	FTR Essen 12/13.4.42.
X3597 KO-Q	From 75Sqn. FTR from mining sortie 16/17.11.42.
X3601	Lost 31.8.42. Details unknown.
X3602 KO-Z	Crashed in Norfolk while training 11.5.42.
X3604 KO-Y	FTR Essen 26/27.3.42.
X3633 KO-Y	FTR Rostock 25/26.4.42.
X3635 KO-J	FTR Bremen 3/4.6.42.
X3639 KO-K	FTR Cologne 27/28.4.42.
X3642	To 101Sqn.
X3644 KO-A	FTR from mining sortie 17/18.5.42.
X3647 KO-A	From 101Sqn. FTR Nuremberg 28/29.8.42.
X3662	To 20 OTU.
X3666	From 9Sqn. To 23 OTU.
X3675 KO-D	FTR Nuremberg 28/29.8.42.
X3718 KO-Q	From 9Sqn. FTR from mining sortie 18/19.9.42.
X3721 KO-F	FTR Essen 1/2.6.42.
X3724 KO-T	FTR Bremen 3/4.6.42.
X3726 KO-A	From 57Sqn. FTR Duisburg 21/22.7.42.
X3749 KO-D	Crash-landed at Marham on return from Bremen 4.6.42.
X3750 KO-B	FTR Duisburg 21/22.7.42.
X3878	From 156Sqn. To 15 OTU.
X3924	To 26 OTU.
X3936 KO-X	From 156Sqn. Abandoned over Gloucestershire on return from a mining sortie 28.1.43.
X3946 KO-Q	From 75Sqn. FTR from mining sortie 16/17.10.42.
X3989 KO-V	FTR from mining sortie 20/21.8.42.
X9616	From 301Sqn. To 26 OTU.
X9632	To 20 OTU.
X9663 KO-R	From 218Sqn. To 149Sqn.
X9671 KO-F	To 21 OTU.
X9672 KO-U/F	From 218Sqn. Abandoned over Norfolk on return from Mannheim 28.8.41.
X9673 KO-B	FTR Hamburg 29/30.9.41.
X9677	To 218Sqn.
X9733 KO-L/E	To 149Sqn.
X9742	From 75Sqn. To 215Sqn.
X9751 KO-A	To 218Sqn.
X9755 KO-H	To 218Sqn.
X9826 KO-D	Shot down by intruder over Suffolk on return from Mannheim 30.8.41.
X9831	To 1505BAT Flt.
X9871	From 218Sqn. To 215Sqn.
X9873 KO-P	FTR Bremen 31.10/1.11.41.
X9875 KO-J	To 218Sqn and back. To 23 OTU.
X9877	To 149Sqn.
X9888 KO-F	From 311Sqn. FTR Emden 15/16.11.41.
X9909	To 40Sqn.
X9910 KO-Y	FTR Hamburg 29/30.9.41.
Z1069	To 218Sqn.
Z1070 KO-B	To 218Sqn.
Z1084 KO-A	From 40Sqn. To 99Sqn.

Z1563 KO-G	Crashed in Marham circuit while training 15.1.42.
Z1572	To 75Sqn.
Z1574 KO-S	Damaged beyond repair during operation to Genoa 23/24.10.42.
Z1605 KO-R	FTR Hamburg 28/29.7.42.
Z1606 KO-J	FTR Duisburg 25/26.7.42.
Z1607 KO-T	Crash-landed in Norfolk on return from Nuremberg 29.8.42.
Z1609	From 156Sqn. To 1483Flt.
Z1614 KO-R	FTR Cologne 30/31.5.42.
Z1620 KO-T	From 156Sqn. FTR Hamburg 3/4.3.43.
Z1624 KO-D	FTR Hamburg 28/29.7.42.
Z1648 KO-A	To 23 OTU.
Z1649	To 83 OTU.
Z1653	From 57Sqn. To 18 OTU.
Z1657 KO-R	From 57Sqn. To CGS.
Z1663 KO-J	From 57Sqn. FTR Lingen (Dortmund-Ems Canal) 28.9.42.
Z1694 KO-G	To 23 OTU.
Z1738 KO-M	From 75Sqn. FTR Essen 29.10.42.
Z8375	To 218Sqn.
Z8788 KO-H	FTR Mannheim 21/22.7.41.
Z8796	To 20 OTU.
Z8799 KO-R	To 20 OTU.
Z8802 KO-W	To 20 OTU.
Z8804	To 20 OTU.
Z8809	To 20 OTU.
Z8830	To TFU.
Z8835 KO-U	FTR Essen 12/13.8.41.
Z8841	To 20 OTU.
Z8844 KO-S	FTR Munich 13/14.10.41.
Z8846	To 20 OTU.
Z8848 KO-H	Ditched off Yorkshire coast on return from Kiel 16.11.41.
Z8852	To 20 OTU.
Z8853	From 9Sqn. To 40Sqn and back. To 218Sqn.
Z8857	To 20 OTU.
Z8863 KO-G	Crashed in Cambridgeshire while training 24.11.41.
BJ584	From 75Sqn. To 36 OTU.
BJ589	To 156Sqn.
BJ595 KO-S	Ditched off Lincolnshire coast during operation to Duisburg 23/24.7.42.
BJ615 KO-G	FTR Hamburg 26/27.7.42.
BJ660 KO-H	FTR Essen 29.10.42.
BJ663 KO-N	FTR Bremen 4/5.9.42.
BJ670 KO-K	FTR Hamburg 26/27.7.42.
BJ688 KO-R	From 9Sqn. FTR Nuremberg 28/29.8.42.
BJ693 KO-J	FTR Wilhelmshaven 14/15.9.42.
BJ706	To 22 OTU.
BJ710 KO-L	FTR Kassel 27/28.8.42.
BJ722	To TFU.
BJ723 KO-B	FTR Hamburg 26/27.7.42.
BJ724 KO-P	Blew up in the air over Norfolk when bound for Duisburg 6.9.42.
BJ756 KO-Q	From 75Sqn. FTR Essen 12/13.3.43.
BJ770	From 57Sqn. To 18 OTU.

BJ771 KO-L	From 57Sqn. FTR Bremen 4/5.9.42.
BJ796 KO-H	From 101Sqn. Ditched in North Sea off the Suffolk coast during operation to Bremen 29/30.6.42.
BJ797	From 101Sqn. To 17 OTU.
BJ832 KO-F	To 75Sqn and back. To 29 OTU.
BJ833	From 57Sqn. To 26 OTU.
BJ842 KO-W	FTR Stuttgart 22/23.11.42.
BJ879	To 26 OTU.
BJ880	To 82 OTU.
BJ893 KO-C	FTR Saarbrücken 1/2.9.42.
BJ898 KO-C	From 75Sqn. FTR Mannheim 6/7.12.42.
BJ962 KO-D	FTR from mining sortie 21/22.9.42.
BJ965	To 12 OTU.
BJ990	To 17 OTU.
BK127 KO-D	FTR Hamburg 3/4.2.43.
BK128	To 30 OTU.
BK166 KO-C	FTR Lorient 13/14.2.43.
BK206 KO-R	From 75Sqn. FTR Stuttgart 22/23.11.42.
BK271 KO-A	FTR Krefeld 2/3.10.42.
BK272	To 17 OTU.
BK274 KO-T	From 75Sqn. FTR Fallersleben 17/18.12.42.
BK275	From 75Sqn. To 26 OTU.
BK306 KO-K	FTR Milan 24/25.10.42.
BK307	To 29 OTU.
BK312	FTR from mining sortie 16/17.10.42.
BK313 KO-B	FTR Osnabrück 6/7.10.42.
BK314	To 17 OTU.
BK336 KO-D	FTR Fallersleben 17/18.12.42.
BK338 KO-A	FTR Frankfurt 2/3.12.42.
BK362	From 75Sqn. To CGS.
BK495 KO-N	FTR from mining sortie 2/3.3.43.
BK513 KO-V	FTR Mannheim 6/7.12.42.

LANCASTER.	**From March 1943.** (MkII *)

DS603*	From 61Sqn. No operations. To 1657CU.
DS604* KO-B	From 61Sqn. FTR Frankfurt 10/11.4.43.
DS607*	From 61Sqn. To 1657CU.
DS608* KO-C	From 61Sqn. To 1657CU.
DS609* KO-M	FTR Duisburg 26/27.4.43.
DS610*	From 61Sqn. To 1657CU.
DS612* KO-F/H	From 61Sqn. To 426Sqn.
DS613* KO-Y	From 61Sqn. To 1668CU.
DS614* KO-A	To 1666CU.
DS615* KO-N	To 1659CU.
DS616* KO-G	Crashed on landing at East Wretham on return from Wuppertal and collided with DS618 (115Sqn) 30.5.43.
DS617* KO-N	To 1657CU.
DS618* KO-P	From 1657CU. Destroyed on ground in accident at East Wretham 30.5.43. (See DS616).

DS619*	To 1657CU.
DS620*KO-V/W	To 1668CU.
DS621*KO-U	From 61Sqn. To 426Sqn.
DS622*KO-F/Q/T	To 1668CU.
DS623*KO-R	To 1678CU.
DS624*KO-L	To 426Sqn.
DS625*KO-W	FTR Berlin 29/30.3.43.
DS626*KO-J	To 426Sqn.
DS627*A4-D/KO-R	From 1657CU. FTR Wuppertal 29/30.5.43.
DS629*KO-D/M	Crash-landed at Coltishall on return from Frankfurt 19.3.44.
DS630*KO-H	FTR Peenemünde 17/18.8.43.
DS631*KO-Z	To 1679CU.
DS633*	From 432Sqn via 1678CU. To 514Sqn.
DS634*KO-K	To 426Sqn.
DS635*KO-G	To 1679CU.
DS647*KO-N	FTR Düsseldorf 11/12.6.43.
DS652*KO-B	FTR Bochum 12/13.6.43.
DS653*KO-S	To 1679CU.
DS654*	To 1657CU.
DS655*KO-M	FTR Essen 27/28.5.43.
DS656*KO-X	To 426Sqn.
DS657*	To 426Sqn.
DS658*KO-K	Wrecked on landing at Little Snoring on return from Berlin 4.9.43.
DS659*KO-T	FTR Nuremberg 27/28.8.43.
DS660*KO-P	FTR Aachen 13/14.7.43.
DS661*KO-F/Z	Crashed on take-off from Witchford while training 20.3.44.
DS662*KO-L	FTR Cologne 3/4.7.43.
DS663*KO-C	FTR from mining sortie 25/26.6.43.
DS664*KO-X/D A4-K	FTR Berlin 24/25.3.44.
DS665*KO-N	Crashed near Cambridge on return from Nuremberg 11.8.43.
DS666*KO-J	FTR Gelsenkirchen 25/26.6.43.
DS667*A4-G	FTR Berlin 2/3.1.44.
DS668*KO-R	FTR from mining sortie 19/20.6.43.
DS669*KO-L	To 514Sqn.
DS670*KO-U	To 1678Sqn.
DS671*	To BDU 6.43.
DS672*	To BDU 6.43.
DS673*KO-V	FTR Hamburg 2/3.8.43.
DS675*KO-E	FTR Hanover 22/23.9.43.
DS678*KO-J	FTR Berlin 24/25.3.44.
DS680*KO-L	FTR Berlin 18/19.11.43.
DS682*KO-Y/A	FTR Laon 22/23.4.44.
DS683*KO-R	Crash-landed at Little Snoring on return from Hanover 18.10.43.
DS684*KO-M	FTR Turin 16/17.8.43.
DS685*KO-A	FTR Hamburg 2/3.8.43.
DS690*KO-P/C	FTR Aachen 13/14.7.43.
DS691*KO-F/B	FTR Hanover 8/9.10.43.
DS715*KO-Q	FTR Hamburg 2/3.8.43.
DS720*KO-D	FTR Brunswick 14/15.1.44.

DS721*KO-U	FTR from air-sea search sortie 4.10.43.
DS722*KO-N	From 426Sqn. FTR Berlin 23/24.8.43.
DS725*KO-F	FTR Leipzig 20/21.10.43.
DS728*KO-P/C/T	FTR Cologne 20/21.4.44.
DS734*KO-Y	FTR Karlsruhe 24/25.4.44.
DS761*KO-W	To 408Sqn.
DS764*KO-S	FTR Berlin 22/23.11.43.
DS765*KO-A	FTR Leipzig 3/4.12.43.
DS766*KO-Q/R	Crashed on approach to Woodbridge on return from Frankfurt 23.3.44.
DS769*KO-H	FTR Hanover 18/19.10.43.
DS773*KO-T	FTR Berlin 23/24.12.44.
DS777*A4-C	FTR Magdeburg 21/22.1.44.
DS780*	Crashed in Norfolk during air-test and training 14.9.43.
DS781*KO-W	FTR Duisburg 21/22.5.44.
DS782*KO-K	FTR Berlin 22/23.11.43.
DS784*	To 514Sqn.
DS793*KO-L	FTR Berlin 26/27.11.43.
DS795*A4-E	To 514Sqn and back. To 38MU.
DS796*KO E	From 514Sqn. Force-landed in Cambridgeshire on return from Berlin 2.1.44.
DS825*	From 514Sqn. Crashed on take-off from Little Snoring when bound for mining sortie 8.11.43.
DS827*KO-B	Crashed in Essex during bombing practice 5.2.44.
DS833*KO-S	FTR Berlin 28/29.1.44.
DS834*KO-F	From 514Sqn. FTR Berlin 29/30.12.43.
DS835*KO-K	FTR Berlin 16/17.12.43.
DS836*KO-R	To 514Sqn.
ED491	From 50Sqn. To A&AEE Boscombe Down.
ED631 KO-B	From 617Sqn. To 1651CU.
HK541 KO-P	From 75Sqn. To 3LFS.
HK542 KO-J	From 75Sqn. FTR Karlsruhe 24/25.4.44.
HK544 KO-U	From 75Sqn. FTR Bonn 18.10.44.
HK545 KO-E	From 622Sqn. FTR Gelsenkirchen 12/13.6.44.
HK546 A4-H	To 149Sqn.
HK547 A4-F	FTR Le Mans 19/20.5.44.
HK548 KO-W	FTR Chevreusse 7/8.6.44.
HK549 KO-Q	To 149Sqn.
HK550 KO-Y	FTR Valenciennes 15/16.6.44.
HK551 A4-E	From 75Sqn. To 149Sqn.
HK552 KO-J	FTR Chevreusse 7/8.6.44.
HK555 KO-E	To 149Sqn and back. Collided over Germany with RA533 (186Sqn) while returning from Leuna 4/5.4.45
HK556 A4-F	FTR Kiel 26/27.8.44.
HK559 A4-H	FTR Montdidier 17/18.6.44.
HK560 A4-K	FTR Kiel 27.8.44.
HK564	To 75Sqn.
HK565 KO-L	From 75Sqn. To 1659CU.
HK566	To 1654CU.
HK572 KO-Y	To 149Sqn and back. To 1661CU.
HK578 IL-C	To 149Sqn.
HK579 A4-B	FTR Le Havre 8.9.44.

HK595 KO-A	FTR Dortmund 15.11.44.
HK598	To 149Sqn.
HK599 KO-K	FTR Duisburg 14.10.44.
HK624 IL-J	From 149Sqn. FTR Cologne 27.11.44.
HK653	From 149Sqn. Returned to 149Sqn.
HK656 KO-Q	From 149Sqn.
HK691 KO-R	
HK696	From 90Sqn.
HK698 IL-A/K	
HK766 KO-F	
HK768	
HK790 KO-Y	
HK798 KO-H/L	
IL-L	
LL621*	To 426Sqn.
LL622*A4-F/KO-J	FTR Nuremberg 30/31.3.44.
LL624*KO-D	To 514Sqn.
LL626*A4-N	
LL639*	To 514Sqn.
LL640*A4-C	FTR Frankfurt 18/19.3.44.
LL644*KO-N	From 514Sqn. FTR Schweinfurt 24/25.2.44.
LL646*KO-G	To 46MU following forced-landing.
LL648*A4-B	FTR Berlin 30/31.1.44.
LL649*A4-G	FTR Berlin 28/29.1.44.
LL650*A4-J	From 514Sqn. FTR Berlin 20/21.1.44.
LL651*A4-A	FTR Berlin 15/16.2.44.
LL652*A4-Q	To 514Sqn.
LL666*KO-U	To 514Sqn.
LL667*KO-R	Shot down by intruder over Witchford on return from Rouen 19.4.44.
LL668*A4-H	FTR Berlin 27/28.1.44.
LL669*	To 514Sqn.
LL670*	To 514Sqn.
LL673*KO-G	FTR Brunswick 14/15.1.44.
LL678*	To 514Sqn.
LL680*	To 514Sqn.
LL681*A4-A	FTR Leipzig 19/20.2.44.
LL682*KO-P	FTR Berlin 27/28.1.44.
LL685*	To 514sqn.
LL687*	From 426Sqn. To 408Sqn.
LL689*KO-P	FTR Berlin 15/16.2.44.
LL691*	To 514Sqn.
LL692*KO-F	FTR Stuttgart 28/29.7.44.
LL693*KO-I/A4-K²	FTR Stuttgart 15/16.3.44.
LL694*KO-N	FTR Berlin 24/25.3.44.
LL695*	To 514Sqn.
LL701*KO-F	FTR Schweinfurt 24/25.2.44.
LL702*	Damaged in accident and SOC 15.1.44.
LL704*KO-H	FTR Nuremberg 30/31.3.44.
LL716*	To 514Sqn.
LL726*KO-G	To 514Sqn.

	A4-A	
LL729*A4-B	Crashed in Bedfordshire on return from Stuttgart 21.2.44.	
LL730*KO-G	From 514Sqn. FTR Berlin 24/25.3.44.	
LL734*	To 514Sqn.	
LL804	To 300Sqn.	
LL864 A4-H	From 75Sqn. FTR Chevreusse 7/8.6.44.	
LL867 KO-U/A4-J	From 75Sqn. Shot down by intruder over Witchford on return from Rouen 19.4.44.	
LL880 KO-D	From 75Sqn. FTR Dortmund 6/7.10.44.	
LL921	To 75Sqn.	
LL923	To XVSqn.	
LL935 KO-N	From 57Sqn. To 3LFS.	
IL-N		
LL936 KO-V	FTR Trappes 31.5/1.6.44.	
LL943 KO-C	FTR Aulnoye 18/19.7.44.	
LL944 KO-Z	FTR Siegen 16.12.44.	
LM127KO-H	FTR Kiel 26/27.8.44.	
LM166KO-Y	FTR Foret de Lucheux 8/9.8.44.	
LM510KO-A/K	From 75Sqn. Crash-landed at Woodbridge on return from Homberg 21.7.44.	
LM533KO-T	From XVSqn. FTR Lisieux 6/7.6.44.	
LM534	To XVSqn.	
LM544	To 75Sqn.	
LM616KO-J	Crashed in Hertfordshire on return from Emieville 18.7.44.	
LM693KO-T	FTR Moerdijk 16/17.9.44.	
LM696KO-F/U		
A4-F		
LM725KO-X	FTR Chemnitz 14/15.2.45.	
LM734IL-J	From 514Sqn.	
LM738A4-B	FTR Calais 27.9.44.	
LM743	To 195Sqn.	
LM744	To 195Sqn.	
LM753	To 195Sqn.	
ME692 KO-G	From 75Sqn. FTR Wilhelmshaven 15/16.10.44.	
A4-G		
ME718 KO-G	FTR Stettin 29/30.8.44.	
ME751	To 75Sqn.	
ME752	To 75Sqn.	
ME753	To 75Sqn.	
ME754	To 75Sqn.	
ME756 A4-U/V	To 1651CU. 11.44.	
ME803 KO-D/L		
A4-D/IL-B		
ME834	From 75Sqn.	
ME836 KO-S	Completed 99 operations.	
A4-C		
ND677 KO-X	From 49Sqn.	
ND745 A4-D	From 75Sqn. FTR Dortmund 22/23.5.44.	
ND753 KO-K	From 75Sqn. FTR Düsseldorf 22/23.4.44.	
ND754 KO-F	From 75Sqn. FTR Duisburg 21/22.5.44.	
ND758 KO-Y	From 75Sqn. To 3LFS 11.44.	

	A4-A	
ND760	A4-K	From 75Sqn. FTR Chevreusse 7/8.6.44.
ND761	A4-C	From 75Sqn. FTR Chevreusse 7/8.6.44.
ND790	KO-H	FTR Chevreusse 7/8.6.44.
ND800	A4-C	To 75Sqn.
ND803	A4-D/B	FTR Friedrichshafen 27/28.4.44.
ND805	A4-J	FTR Duisburg 14.10.44.
ND900	KO-S	To 1651CU.
ND904	KO-M	To 75Sqn.
ND913	KO-N	FTR Homberg 20/21.7.44.
	A4-M²	
ND917		To 75Sqn.
ND920		To 75Sqn.
ND923	KO-C	FTR Louvain 11/12.5.44.
ND927	KO-B	FTR Brunswick 12/13.8.44.
NE148		To 75Sqn.
NF960	KO-R	FTR Cologne 28.10.44.
NG122		
NG124	KO-U	
	A4-L	
NG130	IL-V	
NG162		To 195Sqn.
NG168		
NG205	KO-K	
	IL-D	
NG332	IL-D	FTR Vohwinkel 1/2.1.45.
NN706	KO-B	FTR Dortmund 15.11.44.
NN754	IL-F/J	
NN755		To 195Sqn.
NN761		
NN762		
NN806		From 576Sqn. Crashed on take-off from Fiskerton 8.5.45.
NX559	KO-D	
PA181	KO-A	
PA224	KO-L	
PA967		To 75Sqn.
PB127	KO-T	FTR Brunswick 12/13.8.44.
PB130	KO-A	FTR Amaye-sur-Seulles 30.7.44.
PB131	KO-W	FTR Stettin 29/30.8.44.
PB373		From 49Sqn.
PB433	KO-E	From 49Sqn.
PB455		From 49Sqn.
PB524	KO-C	To 1659CU.
PB571		From 49Sqn.
PB577		To GH Flt at Feltwell.
PB647		From 227Sqn.
PB686	KO-D	FTR Dresden 14.2.45.
PB721	KO-U	From 218Sqn.
PB756	IL-A/H	
PB757	IL-E	

PB767 KO-T   From 514Sqn.
PB789 KO-C   From 514Sqn.
PB798 IL-G   From 514Sqn.
PB818 KO-X   To 195Sqn.
PB907 KO-O   From 49Sqn.
PD274 KO-Y   FTR Rüsselsheim 26/27.8.44.
PD276 KO-X   FTR Essen 25.10.44.
PD277 KO-C   From 218Sqn.
PD293 KO-O   FTR from training sortie 26.11.44.
PD344 KO-M   FTR Saarbrücken 5/6.10.44.
PD345   From 227Sqn.
PD367 KO-H   FTR Osterfeld 30.11.44.
PD370   To 138Sqn.
PD400   To 90Sqn.
PD401
PD402   To 90Sqn.
PD444   From 1662CU.
PP666 KO-W
      IL-K
PP670
RF190   To 75Sqn.

HEAVIEST SINGLE LOSS.

7/8.6.44. Chevreusse. 6 Lancasters FTR.

Printed in Great Britain
by Amazon